FROMMER'S FOOD LOVER'S COMPANION TO

ITALY

FROMMER'S FOOD LOVER'S COMPANION TO

ITALY

BY
MARC AND KIM MILLON

Macmillan • USA

To the memory of my mother,
Lori, who loved Italy

Macmillan Travel
A Simon & Schuster
Macmillan Company
1633 Broadway
New York, NY 10019

ISBN 0-02-860926-3
Library of Congress Catalog Card No.:
95-81806

Manufactured in Italy by
Rotolito Lombarda
Color separations by Global Colour

Conceived, edited, and designed by
Websters International Publishers
Axe and Bottle Court
70 Newcomen Street
London SE1 1YT

10 9 8 7 6 5 4 3 2 1

First Edition

Project Editor Shirin Patel • *Art Editor* Joanna Pocock

Designer Adelle Morris • *Editors* Julia Colbourne, Hugh Morgan, Pauline Savage

Index Naomi Good • *Production* Charles James

Illustrations James G. Robins • *Design Manager* Jason Vrakas

CONTENTS

Eating outdoors, Italian-style, at a mountain refuge in Calabria

Introduction
LA DOLCE VITA

THAT EASY ITALIAN WAY OF LIFE that we visitors to Italy find so alluring and enviable — *la dolce vita* — is undoubtedly linked to the Italians' inherent knowledge of how to eat and drink well. Though we feel we are all familiar with Italian foods and wines, this book will take you beyond the obvious and internationally known so you can taste and enjoy the real gastronomy of Italy — the gastronomy of regional Italy.

For Italy today, more so than any nation in Europe, still maintains its distinct regional and local characteristics and traditions, and many of its greatest foods and wines may rarely be encountered outside their area of production: many are known only by their names in the local dialect; and, in other cases, familiar Italian names mean different things in other parts of the nation. Some such specialties may be the sort of precious and rare foods that gourmets travel the world to enjoy on the spot. Genuine *aceto balsamico tradizionale di Modena* (traditional balsamic vinegar) is produced in minute quantity and at exorbitant expense, yet this viscous and concentrated condiment, aged in batteries of small wood casks for 25 years or longer, really must be tasted to be believed; the best way to do this is to track it down to an *acetaia* in Modena, or enjoy it in country restaurants around that great gastronomic city. *Tartufi bianchi* (white truffles) from Alba and Asti are, quite simply, one of the greatest, most incredibly intense and sensuous — even addictive — foods in the world, but their mind-blowing aroma and their subtle, inimitable earthy flavor are fleeting, impossible to capture and conserve, so they must be enjoyed fresh, on the spot, during their brief but glorious fall season in Piemonte. Simpler, but no less delicious, are fresh and juicy tomatoes during their summer glut in Campania and Calabria; the concentrated flavors of lemon or coffee in a *granita* ice from a roadside stand in Sicily; a shot of *grappa di monovitigno* after a day's skiing in the Dolomites; or a sheet of crunchy *pane carasau* topped with pungent ewe's milk *ricotta* cheese and dribbled with honey in Sardinia.

We will introduce you to the general principles of Italian gastronomy in the first part of this book: from shopping for food and drink in markets and specialist shops or putting together the components for a picnic in the vineyard, to eating in simple *osterie* and *trattorie* or in grand *ristoranti*. In the second part, we divide Italy into broad geographical areas and explore in detail local and regional foods, wines, and specialties.

With this guide, you will enjoy the real gastronomy of Italy: in a local *trattoria* or a mountain refuge, at a cheese dairy or in vineyard and *cantina,* making, we are sure, many discoveries and new friends along the way.

Buon viaggio e buon appetito!
Marc and Kim Millon

Variety and Integrity

REGIONAL AND TRADITIONAL ITALY

ITALY IS MADE UP of twenty regions, all of which demonstrate remarkable individuality and integrity in terms of culture, language, customs and traditions, architecture, and, of course, food and wine. In this era of social mobility, where the regional differences of many nations tend to blur as people constantly move and settle in new areas, the way in which local traditions and foods and wines in Italy have stayed tenaciously intact is as surprising as it is admirable.

From the snow-covered Alps of the French-speaking Valle d'Aosta, the Dolomites of the Austrian-influenced Alto Adige, and the alpine arc of Veneto and Friuli-Venezia Giulia, this narrow, spiny peninsula plunges ever southwards. The great, broad Po Valley is something of a watershed,

 the river meandering across some of the nation's richest and most fertile land, as well as through the industrial heartland of Piemonte, Lombardia, Emilia-Romagna, and Veneto.

Below the Po, the Apennines divide the nation into east and west, for this formidable barrier extends the entire length of the peninsula, separating regions that otherwise would be relatively close in distance. On the western side, Liguria and Tuscany extend from their high slopes across to the Tyrrhenian

Garda, a popular lakeside town, whose vineyards produce light, thirst quenching Bardolino wine

Sea; Umbria straddles the range, meeting the pretty but isolated Le Marche to the east; and, further south, lie rugged Abruzzo and Molise.

Lazio, the region which encompasses Rome, serves as something of a transition, its northern provinces not too dissimilar to the rest of Central Italy. But by the time you are south of Rome, you know you have definitely entered the *Mezzogiorno,* Italy's wild and wonderful "deep south," which comprises Campania, Calabria, Basilicata, and Puglia, each with distinctive identities and rich and colorful gastronomic traditions.

Finally, offshore Sicily and Sardinia stand alone, with heady mixes of the indigenous and foreign, proud traditions, and strong regional identities.

SMALL IS *BELLISSIMO*

There is a deep-seated belief throughout almost all Italy that the handmade, the artisan-produced, or the homemade is infinitely superior to the industrially produced. Though this thinking applies across the board to any number of products (from shoes to furniture), it is nowhere more evident than in the area of food and wine.

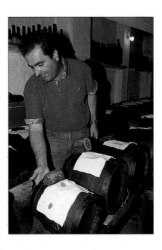

Whether it is in the production of a hand-made *salame;* cheeses from small, independent dairies; fresh *pasta* in simple or grand restaurants; bread baked in a *forno a legno* (wood-fired oven); olives, ground by slowly revolving granite stones to produce peppery, cold-pressed, extra-virgin olive oil; or the infinitely slow, authentic production of *aceto balsamico tradizionale di Modena* in minuscule quantities, Italy is nothing if not a nation of artists and artisans, producers of fine products who take infinite care and pride in their work.

Examining a sample of real balsamic vinegar at the Consorzio Produttori di Aceto Balsamico Tradizionale di Modena

This book, in great measure, aims to define those artisan products worth seeking out, and to direct you to some of the nation's most committed makers of them. For we share with them the essential belief that unless we keep our senses alive to the really excellent, we risk losing our capacity to distinguish and appreciate the best from the mediocre.

ARCIGOLA: "SLOW FOOD, PLEASE, WE'RE ITALIAN"

While the rest of the world has embraced fast food, Italy has given birth to the world's first "slow-food" movement. When the first McDonald's opened in Italy in the late 80s, a group of committed individuals in Piemonte felt compelled to create the "slow food" movement, its symbol, the snail — both slow and delicious!

Arcigola Slow Food caught the imagination of the Italian people and even the world. Today, it has over 20,000 members and 240 volunteer chapters in 18 nations.

Arcigola Slow Food defends and champions genuine regional food traditions by organizing conferences, food and wine tastings, and publishing books and guides which highlight the best and most authentic regional food and wine.

Arcigola Slow Food
Via della Mendicità Istruita, 14
12042 Bra CN
tel: 0172/411273
fax: 0172/421293

Slow Food

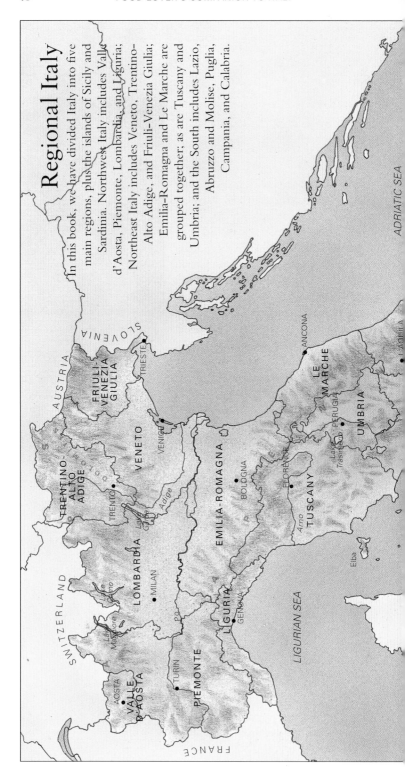

Regional Italy

In this book, we have divided Italy into five main regions, plus the islands of Sicily and Sardinia. Northwest Italy includes Valle d'Aosta, Piemonte, Lombardia, and Liguria; Northeast Italy includes Veneto, Trentino–Alto Adige, and Friuli-Venezia Giulia; Emilia-Romagna and Le Marche are grouped together; as are Tuscany and Umbria; and the South includes Lazio, Abruzzo and Molise, Puglia, Campania, and Calabria.

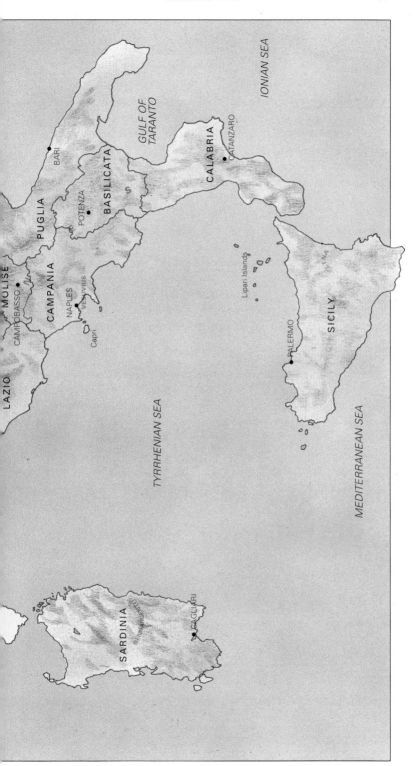

A National Obsession

THE GASTRONOMY OF ITALY

W HILE THE REST OF THE WORLD eats to live, Italians, it is said, live to eat. Food — good food — and wine are of immense importance to all Italians across generations and regions, social classes, and occupations. While wealthy industrialists in the North still find time to enjoy extended business lunches, less well-off *contadini* (country folk) in the South sit down to a Mediterranean diet of homegrown and home-produced food that has become the envy of the Western world. The issue of eating well and copiously in Italy is not really about whether one can afford to or not, because to do otherwise would indicate a poverty of spirit beyond even the meanest imagination. Why else, in Italy, would even prisoners be given a healthy daily ration of wine to accompany their *pasta asciutta* (*pasta* with sauce). Why not indeed, for surely to provide food without wine is nothing short of a cruel and unusual punishment.

In a nation notoriously torn by regional divisions, even rivalries, the obsession with food is one national characteristic that unifies Italy.

AN INBRED APPRECIATION

From the moment a baby takes its first spoonful of *pappa al pomodoro* (a Tuscan tomato and bread mush made with the finest extra-virgin olive oil), *riso in bianco* (soupy *risotto* made with rich chicken stock and grated *parmigiano reggiano* cheese), or *maccheroni col pomodoro* (maccaroni with tomato sauce), a process begins whereby mothers (and fathers) the Italian world over imbue in their offspring a love of good, home-prepared food. Thus, from the earliest age, Italians acquire an appreciation of the

Lazy days on the Zattere, Venice

A simple feast laid out for an open-air buffet in the mountains in Sardinia

importance of good food, and an unquestioning belief that eating well and regularly (preferably at least two large meals a day) is part of good living and life itself.

All those little Italian princes and princesses, spoon fed on the finest milk-fed *vitello* (veal), paper-thin slices of *prosciutto di Parma* (Parma ham), not to mention countless cups of *gelato* (ice cream), grow up naturally discerning. Italy is nothing if not a nation of passionate critics, with most considering themselves qualified to pontificate at length on politics, Renaissance art, football, sex, last night's performance at La Scala, and, by no means least of all, the quality of food and wine.

Yet, it must be said that too much passion, like too much wine, can sometimes obscure vision. The result is a profound, self-admitted ignorance and lack of interest on the part of most Italians toward anything from the rest of the nation outside their own locality, province, or region. Of course, in the broadest sense, the North-South divide that creates much tension in the nation is highly divisive socially. Yet, even when it comes to food and wine, this tunnel vision, this lack of interest, this inability to see beyond the merely local or, at best, the regional, is surprising. Perhaps it is because prior to the Risorgimento and the subsequent unification of Italy in the late 19th century, the Italian Peninsula was hopelessly fragmented, made up of disparate republics, vassal states under foreign domination, not to mention the legacy of medieval city-states that once fiercely vied for power and influence against one another. An inbred skepticism remains, an essential conservatism that refuses to believe that something different, from somewhere else — anywhere else — could possibly be good or worthwhile.

TRAVEL BROADENS THE MIND

On the other hand, we travelers to Italy find ourselves in a curiously fortunate position, for we are able to stand back and view the nation as a whole from a more objective and dispassionate point of view.

Bar-cum-shop in Friuli-Venezia Giulia, for a drink with a quick snack

And what we see is incredibly exciting, varied, and rich.

During the course of our research, we have been out to lay nets on Lake Como with professional fishermen in search of *pesce persico* (perch) and other freshwater fish, and we have witnessed cheesemakers in Campania undertake the miraculous daily transformation of fresh buffalo milk into glistening balls of *mozzarella* cheese. We have hiked to mountain refuges in Southern Calabria where the guides then cooked for us meals of roast kid and wild mushrooms, and we have made our way to similar refuges in Northern Trentino to eat *polenta,* cooked in the open air in huge copper pots.

In Puglia, we discovered a magnificent vegetarian cuisine made up of a profusion of fresh produce ripened in the sun; in Tuscany, we enjoyed immense Florentine T-bones, grilled over the ever present wood fire. Way up by the border with Slovenia, we ate boiled meats and *sauerkraut,* followed by pastries inspired by the former Austrian Empire; down in Sicily, on the other hand, we enjoyed food, wine, and sweets that betrayed the spicy, sweet, oriental influences of the Levant. On the Adriatic seaboard, we enjoyed the smallest, sweetest fish and shellfish and, by contrast,

The chef from the Hotel Cipriani selecting fish at Venice's Rialto Market

along the southern Tyrrhenian, we feasted on great, barbecued tuna and swordfish

---

RECOMMENDED ESTABLISHMENTS

This book does not aim to be a comprehensive restaurant or shopping guide, but, throughout, we do include the addresses of places that we consider to be essential points of reference for the finest Italian foods and drinks at any level. Such establishments range from the greatest (and most expensive) restaurants in Italy to humble and genuine *osterie* and *trattorie* serving authentic local foods; from world class and famous wine producers to rustic rice and *polenta*

mills. Visit them and you will begin discovering your own personal favorites to the finest Italian gastronomy.

We also suggest you consult the guides we recommend (see p.45) for more detailed listings for eating out.

As a rough indication only, we have included the following price coding:

$ = Inexpensive
$$ = Moderate
$$$ = Expensive
$$$$ = Very expensive

steaks. In Emilia-Romagna, we witnessed *pasta all'uovo* being made by hand, the yellow, elastic sheet of eggy dough rolled out and cut into a joyous array of forms; while, in the South, we were equally impressed by the variety of *pasta* shapes made from no more than hard durum wheat, water, and manual dexterity.

REGIONAL ITALY TODAY

In Italy, you never need go too far to come across local foods and wines. They are all around you in each region because Italians would have it no other way. For that reason, Italy probably boasts the most fully intact and richest traditional and regional gastronomy of any nation in Western Europe.

Meats, cheese, and schuttelbrot *at an informal wine garden in the German-speaking Alto Adige*

The aim of this book is to define that gastronomy for the visitor, with an appetizing and up-to-date portrait of contemporary food and wine as it really is in Italy. After the thousands of miles on the road covering the length and breadth of the peninsula; the scores of meals eaten and enjoyed; the liters of wine tasted, spit (and, OK, we admit, sometimes swallowed); and the many friends encountered, new and old, who were so kind to us; we keep returning to a nation that is, essentially, the warmest, friendliest, and most hospitable on earth. And, in Italy, hospitality begins, as always, with a glass of wine, a plate of food.

THE MEDITERRANEAN DIET

It's official: eating and drinking in Italy is good for you! Studies undertaken by eminent bodies such as the World Health Organization, the French Institut National de la Santé et de la Recherche, and Rome's Institute of Nutrition have now concluded that the Mediterranean diet makes for a longer life and lessens the chances of heart disease. This is one of the few cases where what is good for us is desirable, fashionable, and delicious.

These studies call for a diet of *pasta* and carbohydrates, plenty of anti-oxidizing fresh fruit and vegetables, more fish in place of red meat, less butter and cream in favor of monosaturated olive oil, and regular, moderate, consumption of red wine with meals: in short, the traditional diet of most of Italy.

Pasta, Bella Pasta
THE NATIONAL STAPLE

IS THERE A MORE PERFECT food than *pasta?* It is at once one of the simplest as well as the best foods for us. Guidelines given by the World Health Organization are based on a food pyramid that has, at its base, carbohydrates such as *pasta* to form the bulk staple of our ideal diet (with such high protein food as meats eaten only occasionally). If *pasta* is good for us, it is also one of the most delicious and varied of all foods. And, of course, in no other nation is a greater wealth of types and forms daily enjoyed than in Italy.

Rudimentary forms of *pasta* have existed in Italy since at least Roman times, and possibly even as far back as the Etruscan epoch. The Romans, for example, were fond of making up a paste of flour and water which, after frying, they cut into strips and seasoned with sauce and chickpeas (*laganum et ciceris,* similar to the *laganam e ceci* still enjoyed today in Calabria). The belief that Marco Polo brought back *spaghetti* with him from his travels overland to China is probably not wholly true, though the development of the numerous forms and shapes of *pasta* as we recognize them today could well have found their way to Italy from the Orient by way of Arab traders based in Sicily.

Whatever the exact provenance, what is indubitable today is that Italians are simply passionate about *pasta.* It is enjoyed by all, often twice a day: indeed, a meal without *pasta* to many is hardly

worth contemplating. Witness the alleged suffering of the great tenor Pavarotti during one of his well-publicized diets when he was reported to be rationed to a mere quarter pound (about 100 g.) per day!

TYPES OF *PASTA*

Today, *pasta* is produced in three forms: dried, fresh machine-made, and home-made or hand-made. Dried *pasta,* is, of course, the most common, produced in more than 600 different sizes and shapes, mainly industrially, whereby a paste of hard durum wheat and water is forced mechanically through bronze extruders, then quickly dried in the process. Italian dried *pasta,* even the industrially made, is a very fine food, and there are now smaller companies producing high quality dried *pasta* that can be outstanding, made from selected wheat utilizing slower artisan processes.

Fresh machine-made *pasta* is made from mixtures of either durum wheat, semolina, or soft cake flour, with eggs and water added. Though it is made in machines to ease the work load, the best producers work on a relatively small scale, producing a variety of shapes and sizes. Such *pasta* is consumed daily throughout Italy, needing no more than a simple sauce to complement it.

The finest *pasta,* however, continues to be made by hand, from hard semolina or soft flour *(tipo 00),* eggs, and nothing else, rolled out dexterously with a wooden roller, then cut and formed into an amazing variety of shapes and forms. Good as fresh machine-made *pasta* can be, it is not a patch on fresh hand-made, as still served in restaurants and at home in Italy today. If you have never had the chance to enjoy fresh, handmade *pasta* before, you have a real treat in store, for it is infinitely finer, fresher, and lighter.

There is something of a North-South divide when it comes to *pasta.* The North, influenced by the great gastro-nomic region of Emilia-Romagna, favors

Tortellini, *Emilia-Romagna's favorite* pasta

fresh egg *pasta,* such as *tagliatelle* and stuffed forms like *tortelli* and *ravioli;* the South, however, prefers mainly dried *pasta.* Even when fresh *pasta* is made in the South, it is usually made from a paste of hard durum wheat and water, with no egg added — yet, from humble ingredients, what ingenious variety is created.

Tagliatelle verde, *flat egg noodles with spinach added*

ENJOYING *PASTA*

Pasta in Italy is almost always eaten not as a main course, but as a *primo piatto* (first course), either as *pasta asciutta,* served "dry" with a sauce, or as *pasta in brodo,* that is, small *pasta* shapes added to broth or soup.

Farfalle primavera, *brightly colored "butterfly" pasta*

Yet, within that broad framework, there is such incredible variety that it is hard even for the self-confessed *pasta* fanatic not to get confused and overwhelmed. While we discuss many regional and local *paste* in the second part of this book, the following is a brief guide to *pasta* shapes and sauces usually encountered throughout Italy.

Tagliatelle alla rapa, *flat noodles with rape, a violet root vegetable*

Cannelloni Squares of *pasta* rolled around a stuffing and baked.
Farfalle Butterfly shapes.
Fettuccine Long, thin, ribbon noodles.
Fusilli *Pasta* spirals, though, in the South, often indicates any *maccheroni* type.
Gnocchi Not strictly *pasta:* little dumplings made of potato and flour or semolina, served with sauce.
Lasagne Broad strips of egg *pasta,* often layered and baked. In the South, the term can often be used for any type of broad fresh noodle.
Linguine Thin, flat, *spaghetti*-type noodle.

Maccheroni Stubby tubes of *pasta,* though, in the South, can indicate any type of *pasta.*
Pappardelle Broad, thick egg noodles.
Pasticciata Baked *pasta.*
Ravioli Any type of stuffed *pasta* shape.
Rigatoni Ribbed *maccheroni.*
Spaghetti Still the Italians' favorite.
Tagliatelle Popular, flat egg noodles.
Tortellini Small, stuffed *pasta;* often served in broth.
Tortelloni Large stuffed *pasta;* often served with sauce.
Vermicelli Fine *spaghetti*-type *pasta.*

POPULAR SAUCES

Aglio e olio Olive oil, fried garlic, and (usually) hot pepper flakes.
Amatriciana Smoked *pancetta* (bacon), onions, garlic, and tomato.
Arrabbiata Tomato and *peperoncino* (chilis).
Boscaiola Cream and mushrooms.
Burro e salvia Butter and fresh sage.
Carbonara Diced *pancetta,* eggs, and *pecorino* cheese.
Lepre, alla Rich sauce made from wild hare.
Marinara Fresh tomatoes, garlic, olive oil, and basil.
Noci Creamy walnut, pine nut, and olive oil sauce.
Pesto Pounded basil, pine nuts, garlic, and olive oil.
Pomodoro Fresh tomatoes.
Ragù Classic meat sauce; sometimes called *alla bolognese.*
Sugo di cinghiale Wild boar sauce.
Vongole, alle Clams in oil, white wine and garlic or in tomato sauce.

Pane
BREAD, THE STAFF OF ITALIAN LIFE

It is almost unheard of for an Italian to sit down to a meal without bread. Even when a meal primarily is made up of a bowl of *pasta, risotto, polenta,* or other starch, bread is always an essential accompaniment.

So basic is bread to Italian gastronomy that when you sit down in a restaurant or *trattoria,* you are immediately levied a bread and cover charge, known as *pane e coperto,* as a matter of course.

Pane carasau, *the fine "music paper bread" of Sardinia*

Italian bread can be outstanding, with a good range and variety found throughout the regions. The overwhelming demand

Pane toscano, *unsalted Tuscan bread, traditionally marked with the baker's initials*

almost everywhere is still for white bread, but this too considerably varies in taste, texture, and style from region to region. In much of the North, softly textured rolls and breads are preferred, while in the South, especially in Puglia, superb dense breads are made from hard durum wheat. In Piemonte, *grissini* (breadsticks) stretched out by hand are baked fresh daily, and, in Liguria, there is a tradition of flat breads flavored with local olive oil. Tuscany and Umbria are noted for their delicious unsalted sourdough country bread. And Alto Adige offers an excellent variety of Austrian-inspired breads made from rye, wheat, and other grains.

Some of the important regional breads are further described in the individual regional chapters, but you may find the following guide useful for the national and regional breads available.

Ciabatta "Slipper" shaped loaf; sometimes flavored with olive oil, dried tomatoes, or olives.

Focaccia Flat, pizza-like bread; usually dimpled and dribbled with olive oil.

Pane carasau Known also as *carta da musica* or music-paper bread, the flat, twice-baked bread of Sardinia.

Pane con le noci Walnut bread.

Pane con l'uva Raisin bread; also made with fresh grapes during the grape harvest.

Pane integrale or **pane bigio** Brown or wholewheat bread; usually made with additional bran.

Pane nero Dark rye bread; specialty of Bolzano.

Pane di segale Rye bread.

Pane tipo Altamura Dense, rustic, bread made from durum wheat, with a crunchy, hard crust.

Pane toscano Unsalted, dense sourdough country bread.

Panino Bread roll. (A filled roll or sandwich is also called *panino.*)

Schuttelbrot Hard, crunchy bread flavored with cumin seeds; a specialty of Alto Adige.

A selection of multi-cereal breads and rolls from Alto Adige

Riso
ITALIAN RICE

THOUGH *PASTA* is undoubtedly the staple food of Italy, in the North, especially in Piemonte, Lombardia, and Veneto, rice runs it a close second. Here, the mighty Po River waters a broad and fertile valley, and rice is grown across all three regions.

Vercelli in Northern Piemonte is the area of the greatest and most important cultivation. The sight of extensive stretches of paddies — the new shoots of rice, verdant green in spring; the ripe ears of grain golden at the time of the fall harvest; with the Alps providing a majestic backdrop — is magnificent.

Risotto alla pescatora, *rice with seafood and shell-fish, a popular* risotto *anywhere along the coast*

Italian rice is almost exclusively cultivated to be eaten as *risotto,* a uniquely Italian method of cooking rice whereby short to medium grain varieties are sautéed with butter or oil, then gradually cooked with any number of different ingredients in a rich stock, and finally finished with butter and grated cheese to give a creamy, rich consistency. The rice absorbs the flavorful cooking liquid, yet remains *al dente* — firm to the bite but cooked through — and it is usually served *all'onda,* "wave-like" or moist, to be eaten as a *primo piatto* (first course).

TYPES OF RICE

Only certain varieties of rice have the tenacity to respond well to such treatment and, for this reason, virtually only that which is cultivated and processed in Italy is consumed there.

Italian rice is classified into four categories, depending not on quality but on the length and form of the grain, ranging from the small *ordinario* or *comune* through *semi-fino* and *fino* to *superfino*. The better the quality of the rice, the longer it will take to cook and will absorb more of the cooking liquid. *Riso*

Paddies of Vercelli, Italy's most important rice growing region

integrale (brown rice) is rarely eaten in Italy, considered fit only for those with dietary problems.

The finest Italian rice comes from artisan *riserie* (rice mills) where the rice is milled and polished by slow, traditional methods that do not damage the grains. It is milled and processed only as required so that it can be sold fresh with no need for chemical preservatives.

Carnaroli This *superfino* is cultivated in only tiny quantities, but many rice connoisseurs consider it to be the greatest single variety, most noteworthy for its texture, flavor, and *al dente* bite.

Vialone Nano Another great rice cultivated in minuscule quantities, this *semi-fino* has a shorter, fatter grain than Carnaroli, but is most noteworthy for its capacity to absorb great quantities of cooking liquid (see p.106).

Arborio The best-known and most widely available Italian rice (but not the best), this *super-fino,* nonetheless, is used by many to make excellent *risotti.*

Other good Italian rice varieties are **Baldo, Razza 77,** and **Sant'Andrea.**

Frutta e Ortaggi

A   RICH   HARVEST   OF   FRUITS   AND   VEGETABLES

ITALY ENJOYS a year-round selection of seasonal fruits and vegetables. Fresh produce from the South and Sicily brightens up the markets of Northern Italy in winter, and also those of most of Europe.

But, whereas produce from the South may supplement local and regional produce elsewhere, most markets in Italy prefer the homegrown, the local, and the really fresh. Thus, apart from the basic standard produce found everywhere, there are often items found only in particular regions or localities, such as *cardi gobbi* (cardoons) from Piemonte's Nizza Monferrato; *cavolo nero,* a unique type of winter cabbage only found in Tuscany; or Liguria's favorite *zucchina trombetta* (fine, long, thin zucchini) and *melanzana violetta* (round, white and purple eggplant).

Because produce is, on the whole, local and seasonal, it reaches the consumer while still vividly fresh. This, I believe, is the principal reason why fruits and vegetables have so much more taste in Italy. The other reason, of course, is the sun, which puts such flavor into both. Here, it is true, tomatoes still *taste,* intensely, deliciously of — what else? — tomatoes, especially during their summer glut when they are at their most delicious and can be purchased in markets for a bare pittance. At such times, prudent

Fico d'India, *Indian fig or prickly pear, the popular cactus fruit of Southern Italy*

housewives and *buongustai* (connoisseurs) cart them home by the trayloads to conserve and bottle, not because they save any money by doing so (canned and bottled tomatoes in Italy are of high quality and still inexpensive), but because the quality and flavor of the home product is so superior. Not only are tomatoes conserved in this manner: in the South, especially, there is a great tradition of preserving an enormous range of vegetables *sott'olio* (in jars filled with olive oil) to last through the winter.

Like everything else in this region, natural produce has its own time and rhythm, each product a principal player in a sequence. If summer brings tomatoes followed by zucchini, bell peppers and eggplant, then fall brings the eagerly awaited season of *funghi* (mushrooms), especially the rare and prized *porcini* (cepes), chestnuts for roasting as the nights draw in, and the new season apples.

Winter inevitably leads to leeks and other root vegetables, kale, and cabbages, as well as the first crop of juicy blood oranges from Sicily.

Spring has its own treats, from *baccelli* (tiny fava beans) tender enough to eat raw with *pecorino* cheese, new season *asparagi,* and, of course, soft fruits, such as *fragole* (strawberries) and *lamponi* (raspberries).

Ciliegie, *cherries*

Pomodori, *tomatoes*

Here is a list of fruit and vegetables available nationally; where possible, their approximate seasons are indicated.

LA FRUTTA — FRUITS
Albicocche Apricots (early summer).
Arance Oranges (Oct–Jun).
Castagne Chestnuts (Sep–Nov).
Ciliegie Cherries (May–Jul).
Cocomero Watermelon (Jul–Aug).
Fragole Strawberries (Apr–Jun).
Kiwi Kiwi fruit (Nov–Mar).
Lamponi Raspberries (Jun–Aug).
Limone Lemon (throughout the year).
Mele Apples (Sep–Dec).
Melone Melon (Jun–Aug).
Noci Walnuts (Oct–Nov).
Nocciole Hazelnuts (Oct–Nov).
Pere Pears (Jul–Nov).
Pesche Peaches (Jun–Aug).
Susine Plums (Jul–Sep).
Uva Table grapes (Aug–Nov).

GLI ORTAGGI — VEGETABLES
Aglio Garlic (Jun–Sep).
Asparagi Asparagus, usually the green variety (mid-May–Jul).
Carciofi Artichokes (Apr–Jun).
Cardi Cardoons (fall).
Carote Carrots (most of the year).
Cavolfiore Cauliflower (most of the year).
Cavolo Cabbage (fall–winter).

Cetrioli Cucumbers (Apr–Nov).
Cipolle Onions (throughout the year).
Fagiolini verdi Green beans (Jun–Aug).
Finocchi Bulb fennel (Jun–Sep).
Funghi Mushrooms (cultivated varieties throughout the year; others, summer and fall).
Lattuga Lettuce (various types throughout the year).
Melanzane Eggplant (Jun–Sep).
Patate Potato (throughout the year but new potatoes spring–early summer).
Peperoni Bell peppers, usually red or yellow (May–Oct).
Piselli Peas (early summer).
Pomodori Tomatoes (May–Sep).
Porri Leeks (fall–winter).
Radicchio Round, bitter red lettuce (throughout the year); **radicchio di Treviso** long-leaved red lettuce (fall–winter).
Rape Turnips (winter).
Sedano Celery (spring–summer).
Spinaci Spinach (summer).
Zucchine Zucchini (Jun–Sep).

Cipolle, *onions*

ERBE AROMATICHE — HERBS
Basilico Basil.
Maggiorana Marjoram.
Origano Oregano.
Prezzemolo Flat-leaved parsley.
Rosmarino Rosemary.
Salvia Sage.

Cardi, *cardoons*

Carciofi, *artichokes*

Al Mare

FOOD FROM THE SEAS

THE NARROW Italian Peninsula, extending nearly 1,120 km. (700 miles) from the Alps to almost the northern coast of Africa, is bordered by the Adriatic Sea to the east, and the Tyrrhenian Sea to the west, as well as by the less important Ligurian Sea in the northwest and the Ionian Sea on the instep of the Southern Italian boot. Offshore, Italy includes the large islands of Sicily and Sardinia, the islands of Pantelleria, Linosa, Lampione, and Lampedusa in the Mediterranean between Sicily and North Africa, as well as Capri and Ischia (off the Bay of Naples), Elba, and the Aeolian Islands north of Sicily.

A fish market in Milazzo, Sicily

With such extensive national coastlines, it is not surprising that fishing is an important industry, so the visitor, especially near coastal resorts, should have no difficulty in finding plenty of fresh fish and shellfish. However, as many of Italy's fishing ports are small, often worked by tiny boats using outdated equipment, the catch is insufficient to satisfy the national appetite and, so, fresh fish is inevitably expensive. As the most general of generalizations, fish from the Adriatic is often extremely small but the best can be amazingly sweet compared to larger fish from the Tyrrhenian.

While some large fleets fish in North Atlantic waters, the greater bulk of the catch comes from the Mediterranean, a rich source of some common fish varieties also encountered elsewhere, as well as of, literally, scores of often strange-looking species that have no counterparts

anywhere else. This undoubtedly can cause difficulties in giving precise translations of names and the problem is further complicated by the fact that in many regions, different or local dialect names may also be used. Zoological names or even English equivalents, when they exist, may be of little use to the lay person, if only because it is difficult to correlate one species to the other, since points of reference differ depending on what we are ourselves accustomed to (in North America, for example, the varieties of fish available on the East Coast differ widely from those found either in the Gulf or the Pacific). Where necessary, we have given an indication, at least, of the family or group that a fish belongs to (porgy or sea bream, bass, tuna, etc.), as a rough indicator of what to expect.

The first rule, as always, whether eating fish in a restaurant or buying in a market, is to ask to see the fish, both to get an idea of what it actually is as well as to ensure that it is fresh (eyes clear and bright, gills moist, flesh firm to the touch and the smell pleasant and sea fresh, not strong).

Given the polluted state of much of the Mediterranean, as a general rule, we avoid eating raw fish or shellfish.

In addition to fresh sea fish, Italy's lakes and rivers provide an excellent catch of freshwater fish (see p.79), and salted and/or air-dried cod from Norway and Newfoundland remains a favorite staple throughout the nation.

TYPES OF FISH

Acciuga, alice Anchovy; often best served fresh, not conserved. Semi-salted anchovies can be bought loose in markets.

Agone Freshwater shad from the lakes of Lombardia.

Alalunga or **albacore** Long fin tuna, the prized white tuna considered by many the finest of the tuna family.

Anguilla Eel.

Baccalà Dried salt cod (see p.24).

SOME FAVORITE WAYS OF COOKING FISH

Arrosto Roasted whole.
Bollito or **lessato** Boiled.
Brodetto Adriatic fish stew.
Carpione, in Fried fillets soused in vinegar and eaten cold.
Cartoccio, al Baked in parchment paper.
Ferri, ai Grilled, often over charcoal.
Forno, al Baked.
Fritto Fried.
Griglia, alla Char-grilled or broiled.
Ripieno Stuffed.
Umido, in Stewed; usually in wine with herbs.

Branzino Sea bass, one of the great fish of the Mediterranean; expensive, but when fresh, outstanding.
Cappone Sea robin or gurnard.
Cavalla Chub mackerel.
Cefalo Gray mullet.
Cernia Grouper.
Dentice Dentex, a type of porgy or sea bream; excellent grilled.
Grongo Conger eel.
Merlano Silver hake, Pacific hake, whiting.
Merluzzo Hake, an important and plentiful Mediterranean fish.
Orata Gilt-head bream, the finest fish from the porgy or bream family.
Parago Red porgy or sea bream.
Pesce persico Royal perch, a prized freshwater fish.
Pesce sciabola Scabbard fish, a silvery, long, eel-like fish which can be excellent.
Pesce serra Bluefish.
Pesce spada Swordfish; one of the great fishes of Southern Italy, best cut into steaks and grilled.
Pesce volante Flying fish.
Rana pescatrice Monkfish or angler-fish (known also as *rospo*).

Razza Ray.
Ricciola Amberjack, a large, superbly flavored fish; often treated like sword-fish, cut into steaks and grilled.
Rombo Turbot, a fine, large flatfish.
Rospo, coda di rospo Monkfish or angler-fish; only the tail of this large-mouthed monster is eaten, but it is truly excellent, firmly textured, its flavor not unlike that of lobster.
San Pietro John Dory, an ugly but outstanding, firm-fleshed fish.
Sarago, sargo Striped porgy or sea bream.
Sardina, sarda Sardine or, if large, pilchard.
Sgombro Mackerel.
Sogliola Dover sole, the finest flatfish.
Spigola Sea bass (also called **branzino**).
Suro Horse mackerel.
Tonnetto Little tunny, a true member of the tuna family, though often caught when mackerel-sized; outstanding in flavor and generally quite inexpensive.
Tonno Bluefin tuna.
Tordo Wrasse; often used in fish soups.
Tracina dragone Weever, a poisonous fish; delicious in fish soups, once its spines have been carefully removed.
Triglia Goatfish or red mullet, one of the great fishes of the Mediterranean; excellent char-grilled or *in umido* (stewed).
Trota Trout; a favorite from freshwater lakes and rivers.

Fishermen idling away the hours on Lipari, one of the Aeolian Islands in the Tyrrhenian Sea

Frutti di Mare

SHELLFISH AND SEAFOOD

ITALIANS, IT IS SOMETIMES SAID, will eat just about anything that moves, and this is certainly true of shellfish and seafood. There is a wide, and sometimes bewildering, variety gathered and (in some cases) cultivated around the nation's shores, consumed with gusto as *antipasti* or served over steaming bowls of *pasta*.

Though we ourselves have never suffered any ill effects from eating shellfish in Italy, avoid eating raw shellfish or anything that does not look or smell absolutely fresh.

Aragosta Spiny lobster or crawfish; similar to lobster but without claws.

Astice Lobster.

Calamari Squid.

Cappesante Scallops (known also as *pettini, ventagli, pellegrine*).

Cannocchia Mantis shrimp, similar to small *cicala*.

Cannolicchio Razor-shell clam.

Cicala Flat lobster, highly prized, well-flavored variety.

Cozze Mussels.

Dattero di mare Sea date; a delicious bi-valve eaten raw or used to make *zuppa* (soup).

Gamberetto Brown shrimp.

Gambero Large shrimp or prawn.

Grancevola, granseola Spider crab; no claw meat, but regarded highly for its sweet body flesh.

Granchio Soft-shelled crab.

Granciporro Common edible crab.

Muscoli Mussels.

Ostrica Oyster.

Polipo, polpo Octopus.

Riccio di mare Sea urchin.

Scampi Norway lobster or langoustine.

Seppia Cuttlefish.

Tartufo di mare Sea truffle is a more appetizing name than the English, Warty Venus; a fine, highly prized bivalve, eaten raw or steamed over *pasta*.

Totano Flying squid; reddish and populous in southern waters.

Vongole Clams; the finest are *vongole veraci*, excellent steamed and served over hot *spaghetti*.

Grigliata mista di pesce, *mixed grill of seafood and shellfish*

STOCCAFISSO AND BACCALA

Given the wide availability of fresh fish in Italy, it is perhaps surprising that *baccalà* (salt cod) and *stoccafisso* (air-dried cod or stockfish) are still so popular throughout the nation.

Cod is not native to the Mediterranean, but there has been a centuries-long lively trade in preserved fish with the Scandinavian countries as well as Newfoundland.

In this Roman Catholic nation, where it was and remains necessary to eat fish on days ordained meatless, in times past, dried or salt cod was often all there was available. Old tastes die hard, and today, *baccalà* and *stoccafisso* continue to be widely eaten out of choice, not necessity.

Stoccafisso is considered the finer of the two, better in flavor, more delicate, and less salty than *baccalà*. The best still comes from Norway and is referred to as *ragno*.

Both *baccalà* and *stoccafisso* should be soaked in several changes of fresh water for more than 48 hours before cooking, though, often, they can be bought pre-soaked and ready to cook.

Meat and Poultry
QUALITY IS ALL

A DOMINANT feature of the Mediterranean diet is that *pasta* and other carbohydrates as well as plenty of fresh vegetables are eaten in much greater quantity than high protein meat. Italians are not, on the whole, great carnivores.

Pork butcher's sign

They are, however, particularly fastidious and discerning when it comes to buying and consuming meat: as always, only the best will do. As a consequence, butchers go to great ends to cut precisely and trim exactly whatever their customers require, even for purchases of as little as 200 g. (7 oz.). Meat, if excellent in quality, remains relatively expensive, another reason why it is purchased with care.

Though Italy cannot boast a system of controlled denominations as intricate or well-defined as France's system of *appellation d'origine contrôlée,* there is a growing awareness that traditional food must be safeguarded. Thus, with *manzo* (beef) for example, under the *Cinque Razze* scheme, five races of indigenous cattle have been picked for the superior quality of their meat: Chianina, Romagnola, Marchigiana, Maremmana, and Podolica. It is certainly worth looking out for meat from any of these superior and distinctive breeds.

Vitello (veal) is as popular or even more so than beef, in spite of its high cost. The best is *vitello da latte* (from a milk-fed calf no older than four to six weeks). *Vitellone* comes from an animal that is too old to be *vitello* but not yet old enough to be considered beef. It can be exceptionally tender and flavorful as in the cut from the Chianina cattle used for Tuscany's most famous meat dish, *bistecca alla fiorentina* (see p.168).

Given that sheep rearing is still an important nationwide activity, it is not surprising that *agnello* (lamb) and *castrato* (mutton from a castrated animal) are also regularly enjoyed. The best lamb, like veal, comes from baby animals still feeding on milk *(abbacchio). Capretto* (kid) is also popular, especially in the South, and is excellent roasted.

Pigs in Italy are raised primarily to be transformed into *salumi* (cured pork products), but *maiale* (fresh pork) is also widely consumed. A national favorite is *porchetta* (roast suckling pig).

Pollame (poultry) is plentiful, too, and eaten throughout the nation. As always, the best often comes from small individual farms where the free-range animals are allowed to live and run around outdoors. A visit to such a farm can be a sobering experience: we stopped once where a roadside sign indicated that *polli ruspanti* were available and we, and especially our children, were appalled to be reminded of the realities of the food chain when the proud cockerel we had admired happily running around outside was dispatched and made "oven-ready" in front of our eyes in no more than five minutes (to top it all, the meat was as tough as old boots).

Tacchino (turkey) is also popular, primarily to provide cuts of breast to serve as an inexpensive alternative to veal. *Cappone* (capon) is enjoyed at Christmas and other festive occasions and *faraona* (guinea hen), *anitra* (duck), and *oca* (goose) are also available.

Whole suckling pigs and spring lamb cooking over an open wood fire in Sardinia

Salumi

CURED PORK AND OTHER MEAT PRODUCTS

THE GENERIC TERM for Italian cured meat products is *salumi*, of which *salame* (salami as we know it) is but one item. Curing pork by salting and aging it is one of the oldest and most important traditional ways of preserving meat, a technique highly developed in Italy.

Of course, the home curing of pork goes back to the time not that long ago of the *mezzadria* (a feudal form of share-cropping) whereby, in return for a house and a piece of land, the *mezzadraio* shared half his crops with the *padrone* (land-owner). In addition to a few rows of vines, grain, or olives, there would always be a pig or two, raised to be slaughtered before winter, then salted to preserve for the cold months. The best *salame* and *prosciutto* were always delivered to the *padrone* out of respect.

Today, the widescale production of *salumi* is carried out by artisan individual butchers as well as on an industrial scale, as these products are considered essential to the Italian diet and are consumed in great quantities.

Basically, *salumi* fall into two principal groups: those products made by curing a large whole section of meat *(prosciutto, spalla, capocollo),* and those made by grinding the meat to varying degrees of texture, then mixing it with other ingredients (fresh and cured sausages, such as *salami, mortadella,* etc.). On the whole, pork is the meat most widely used, though *cinghiale* (wild boar), *cervo* (venison), and *capra* (kid) are also used when available, and beef tenderloin is cured to produce *bresaola.*

An enormous and imaginative range of products is concocted throughout the nation, many available only locally or regionally (and covered in individual chapters in the second part of this book).

TRY TO SAMPLE

Bresaola Salted, air-dried tenderloin of beef; the best is produced in Lombardia's Valtellina.

Capocollo Meaty, cured pork product made from the upper neck and shoulder, kept whole, cured in salt and spices and aged until quite hard and dry; mainly a product of Central and South Italy.

Coppa Cylindrical cured *salumi* made with large pieces of pork from the head and shoulder; usually highly seasoned with black pepper, then aged for upward of six months. To be eaten sliced or used in cooking.

Cotechino Boiling *salame.*

Culatello Prized cured pork product made from the rump of the pig rubbed in spices and cured in a pig's bladder.

Finocchiona Outstanding Central Italian *salame* with a characteristic loose texture and the distinctive flavor of wild fennel seeds.

Guanciale Cured pig's cheek or jowl, rather fatty, mainly used in cooking.

Lingua Pig's or lamb's tongue, cured in brine.

Lonza Meaty loin of pork cured in salt and garlic.

Lucanica Spicy pork sausage for grilling.

Mortadella The original "baloney" of Bologna, a large sausage made from a

Prosciutto di Parma *airing in a ham loft in the hills of Langhirano, south of Parma*

mix of lean, finely ground pork dotted with large nuggets of smooth fat.

Musetto Another name for *cotechino* or boiling *salame*.

Pancetta Cured belly pork, the closest equivalent to what we know as bacon. *Pancetta* is essentially used as a flavoring ingredient in cooking, though superior, lean versions are sometimes rolled to be cut into thin slices and eaten like *salami*.

Prosciutto Ham.

Prosciutto cotto Cooked ham.

Prosciutto crudo Salted, air-dried ham, the most famous of which comes from Parma and is consumed raw *(crudo)*. Similar cured and aged hams are produced throughout Italy. Many local versions, which can also be excellent, are *prosciutto crudo salato* (in contrast to the sweet *prosciutto crudo dolce* of Parma or San Daniele), produced by utilizing a longer period of salting, followed by a shorter period of aging. (see pp.109, 141, and 163).

Prosciutto crudo di cervo Air-cured venison *prosciutto*.

Prosciutto crudo di cinghiale Salted, air-cured ham made from the hind leg of *cinghiale* (wild boar).

Salame Finely ground lean pork and fat, mixed with other seasonings and stuffed in skins of varying sizes, then left to age and dry. A huge range of individual, local, and regional variations

Smoked speck

Pancetta

Salsicce

Capocollo

exist, the best of which are highlighted in individual chapters in the second part of this book. Italian *salami* often encountered nationally include *salame milanese* (finely ground, small-grained mix of pork and sometimes beef); *salame genovese* (tasty, well-flavored mix of finely ground pork, pork fat, and veal); *salame napoletano* (slightly coarser texture with larger pieces of pork fat mixed with lean in a well-seasoned mixture of pork and sometimes beef). *Salame nostrano* indicates locally produced *salami*.

Salamino Small *salame*.

Salsicce Fresh sausages.

Salsicce piccante Spicy sausages.

Salsiccce di cinghiale Wild boar sausages; can be either cured for eating raw or fresh for cooking.

Soppressa Large *salame* made from mix of coarsely ground lean and fatty pork.

Soppressata Pressed, meaty *salame* mainly from South Italy, often flavored with *peperoncino*.

Spalla Shoulder of pork cured in a similar manner to both *prosciutto cotto* and *crudo* — fattier but less expensive.

Speck Cured, smoked *prosciutto crudo;* the best of which comes from Trentino-Alto Adige (see p.108).

Violino Air-cured hind leg of goat (or sometimes mutton); a mountain specialty.

Zampone Boiling *salame* stuffed into a pig's trotter, a specialty of Modena.

Selvaggina e Selvatici
WILD FOOD FOR FREE

SOMEWHERE IN the Italian psyche, I conjecture, there lurks a vestigial folk memory of a prehistoric life that relied on hunting and fishing as well as gathering edible wild plants: for the fact is many Italians enjoy nothing more than heading out into the

Fresh funghi porcini, *cepe mushrooms*

country to hunt or fish, or simply to collect wild food — from berries and chestnuts, to precious *porcini* (cepes) and other mushrooms, or even the rare black and white *tartufi* (truffles). No doubt, the already emphatic flavors of such foods are further intensified by the knowledge that they were gathered gratis.

Such activities are not entirely without their hazards. Italian *cacciatori* (hunters) are

Castagne, *chestnuts*

nothing if not enthusiastic, and are notorious for taking a pot shot at almost anything that moves: so ramblers beware, as signs in the hunting season will warn. (It is always a good idea to wear bright clothing.)

Those in search of *funghi,* meanwhile, must really know what they are looking for: numerous varieties that are highly sought, alas, have deadly lookalikes. Every year, there are fatalities from eating poisonous mushrooms. In most towns in Italy, there are public health offices where one can take gathered mushrooms to be checked officially. But, Italians being Italians, we have found that macho pride does not always allow such precautions, for there are few mushroom gatherers who would readily admit to anything less than expertise. So, if in doubt, let the "experts" sample first. Wild mushrooms on sale in markets and as served in restaurants are almost always safe to eat, so have no fears.

Of course, there are other less hazardous but equally enjoyable country pursuits. In fall, one of the most popular activities is gathering *castagne* (chestnuts) to take home to roast over an open fire, preferably accompanied by either *mosto* (partially fermented wine), or the first new wine in November.

TYPES OF GAME
Beccaccia Woodcock.
Capriolo Roe buck.
Cervo Venison.
Cinghiale Wild boar.
Coniglio selvatico Wild rabbit.
Fagiano Pheasant.
Lepre Hare.
Pernice Partridge.
Piccione Pigeon.
Quaglia Quail.
Uccelletti Small songbirds. The penchant for eating just about anything, including small songbirds, has been tempered in recent years by stricter conservation laws.

TYPES OF *FUNGHI*
Chiodino Conical shaped, ochre-colored mushroom widely gathered and consumed.
Finferlo Bright orange, finely flavored mushroom, similar to French *chanterelles*.
Ovulo Egg-shaped mushroom appreciated since Roman times and called "food of the gods" by Nero.
Porcino *Boletus edulis* or cepes, the most prized of all wild mushrooms; delicious fresh and dried for use all year round.
Trombetta da morto Chestnut brown, with a fine but resistant cap.

Olio d'Oliva

THE ESSENCE OF THE MEDITERRANEAN DIET

FROM THE LIGURIAN COAST, past the shores of Lake Garda, through Le Marche, Tuscany, and Umbria, way down to Puglia and Calabria, and beyond to Sicily and other islands, the olive tree flourishes happily. This sturdy Mediterranean plant provides fruit for eating as well as for its precious oil.

Today, supermarkets the world over stock enormous ranges and varieties of olive oils, for the health claims made on behalf of this fashionable monosaturated fat are legion: studies claim that it may help to reduce coronary disease by lowering blood cholesterol, control obesity, assist digestion, and act as an anti-oxidant and general panacea.

Granite millstones, traditionally used to grind olives before pressing

The main reason olive oil is so popular, however, is that it is delicious — raw-processed as a dressing as well as an ingredient in Mediterranean-style cooking.

The finest and most expensive Italian olive oil is *olio extra vergine d'oliva,* (extra-virgin olive oil), which must be extracted from the first cold pressing of olives and contain less than one per cent oleic acid. The lower the acid content, the fruitier and fuller the flavor and aroma. The best of such oils are traditionally produced from hand-harvested olives ground to a pulp by granite millstones, cold-pressed, i.e., without heating, then filtered.

Olio vergine d'oliva (virgin olive oil) is similarly cold-pressed and may contain up to two per cent oleic acid. Plain *olio d'oliva* is usually a mix of inferior oils that have been heat treated to extract more oil then refined.

Fine single-estate extra-virgin olive oils, especially from Tuscany, have become as precious as fine wine (see p.161). But affordable superb cold-pressed traditional oils also come from Liguria (excellent with fish), Le Marche (very fruity, with considerable finesse), Lake Garda (fine, peppery when new), and Puglia (Italy's largest source, producing fat, dense, fruity oils that can be outstanding and still quite inexpensive).

Olive trees, an essential feature of the Italian landscape

Formaggi
C H E E S E

ITALIAN CHEESES may be less well-known internationally than those of France, but they are equally rewarding in variety of type and style and quality. Throughout the nation, milk from cows, sheep, goats, and water buffalo is transformed into an array of glorious, exciting, and often world-class cheeses.

Cheese has been made in Italy since its earliest days. Indeed, when Homer's Odysseus in his wanderings came to what is generally regarded as the island of Sicily, the cyclops Polyphemus was already making ewe's milk cheese in his grotto. The Etruscans mastered the art of coagulating fresh milk by using a vegetable rennet, probably made from wild artichokes: *Marzolino,* an excellent ewe's milk cheese from Chianti, is still produced today in the same way. The ancient Romans certainly enjoyed a variety of cheeses, and new methods and styles were perfected and developed during the Middle Ages, often in Cistercian and Benedictine monasteries.

The *Istituto Nazionale di Sociologia Rurale* has estimated that there are some 400 classified Italian cheeses and probably many more made only locally: wherever you are in Italy, try to sample local specialties. The great regional cheeses of Italy are described in individual chapters in the second part of this book; the following is a list of the types and styles of Italian cheeses you will come across.

"DOLCE O STAGIONATO?"

When choosing cheese, you may be asked whether you prefer *dolce* (fresh, unaged), *semi-secco, mezzano,* or *semi-duro* (medium aged, for four–six months, depending on the type of cheese), *stagionato* (aged for 12 months or even longer), or *stravecchio* (well-aged, in some cases, for two years or more). If in doubt, ask for a taste *("un assaggio")* before buying.

TYPES OF ITALIAN CHEESES

Ricotta A fresh cheese produced by reheating the whey left over in the cheesemaking process, resulting in a fresh, light, lowfat cheese which can be eaten immediately, used in cooking or in desserts, or left to age to become *ricotta salata,* a favorite cheese for grating over *pasta* in Puglia, Sardinia, and Sicily. *Ricotta* can be made from cow's, ewe's, or buffalo's milk.

Pasta filata The term used to indicate a uniquely Italian family of layered cheeses, including *mozzarella,* produced primarily in the South. They are eaten extremely fresh, either on the day or, at most, within days of production; or else, they are aged for a few months and sometimes smoked. Such cheeses are produced by chopping or cutting strips of solidified fresh curd, which are then mixed in boiling water and formed into shapes held together by an elastic cheesy skin. Cheeses included in this family are *provolone, caciocavallo, scamorza,* and *mozzarella di bufala* and its derivatives.

Pecorino The general term for any variety of ewe's milk cheese produced throughout Italy, and in a number of different styles, to be consumed young and fresh, medium-aged, or aged for more than a year. Though some of the finest *pecorino* for eating comes from Tuscany and Umbria, excellent *pecorino romano* is produced in Lazio (the Romans' favorite grating cheese). Sardinia's *pecorino sardo* is also outstanding, as are Sicilian versions, such as the hard *pecorino pepato,* studded with black peppercorns.

Stracchino This term is applied to rich, buttery cheeses from Northern Italy, containing up to 50 per cent fat and which are usually eaten while fresh and young. *Gorgonzola,* Italy's greatest blue-veined cheese, available both *dolce* (fresh) and *piccante* (sharp), is a member of this family, as is creamy *taleggio,* and the exceedingly fresh *stracchino* itself, a favorite dessert cheese.

Mountain cheeses Cheeses produced on the alpine slopes of Northern Italy, as well as on the lower pastures leading up to the Apennines, Alps, and Dolomites include such hard-pressed classics as *asiago* and *vezzena* from Veneto, creamy *fontina* from Valle d'Aosta, and pungent ewe's and goat's milk *tome* from Piemonte. *Tome* are sometimes further aged with oil, truffles, mushrooms, *peperoncino* (chili pepper), or other flavorings. The finest mountain cheeses are made from unpasteurized milk from animals that have grazed in summer in high pastures redolent with wild flowers and herbs.

Grana These cooked, hard cheeses rank among the great cheeses of the world; concentrated in flavor, matured for more than a year, acquiring a granular texture that makes them excellent for eating as well as grating. *Parmigiano reggiano* (see p.144–145) and *grana padano* are the two outstanding examples of this family. So valuable are these great *grana* cheeses that they are traditionally aged in cheese vaults owned by banks.

Marzolino, *a ewe's milk cheese of Chianti Classico, Tuscany, made traditionally using wild artichokes to coagulate the milk*

Ewes being milked in Sardinia, where their milk is used to make an outstanding range of *pecorino sardo cheeses*

Vats of curds being cooked for *parmigiano reggiano, one of the great cheeses of the world*

Provolone *and* caciocavallo, *two typical cheeses of Southern Italy*

Condiments and Conserves
AGE-OLD METHODS OF CONSERVING

ITALY IS THE SOURCE of so much good and delicious seasonal produce that Italians long ago devised ways of preserving this bounty for later use by employing traditional and modern methods of conservation side by side.

The *pomodoro* — golden apple, as the tomato was named in the 16th century when it reached Italy from Mexico — has come to be something of a symbol of Italian food at home and abroad. When field upon field of outdoor-grown tomatoes ripen on the vine in June and July, especially in southern regions such as Puglia and Campania, it is awe-inspiring to witness the

Dried chili peppers fried in hot oil, a piquant accompaniment to drinks

almost military precision with which they are picked, loaded carefully in crates, and dispatched quickly to the immense canneries for processing. Indeed, Italian canned plum tomatoes are the finest in the world. But even at the artisan and domestic level, tomatoes are cooked into conserves and concentrates, split open and salted then left to dry in the sun, or simply strung up for use all winter long.

When other vegetables enjoy their flush of seasonal plenty, they too are harvested and conserved to be eaten throughout the year. *Fave novelle* (baby

Sun-dried tomatoes, to be eaten as an antipasto *with* salumi *or added to sauces*

fava beans), *funghi* (mushrooms), *carciofini* (baby artichokes*)*, zucchini, and *melanzane* (eggplant) are all preserved in jars *sott'olio* (in olive oil), while other fresh seasonal vegetables are pickled *sott'aceto* (in vinegar).

In the South, especially, the *peperoncino* (chili pepper) is widely cultivated and harvested, and then strings of colorful peppers are hung out to dry in the sun. For the *cucina povera* — poor folk's food — of the South has necessitated that chili peppers were and still are consumed in abundance, as a way of inexpensively adding flavor and fire to foods when no other more substantial ingredients were available. *Peperoncini,* as well as being available dried in strings, are converted in oil, vinegar and made into a range of bottled pastes and sauces.

Fresh fruits are transformed into concentrated *sciroppi* (syrups) for refreshing drinks, infused in alcohol, or made into sweet preserves and marmalades. And, of course, pungent and flavorful condiments such as *mostarda di frutta* (fruit mustard) add a classic *agrodolce* (sweet-and-sour) accent to the foods they accompany.

Good things come from the mountains and woods too. Fresh wild mushrooms are gathered, then carefully dried for use all year round. *Tartufi* (truffles) are one of the most fleeting and elusive of all foods, but in Piemonte, Umbria, and Le Marche, artisan conservers attempt to capture their haunting aroma and lingering flavors in a range of truffle-scented pastes, oils, and sauces.

Traditionally conserved and preserved vegetables and fruits have been part of the great gastronomic heritage of Italy. Such items may also make great food gifts to take back home.

Gelati

ITALIAN ICE CREAM

ONE OF THE MOST consistent — if simplest — of pleasures in Italy is *gelati*, its world-famous ice cream. No matter where you are in the country, there is always a good, artisan *gelateria*, producing a staggering range of home-made ice creams, ices, *semifreddi*, and other iced specialties.

The reason Italian ice cream is so outstanding — in our opinion, the best in the world — is because it is not dependent on novelty or a rash of weird combinations of flavors or ingredients. Italian ice cream is exceptional quite simply because it does not compromise the purity and quality of its ingredients. It is the concentration and intensity of flavors that is so wonderful, so that even a small cup or cone explodes with flavor in the mouth.

Essentially, there are two main types of ice cream: *gelati alla crema*, made from a base of milk, egg yolk, and sugar to which other flavorings are added (vanilla, chocolate, coffee, mocha); and *gelati alla frutta*, made with a high proportion of fresh fruit or the pulp of conserved fruit

A selection of granite, *from left:* pesca *(peach),* caffè *(coffee), and* limone *(lemon)*

and sugar syrup.

Semifreddo has a mousse-like consistency because of the addition of whipped egg white, which, because it does not freeze, keeps the ice cream in its *semi-freddo* (not-quite-frozen) state.

Elaborate cream cakes, *bombes,* and other frozen specialties are also enjoyed. The *tartufo,* an intense chocolate creation shaped like a truffle, is a particularly popular dessert in restaurants and should be tried. *Granite* (the best come from the South) are slushy ices made with fresh fruit pulp or juice or coffee.

GELATI VARIETIES

Amaretto With *amaretti* macaroons and Amaretto liqueur.
Banana Banana.
Caffè Coffee.
Cassata Based on the famous Sicilian cake: an ice cream *bombe* with candied fruit, *ricotta*, and pieces of chocolate.
Cedro Citron; bitter-sweet citrus fruit from the South.
Cioccolato Chocolate.
Fior di latte Cream.
Fragola Strawberry.
Frutti di bosco Mix of wild berries.

Gianduia Chocolate and hazelnut.
Limone Lemon.
Malaga With rum and Malaga raisins.
Mirtillo Bilberry.

Nocciola Hazelnut.
Pesca Peach.
Pistacchio Pistacchio.
Stracciatella Chocolate chip.
Tartufo Chocolate ice cream that looks like a truffle.
Tiramisù Based on the Venetian cake; with biscuits, liqueur, and cocoa.
Torroncino With honey-and-almond *torrone* (nougat).
Zabaione Egg yolk-thickened ice flavored with Marsala.

Sagre e Feste

CELEBRATING WITH FOOD

SOMEWHERE IN ITALY there is probably a *sagra* or a *festa* on any day of the year. From solemn religious processions to joyous harvest festivals, from traditional annual gatherings to new events designed to celebrate as well as promote the labors of a year: Italy is a nation that likes nothing so much as an excuse for a good communal party. And in typical Italian fashion, no party in Italy would be complete without the chance to eat, drink, and be merry.

Pane di Santa Rita, *specially prepared for a religious festival in Oliena, Sardinia*

There are, literally, scores of food and wine festivals throughout the nation. As such, they provide an excellent opportunity get to know an area and its people as well as its products. For Italians, always friendly and open to outsiders, are even more so at their own festivals.

Some festivals are of national and even international importance, such as the remarkable month-long *Fiera del tartufo* or Truffle Fair of Alba in Piemonte, where restaurateurs and gourmets from all over the world come to taste and buy the rare white truffles of Alba. Others are so local that they are really little more than gatherings of groups of like-minded friends.

In each regional chapter in the second part of this book, we include the dates of some of the more significant food festivals: a *peperoncino* festival in Calabria takes the meaning of *piccante* to new levels by celebrating not only hot peppers but also erotic art in all forms, while at the *Fiera del riso* at Isola della Scala near Verona, thousands of portions of fresh *risotto* are prepared daily for the public. Among other food celebrations, there are festivals dedicated to *polenta,* strawberries, the famed grilled Tuscan T-bone steak, *pizza, prosciutto,* fish, *radicchio di Treviso,* beer, mushrooms, and even new season peas.

In other cases, religious festivities provide an opportunity for a communal "let-it-all-hang-out" party, with games and, of course, plenty of serious eating and drinking. Some of the best food and/or drink festivals may be worth planning a special visit for, especially if you have a passion or great interest in that particular food or drink. Inquire at your nearest Italian State Tourist Office for up-to-date information.

On the other hand, the hundreds of festivals that are primarily of local, sometimes even only of neighborhood, interest can be equally satisfying to drop in on whenever you discover one in full swing. Check at the local tourist office if anything is going on, ask local residents, or look out for posters advertising village or local *feste* or *sagre.* In September and October, particularly, there are wine and grape festivals throughout most of Italy, and these are invariably joyous and raucous affairs. So, roll up your sleeves, wade right in, and simply join in the communal festivities.

The Sagra della bistecca, *feast of the celebrated Tuscan T-bone steak, at Cortona, Tuscany*

Shopping for Food and Drink

WHERE AND WHAT TO BUY

WHETHER YOU ARE staying in rented, self-catering accommodation, putting together a picnic, window shopping, or looking for edible gifts to take back home, there will be no shortage of opportunities to buy food and drink in Italy.

This is a nation still made up primarily of small, independent, traditional specialist shops, and visiting them is one of the true joys of daily life. Of course, there are supermarkets and self-service stores where you can find things more quickly and without recourse to struggling with a foreign language. But if you are looking for quality, if you care about what you eat, and if you want to get the feel of daily Italian life and really shop like a local, then you must take the time to visit the traditional food shops of Italy.

The essential thing to remember is to take your time. To shop in small, individual establishments is to enjoy the opportunity to participate in the daily life of a community. As a result, shopkeepers rarely serve customers without having a brief conversation. If there are a few people in front of you, have patience, for when it is your turn, you, even as a foreigner, will be treated similarly with courtesy and respect. Even if you are just buying tiny quantities — say an *etto* (100 g. or about ¼ lb.) each of different *salami* or cheeses — the shopkeeper will slice and wrap your purchases as carefully as he would for his most prized customers. Indeed, if you are staying in the same place for a while, after your first visit, *you* will be made to feel the prized regular. Be patient and polite, greeting with a *buon giorno/buona sera* and leaving with an *arriverderci;* ask or gesture if you do not know what something is; and always seek advice or a taste if you are unsure. And

A general store in Rome selling daily necessities

always check "sell-by" dates on any packaged goods, as we have found that Italians are not always attentive to them.

LO SCONTRINO

In Italy, by law, customers must always receive *lo scontrino* (the receipt) for their purchases. You must keep this until you reach home or your hotel. If stopped by a member of the *Guardia di Finanza* (police charged with stamping out fraud and the "black economy"), failure to produce the *scontrino* could result in a fine for both you and the shopkeeper.

SPECIALIST FOOD SHOPS

Alimentari or **generi alimentari** This is the Italian corner shop, found in every town, village, or local neighborhood, stocking just about everything, from cans and packaged food (even cornflakes) to fresh eggs, *salumi* and cheeses, wines, or

---

SHOPPING HOURS

Food shops in Italy are generally open five-and-a-half days a week, from about 8:30 a.m. until 12:30 or 1 p.m., then again from about 3:30 or 4:00 p.m. until 7:30 or 8:00 p.m. In summer and the farther south you go, the midday break is longer, with some shops not reopening in the afternoon until as late as 5:00 or 5:30 p.m.

Many food shops are open Sunday mornings, especially *pasticceria* (selling pastries and desserts for Sunday meals), bakeries, and delicatessens. All shops close one day a week, as posted on the door: for example, *Giorno di chiusura lunedì* (closed Monday).

spirits. Often, there is a bar attached where you can enjoy an *espresso* while waiting to be served.

Caseificio or **latteria** The *caseificio* or *latteria* sells *formaggio* (cheese), *latte* (milk), and other dairy products, including *burro* (butter) and *panna* (cream). Sometimes, the *caseificio* is the actual dairy where such products are processed. *Latte fresco* is fresh milk (as opposed to U.H.T. — heat treated milk sold in tetra-brik cartons). *Latte scremato* and *latte parzialmente scremato* are, respectively, skimmed milk and semi-skimmed milk. Most *latterie* sell *uova* (eggs) by *una dozzina* (a dozen).

Enoteca The specialist wine shop may sell a good selection of fine wines by the bottle, three-bottle box, or 12-bottle case, as well as inexpensive *vino sfuso* (bulk wine on tap), to fill your own 5- or 10-liter (1¼- or 2½-gal.) container.

Shopping at a pescheria for fresh fish and shellfish

Frantoio This can be either the olive-oil mill or a shop that specializes in a range of olive oils (sometimes such shops also sell wine and simply call themselves *vini e olii*). In a *frantoio*, olive oil may usually be bought by the bottle or can, as well as *sfuso*, decanted into your own container.

Frutte e verdure Fruit and vegetable shops sell unpackaged produce, usually purchased by weight or individual item. You can usually, but not always, select or choose what you want yourself without incurring the wrath of the *fruttivendolo* (greengrocer). Always buy seasonally and preferably from local producers.

Gelateria The ice cream shop sells not only cones or cups of *gelato* for eating on the spot but also ice cream packed in tubs to take away as well as specialties such as ice cream cakes.

Macelleria Butchers sell fresh meat, poultry, and sometimes a limited selection of *salumi* (cured pork products). A shop selling exclusively poultry is called a *polleria*.

Norcineria Butchers who are particularly proud of their range of homemade *salumi* may call themselves *norcinerie*, after Norcia, a town in Umbria famous for its cured pork products.

SOME USEFUL SHOPPING PHRASES, WEIGHTS, AND MEASURES

Vorrei ... I would like ...
Per piacere, per favore Please
Grazie Thank you
Una fetta (... fette) A slice (... slices)
Una dozzina A dozen
Un pacchetto A packet
Una scatola A can
Tutta la forma The whole thing (as for a whole cheese or *salame*)
Mi dà ... per favore Please give me ...
Quant'è? How much (does it all come to)?
Un etto 100 g. (3½ oz.) (useful when buying *salami* or *prosciutto*)

Mezzo chilo Half a kilogram (approximately 1 lb.)
Un chilo A kilogram (approximately 2¼ lbs.)

APPROXIMATE CONVERSIONS
200 g. = 7 oz.
500 g. = 1 lb.
1 kg. = 2¼ lbs.
1 liter = 1 (U.S.) quart or 1¾ Imperial pints
1 (U.S.) pint = 0.5 liter
1 (Imperial) pint > 0.5 liter

Freshly baked pastries and breads at a panificio *in Camucia, near Arezzo, Tuscany*

Panetteria, panificio, or **forno**
The bread shop or bakery sells a range of fresh baked breads, *biscotti* (twice-cooked sweet biscuits or cookies), *grissini* (breadsticks), *panini* (rolls), and sweet pastries. Though the overwhelming preference throughout Italy is still for white bread, *pane integrale* (brown bread) and *pane di segale* (rye bread) are increasingly available, together with other specialty breads (see p.18).

Pasticceria The pastry shop is one of the most important local institutions in every town or village, the source of everyday cakes, cookies, and pastries as well as amazing creations for special celebrations. There is always one shop that is considered the best in town, so ask around.

Pastificio or **pasta fresca** Fresh and freshly stuffed *paste* made on the premises. Buy by weight or simply say for how many. Most *pastifici* also sell a selection of homemade sauces.

Pescheria The fishmonger; source of fresh fish and shellfish. (Always examine fish for freshness before buying.)

Pizza a taglio The take-out *pizzeria* sells *pizze* by the slice (or sometimes by the meter). Often open evenings only.

Rosticceria A useful food shop, selling hot and cold foods to take out. Often, a superb selection of restaurant-quality food is available which you can put together for meals at home or delicious, elaborate picnics.

Salumeria or **salsamenteria** Shop-cum-delicatessan selling cured *salumi,* cheeses, prepared salads, specialty condiments, fresh *pasta,* and specialty foods.

Torrefazione The coffee shop; where, traditionally, coffee is roasted on the premises and sold as whole beans or ground to order to your specifications. Usually, there is also a limited selection of teas available.

Shop selling local specialties of funghi porcini *(cepes) and* grappa *in Bassano del Grappa, Veneto*

Vendita Diretta
BUYING AT SOURCE

Direct sale of wines, olive oil, fresh produce, and local specialties

BY FAR THE BEST WAY to buy food and drink in Italy is to track it down to its original source. There are scores of opportunities for doing so throughout the nation, and for any number and range of excellent fresh produce and products: including fresh fruits and vegetables; cheese and other dairy products; artisan-cured *salumi* and *prosciutto;* farm-fresh, free-range poultry and eggs; stoneground flour, cornmeal, or rice direct from the mill; fish and shellfish straight off the boats; rare specialist products such as *aceto balsamico tradizionale di Modena;* extra-virgin olive oil; and, of course, wines and *grappe.*

Buying directly at source has many advantages. Most importantly, it establishes a direct link between producer and consumer, who benefits from fresher produce with no recourse to middlemen.

Cornmeal for polenta *for sale at a traditional mill in Friuli-Venezia Giulia*

Often, it is also a considerably cheaper method of buying.

We are great believers, as well, in the simple concept that the fewer "food miles" produce or products have to travel, the better. It may be well and good at any time of year to be able to enjoy produce that has traveled halfway round the world (such as unseasonal strawberries or asparagus in January), but for our money, we'd opt for the local, the fresh-picked, the truly seasonal every time. Buying direct at source guarantees that. Moreover, buying direct, whatever the produce or product, is a way of making sure that you experience the truly local, what the people of the area you are in most enjoy themselves.

Furthermore, in some cases, buying

Wines to taste or buy at the Serègo Alighieri estate, Valpolicella, near Verona

direct can be the only way to track down genuine and rare products. *Culatello di Zibello,* possibly the greatest cured ham in the world, is made only by a handful of artisan curers in the Bassa Parmense of Emilia-Romagna: to sample or purchase it, it really is essential to come directly to the source (see p.142). Similarly, visit an *acetaia* in Modena or its surrounds to taste and buy direct that esoteric and mysterious product, *aceto balsamico tradizionale di Modena* (see p.137). It will cost you an arm and a leg, but you will be guaranteed the genuine article.

Whether you are buying a box of apples from a roadside stand next to the orchard, or a whole *parmigiano reggiano* cheese to last you months, buying direct is not only the smart thing to do, it is also most enjoyable and satisfying.

Al Mercato

TO MARKET, TO MARKET

WE HAVE A FRIEND who lives in an apartment overlooking Padua's Piazza delle Erbe, a large and elegant square lined each morning with a sprawl of traders' stalls selling the finest and best display of seasonal fruits and vegetables that you are ever likely to see. Whenever we visit her, we enjoy nothing more than leaning out from the upstairs window and simply gazing down wide eyed at the bustle and activity of it all. Then, in anticipation of *pranzo* (the midday meal), we descend to street level for a closer examination of the profusion of produce laid out so beautifully and carefully: tiny, neatly trimmed and ready-to-cook *carciofini* (baby artichoke hearts); a stall overflowing with *porcini, finferli,* and other wild mushrooms; onions, lettuce, and carrots from nearby Chióggia; *radicchio* from Treviso; a mountain of *tarocco* oranges — the first blood oranges, just up from Sicily; varieties of table grapes; and, in fall, vivid orange *zucca* (pumpkin), not to carve into jack-o'-lanterns but to cook into rich, filling soups or to make a stuffing for homemade *ravioli.*

Shopping in markets essentially re-

Seasonal produce, piled high for sale

quires a different mentality and approach to that required when shopping in supermakets. When shopping in a supermarket, you go hurriedly, with preconceived ideas of what you want, usually scribbled on a shopping list. In markets, by contrast, you can stroll at a leisurely pace, noting what is fresh and seasonal, attractive and keenly priced, and only then decide what you need or would like to buy and eat.

In Italy, there is still time for this more spontaneous, leisurely approach, if not on a daily basis, then, at the least, on a weekly one. By visiting markets, we are thus able to gain not only an appreciation of the wealth of fine seasonal produce and products available, we also learn to see and to appreciate that which is often, literally, right before our eyes — reminded by the vendor's cry of *"buonissimo"* or an alert shopper's hand reaching out for the perfect *pesca* (peach) or *mela* (apple).

We have supplied the market days for many of the towns and villages covered by this book, but these lists are by no means comprehensive. So, ask around when and where local markets take place. Even if you don't have cooking facilities to prepare the beautiful produce, you will gain a good idea of the local and seasonal produce available when you eat out.

The market in Padua's Piazza delle Erbe — a colorful and welcoming sight from any perspective

Buona Forchetta

EATING AND DRINKING IN ITALY

ITALY HAS MUCH TO OFFER THE VISITOR in terms of art, architecture, culture, and history, but, arguably, the most popular motive for visiting the country is the attraction of eating, drinking, and living well Italian-style. This is still a country for hedonists, where, as in the days of the ancient Romans, the sensual pleasures of the table have not been forsaken. For us all, in Italy, meals, whether at home or in restaurants, are always keenly anticipated. Italians care for food as much as people from any nation that we know (France included) and food is taken as seriously as it is enjoyed, as passionately discussed as it is carefully prepared. Indeed, the term *buona forchetta,* denoting a hearty and enthusiastic eater, is used with universal approbation.

BREAKFAST, LUNCH, AND DINNER

Perhaps it is not surprising, given the amount of time spent over food at midday and evening meals that *la prima colazione* (breakfast) is such an insubstantial and unimportant meal. The great saving grace, of course, is Italian coffee — undoubtedly the best in the world. At breakfast, it is usually taken as *caffèlatte* (a concentrated measure of *espresso* coffee topped with plenty of scalding hot milk). At home, this may be accompanied by no more than breakfast *biscotti* (sweet graham-cracker-like biscuits) eaten in enormous quantity, often dipped or even crumbled into the coffee. In bars or hotels, fresh bread and jam, or French-style *brioches* may be served.

But, all in all, breakfast in Italy is actually a pretty dismal affair (cooked breakfasts are rarely taken, though international hotels will serve up an American or English cooked breakfast with all "the works" for an astronomical sum).

Yet, if breakfast is nothing to write home about, *pranzo,* the midday meal, more than makes up for it. Indeed, this has long been considered the main meal of the day, and though Italian eating habits are evolving as increasingly both partners go out to work, *pranzo* still remains sacrosanct for many, a truly substantial

Sharing food and conversation at the Ca' de Be' drinking house in Bertinoro, Emilia-Romagna

meal, at home or in a restaurant, lingered over for two hours or longer.

A proper meal might begin first with some *antipasti* (appetizers), followed by the *primo piatto* (first course) which is usually *pasta, risotto,* or soup. A substantial *secondo piatto* (main course) is next with *contorni* (vegetables) ordered on the side. Afterward, one might indulge in a *dolce* (dessert), or else finish with a piece of *frutta* (fruit) or *formaggio* (cheese). Naturally, wine accompanies the meal, and *espresso* (concentrated black coffee) is always taken at the end. In restaurants, *pranzo* is usually served from 12:00 to 2:00 p.m.

Cena (the evening meal) can be very similar to *pranzo,* consisting of at least a *primo piatto* and a *secondo piatto*. Menus in restaurants rarely differ much between lunch and dinner (though, often, foods such as *pizze* are served only in the evenings). At home, the first course is usually

Simply elegant — bread, salame, and wine in the Oltrepò Pavese, Lombardia

pasta in brodo (broth or soup with *pasta*) as opposed to *pasta asciutta* (pasta served with sauce) which is usually eaten only once a day. Restaurants open in evenings from about 7:00 until approximately 10:00 p.m., though hours vary depending on the time of year and location: the farther south, the later you go out to eat.

ENJOYING FOOD HOW AND WHEN WE WANT TO

If Italians are among the heartiest eaters of the world, they are also, it must be added, among the most intolerant and fussiest. When abroad, most Italians invariably seek out local Italian restaurants. The assumption is apparent: nobody knows how to eat like Italians.

Such attitudes could lead to problems for the visitor. For if Italians, on the whole, wish to eat only Italian-style wherever they are in the world, they, nonetheless, expect visitors to adapt to their way of eating when in Italy. Of course, this book exists in great measure to help you to do so. However, there will be times when you will wish to eat as you please, not as Italians expect you to. Often, at lunchtime, for example, you may be more than happy with just a bowl of *pasta* accompanied perhaps by a salad. Or maybe the *antipasti* buffet looks so appealing that you would rather have a selection of that and nothing else. Our advice is: let the waiter know your requirements and eat whatever you want when you want — and enjoy the experience.

La Cucina Italiana

TYPES AND STYLES OF ITALIAN COOKING

ITALIAN CUISINE is infinitely richer and surprisingly more varied than even the most imaginative "new wave" Italian restaurants would have us believe. And yet, it remains unselfconsciously so, not least because its wealth and variety are not imposed upon or even much influenced by new food trends but remain strongly based on regional tradition.

For, unlike French cuisine, there is no national or classical Italian school of cooking that can compare with the *haute cuisine* traditions that form and fashion food at all levels in France. The formal and rigid precepts as defined by Escoffier that influenced generations of French chefs have no counterparts in Italy. Here, true to national character, the best of *la cucina italiana* at its highest level remains, above all, a forum for individual and imaginative expression where anything, literally, goes.

At its more basic and everyday level, meanwhile, *la cucina italiana* has come to signify those dishes that transcend regional, even national borders, and which are loved and enjoyed by all, such as *spaghetti al ragù, scalloppine alla milanese,* or the world's favorite finger food, *pizza* (eaten almost always with a knife and fork in Italy).

CUCINA REGIONALE

The most important and vivid expression of Italian cooking is *cucina regionale*

Elegant creative cuisine at Vissani, Baschi, one of Italy's top restaurants

(regional cooking). For if every Italian remains first a citizen of his town or village, secondly of his region, and only lastly of Italy, it stands to reason that the regional character of food remains strongly and unselfconsciously intact.

The cuisine of Italy is markedly different and distinct from region to region. In the Veneto, it is hard to have a meal without *polenta* in some form, and many meals start with *risotto* in place of *pasta asciutta*. The range of elaborate *antipasti* as served in Piemonte, has no rivals, except, perhaps, for the great arrays of mainly vegetarian appetizers encountered in Puglia. In Tuscany, a unique range of bread soups is regularly served, seasoned, of course, with the finest Tuscan extra-virgin olive oil.

Rome, the nation's capital, has even managed to maintain purely local food traditions: in districts like Testaccio or Trastevere, dishes such as *pagliata* (calf's innards poached and served over *pasta*), *coda alla vaccinara alla romana* (stewed oxtail), or *carciofi alla giudìa* (baby artichockes fried in olive oil) are served in a wholly distinctive manner not found anywhere else in the country.

Consider for a moment the sheer variety and diversity of regional cuisines as distinct as the Germanic foods of the Alto Adige, where dumplings and smoked meats are served alongside steaming platters of *crauti (sauerkraut);* the mountain foods of the Valle d'Aosta, such

Seppie alla veneziana — cuttlefish cooked in its own ink and served with polenta, *a great regional dish of Northeast Italy*

as *fonduta* (a creamy hot cheese mixture made with local *fontina* cheese) and the Valtellina with its buckwheat *pizzocheri* and air-dried *bresaola* (cured beef tenderloin); or the Austrian-inspired pastries and *dolci* of Friuli-Venezia Giulia.

We tend, of course, to paint a nation with broad, clumsy strokes, and make casual, sweeping generalizations between, say, the north and the south. But look closely at the *Mezzogiorno,* and the distinctive and vivid cuisines of diverse regions stand out sharply: Calabria, noted for its liberal use of fiery *peperoncino* on just about everything; Abruzzo, a little-known and visited region, with its rich regional *cucina* that extends well beyond its most famous dish, *spaghetti alla chitarra;* the stupendous and highly developed vegetarian cuisine of Puglia; and the classic tomato-tinted southern dishes of Naples and the rest of Campania.

Perhaps only Emilia-Romagna, by sheer dint of its great regional kitchen, remains closest to a classic Italian ideal. This great gastronomic region is the source of so much that is good and wholly familiar — egg *paste, ragù* (meat sauce), *prosciutto di Parma, parmigiano reggiano* cheese, balsamic vinegar, and much else. Yet, here, too, the visitor finds that the real food as enjoyed in the region is infinitely finer than bastardized versions that have spread throughout the world. Even its local wine, Lambrusco, can be sensational drunk on the spot, vividly foaming, raspingly dry, and a perfect accompaniment to the hearty cuisine of the region.

CUCINA REGIONALE RINNOVATA

If regional cooking is essentially *casalinga,* the sort of food regularly cooked at home, it stands to reason that when many Italians go out to eat they are looking for something exciting, something a bit more special. "*Pappa al pomodoro* may be a novelty for you," a Tuscan friend told me, "but when we go out to eat we often

want something different."

Therefore, a more refined style of regional cooking has evolved — *cucina regionale rinnovata* — which, while firmly based in local and regional tradition, takes a fresh look at such foods, either by adapting recipes or creating new ones using fresh local ingredients. Such stylish regional variations, prepared creatively and presented carefully, can be among the most exciting in Italy.

CUCINA CREATIVA

Italy, let's face it, was never going to fall for *nouvelle cuisine.* People here like eating too much, so there was bound to be resistance if restaurateurs tried to serve minuscule portions on extra-large plates, no matter how prettily arranged.

Moreover, if *nouvelle cuisine* (in the original French sense) liberated chefs from rigid classical precepts, Italy never had such a classical tradition to escape from. Thus, here the so-called *cucina novella* movement went off at a tangent that has resulted in *cucina creativa* — individual creative cooking of the highest

Gianfranco Vissani — superstar chef, preparing fresh, seasonal food in his own inimitable and exciting style

order. Eschewing the rather rigid Italian eating formula of a meal consisting of *antipasto* followed by *primo* and *secondo,* meals are created that become occasions or happenings, a succession of small but elaborate *assaggi* ("tastes" consisting of no more than a forkful or two), perhaps as many as seven or eight in a full-blown *menù di degustazione.*

It is taken for granted that in this post-modern age, most of us no longer go out to restaurants simply because we are hungry and are in need of sustenance. Rather, the supposition is that a meal in a great restaurant should be an exciting, new, and always unexpected experience. Certainly, in the hands of such brilliant artist-chefs as

Antipasti — *appetizers eaten before a meal*

Gualtiero Marchesi in Milan or Gianfranco Vissani near Orvieto, meals can approach this ideal.

Cucina casalinga

Yet, contrary to the above, and for most of us when we are traveling, meals are taken in restaurants out of necessity as well as pleasure, quite simply because we *are* hungry and in need of replenishment. Thus, there are times when there can be nothing more satisfying than the simplest *cucina casalinga* (basic home cooking) as served in humble *trattorie* and *osterie* throughout the country. At such places, you take potluck and

Cucina casalinga, *simply good home cooking*

enjoy whatever is available that day — there is usually no menu — and if such food is not anything special or refined, it should at best be filling as well as inexpensive — and thoroughly satisfying.

Wine with food

Fortunately, in Italy, far less fuss is made about wine with meals than in many other countries. At its most basic level, wine is just a natural accompaniment to food, as essential and as noteworthy as the salt, pepper, and grated cheese on the table. In such instances, the most difficult choice may be simply whether you care for *rosso* (red) or *bianco* (white). Indeed, such anonymous house wines, served by the jug or carafe, can be quite acceptable, sometimes, even enjoyable.

There are few hard and fast rules regarding matching wine with food in Italy. Taste, as always, is a highly personal matter. One abiding principle to remember is to drink locally, especially when accompanying regional or local foods. Most restaurants, even the humblest, have, at the least, a limited selection of bottled DOC and DOCG wines available at moderate prices. Wine in Italy is rarely marked up as extortionately as we are accustomed to. For special meals and occasions, one of the so-called *"super vini da tavola"* (see p.58) might be appropriate. Don't overlook, either, for those special moments, some of the great sparkling wines of Italy.

And don't be too timid to try styles of wine you might not usually consider — *rosato,* semi-sparkling reds, sweet dessert wines, for example — you will be sure to make some exciting discoveries.

Mangiar Bene
EATING OUT IN ITALY

Eating out is one of the nation's consummate passions and Italians enjoy going out to restaurants on a regular basis. Cooking good Italian food, after all, is labor intensive, so everybody deserves a break from time to time. Moreover, since many urban Italians live in apartments, entertaining is more often done in restaurants than at home.

Dining outdoors, one of the pleasures of eating in Italy

Choosing a Restaurant

There are, literally, thousands of restaurants throughout Italy, so you will never have a problem in finding somewhere to eat. The difficulty usually is deciding on which to choose.

The cardinal rule is always to go where the locals are as well as to frequent restaurants or *trattorie* that are crowded. If you do this, you will probably not go too far wrong.

Of course, you must decide which type of restaurant you wish to visit and how much you want to spend, considerations that can limit your choice quite a bit. We also suggest that you consult one of the guidebooks below (you may have to purchase one or two while in Italy, but a reliable guidebook more than pays for itself).

Types of eating establishments

Ristorante This is the all-embracing term for restaurant and it can include those at the highest level as well as far simpler everyday eating establishments. Generally speaking, the service in a *ristorante* should be a little more formal, the dishes prepared to order or more elaborately than in a *trattoria*.

Trattoria/osteria Our favorite restaurants invariably fall into this category: the traditional *trattoria* or *osteria* is a family-run establishment generally serving homecooked food (often, home-made *pasta*), together with local wine at

---

A GUIDE TO THE GUIDES

The best Italian restaurant guides are written in Italian. The following are our favorites (publication details in the bibliography p.247).

Ristoranti di Veronelli (annual) Though Luigi Veronelli has handed over the day-to-day reins of this guide to others, it is recognized as one of the best guides to Italian restaurants. I have long admired its idiosyncratic and opinionated approach and well laid-out, easy-to-consult entries.

Ristoranti d'Italia del Gambero Rosso (annual) The "pink shrimp" is a big fish in food and wine publishing

in Italy, and this is a guide to serious Italian restaurants at all levels; gives *qualità/prezzo* ratings for best value.

Osterie d'Italia (annual) Arcigola (see p.9) publishes this outstanding guide to inexpensive *trattorie* and *osterie* serving, above all, typical regional foods. We consider this guide essential for all *buongustai* (gourmets) on a budget: don't visit Italy without it.

Michelin Red Guide (annual) This famous annual reference is useful to have on hand for comprehensive listings of reliable hotels and restaurants.

Eating out in Italy — always done with style

affordable prices. There are thousands throughout Italy.

Tavola calda/rosticceria   The *tavola calda* or *rosticceria* is extremely useful when you do not want a full three-course meal. Informal, often self-service or even bar service, food in such establishments is usually pre-prepared and you simply choose from a displayed selection.

Pizzeria   The *pizzeria* in Italy is frequented generally in evenings only, and may stay open and serve food until very late. In addition to a range of *pizze,* most also serve a selection of *pasta* dishes.

Ristorante agrituristico   There are now scores of good farmhouse restaurants throughout Italy, usually on working farms, serving meals consisting primarily of their own or neighboring farms' produce, prepared to local recipes. These restaurants can range from very simple, rustic affairs to much more elaborate restaurants. In many cases, they are open by reservation only, so it is essential always to telephone first. This book highlights some of the best; visit at least one of them for a dining experience with a difference.

Rifugio di montagna   Italy is an extremely mountainous country and there is a growing number of mountain refuges you can hike to where, in some cases, quite exceptional meals are presented. We point the way to a few such places, but this is certainly one area worth further exploration and legwork.

PAYING AND TIPPING

Credit cards are not universally accepted in Italy. Most smart and more expensive restaurants, including many hotel restaurants, may accept Visa, Mastercard, and American Express but many smaller places may well not.

In theory, service is included in most meal prices, but a further tip is expected, especially for good service; five to ten per cent is about right.

LA RICEVUTA FISCALE

In Italy, you are required by law to retain receipts from a restaurant, bar, or shop. A member of the *Guardia di finanza* can at any time ask for your *ricevuta fiscale* (restaurant receipt) and if you are unable to produce it, then both you and the owner can be liable for a hefty fine.

RESTAURANT SPEAK — SOME USEFUL PHRASES

Per favore/piacere Please
Vorrei ... I would like…
Vorrei un tavolo ... I would like a table ... **per due** for two; **per quatro** for four
Come primo (secondo), prendo (prendiamo) ... For the first course (main course), I (we) will have ...
Cos'è la specialità della casa? What is the house specialty?

Un po' di più, per piacere A little more, please
Per tutti For all of us
Dov'è il bagno/la toiletta? Where is the restroom?
Il conto, per piacere The check, please
E compreso il servizio? Is service included?
Buon appetito! Enjoy your meal!

Al Bar
A NATIONAL INSTITUTION

THE BAR IN ITALY is central to its way of life. It serves as the focus of a community or neighborhood, as well as somewhere to pop into whenever you need liquid refreshment in any form.

In the morning, bars are no less than lifesavers for those of us who cannot function without our daily kick-start of strong, concentrated *espresso*. In mid-mornings, people sit for hours, gossiping, reading the papers, sitting in the sun enjoying *brioche* and a foamy *cappuccino*. Workers pop in for a *rosso* and a *panino* — a tumbler of red wine and a roll filled with *salame*. In the afternoon, youths hang out after school or college drinking cola or beer, listening to loud music, and the evening often belongs to old men playing cards and drinking wine, *grappa,* or *amaro*.

Wherever you are in Italy, and for however brief a time, it is well worth finding your own bar; after just a few visits, you too may be accepted as a regular, your favorite drink served almost before you order it.

There is a certain bar etiquette which it is well to know. The most important is that, in many bars, the cash desk sits apart, usually by the door of the establishment, often attended by the owner. Say what you require, pay for it, and you will be given a *scontrino* (receipt). Present this piece of paper at the bar and state your order. If you like, you can place a 100- or 200-*lira* coin on the slip as a tip. Though the slip may be torn up to show you have been served, by law you must retain the receipt as proof that you have paid.

It is almost always cheaper to stand at a bar to have your drink or snack, sometimes considerably more so than sitting at a table, inside or outside. Sitting out in one of Venice's Piazza San Marco or Rome's Piazza Navonna *caffès* is nothing short of a wild extravagance, unless you plan to nurse your *cappuccino* for an hour or longer, while soaking in the sights.

SOFT DRINKS

Acqua minerale Mineral water; **gassata/non gassata** sparkling/still.
Aranciata Orange soda.
Limonata Lemon soda.
Spremuta Freshly squeezed fruit juice; **spremuta di limone** freshly squeezed lemon juice topped up with water or seltzer; **spremuta di arancia** freshly squeezed orange juice; **spremuta di pompelmo** freshly squeezed grapefruit juice.
Succo di frutta Bottled fruit juice, often very thick and concentrated fruit pulp; **albicocca** apricot; **mela** apple; **pera** pear; **pesca** peach; **pomodoro** tomato.

Coffee, of course, is one of the most frequently consumed beverages in bars (see p.53). Additionally, white and red table wines are served by the glass, as are fortified wines, Italian drinks such as *amaro,* and international spirits such as whiskey, malt whisky, Cognac, and the like. Measures are invariably generous. Italian beer may be available either *alla spina* (draft) or in bottles. Favorites include Peroni, Nastro Azzurro, and the cultish Moretti. If you prefer imported beer, ask for *birra èstera*.

In addition to drink, bars usually also serve simple snacks.

Cantina Do Mori, a typical bar near the Rialto market, Venice

Al Ristorante
TYPICAL MENUS

DEPENDING ON where you choose to eat in Italy, you may or may not be offered a menu. Either way, meals follow a certain pattern.

As soon as you sit down, you incur a cover charge, known as *pane e coperto,* which is supposed to cover the cost of bread and *grissini* as well as of providing the table linen. This may range from just 1,000 *lire* in a simple *casalinga* restaurant to perhaps as much as 6,000 *lire* in a fancier one, and it usually applies to everyone, even small children (fair enough, we feel, given that our two-year-old usually eats as much bread as any of us, and also in her enjoyment can make a considerable mess both on and below the table). If there is no menu, the waiter will usually tell you what there is to eat, beginning with the *anti-pasti* and *primi piatti* courses. Often, waiters reel off a list of dishes at breakneck speed which can be hard to follow even for those who consider themselves reasonably fluent, many dishes may be unfamiliar or local. In such instances, it is all too easy, for the sake of avoiding embarrassment, just to order the easiest or most familiar. But this is also often the least interesting. Better to take your time, ask the waiter to repeat what is on offer, and if you still can't understand, then ask or motion that you would like to go into the kitchen to see what is on offer. Alternatively, take potluck and ask to try a local dish *(un piatto tipico)* or *la specialità della casa* (house specialty).

Grissini and a glass of wine, to start with

ANTIPASTI

Italian *antipasti* are often the most attractive items in many restaurants, humble and grand alike, and we can rarely resist sampling a good array. Unless you are very hungry, you may decide that you will have *antipasti* in place of the *primo piatto* or else, perhaps, *antipasti* followed by a *primo* with no *secondo* to follow. This is always acceptable. A few typical non-regional *antipasti* include:

Affettati misti Mixed selection of *salumi, prosciutto,* and other cold meats.
Antipasto di mare Selection of seafood and shellfish appetizers.
Bruschetta Toasted country bread rubbed with garlic and dribbled with olive oil.
Caprese Sliced tomatoes layered with fresh *mozzarella* cheese and basil.
Carpaccio Finely sliced raw beef tenderloin served with a sauce and some-times shavings of *parmigiano reggiano* cheese.
Peperoni arrostiti Roasted red peppers, peeled then dressed with olive oil and vinegar.

I PRIMI PIATTI

While we are perhaps more used to eating *pasta* as a main course, in Italy it is almost always eaten as a *primo* or first course (see p.17). If you consider *pasta* too filling to have as a starter, ask instead for a bowl of *minestra* or *zuppa* (soup), invariably homemade and often excellent. *Risotti* are also always eaten as a first course, with the exception of the famous saffron-scented *risotto alla milanese,* the traditional accompaniment to *ossobuco alla milanese* (shin of veal). Some non-*pasta* starters include:

Crema Creamed soup; **crema di gallina** cream of chicken; **crema d'asparagi** cream of asparagus.
Minestra di verdura Vegetable soup.
Pasta e fagioli Bean soup with *pasta.*
Risotto ai funghi Mushroom *risotto* (usually made with dried *porcini* or cepes).
Risotto di pesce Seafood *risotto.*
Risotto primavera Vegetable *risotto.*
Zuppa pavese Clear broth with a poached egg.

I SECONDI PIATTI

If you have already enjoyed some *anti-pasti* followed by a bowl of *pasta* or *risotto*, you may not have much room left for the *secondo*, or main course. However, the *secondo* is often a relatively small portion of meat, poultry, game, or fish, served on a plate on its own, with any vegetables to be ordered on the side. In that sense,

Coniglio al Brunello, *rabbit stewed in and accompanied by Brunello di Montalcino*

it is not really the focal point of a meal, as our translation "main course" implies. Some basic *secondi* available nationwide include:

Bistecca alla brace Char-grilled steak: be sure to specify *al sangue* (rare), *cotta a puntino* (medium), *ben cotta* (well done).
Bollito misto Mixed boiled meats; much more delicious than it sounds.
Braciola di maiale/costoletta di maiale alla griglia Broiled pork chop.
Fritto misto Mix of either meats or fish, dipped in batter or flour and deep-fried.
Pollo arrosto Roast chicken.
Pollo alla cacciatora Chicken stewed "hunter's style," in tomatoes and wine.
Salsiccia Fresh sausage.
Scaloppine alla milanese Breaded veal escalopes fried in butter or olive oil.
Spezzatino di vitello Sauté of veal pieces.
Stracotto Beef or veal, whole or chunks, braised in wine.

I CONTORNI

Vegetables or other side dishes are always ordered (and paid for) separately. Common accompaniments include:
Insalata mista Mixed salad; **insalata verde** green salad.
Melanzane Eggplant.
Patate arrostiti Roast potatoes, usually in olive oil; **patate fritte** french fries.
Peperonata Sort of Italian *ratatouille:* a stew of red bell peppers, onions, and tomatoes.
Spinaci Spinach; **all'agro** stewed with garlic in olive oil and lemon juice; **al burro** with butter.

I DOLCI

Meals in Italy finish either with a *dolce* (dessert) or with *frutta* (fruit). Occasionally, cheese is served after the main course, though nowhere near as often as in France.

Regional *dolci* are covered in the second part of this book. Some typical desserts and fruits often offered include:
Fichi freschi Fresh figs (not to be missed in season).
Macedonia Fresh fruit salad.
Panna cotta A delicious, delicate cooked cream dessert rather like a light *crème caramel*.
Profiteroles Not strictly Italian, but highly popular: small *choux* pastry buns filled with cream and covered with melted chocolate.
Tiramisù The famous Venetian "pick me up" dessert, a wickedly delicious cake made with sponge cake soaked in Marsala, then layered with creamy *mascarpone* cheese and dusted with cocoa powder.
Torta Cake.
Zabaione Delicious custard-like sauce made with beaten egg yolks, sugar, and Marsala wine.

Panna cotta al vin santo, *a rich dessert of cooked cream with a sauce made from* Vin Santo

La Pizzeria

FOR THE WORLD'S FAVORITE FAST FOOD

*P*IZZA IS PROBABLY the best-known Italian food in the world. This simple street snack from Naples has spread so far beyond its homeland that it has virtually become synonymous with fast food, alongside such international stand-bys as the hamburger, *taco*, or hot dog.

Yet *pizza* is as Italian as, well, *torta di mela* (apple pie). If its spiritual birthplace remains the backstreets of Naples (the source still of probably the best *pizze* in the world — see p.198), it is, nonetheless, found and enjoyed throughout the nation, often best prepared by Neapolitan *pizzaiuoli* who have opened restaurants far from their native homes.

At its most basic, *pizza* is no more than yeasty bread dough, flattened out by hand, spread with a bit of tomato sauce and olive oil, perhaps a few shreds of garlic and a

Top: Pizza alla capricciosa
Bottom: Pizza margherita

dusting of oregano, then popped into an intensely hot wood-fired oven for no more than a minute and a half, maybe two at the most. The thin dough cooks through quickly, while the smoke from the still burning wood singes and flavors the crust which acquires a characteristic burnt edge (the hallmark of *pizza* cooked in a wood-fired oven).

We prefer the simpler *pizze*, especially the two classics, *margherita* and *marinara*. But, today, a huge array of *pizze* with any number of unusual toppings are offered the length and breadth of the nation.

There are basically two types of *pizzerie* in Italy, the more refined sort where you sit down and eat individually ordered *pizze* with a knife and fork, and the "holes-in-the-wall," selling *pizze* to go by the slice *(al taglio)* or meter.

PIZZE MENU

Marinara In spite of its name, this simplest of *pizze* has no seafood or shellfish, just tomato sauce, garlic, and oregano.

Margherita Named in honor of Queen Margherita, and made in the colors of the Italian flag with red tomatoes, white *mozzarella* cheese, and green fresh basil.

Napoletana Another exceedingly simple *pizza*, topped with tomato, *mozzarella*, and anchovy fillets.

Quatro stagione The "Four Seasons" has each quarter of the *pizza* topped with something different: perhaps *prosciutto* (ham), mushrooms, artichokes, and olives.

Capricciosa Similar mix of toppings to *quattro stagione*, but layered "capriciously" all over.

Funghi With mushrooms.

Funghi porcini In season, sometimes fresh *porcini* mushrooms are used.

Prosciutto With cooked ham.

Calzone *Pizza ripiena*, a stuffed *pizza*. Strictly speaking, should contain *ricotta* and *mozzarella* cheeses, and pork, but often it is filled with any number of ingredients, then folded over and sealed like a giant turn-over before baking.

Ortolana Topped with a mix of fresh garden vegetables.

Ai frutti di mare Tomatoes and shellfish, including shrimp and mussels.

La Merenda

PICNICS AND SNACKING ITALIAN-STYLE

ITALY IS A GREAT COUNTRY for picnics and for snacking. In the middle of a day's sightseeing, there is little to match a stand-up snack of a *panino* — a crusty roll — stuffed with tissue-paper thin slices of *prosciutto crudo,* washed down with a tumbler or two of *vino rosso.*

We love to picnic, too, and half the fun is putting one together: visiting first a *salumeria* to choose a selection of cured meats, then sniffing out the *panetteria,* where the aromas of breads, rolls, and *grissini* fresh out of the oven are irresistible. We then cross the road to the fruit and vegetable shop, and finally seek some place selling wine or water. So equipped, we can be guaranteed that this simplest of repasts will be a picnic to remember.

Of course, it is also possible to picnic in more elaborate fashion. When Italians get together for meals outdoors, they invariably find some way to boil water to cook *pasta* (or failing that, transport *pasta* already cooked to eat lukewarm or even cold). Tables are laid, wine bottles are opened, and fires are lit for grilling meats and sausages.

For those of us who may be less ambitious but no less hungry, a visit to a *rosticceria* can provide the makings for a quite delicious meal effortlessly: perhaps some *crostini* or bits of fried *polenta* to start, followed by sliced roast veal or pork, together with a selection of cold salads and dressed vegetables. All you need to find now is the perfect picnic spot.

Travelers are often in need of quick snacks, a bite here, a bite there, to stave off hunger between the next visit to a restaurant or *trattoria.* Fortunately, there is

A selection of panini *and* tramezzini

never any difficulty in finding good things to eat and drink in Italy. Even in railway stations, the carts pushed alongside trains ready to pull away usually offer quite decent *panini* (filled rolls) along with quarter bottles of wine or mineral water.

Elsewhere, bars may have more elaborate offerings: in addition to a variety of *panini,* a selection of *tramezzini* (crustless sandwiches usually filled with mayonaissey mixtures of various fillings), *focaccia* (flattened bread dough) sprinkled with olive oil and salt, or *bruschetta* (toasted bread) classically topped with garlic and oil, though often with more elaborate fillings, such as meat or cheese.

Street stalls sell *porchetta,* roast suckling pig stuffed with garlic and wild fennel, and markets are the source of delicious hot *pollo arrosto* (roast chicken), one of our favorite finger foods.

In Trieste, we've popped into *"buffets"* for boiled sausages and meats straight from the *caldaio,* and in Sardinia, we've staved off hunger with a sheet of the local *pane carasau* topped with *ricotta* cheese and honey.

Hot boiled meats and sauerkraut, *served in Trieste* "buffets" *with local beer*

Acqua Minerale
TAKING THE WATERS

Tap water may be safe and perfectly drinkable just about anywhere in Italy, but Italians continue to consume mineral waters in enormous quantities. No meal, at home or in a restaurant, is complete without a bottle of *acqua minerale* on the table, an essential element in the holy trinity of food together with wine and bread.

Italians, of course, have a tradition of drinking mineral water that goes at least as far back as classical times. It was the Romans, with their obsession for baths fed by hot mineral springs, who established spa towns not only throughout Italy but all of Europe. Spas such as Montecatini Terme, Saturnia, or Abano Terme are popular not least because people go there to be treated for a number of ailments, both by drinking the waters as well as by bathing in them.

Italy is a volcanic country, and there are still scores of natural springs almost everywhere. It is not uncommon to come across Italians lining up along the road where water emerges from the ground to fill gratis their own collection

of bottles, demijohns, and jars.

Natural mineral waters that are bottled are rigorously controlled by the state to ensure purity. They must undergo clinical analyses and are defined as having certain therapeutic and hygienic properties, though the long list of minerals in each, together with their respective health claims, might be enough to put you off.

But the main reason for consuming mineral water — *acqua gassata* (sparkling), *acqua non gassata* or *naturale* (still) — is merely as an accompaniment to meals, alongside wine (rarely in place of it), as an aid to digestion.

There are many local and regional Italian waters, few of them known internationally, so it is usual in restaurants not to specify which you like. Some better-known mineral waters include:

Claudia This lightly sparkling mineral water comes from a source known since Roman days, located at Anguillara, off the ancient Via Cassia near Rome.
Ferrarelle Naturally carbonated, with a medium mineralization, this is one of the best for accompanying meals; the source is located northeast of Naples.
Fiuggi Still water famous since medieval times as a health-giving elixir, said to be particularly beneficial for those suffering from kidney or urinary problems.
Panna Very popular and pure still mineral water, widely used for mixing baby formulas.
Recoaro Our favorite bottled sparkling water in the Northeast, from a source between Verona and Vicenza.
Sangemini Extremely pure — low in mineral content — water available both still and lightly sparkling; particularly favored for newborn babies and invalids.
San Pellegrino Italy's internationally known sparkling mineral water, widely exported throughout the world; it comes from a source in the foothills of the Italian Alps near Bergamo and has a marked mineral taste.

Pure spring water bubbling up from deep within the earth at Su Gologone in Central Sardinia

Caffè

THE BEST COFFEE IN THE WORLD

ITALY IS NOT a coffee producing country, but it is a country where the culture of coffee and coffee drinking is highly developed. Italians demand real coffee, carefully prepared and properly served. We have never been offered instant

coffee anywhere in Italy: the ritual itself of making coffee, either at home or in bars or restaurants, is part of Italian hospitality and culture.

A perfect espresso, *dark and concentrated, with a creamy foam*

Coffee beans were introduced into Europe by the Venetians in about 1615, and it was the Venetians who began the business of *torrefazione,* the roasting of the green coffee beans. Thus processed, these were subsequently dispersed throughout Europe. Of course, Venice soon established the *caffè* or coffee shop where people came to enjoy this novel beverage, such as the historic Caffè Florian, founded in 1720 by Floriano Francesconi.

Today, the best Italian coffee comes from pure *arabica* coffee beans (milder in flavor and aroma than *robusta,* less astringent, rounded in character, and slightly acidic) roasted to varying degrees of darkness depending on taste (the darker the roast, the more bitter but less acidic the resulting coffee).

To make a perfect *espresso,* the coffee is carefully and finely ground. Then, in special Italian *espresso* machines, very hot water is forced under pressure through the measured dose of coffee to result in just a gulp or two of concentrated, rich, dark coffee with a walnut-brown, foamy cream on the top and a quite incredible intensity of flavor. Paradoxically, *espresso* properly made in this fashion is actually relatively low in caffeine, as the infusion time is so brief.

COFFEE BREAK

Caffè Order merely "coffee" and you will get *espresso,* a tiny quantity of concentrated coffee.

Caffè corretto *Espresso* "corrected" with the addition of a splash of strong alcohol, usually *grappa* or brandy.

Caffèlatte Small quantity of *espresso* topped up with a large amount of hot milk, the favorite at breakfast.

Caffè lungo *Espresso* made with more water, to dilute it a little.

Caffè macchiato *Espresso* "stained" with just a dapple of milk.

Caffè ristretto Even stronger *espresso.*

Cappuccino *Espresso* topped up with steamed, frothy milk, often dusted with cocoa powder — so called, because the brown color of the surface is the same as that of the habits worn by Capucin monks.

Caffè decaffeinato Decaffeinated coffee; often made as *espresso* from freshly ground decaffeinated beans.

A quiet moment after a caffè *freddo at a sidewalk café in Bolzano*

Cin Cin

THE WINES OF ITALY

ITALY IS A NATION LITERALLY AWASH IN WINE, millions and millions of liters of it. Admittedly, much of it may be indifferent and anonymous, with no higher ambition than to swell an already overflowing European wine lake. Yet, today, more than ever before, so many good, interesting, and individual wines are being produced throughout Italy that the curious wine lover, as well as the traveler simply in need of quenching thirst is almost flooded with choice.

Wine, after all, is part and parcel of Italian life and culture. It courses through the veins of most Italians it would seem, almost from birth: from the moment when a new arrival is toasted liberally with sparkling Ferrari, Ca' del Bosco, or even good old Asti Spumante. Long before first communion, children are introduced to wine drinking by having a little to sample, well watered down, of course, with meals. Special wines mark landmark occasions, while ordinary table wines lubricate everyday meals and help to smooth the daily trials and tribulations — even in Italy, alas.

And yet, wine can be so inherent to the Italian way of life as to be taken for granted. For those of us from nations without a tradition of the casual acceptance of wine in daily life, it may seem nothing less than some magical elixir, to be studied, analyzed, discussed endlessly. Italians, however, are much more at ease and relaxed about wine, their enjoyment of it is as unselfconscious as their appreciation of Renaissance art, the history of ancient Rome, or Dante's *Inferno* — all of them elements of a precious national heritage. In Italy, there is no mystique attached to wine: it is principally an accompaniment to food, rarely drunk merely to

Past rooftops into the vineyards of Serralunga d'Alba, in the heart of Piemonte's Barolo country

Vines trained as pergolas in the vineyards of Verona

intoxicate; in fact, drunkenness in Italy is rare, a state most Italians find intensely distasteful.

The range of Italian wines widely available today is quite staggering. Good wines are produced in every one of Italy's 20 regions, from the Valle d'Aosta and the German speaking Alto Adige to Pantelleria, almost off the coast of North Africa. Of course, the image of Italian wine outside Italy was formed decades ago by the success of such popular wines as Chianti, Soave, Verdicchio, Frascati, Lambrusco, and Asti Spumante. If such easy-to-drink wines introduced millions the world over to the delights of wine drinking, then surely this is an achievement to be proud of. But Italian wines during the last decades have left the image of the straw-covered Chianti *fiasco* far behind.

I consider that today Italy is producing some of the most exciting wines anywhere in the world, both traditional as well as new-wave "designer" wines that are at once modern and of the highest quality. Such wines, in their antique bottles with deep punts and their minimalist labels, can be truly serious and exciting. Yet, at the same time, I can't help but feel a certain lingering fondness for the Chianti *fiasco* of old, symbol of the fun, uncomplicated, inexpensive, if one-dimensional, pleasure of wine.

Italians approach wine as they do everything else: from a local or regional standpoint. This means that many, even self-appointed cognoscenti, rarely drink wines from outside their own region. In some cases, the distinctions are even more local — few from Alba, for example, drink wine from nearby Asti, and Florentines rarely drink Chiantis produced in the vineyards of Siena. However, visitors, devoid of local, regional, or national prejudices, can happily wander through Italy glass in hand, appreciating and enjoying the full range of the country's vineyards.

Above all, remember that in Italy, wine is not fussed over, pontificated about, or over analysed: it is there simply to be enjoyed — preferably with good friends and food.

The cellars of the Fattoria dei Barbi, Montalcino

Tradition and Innovation
THE CLASSICS AND THE ULTRA-MODERN

ITALY IS ONE OF THE WORLD'S oldest wine-producing nations. Long before the ancient Romans, even before the Greeks colonized Sicily and the South, the mysterious, indigenous Etruscans cultivated the vine, made and consumed wine, and even traded it as far as Gaul and beyond. The picturesque Etruscan system of promiscuous cultivation, whereby vines were trained up trees or other vegetation, can still be seen throughout Central Italy.

Wine amphora recovered from the sea bed

Today, Italy remains one of the world's most traditional winemaking nations, both in terms of taste as well as in styles of winemaking. That is not to say that wine made and enjoyed by the ancient Romans would even be remotely similar in taste to wine made today — the Roman taste was for concentrated and extremely aged wine that had to be diluted and often flavored with seasonings, honey, and spices before drinking. But winemaking methods and styles of wines developed by the Romans have continued, with variations, even till today.

Some of Italy's greatest and most individual wines, for example, are *passito*

Many Italian "new wave" wines are aged in new French oak barriques *or barrels*

wines, made from grapes that have been dried to almost raisins before pressing. A similar method was certainly used in Roman times, though it is found in few other places in the world today. Wine such as Recioto and Amarone della Valpolicella, or Vin Santo rank among the world's classics.

Elsewhere, historical antecedents, if not actual roots, go back centuries, or even millenia. Antonio Mastroberardino and the Avallone family, both in Campania, have recuperated grapes and vines once cultivated by the ancient Greeks and Romans. In Tuscany, the Frescobaldi family have been winegrowers since 1300, and near Verona, Count Pieralvise Serègo Alighieri, a direct descendant of the poet Dante, continues to produce wine on the estate founded by the poet's son in 1353.

Yet, Italians also have been quick to modernize their cellars and take on board state-of-the-art techniques of modern winemaking, learning from successes as far flung as Davis, California and Marlborough, New Zealand.

Stainless steel vats for vinification alongside new French oak *barriques* (225-liter or 55-gallon oak casks) for aging and finishing wines have become *de rigueur* in any winery with aspirations for national and international recognition. Traditional wines have been modernized by new vinification techniques, and many outstanding new wines are created almost by the day. Meanwhile, Italian grape varieties found nowhere else in the world grow beside ever larger plantations of brought in "foreign" varieties. This continuous flux between tradition and innovation, local and regional tastes and the demands of the international market, is one of the most fascinating aspects of the Italian wine scene today.

DOC and DOCG

LAWS TO PROTECT AUTHENTICITY

THE VINEYARDS AND WINES of Italy were classified and categorized in Roman times, and in the 18th century, a granducal decree by the Medici Cosimo III identified the delimited zones and rules of production for some of Tuscany's best. Today, the nation's system of *denominazione di origine controllata* (DOC) tries to serve the same purpose: to define and delimit zones of production for quality wines, and to lay down strictures and rules relating to permitted grape varieties, maximum yield per hectare, minimum alcohol levels, and aging disciplines and production methods.

There are, at present, some 220 wines that qualify for DOC. Furthermore, a higher tier has now been created, *denominazione di origine controllata e garantita* (DOCG), granted to some of the country's finest wines. DOCG lays down even stricter disciplines and rules of production. Wines that have so far qualified for DOCG include Barolo, Barbaresco, Chianti Classico, Brunello di Montalcino, Torgiano, Carmignano, and Albano di Romagna, among others.

Paradoxically, Italy being Italy, some of the nation's greatest wines, because they do not conform to the DOC/DOCG strictures, are still labeled and marketed under the humble *vino da tavola* label, Italy's lowest category.

Meanwhile, a new category has just been introduced, *indicazioni geografiche tipiche* (IGT), which aims to serve as an Italian equivalent of the French *vin de pays* (regional country wine) and is applied to some 150 new wines.

There have been critics of Italy's DOC system. Certainly, there are too many DOC wines with only limited or minor local interest. However, DOC and DOCG do serve an important role for the consumer and can be taken as a guarantee of a wine's authenticity. As always, however, the best guarantee of quality is the reputation of the producers themselves.

Sangiovese di Romagna, a DOCG wine from Emilia-Romagna

THE LANGUAGE OF THE LABEL

Abboccato Medium-dry.

Amabile Medium-sweet.

Annata Year of harvest; sometimes **vendemmia** (harvest) may precede the date.

Azienda agricola Private wine estate.

Cantina sociale, cantina cooperativa Cooperative winery.

Classico The heart or classic zone of a DOC area.

Dolce Sweet.

Frizzante Slightly fizzy, usually from a natural secondary fermentation.

Imbottigliato all'origine Estate-bottled.

Liquoroso Fortified dessert wine.

Metodo classico Classic method of making sparkling wine, by secondary fermentation in the bottle.

Riserva DOC wine matured for a longer specified period.

Secco Dry.

Spumante Fully sparkling.

Superiore Higher specified degree of alcohol than normal.

I Super Vini da Tavola
EXCEPTIONAL "TABLE WINES"

IN THIS NATION of individualists, it is not surprising that many wine producers have chosen to go their own way, to eschew the benefits of DOC status, and to produce, instead, highly individual wines outside the scope of the system: paradoxically, such wines are thus entitled only to lowly *vino da tavola* status.

Sangiovese grapes, a principal component of many Tuscan super vini

Today, there are hundreds of such superior table wines, the *super vini da tavola* — Italy's so-called "super table wines" — the best of which undoubtedly rank alongside the greatest wines of Italy and even the world.

The idea of producing such wines arose originally in Tuscany, in part due to disillusionment with poor quality wine produced under the aegis of the Chianti DOC (though this is no longer the case now that the requirements have been tightened). There, wine producers have chosen to produce either predominantly Sangiovese-based "super wines" or else wines made from Cabernet Sauvignon. White wines, largely from Chardonnay and Sauvignon, are also being produced. Most "super wines" invariably spend some time in new French oak *barriques* (225-liter or about 55-gallon casks of French oak).

Such wines are not confined to Tuscany. Today, *super vini da tavola* are produced throughout Italy, from Piemonte and Veneto to Basilicata and Sicily. Many producers of DOC wine seem to feel the need to produce a "super wine" almost as a matter of pride and prestige.

Undoubtedly, there are far too many indifferent wines masquerading under false pretences. Given that such "super wines," with their heavy bottles and designer labels, always attract a considerable premium, it can be easy to make a mistake. When in doubt, try those recommended in the second part of this book, or ask for advice in a good *enoteca* (wine shop) or from an experienced restaurant *sommelier*.

Some of Italy's finest *super vini* include:

REDS
Barbarossa (Emilia-Romagna).
Bricco Manzoni (Piemonte).
Canneto (Basilicata).
Cùmaro (Le Marche).
Darmagi (Piemonte).
Ornelaia (Tuscany).
Pignolo (Friuli-Venezia Giulia).
Sassicaia (Tuscany).
Solaia (Tuscany).
Tignanello (Tuscany).
Toar (Veneto).
Torre Ercolana (Lazio).
Querciagrande (Tuscany).

WHITES
Chardonnay Gaja & Rey (Piemonte).
Feldmarschall (Alto Adige).
Le Busche (Le Marche).
Preludio (Puglia).
Terre Alte (Friuli-Venezia Giulia).
Torcolato (Veneto).
Vecchio Samperi (Sicily).
Vintage Tunina (Friuli-Venezia Giulia).

Vineyard in Chianti Classico, home of the best super vini

In Search of Wine
THE MAIN WINES OF ITALY

Wine is produced in every region of Italy, so the wine loving visitor is never likely to go thirsty for long. In the second part of this book, we discuss in detail the most important Italian wines in each region, and, as always, we urge you, wherever you are, to drink locally.

This map shows suggested principal DOC and DOCG wines worth trying in each area.

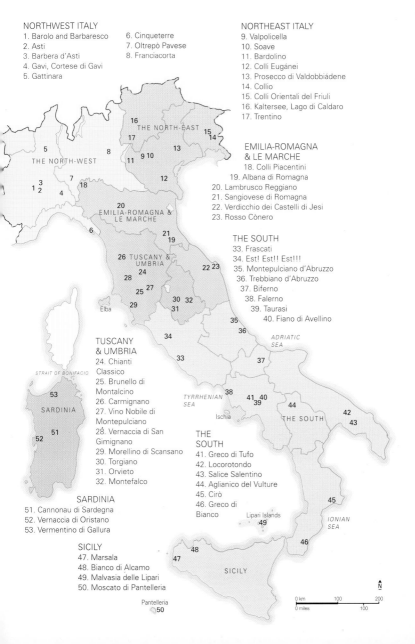

NORTHWEST ITALY
1. Barolo and Barbaresco
2. Asti
3. Barbera d'Asti
4. Gavi, Cortese di Gavi
5. Gattinara
6. Cinqueterre
7. Oltrepò Pavese
8. Franciacorta

NORTHEAST ITALY
9. Valpolicella
10. Soave
11. Bardolino
12. Colli Eugánei
13. Prosecco di Valdobbiádene
14. Collio
15. Colli Orientali del Friuli
16. Kaltersee, Lago di Caldaro
17. Trentino

EMILIA-ROMAGNA & LE MARCHE
18. Colli Piacentini
19. Albana di Romagna
20. Lambrusco Reggiano
21. Sangiovese di Romagna
22. Verdicchio dei Castelli di Jesi
23. Rosso Cònero

THE SOUTH
33. Frascati
34. Est! Est!! Est!!!
35. Montepulciano d'Abruzzo
36. Trebbiano d'Abruzzo
37. Biferno
38. Falerno
39. Taurasi
40. Fiano di Avellino

TUSCANY & UMBRIA
24. Chianti Classico
25. Brunello di Montalcino
26. Carmignano
27. Vino Nobile di Montepulciano
28. Vernaccia di San Gimignano
29. Morellino di Scansano
30. Torgiano
31. Orvieto
32. Montefalco

THE SOUTH
41. Greco di Tufo
42. Locorotondo
43. Salice Salentino
44. Aglianico del Vulture
45. Cirò
46. Greco di Bianco

SARDINIA
51. Cannonau di Sardegna
52. Vernaccia di Oristano
53. Vermentino di Gallura

SICILY
47. Marsala
48. Bianco di Alcamo
49. Malvasia delle Lipari
50. Moscato di Pantelleria

A Wide Variety
TYPES AND STYLES OF WINES

ITALY PROBABLY MAKES a greater range of types and individual styles of wine than any other nation. With over 200 often baffling and little-known names and *denominazioni,* it is easy for the wine drinker to get lost in a haze, if not stupor, along the way. It may be helpful, therefore, to be aware of broad categories and styles of Italian wine.

LIGHT *FRIZZANTE* WHITES
New technology, especially the use of temperature-controlled stainless steel fermentation vats, coupled with early harvesting of grapes, has led to the creation of a range of light, dry, white wines that retain the pleasant *frizzante* prickle of carbon dioxide. Such wines low in alcohol, are to be drunk as fresh and young as possible: at best, they can be thirst quenching beverages. Tuscany's Galestro (made by a number of well-known Chianti producers) is one of the best-known examples.

DRY WHITE WINES
Italy is the source of an immense range of sturdy, dry white wines, vinified traditionally to be drunk with food. Such wines are produced from both traditional, indigenous Italian grapes, as well as, increasingly, from "foreigners" such as Chardonnay and Sauvignon (the latter duo often aged in French oak *barriques*).

Well-known dry white wines include the famous trio of Soave (from Veneto), Frascati (Lazio), and Verdicchio dei Castelli di Jesi (Le Marche). We consider the range of mainly varietal wines from Friuli-Venezia Giulia (vinified utilizing modern stainless steel technology in the classic Italian style) to be outstanding: strong, dry white wines to accompany food. Elsewhere, new wines are being produced from old indigenous grape varieties, such as Arneis in Piemonte and Grechetto in Umbria, and traditional wines such as Vernaccia di San Gimignano (still in some cases vinified in wood) compromise not a jot to international tastes.

MEDIUM-SWEET AND AROMATIC WHITE WINES
If, on the whole, Italian white wines have less obvious, up-front varietal character than their New World counterparts, there is still a penchant for *abboccato* (off-dry) and *amabile* (medium-sweet) white wines which add character and roundness by retaining some residual sweetness in varying degrees. Many white wines are made in off-dry to medium-sweet styles. Traditional classics include Orvieto (usually much better in this style than in the more neutral *secco*) and Frascati's *cannellino,* the traditional term for a delectable, softly sweet wine.

White wines made from intensely aromatic grapes, whether off-dry or fairly sweet, are also worth sampling, often best as an *aperitivo* before a meal. The distinctive Moscato grape is cultivated widely in Italy, and produces excellent, intensely perfumed, slightly *frizzante* (as well as fully sparkling) wines in Piemonte, Veneto, and even way down in Puglia. In Alto Adige, near the national frontier with Austria, and in neighboring Trentino, outstanding aromatic white wines are produced from grapes such as Traminer Aromatico (Gewürztraminer), Riesling, Ruländer, Sylvaner, and

Barrels for Vin Santo *at Frescobaldi's Pomino estate in the Chianti Rufina area, Tuscany*

La vendemmia, *the harvest*

Müller-Thurgau. Such varietal wines may not sound very Italian but they can be superb and are certainly worth trying.

ROSATO WINES

Rosato or rosé wine is not widely drunk in Italy. As elsewhere, this style is considered neither one thing nor another. Yet fine examples are produced throughout the country, including Bardolino Chiaretto, Vin Ruspo from Tuscany's Carmignano, and the outstanding full in color and flavor pink wines from Puglia's Salento Peninsula. On the right occasion, say, an outdoor lunch, they can be perfect.

LIGHT, FOAMING, FRIZZANTE REDS

One category of wine almost uniquely Italian in style is that of young, *frizzante* (slightly sparkling), red wines. Of course, much damage has been done to the image of such wines by the sweet, soda-pop Lambrusco flooding international markets for so long that you would be forgiven for wanting to avoid them. But to do so would be to miss some of the most original and delightful wines in Italy.

In Piemonte, for example, red wines are often vinified to be drunk while young and at their freshest and most vivid (as opposed to being vinified for aging), and *frizzante* examples from grapes such as Barbera, Dolcetto, and Grignolino can all be most enjoyable. Brachetto d'Acqui, on the other hand, is vinified almost exclusively in this fashion, the fleeting, strawberry perfume intensified by the residual sugar and the sparkle.

Real Lambrusco does exist, and visitors to Emilia-Romagna should not miss sampling it: deep in color, wildly effervescent, bone dry, and an excellent accompaniment to the rich cooking of that great gastronomic region.

MEDIUM-BODIED RED TABLE WINES

So many good, medium-bodied, and medium-priced red table wines are produced in Italy that it is difficult to know where to start. From Barbera and Nebbiolo in Piemonte, across to Valpolicella Classico in Veneto and Cabernets from Friuli and Trentino, to the Sangiovese-based wines of Tuscany; and from little-known but fine wines such as Rosso Cònero in Le Marche and Torgiano and Rosso di Montefalco in Umbria, down south to such ancient and

Vineyards of Bolzano, in the German-speaking Alto Adige

Valpolicella vineyards near Verona

historic wines as Falerno in Campania and Cirò in Calabria: wherever you are in Italy, there is no shortage of good, regional red table wines. The main thing to remember is not to fall back on the familiar: try the unusual, the local; you will be surprised by the range and quality available.

BIG RED WINES

We love big, traditional, full-flavored red wines packed with concentrated fruit and the complex bouquet and flavors that come only after lengthy aging in casks (usually large Slavonian oak, not small French *barriques*) followed by years or even decades in the bottle. Italy produces some of the world's greatest, big, serious red wines, including Barolo and Barbaresco from Piemonte, Brunello di Montalcino from Tuscany, Torgiano Riserva from Umbria, Taurasi from Campania, Aglianico del Vulture from Basilicata, and Salice Salentino from Puglia.

PASSITO RED WINES

Some of Italy's greatest and most distinctive and original wines are *passito* wines, produced from grapes that have been laid out to dry for months. In addition to sweet white dessert wines, outstanding red wines are also made, most notably Amarone and Recioto della Valpolicella, as well as the rare Umbrian wine, Sagrantino di Montefalco *passito*.

SWEET DESSERT WINES

Luscious, sweet dessert wines are produced from freshly pressed grapes (Picolit), late harvested grapes affected by noble rot (Muffato della Sala from Umbria), and dried grapes (Vin Santo, Recioto di Soave, Moscato di Pantelleria *passito*). At best, such wines are among Italy's greatest and most individual.

SPARKLING WINES

Once noted mainly for medium-sweet sparkling Asti Spumante, Italy is today the source of an impressive range of sparkling wines made by the classic method of secondary fermentation and *dégorgement* (removal of the yeast sediment) in the bottle. Great classic sparkling wines, mainly using an *uvaggio* (blend) of grapes that includes Chardonnay and Pinot Nero, are produced in Lombardia (Berlucchi, Ca' del Bosco), Trentino (Ferrari), Umbria (Lungarotti), and elsewhere. Prosecco di Conegliano-Valdobbiádene is the favorite sparkling wine of Veneto.

ORDERING WINE

In many restaurants in Italy, you may not even be offered a *carta dei vini* (wine list) unless you ask for one. Instead, you simply indicate whether you would prefer *rosso* or *bianco* — house red or white. Your choice may depend not only on what you are eating, but on where you are. Zones noted for their white wines (the Colli Albani, Friuli, or the vineyards of Verona) might well offer passable house whites, but elsewhere it is usually safer to stick to red.

When there is a wine list, always ask for a recommendation for good local wines. This may lead to many unexpected surprises and wines that you would otherwise not have come across. Invariably, local wines are the best partner to local foods.

Cantine Aperte

TASTING AND BUYING WINE AT SOURCE

U NLIKE FRANCE, Italy does not have a tradition of welcoming visitors at vineyards and wine estates. The reason is not lack of hospitality in this most welcoming of nations, but that, until recently, wine was considered just another agricultural product, of no more interest to the visitor than, say, last season's crop of corn or tomatoes.

There were few organized opportunities for visiting vineyards, but if you took potluck and knocked on the door of a wine estate, even a famous wine estate, you were more often than not made extremely welcome, not just for any sale that might result, but as much for the chance to share likeminded passions.

Today, Italians have a new self-awareness and appreciation of their wine industry. Wine is not only big business, it is prestigious big business and many wineries,

Enoteca *or "wine library,"*
offering local wines

large and small, are happy to welcome foreign visitors. Thus, there are scores of opportunities for visiting wine estates to taste and purchase wines direct.

Whenever you are in a wine region (and most of Italy is one), you should enquire locally, seek out the sources of wines that you have enjoyed, then go and visit the properties where they are made. It is always a good idea to telephone in advance before making an out-of-the-way trip, if only to ensure that someone is on hand to receive you (in small family concerns, everybody might be out tending the vines). On the other hand, if there is a particular Italian wine producer whom you would really like to visit, try to make arrangements in advance, either by writing to them directly, or by making contact with their agent or importer in your own country.

IL MOVIMENTO PER IL TURISMO DI VINO — WINE TOURISM

Even for Italians, the concept of "wine tourism" is novel, as wine has been utterly taken for granted by Italians for so long. They may have gone to winegrowers direct to purchase *vino sfuso* (unbottled wine) drawn directly from the vat into demijohns for bottling at home. But they rarely visited estates to learn about winemaking, taste wine at source, or to purchase prestigious bottles by the case.

To encourage intelligent wine touring, the *Movimento per il turismo di vino* has been created, which encourages wine producers to welcome visitors. It has published a series of regional booklets which give suggested itineraries, with names and addresses of wine estates that welcome visitors. But, in most cases, it is still necessary

to telephone in advance of a visit as few private wineries have staff on hand dedicated to receive casual visitors.

Each May, the movement organizes a *cantine aperte* day, when some 500 wine estates throughout Italy keep open house. This has proved phenomenally successful: recently, in Friuli-Venezia Giulia, some 40,000 visitors came, saw, and tasted wine at 63 estates on a single day, and, apparently, a good time was had by all.

For further information on wine tourism, contact:

Movimento per il turismo di vino
c/o Donatella Cinelli Colombini
Fattoria dei Barbi
53024 Montalcino SI
tel: 0577/849421
fax: 0577/849356

Aperitivi e Digestivi
PRE- AND POST-PRANDIAL DRINKS

A N *APERITIVO* SHOULD WHET the appetite in anticipation of a fine or extensive meal. Pungent drinks made from infusions of herbs, peel, and spices, literally, set the gastric juices flowing. A *digestivo,* by contrast, aids digestion at the end of that same meal. In Italy, both pre- and post-prandial drinks are enjoyed, especially when dining in restaurants.

A selection of homemade liqueurs infused with fruits and herbs, highly enjoyable — in small doses — before or after a meal

APERITIVI

Aperitivo analcolico della casa
Non-alcoholic house *aperitivo,* perhaps fruit-juice based, flavored and colored with syrup.

Aperitivo della casa Many bars and restaurants offer a house *aperitivo* based on wine or sparkling wine, with added spirits, fruit juice, or other ingredients. Ask what it is if you are unsure *("Cos'è l'aperitivo della casa?")*

Aperol Brand of low alcohol bitter drink with a characteristic orange finish; enjoy as a long drink, topped up with seltzer and plenty of ice. Other low or alcohol free bitter-type *aperitivi* include **Bitter San Pellerino** and **Crodino.**

Bellini A delectable favorite of Northeast Italy: sparkling Prosecco wine with fresh white peach juice.

Campari The classic Italian bitter drink, usually enjoyed as a long drink, Campari soda, topped up with seltzer, plenty of ice, and a twist of lemon.

Limoncello Infusion of fresh lemons, sugar, and alcohol. Always served ice cold; can be exquisite.

Negroni A powerful cocktail made from a mixture of Campari, Punt e Mes, and gin, served with ice and an orange slice, optionally topped up with seltzer.

Punt e Mes Classic and popular *aperitivo* created from a mixture of sweet red vermouth and red wine, lighter and slightly drier than the vermouth on its own. Enjoy straight or with seltzer on the rocks.

Spremuta di frutta Ask for a *spremuta* (freshly squeezed fruit juice) — usually orange — for a refreshing, non-alcoholic pre-dinner drink.

Vermouth Classic herbal *aperitivo* in a fortified wine base. **Martini Dry** is the best-known dry version. **Cinzano Bianco** is a sweet white; **Vermouth Rosso** is a sweet red.

DIGESTIVI

Amaretto Quite sweet, almond flavored liqueur.

Amaro Dense, viscous drink with a strongly bitter flavor of herbs and other flavoring in a base that is both strong and sweet: **Fernet Branca** is one of the best-known brands, but there are always scores of local varieties to sample.

Grappa Distillation made from the left-over residue after the winemaking process (see opposite).

Liquori casalinghi Homemade liqueurs made by infusing fruits, spices, herbs, or other ingredients in alcohol with sugar.

Nocino Dense, sweet infusion of green walnuts, alcohol, sugar, and flavorings; often homemade.

Sambuca Anise-flavored liqueur, often served with *"la mosca,"* a coffee bean or two in the glass to add flavor. Some eat the bean, some do not. In Italy, Sambuca is never ignited.

Vecchia Romagna Popular, slightly sweet, grape brandy.

Grappa

THE SPIRIT OF ITALY

Y OU'LL EITHER love *grappa* or hate it — there is no in-between. *Grappa* has a distinctive character and kick that is wholly Italian, and we consider it almost obligatory to sample it when in the country — or, at least, that's my excuse. Many consider *grappa* an acquired taste not worth acquiring. I disagree. Try a good *grappa* and you will be converted, I am sure.

Paolo Marolo, producer of an outstanding range of single variety grappe, at his distillery near Alba

There is, of course, *grappa* and there is *grappa*. The best, produced by no more than a handful of artisan distillers mainly located in the north of Italy (the necessity for such high-alcohol spirits has always been greater in cold, northern countries), really can be ethereal drinks, the true essence of the grape in its purest, strongest form. The worst ... well, the worst *grappa* really can be quite horrible and is best avoided.

Grappa is produced by distilling the *vinacce,* the residue of grape skins, seeds, and pulp left over after winemaking. The best *vinacce* come from select single-grape varieties, and arrive fresh from the press, still wine-drenched and rich in potential or already converted alcohol.

Bassano del Grappa, Northeast Italy, famed town of Italian firewater

From this point on, there are a number of ways of proceeding, for *grappa* is made on a tiny scale as well as on an immense, industrial one.

Paolo Marolo of Alba is one of the most respected artisan distillers in the nation. Marolo was one of the first in Italy to pioneer the distillation of prestigious *grappe di monovitigno* (that is, *grappa* from single grape varieties). Today, such *grappe* from the *vinacce* of prestigious wines such as Barolo, Barbaresco, Brunello di Montalcino, Gavi dei Gavi, and Fiano di Avellino are highly sought for their full flavor and smoothness. Aromatic single grape varieties such as Moscato, Müller-Thurgau, Traminer, and Verdicchio also yield outstanding results.

Marolo believes that the use of a *bagno maria* (double boiler) gives the best results, so he charges his small, discontinuous pot stills with between 300–600 kg. (660–1,320 lbs.) of *vinacce,* then heats them indirectly through a blanket of hot water. This process allows for a very slow and gentle vaporization (direct heat would scorch the *vinacce*), and the subsequent condensed liquid passes once more through another system of rectification, discarding both the heads and the tails (the first and last fractions), and keeping only the *cuore* (heart) of the distillate. The end yield is a miniscule three to four per cent of the original volume of the *vinacce,* but what is left is pure colorless *grappa* of the highest quality.

Grappe may either be colorless and unaged, or amber through aging in wood casks. There are also *grappe aromatizzate* (flavored *grappe*), made by infusing the distilled spirit with various mixtures of herbs, fruit, or other flavorings.

The Northwest

VALLE D'AOSTA

PIEMONTE

LOMBARDIA, LIGURIA

NORTHWEST ITALY IS RICH in every way — economically, socially, gastronomically. Milan, the banking capital of Italy, is one of the great financial centers of Europe. Turin, capital of Piemonte and a great historic city, has both traditional heavy industry as well as much new high technology and investment. Genoa, birthplace of Christopher Columbus, is today a vibrant and chaotic city, one of the busiest Mediterranean ports. Coastal towns along the Italian Riviera, such as fashionable Portofino, attract well-heeled tourists from throughout Europe. Elsewhere, in Lombardia and Piemonte, smaller towns like Ivrea, Brescia, Bergamo, Varese, Novara, and Vercelli are busy and self-important, demonstrating the prosperity and industry of the region.

The people of the Northwest are nothing if not hardworking — they like to make money, and they like to spend it. This is the Italy of conspicuous consumption, of *la bella figura*, where you are, what you wear, what you drive, where you live, what you eat. No wonder that Northwest Italy is the center of Italian fashion, car manufacture, design, publishing, *cucina novella,* and designer wines. Yet, outside urban areas, there is still much quiet and beautiful country where you can eat good, genuine, and unpretentious regional food.

Vernazza, one of the five fishing villages called the Cinque Terre, Liguria

VALLE D'AOSTA — A FRENCH CORNER OF ITALY

Though separated from France by the Alps, the Valle d'Aosta, Italy's smallest region, is regionally autonomous and bilingual, its inhabitants as comfortable speaking French as Italian. This is one of the most dramatically scenic stretches of the Alps, and many visitors come to the Valle d'Aosta in winter to ski in fashionable resorts such as Courmayeur and Cervinia, while others come in summer to walk through the verdant pastures of the lower slopes leading up to the high peaks of the Gran Paradiso National Park. Many visitors may cross into the region either through the 24-km. (15-mile) long Monte Bianco (Mont Blanc) tunnel or through the San Bernardo passes, two natural corridors into Italy traversed by invaders and visitors for millennia.

PIEMONTE — A GENEROUS AND AMPLE LAND

Piemonte means "foot of the mountain," and this immense region — Italy's largest on the mainland — encompasses some seven provinces ringed by the dominating Alps to the north and west and the Apennines to the south. Turin, the first capital of a united Italy, is one of Italy's great cities. Birthplace of the 19th-century Risorgimento movement of Italian

Country food and wines outdoors in the Oltrepò Pavese, Lombardia

nationalism, Turin today attracts visitors to its elegant and stylish baroque city center, the Royal Palace of the House of Savoy, and the urn containing the Holy Shroud, said by believers to be the cloth in which Christ was wrapped after the Crucifixion (the shroud itself is only rarely displayed publicly).

Wine and food lovers will certainly wish to tour the Langhe, the Monferrato hills, and Asti, source of not only some of Italy's greatest wines, such as Barolo, Barbaresco, Barbera d'Alba, Asti Spumante, and others, but also of one of its finest, richest, and most ample regional cuisines. Fall is the best time to visit this area, not only for the grape harvest, but also for the chance to sample *tartufi bianchi,* the famous white truffles of Alba. During October, truffle festivals take place throughout the region. Don't, however, overlook the chance to visit Lake Maggiore: Stresa is one of the most picturesque of all lakeside towns, and serves as an excellent base for tours of the beautiful Borromean Islands.

LOMBARDIA — CITY AND COUNTRY

Milan, Lombardia's capital, is no city of gray-suited bankers. True, it is positively sober compared to romantic Venice or the frantic bacchanalia that is Rome, but this is a city where people live well, and visibly so. Most visitors come here for the Teatro La Scala, Milan's world-famous opera house, and to view Leonardo's "Last Supper"; others to shop (or window-shop) in fashionable Via Monte Napoleone or Corso Emanuele. Few come with the sole intention of eating, but Milan is a city with a surprising number of superlative restaurants and *trattorie* of all prices.

Outside Milan, visit Lombardia's beautiful lake country, which includes the eastern shore of Lake Maggiore, Lake Lugano, Lake Como, and the western shore of Lake Garda. Enjoy the Alpine country and mountain foods of the Valtellina. Or tour Lombardia's stretch of the Po Valley, stopping to see Pavia's famous *certosa* (charterhouse), visiting the Oltrepò Pavese, the region's most congenial wine country, and continuing on to Cremona and Mantova, a town with a rich Renaissance heritage and strongly intact local gastronomic traditions.

Tortelli di zucca (pumpkin-filled pasta), a specialty of Mantova, Lombardia

LIGURIA — LAND OF SEA AND MOUNTAIN

The Apennines swing close to the coast in this thin sliver of a region that extends from the French frontier, along the Gulf of Genoa, all the way down to Tuscany: Liguria firmly and decidedly looks out to the sea. Genoa, after all, was once one of the most powerful maritime republics in the Mediterranean, a rival even to Venice; today, it still wears the vestiges of its past glory. Undoubtedly grand if rather faded and chaotic, the region's capital straddles the coast, dividing Liguria's two Rivieras, the Ponente, which extends north to the frontier with France, and the Levante, which ends at La Spezia. The Ponente, known also as the Riviera dei Fiori or the Floral Coast, is particularly beautiful. Where the mountains come straight down almost to the sea, the roads wind down in vertigo-inducing hairpin bends to little villages clustered by the sea, their whitewashed and pastel-colored houses clinging tenaciously to the rocky hillsides. But wherever there is a break in the terrain, a brief stretch of valley or less steeply sloping hills, the ground is covered with greenhouses for the year-round cultivation of flowers and for superb, early-ripening, and flavorful vegetables.

South of Genoa, tiny Portofino is one of the most exclusive resorts on the Italian Riviera. The Cinque Terre are five tiny villages located on terraced, vine-covered slopes between Levanto and La Spezia, some accessible only by foot. Outside the hectic and overcrowded high season, they are among the most charming and delightful places in all of Italy.

Prodotti Regionali
REGIONAL PRODUCE

From the lower slopes of the Alps, down across the rice paddies of Vercelli to the wide Po Valley, and over the Apennines to the steeply terraced shores of Liguria, Northwest Italy is a rich and abundant agricultural land with a wealth of fine, fresh produce.

Market vegetables from Albenga, Liguria

The markets of Liguria are a riot of color: the region is the source of fine early harvested vegetables grown all year round, some in greenhouses built on terraced hillsides to face the sun.

Particularly fine fruit and vegetables come from Albenga, especially *zucchine trombetta,* a local, very fine, thin, and long zucchini, *melanzana violetta,* round, white-and-violet eggplant, *asparagi* (asparagus), *pesche* (peaches), and *albicocche* (apricots). Wild herbs, such as oregano, sage, and rosemary, grow in the hills, but much more important from a commercial point of view is the cultivation all year round of aromatic herbs, outdoors in summer, under glass at other times. Large-leaved *basilico* (basil), when transformed with good yellow Ligurian olive oil, garlic, and pine nuts into *pesto,* is the ultimate aroma of Ligurian cooking.

Piemonte is an immense and important agricultural region. Grapes grow on its hills, the flatter, more fertile plains are cultivated intensively with wheat, corn, and other grains, and, in the flatlands around Vercelli and Novara, vast stretches of flooded rice paddies extend as far as the eye can see, for this is the most important rice growing zone in Italy. Varieties of rice cultivated include the prestigious *carnaroli,* a *superfino* that is considered one of the finest for producing *risotto,* as well as less exalted but still excellent varieties, such as *baldo* and the more widely available *arborio.*

Piemonte, of course, is most famous for the rare and expensive *tartufo bianco* and for *funghi porcini* (*Boletus edulis* or cepe

MOSTARDA DI FRUTTA

A type of fruit condiment, *mostarda di frutta* is one of the most delightful and colorful foods that you will encounter in this part of Italy. The most common version comes from Cremona, and is generally made from whole fruit and pieces of candied fruits, such as pears, pineapple, figs, oranges, cherries, and *cedro* (citron), mixed together in a thick, sweet syrup flavored with white mustard powder. This *mostarda di Cremona* is a delicious accompaniment to *bollito misto* (mixed boiled meats).

Less commonly encountered is Mantova's version, which is made just with pieces of candied apples in a spicy mustard syrup flavored with nutmeg. This is traditionally used when making *tortelli di zucca* (pumpkin stuffed *tortelli*) and adds a distinctive, sweet and spicy flavor. Yet another version is made only with cherries.

Typical of the foods of the Renaissance in their combination of sweet and spicy flavors, fruit mustards are a vivid and piquant taste of Northwest Italy; you can buy jars of them to take back home.

mushrooms) gathered in the fall. Also excellent are *cardi* (cardoons, a type of edible thistle which resembles celery), the best of which comes from Nizza Monferrato. *Nocciole* (hazelnuts) grow extensively in the higher ground and forests, and are widely used in a range of sweets and desserts, famously, *gianduia,* the popular chocolate and hazelnut puree.

The sheer scale and variety of the countryside of Lombardia mean that it yields an abundance of fine produce — a rich variety of good fruits and vegetables. *Zucca* (pumpkin) is a much-loved local vegetable and particularly fine *asparagi* (asparagus) is cultivated on the sandy, alluvial plains around Milan.

TRY TO SAMPLE

Albicocche (Jun–Aug) Apricots; especially from Albenga and Cuneo.
Cardi (winter) Cardoons; eaten raw when young and tender dipped into *bagna cauda* (a pungent anchovy and olive oil mixture; see p.74), or baked in the oven with cheese.

Fragole (late spring to early summer) Strawberries (especially good are the tiny, wild *fragoline*).
Funghi porcini (Sep–early Nov) Fresh wild cepe mushrooms, served over homemade *pasta* or in *risotto*. Dried mushrooms are available all year round. New season dried *porcini,* available in the winter, are good to buy to take home.
Tartufi bianchi (mid-Sep–early Jan) Fresh white truffles, one of the greatest delicacies in the world. Don't miss them at any cost.

Fresh funghi porcini, *available throughout the Northwest in the fall*

PESTO ALLA GENOVESE

One of the most magnificent expressions of Italian cuisine, *pesto alla genovese,* embodies the essence of Liguria. It is best when it is freshly made from torn basil leaves pounded with a mortar and pestle together with crushed garlic, extra-virgin Ligurian olive oil, pine nuts, and freshly grated parmesan and *pecorino* cheeses.

In Liguria, *pesto* may be added to *minestrone* (vegetable soup), rather like the favorite Provençal specialty, *soupe au pistou,* an indication of the close links of these coastal areas. The most typical way of enjoying *pesto,*

however, is to spoon it over hot *pasta.* Here in Liguria, it is usually eaten either with *trenette* (thin, *tagliatelle*-like noodles) or *trionfe* (little homemade *gnocchetti* shaped in spirals), the pasta cooked always with a potato, to thicken it, and a handful of green beans. The pungent aroma and hot, peppery flavor released when the emulsion of garlic, olive oil, and crushed basil combines with the steaming hot *pasta* is irresistible. In summer, freshly made *pesto* may be available in jars, but it must be refrigerated and consumed as quickly as possible.

Tartufi Bianchi

WHITE TRUFFLES FROM ALBA AND ASTI

ONE OF THE RAREST, most prized, and expensive foodstuffs in the world, the *tartufo bianco,* comes from around Alba and Asti in Piemonte. This fungus, which belongs to the genus *Tuber magnatum pico,* is considered the most pungent and odoriferous of all truffles, and grows spontaneously below the surface of the ground under certain conditions only, often among the roots of oak or beech trees. This rare delicacy is gathered by knowledgeable *trifolai* — the local dialect name for truffle hunters — almost always aided by a dog trained to identify the truffles' whereabouts by the odor that emanates from the ground.

Hunting truffles in the woods of the Langhe

Each year in October, a month-long *Fiera del tartufo* (truffle fair) takes place in Alba, and restaurants in the Langhe, Astigiana, and Monferrato country serve delicious local foods liberally garnished with shavings of fresh white truffles, grated with an *affettatartufi,* a special truffle grater that is wielded with great theatricality. Gastronomes from all over Italy, and, indeed, Europe and the world, descend on the region in fall to enjoy this great, prized delicacy at its source.

A 350-g. (12-oz.) tartufo bianco

At the *Mercato del tartufo* (truffle market) in Alba, every Saturday morning from mid-September until the end of December (daily, during the *Fiera del tartufo*), many of the region's *trifolai* gather to sell their truffles in a pavilion off the Via Vittorio Emanuele. This is a rare and heady event worth visiting simply to inhale the, literally, overpowering scent of so many truffles all under one roof.

It is also the place to come to purchase a truffle. Bearing in mind that prices are dependent on supply and demand (when we were last in the area, white truffles from Alba were selling for at least 250,000 lire per 100 g. or ¼ lb.), you still may not be able to resist buying a small one, weighing 30–40 g. (1¼–1½ oz.), plenty for two people to enjoy at a sitting.

Trifolai advise, above all, to smell the truffle — the best have that intense, musky, almost haunting odor which we reckon is positively addictive. And, moreover, the truffle should be hard and not too knobbly or muddy: after all, you are paying for it by weight.

Unless you plan to eat the truffle immediately, wrap it in paper or store it in rice (afterward the perfumed rice makes magnificent *risotto*). But remember: fresh truffles last no longer than a week, and even then, they inevitably lose much of their intense aroma.

Fresh truffles are enjoyed in Piemonte over a range of foods, including *carne cruda all'albese* (raw slices of wafter-thin steak), *bagna cauda* (a pungent anchovy, garlic, and olive oil dip), and on homemade *tajarin* noodles. However, the finest way to enjoy the true and pure character of the truffle, advise *trifolai,* is to simply grate it over a plate of pan fried eggs.

Grating white truffles using an affettatartufi, *the special truffle grater*

Al Mercato

MARKETS

VALLE D'AOSTA

Aosta	Tue–Sat
Courmayeur	Wed

PIEMONTE

Acqui Terme	Tue, Fri
Alba	Sat, Tue, Thu
Alessandria	Mon–Sat
Asti	Mon–Sat
Borgomanero	Tue, Wed
Bra	Wed, Fri
Cuneo	Tue, Wed
Gavi	Sun
Ivrea	Thu, Fri, Sat
Limone Piemonte	Thu
Nizza Monferrato	Fri
Novara	Mon–Sat

Fresh basil plant

Sestriere	Tue
Torino	Mon–Sat
Vercelli	Mon–Sat

LOMBARDIA

Bellagio	3rd Wed of the month
Bergamo	Mon, Sat
Brescia	Sat
Como	Mon, Thu, Sat
Cremona	Wed, Sat
Mantova	Thu
Milan	Mon–Sat
Pavia	Wed, Sat
Sondrio	Wed
Varese	Mon, Thu, Sat

LIGURIA

Alassio	Sat
Albenga	Wed
Genoa	Mon–Sat
Imperia	Mon, Tue, Thu, Sat
Lerici	Sat
Monterosso	Thu
Rapallo	Thu
San Remo	Tue, Sat
Santa Margherita Ligure	Fri
La Spezia	Tue, Fri

Peperoni *or bell peppers*

POPULAR *FESTE*

VALLE D'AOSTA

Aosta: *Fiera del vino (wine)*   Oct

PIEMONTE

Alba: *Fiera del tartufo (truffles)*   Oct

Asti: *Douja d'or (wine and gastronomy)*   Aug

Carrù: *Fiera del bue grasso (beef)*   Dec

LOMBARDIA

Chiuro: *Grappolo d'oro (wine)*   Sep

Bellágio, on Lake Como, Lombardia

Piatti Tipici
REGIONAL SPECIALTIES

Northwest Italy is an enormous and important gastronomic area, providing rich and varied cuisines that demonstrate almost all the flavors and variety of the Italian Peninsula. Mountain traditions and foods come from the Valle d'Aosta and Lombardia's Valtellina. Good fish and shellfish come from Liguria's seaboard and an outstanding catch of freshwater fish comes from the cold, deep waters of Lombardia's lakes. There is sophisticated and cosmopolitan food in the cities, and good, rustic food is found in the countryside.

Bagna cauda

Antipasti

Acciughe al verde (Piemonte) Salted anchovies, first washed, then covered with a dressing of olive oil, lemon juice, and plenty of chopped garlic and parsley.

Antipasti piemontesi (Piemonte) The best selection of hot and cold appetizers in the country; usually a vast trolley or table laden with an astonishing range, including roasted vegetables bathed in *bagna cauda* or *fonduta,* stuffed vegetables, *carne cruda,* stuffed eggs, *vitello tonnato,* trout in aspic, rice salad, *insalata russa,* and much else.

Bagna cauda or **bagna caôda** (Piemonte) Pungent, hot mixture of anchovies, olive oil, and garlic. Can be served fondue-style, i.e., in the *bagna cauda* (hot bath) over a burner at the table, into which a selection of raw vegetables is dipped. Or else, it can be used to top roasted peppers, other roasted vegetables, or meat. Served with grated truffles in season.

Bresaola (Valtellina and all Lombardia) Air-cured tenderloin of beef, eaten in thin slices like *prosciutto crudo;* sometimes dressed in olive oil and lemon juice.

Cappon magro (Genoa and all Liguria) Cold, ample salad consisting of fish, shellfish, hardboiled eggs, and boiled vegetables, mixed with a green sauce of olive oil, plenty of chopped parsley, wine vinegar, garlic, and anchovies.

Carne cruda all'albese (The Langhe and all Piemonte) Very thin slices of raw steak arranged on a plate and served with a dressing of lemon juice and olive oil; sometimes served with shavings of *parmigiano reggiano* cheese, slivers of mushrooms, or, in season, shavings of white truffles.

Carpione (Lombardia Lakes) Fresh-water lake fish, first floured and fried, then marinated in vinegar, white wine, spices, and herbs.

Focaccia all'olio (Liguria) Flat bread, dimpled with the fingers before baking, then doused liberally with Ligurian olive oil, salt, and sometimes fresh rosemary.

Fonduta (Valle d'Aosta and Piemonte) Bubbling mixture of melted *fontina* cheese cooked with milk, egg yolk, and cream, topped with grated truffles in season, and served either fondue-style or as a topping to vegetables, toasted bread, or potatoes.

Insalata alla capricciosa (Piemonte) Salad made from julienned vegetables, slices of tongue and ham, and cubes or slices of cheese, all mixed together in a mayonnaise dressing.

Insalata russa (Piemonte) Popular salad made from boiled carrots, potatoes, green beans, hardboiled eggs, tuna, peas, all mixed together in a rich, homemade mayonnaise.

Missoltini or **missoltitt** or **missortitt** (Lake Como and Lake Maggiore) Small *agoni,* a type of freshwater shad, salted and wind-dried, then pressed in cans with laurel leaves until hard and chewy. They are usually fried or broiled for just a minute, then moistened in the skillet with oil and vinegar. In winter, this is accompanied by *toc,* the local name for *polenta* cooked with butter and cheese.

Mitili (Liguria) Mussels; often served and eaten raw, a practice we avoid.

Moscardini (Liguria) Tiny little octopus; often stewed in tomato, with garlic and rosemary.

Musciame or **mosciame** (Liguria) Air-dried pieces of tuna, soaked in olive oil before eating, to make them soft.

Peperoni con bagna cauda (Piemonte) Roasted red peppers covered in *bagna cauda.*

Torta pasqualina (Liguria) A layered savory pie made with beet greens, artichokes, hardboiled eggs, and herbs. Originally eaten at Easter but now available all year round.

Vitello tonnato or **vitel tonné** (Piemonte) Slices of boiled veal, covered in a rich mayonnaise sauce mixed with tuna, anchovies, and capers.

I PRIMI PIATTI

Agnolini in brodo (Mantova) Small, stuffed *tortellini*-like *pasta*, filled with *salamelle* (see p.80), beef, and grated parmesan cheese. Always served in broth, to which a glass of wine may sometimes be added, a local practice known as *"bevr'in vin."*

Agnolotti al plin (Piemonte) Very small stuffed *pasta* much loved throughout the region; usually filled with a

Carne cruda all'albese

Peperoni con bagna cauda

mixture of ground pork and veal, egg, grated parmesan cheese, and seasonings. Served either in broth or with a meat sauce. The name *"al plin"* in dialect means "folded over by hand."

Busecca (Lombardia) Classic tripe and vegetable soup.

Ciuppin (Liguria) Rich fish soup made with local fish and shellfish, tomatoes, wine, and garlic; usually served with slices of toasted bread.

Minestrone alla genovese (Liguria) One of the great vegetable soups of Italy, made with fresh seasonal vegetables, and always flavored with a generous dollop of pungent *pesto.*

Minestrone alla milanese (Lombardia) Rustic vegetable soup made with whatever is in season — zucchini, carrots, greens, celery, onions, tomatoes, potatoes — always cooked with beans, rice, and *pancetta* (cured belly pork) to give it a characteristically smoky flavor.

Pansoti or **pansotti al sugo di noci** (Liguria) Vegetable- and herb-filled *ravioli*-like *pasta* served with a sauce made from pounded walnuts, garlic, extra-virgin olive oil, and breadcrumbs.

Pizzoccheri (Valtellina) Outstanding local *pasta* made from a mixture of buckwheat and white flour, mixed with water and made into flat noodles. *Pizzoccheri* are usually cooked with winter greens, cabbage, and potatoes, covered with butter and cheese, and baked in the oven.

Polenta taragna (Valtellina) Another heavy mountain favorite: *polenta* made, this time, from buckwheat flour and coarse cornmeal; cooked, then baked with plenty of butter and cheese.

Riso al pesce persico (Lake Como) *Risotto* rice cooked in stock with butter and grated cheese, served with fillets of fried lake perch on top of the rice.

Risotto al Barbera or **al Barolo** (The Langhe and Asti) Classic *risotto* of Piemonte's wine zones, made with either Barbera or Barolo wine, stock, butter, and cheese. The wine gives the rice a lovely color and rich flavor.

Risotto alla certosina (Pavia) This rich and luxurious *risotto,* made with freshwater crayfish, shrimps, peas, mushrooms, sometimes even frog's legs, demonstrates that life for the monks in Pavia's *certosa* was probably not at all bad.

Risotto alla milanese (Lombardia) Classic and simple *risotto,* cooked with butter, bone marrow, rich beef stock, and grated parmesan cheese, and colored yellow with saffron.

Risotto tartufato (The Langhe and all Piemonte) *Risotto* made with butter, broth, and local *murazzano* cheese and served with fresh grated truffles on top.

Tagliarin or **tajarin** (The Langhe and all Piemonte) Very fine, thin homemade egg noodles, served in summer with a fresh tomato sauce and in winter with a rich sauce made from chicken livers. During the *tartufo* season, *tajarin* are often simply served with melted butter and grated white truffles.

Toc (Bellagio) Communal pot of *polenta* made with butter and cheese, to be formed into balls and eaten with the fingers, together with *missoltini* (see above) and fried *alborelle,* a small lake fish.

Tortelli di zucca (Mantova) Large squares of fresh *pasta* filled with cooked pumpkin mixed with candied apple mustard, nutmeg, and parmesan cheese. Usually served with melted butter and grated parmesan cheese.

Trenette al pesto (Liguria) Long, thin noodles, traditionally cooked with potatoes and green beans, served almost always with fresh *pesto alla genovese.*

Trofie (Liguria) Small *gnocchetti* made with flour sometimes enriched with bran or chestnut flour and passed through a press to emerge like little spirals of *pasta.* Usually served with *pesto alla genovese.*

Zuppa alla Pavese (Pavia and all Lombardia) Classic Italian consommé: a freshly broken egg is dropped into the boiling, clear meat broth to poach it.

I SECONDI PIATTI

Alborelle fritte (Lombardia Lakes) Small freshwater fish, no larger than whitebait, dredged in flour and deep fried. **Alborelle fritte in carpione** *Alborelle fritte* marinated in vinegar, wine, herbs, and spices.

Bollito misto alla piemontese (Piemonte) Mixed selection of boiled meats, usually served from a trolley, including beef, chicken, veal, calf's foot, tongue, and *cotechino* (boiling *salame*), accompanied by boiled vegetables, *salsa verde* (chopped parsley, garlic, capers, and olive oil), or *salsa rossa* (fresh tomatoes, vinegar, herbs, olive oil, and *peperoncino*) — or, classically, *mostarda di Cremona* (see p.70).

Brasato al Barolo (Piemonte) Large piece of beef, marinated then braised slowly in Barolo wine with celery, carrots, and herbs.

Burrida (Liguria) Famous, flavorful fish stew made with a variety of the local catch cooked with onions, carrots, celery, anchovies, walnuts, and dried mushrooms.

Alborelle fritte in carpione

Riso al pesce persico — *a specialty of Lake Como*

Cima alla genovese (Liguria)
Elaborate and splendid-to-look-at cold
centerpiece of rolled breast of veal
stuffed with eggs, cheese, peas, and veal
sweetbreads.
Costoletta or **cotoletta alla
valdostana** (Valle d'Aosta) Veal cutlet
layered with a slice of *prosciutto crudo* and
a slice of *fontina* cheese, then dipped in
egg and flour, and pan fried.
Finanziera (Piemonte) Richly extravagant local specialty made with veal
sweetbreads, chicken giblets, chicken
breast, cock's comb, pieces of beef or
veal, mushrooms, all cooked separately,
then mixed in a rich cream sauce and
topped with shavings of white truffles.
Gallo al Barbera (Piemonte) The local
version of chicken-in-wine stew, here
made with a boiling cock, cooked slowly
in Barbera wine.
Lumache (Piemonte and Lombardia)
Snails, often stewed in wine, served with
polenta.
Ossobuco alla milanese (Lombardia)
Great regional specialty consisting of on-
the-bone shin of veal sawn into pieces,
cooked slowly in wine with vegetables,
and always finished with *la gremolada,* a
mixture of finely chopped parsley, grated
lemon rind, and finely chopped garlic.
The bone marrow is considered as great
a delicacy as the meat itself. Traditionally
served with *risotto alla milanese.*
Polenta e osei (Bergamo and
Lombardia) Stew of small birds, served
on a bed of *polenta.*

Rane alla vercellese (Vercelli) Frog's
legs (from frogs in the rice paddies), first
floured and fried, then cooked slowly in
tomatoes and wine.
Salmì (Piemonte) Game in season, wild
hare, boar, or venison, cooked slowly in
wine, garlic, and herbs, usually with
blood added to thicken the sauce which
can be served separately over noodles as
a first course.
Scaloppina alla milanese (Lombardia)
Breaded escalope of veal pan fried and
served with lemon.

I CONTORNI
Asparagi alla milanese (Lombardia)
Boiled asparagus, covered with melted
butter, grated parmesan cheese, and a
fried egg on top.
Cardi gobbi (Nizza Monferrato and all
Piemonte) Bent over, "humpback"
cardoons from Nizza, boiled, then baked
dotted with butter and cheese.
Funghi porcini (Piemonte and
Lombardia) Fresh *Boletus edulis* or cepe
mushrooms, gathered in woods throughout both regions, are greatly enjoyed
during their brief season, served over
homemade noodles as a first course, or
else stewed in olive oil, garlic, lemon
juice, and chopped parsley, as a side dish.
Rattatuia (Liguria) Local version of
Provençal *ratatouille* — eggplant, bell
peppers, zucchini, tomatoes, green beans,
and herbs, stewed slowly in olive oil.
Zucchine ripieni (Liguria) Baked
zucchini stuffed with chopped vegetables
and breadcrumbs.

Fresh fungi porcini *stewed in olive oil*

La Farinata
FAST FOOD LIGURIAN-STYLE

A FAVORITE FAST FOOD of Genoa and all Liguria, *farinata* is a type of thick chickpea pancake. The batter of chickpea flour, extra-virgin olive oil, water, and salt is spread out thinly on *pizza*-shaped platters and cooked quickly in a ferociously hot, wood-fired oven.

It is the sort of street food eaten off paper with fingers, while standing up,

Farinata, *baked in a fiercely hot wood-fired oven at Farinata Puppo, Albenga*

washed down with a tumbler of fresh, cold white wine.

Farinata is similar to *socca*, the chickpea-batter pie of Nice. "But ours is much better," says Maria Puppo, who, together with her sister and husband, has been making *farinata* for decades in Albenga. "*Farinata* must be *croccante sopra e morbida sotto* — crispy on the outside but moist and soft inside," she explains, quickly dusting the hot *farinata* with black pepper, then cutting it into pieces. "For this reason, the *forno* is larger and hotter even than a *pizza* oven. Here, try a piece," she offers. Too hot and too delicious for words … we nod in acknowledgment and take another gulp of the local characterful Pigato white.

Farinata Puppo
Via Torlaro, 20
17031 Albenga SV
tel: 0182/51853

GRISSINI *"STIRATI A MANO"*

Long, thin breadsticks, *grissini* are as stereotypically Italian as the straw-covered Chianti flask. The best come from Piemonte, where they are still baked fresh daily, *"stirati a mano"* — stretched out individually by hand, until they are as long as 1 m. (over 3 ft.) in length. *Grissini* are a simple, everyday food, placed on the table as soon as you sit down. Yet in Piemonte, where they are always made with a little *strutto* (lard) to give them flavor, often still warm from the oven, they are a flavorful and delicious food in their own right — enjoy them fresh from bakeries for picnics or snacks.

Pesce d'Acqua Dolce

FRESHWATER FISH FROM LOMBARDIA'S LAKES

ITALY'S NORTHERN LAKES, carved by glaciers that scoured their way down from the Alps and Dolomites hundreds of thousands of years ago, are today among the most beautiful and popular places in the country. Many come here to enjoy their beauty and tranquillity at stylish resorts such as Bellágio on Lake Como, Stresa on Lake Maggiore, and Riva del Garda and Lugana on Lake Garda.

Lake Como is our favorite, its three narrow legs remote in their grandeur, with mountains rising almost sheer from its shores. It's the deepest lake in Italy, plunging to a depth of more than 450 m. (1,475 ft.) and its cold, clean waters yield some of the finest freshwater fish that we have eaten anywhere.

Today, only a handful of professional fishermen continue to go out night and day laying an intricate system of nets of varying length, depth, and size in order to catch the prized fish of the lake. Silvio and Cristian Ponzini, father and son, take their small boats out daily, throughout even the bitterest cold months of winter, laying nets by day in search of *pesce persico* (royal perch), *agoni* (a type of lake fish related to shad), *lavarello* (the largest fish regularly caught in the lake), and *alborelle* (a small, silvery fish usually caught and eaten when still the size of whitebait).

Each fish inhabits a different area or depth of the lake and must be caught using different methods and nets. Then, in the early hours of the morning, Silvio and Cristian return in the dark to gather in their catch. The fish they have netted is served that day at their restaurant, Albergo-Ristorante Silvio, in Bellágio — in summer, on a terrace

Fishing nets hung out to dry on the terrace of Albergo-Ristorante Silvio at Bellágio, Lake Como

overlooking the lake. When eaten this fresh, lake fish is exquisitely sweet.

In June and October, Silvio and Cristian lay their nets to catch young *agoni,* no larger than small sardines. The *agoni* are salted for 48 hours, then strung up to dry on the restaurant terrace before being conserved and pressed with laurel leaves. This is *missoltini,* one of the great specialties of the Lakes. The air-dried fish are heated up in a pan and seasoned with oil and vinegar. The meat is hard, dry, and very chewy but not at all strong in flavor; served with a winter's portion of *toc,* and a glass or two of Valtellina red wine, it is a simple repast, the taste of Lake Como.

Other lake specialties not to be missed include *riso al pesce persico* (rice with fried fillets of royal perch), *alborelle fritte* (deep-fried *alborelle*), and *lavarello alla griglia* (grilled) or *in carpione* (fried then marinated in vinegar and spices).

Albergo-Ristorante Silvio
Via Carcano, 12
22021 Bellágio CO
tel: 031/950322
fax: 031/950912
$$

Cristian Ponzini on his daily round to lay nets on Lake Como

Salumi

CURED PORK AND OTHER MEAT PRODUCTS

Northwest Italy is one of the nation's richest agricultural areas, but it is not one of the foremost for regional and local artisan *salumi*.

Only in outlying country areas, or on upland farms in the mountains, is there an artisan range of locally cured pork, beef, and game products. Elsewhere, around Milan and other major urban centers, good cured pork products are produced on an industrial scale for distribution regionally and nationally.

Try to sample

Bresaola (Valtellina) Salted and air-cured boneless cut of beef tenderloin. This extremely lean cured meat is eaten raw in thin slices, often garnished with shavings of *grana padano* or *parmigiano reggiano* cheeses, and dressed with lemon juice and olive oil.

Coppa (Lombardia) Meaty *salume* produced from a cut from the upper neck of the pig, salted and left to age for four to six months or longer.

Cotechino (Lombardia) Boiling *salame* made with lean and fat pork and pork rind. Needs to be cooked slowly to remove the fat, and is usually served with *verze* (winter greens) and *lenticchie* (lentils); a real winter warmer.

Luganega (Lombardia) Local version of the spicy, coiled sausage of Basilicata, usually available either *dolce* (mild) or *piccante* (hot and spicy); to be broiled or used to make *risotto*.

Sausages, salami, *and* porchetta — *roast suckling pig — for sale*

Salame mantovane, *a delicious rustic* salame *flavored with garlic*

Mortadella di fegato di maiale (Piemonte and Lombardia) Soft, moist *salame* made with pork liver, spices, and red wine; needs to be boiled, though sometimes available ready cooked.

Prosciutto di capriolo (Piemonte and Valle d'Aosta) *Prosciutto* made from the hind leg of roebuck.

Salame al Barolo (Langhe) Long, rather soft pork *salame* moistened and flavored with Barolo wine.

Salame d'oca (Lombardia and Piemonte) Fresh *salame* made from goose, to be eaten within about ten days of its production.

Salamelle (Mantova) Softly textured *salame* that is either broiled or removed from its skin and used to make *risotto*.

Salame mantovane (Mantova) Large, fairly coarsely ground pork *salame* flavored strongly with garlic.

Salame milanese (Lombardia) Not really a regional *salame,* this has come to be a recognized type produced through-out the country; it describes a *salame* made from a finely ground mixture of pork (sometimes with the addition of a little beef) and has a firm, grainy texture and a mild, not too fatty taste.

Salamin d'la duja (Piemonte) Pure pork *salame* aged in terracotta pots or glass jars under a layer of rendered pork fat, a traditional way of conserving meats.

Violino (Val Chiavenna and all Lombardia) Hind leg of goat (or sometimes sheep), salted and air-cured like *prosciutto crudo;* to be eaten raw and thinly sliced.

Mantova

HISTORIC FOODS AND TRADITIONS

LOCATED IN THE FAR EAST of Lombardia, almost on the borders with both Veneto and Emilia-Romagna, Mantova (Mantua) was for centuries one of Italy's greatest centers of art, culture, and learning. Settled by the Etruscans, birthplace of the poet Virgil, Mantova flourished as an independent dukedom under the patronage of the Gonzagas from the 14th to 16th centuries.

Today, Mantova is an atmospheric and historic town well worth visiting, especially for its Palazzo Ducale which still dominates the town and surrounding country. The Gonzagas brought the painter Mantegna to Mantova, when he was at the peak of his powers, to decorate the ducal palace and famously, the *Camera degli Sposi*, and the Mannerist Giulio Romano to decorate the Palazzo Te with his frenzied, vivid frescoes. Tintoretto, Rubens, and Raphael were also commissioned by the Gonzagas.

Easily reached from Verona, Padua, or Parma, Mantova is also worth coming to for its food, for this small, self-enclosed town has managed to keep intact genuine local gastronomic traditions that reflect not only its splendid period during the Renaissance but also the later influence of the Austro-Hungarians.

Renaissance tastes are evident in the penchant for sweet and savory combinations, as in *tortelli di zucca*, the famous pumpkin-filled *pasta* made with sweet and piquant *mostarda di mela* (see p.70). Boiled capon is served in *salsa di ribes* (blackcurrant sauce), while pigeon is cooked with grapes.

Austro-Hungarian traditions, on the other hand, are evident in a range of whimsical and delicious traditional pastries, cakes, and sweets, including *torta di tagliatelle* (shortcrust pie topped with fine *tagliatelle* noodles), *torta sbrisolona* (a crumbly, very rich and delicious almond and butter cake), or the *anello di Monaco* (a ring-shaped yeast cake made with toasted hazelnuts).

Zucca *(pumpkin)*,
for Mantova's
tortelli di zucca

Mantova is also the source of good local *salumi*, and a dry Lambrusco from surrounding vineyards.

The town sits amid lakes formed by the Mincio River. After sightseeing, walk through the old town and around the lakes, pick up provisions for a picnic if the weather is fine, or dine in typical *trattorie* or restaurants. But whatever you do, it is almost obligatory to stop at the Bar Caravatti in the Piazza delle Erbe and sample the house *aperitivo* under the arched porticoes of the bar.

RECOMMENDED RESTAURANTS, BARS, AND FOOD SHOPS

Gastronomia Zapparoli
Via Cavour, 49
46100 Mantova
tel: 0376/323345
All the gastronomic specialties of Mantova.

Bar Caravatti
Portici Broletto, 16
46100 Mantova
tel: 0376/321653
Historic drinking house.

Panificio Freddi
Piazza Cavallotti, 7
46100 Mantova
tel: 0376/321418;321410
Outstanding tortelli di zucca, cakes, and pastries.

**Ristorante Aquila Nigra
La Ducale**
Vicolo Bonacolsi, 4
46100 Mantova
tel: 0376/327180

Elegant dining in an atmospheric setting in Mantova's historic center.
$$–$$$

Trattoria Due Cavallini
Via Salnitro, 5
46100 Mantova
tel: 0376/322084
Genuine local foods in this friendly family trattoria.
$

Formaggi

THE GREAT CHEESES OF NORTHWEST ITALY

NORTHWEST ITALY is one of the nation's greatest sources of cheeses, produced on an industrial scale for distribution nationally as well as hand-made on a small scale for local consumption.

Lombardia's verdant lower plains are particularly fine dairy country, its herds producing in quantity a superb supply of high-quality milk, rich in flavor and butterfat. This milk is transformed into some of Italy's finest and best-known cheeses, including *gorgonzola, mascarpone, taleggio,* and *stracchino.*

Cheesemaking, of course, is tied to alpine traditions. The great cheese of the Valle d'Aosta is the delectable and creamy *fontina.* The tasty but little-known *scimudin* and the flavorful *magnuc* come from the high alpine hills of the Alta Valtellina in Lombardia.

Piemonte's province of Cuneo is a particularly rich source of fine, distinctive, hand-made cheeses including *castelmagno, bra, raschera,* and *murazzano,* all of which have their own consortiums and are protected by *denominazioni di origine* for authenticity and quality.

Though Liguria's rugged, terraced terrain does not lend itself to raising livestock on a large scale, you can still find some good local cheeses.

Piemonte, this semi-fat cow's milk cheese is made in large rounds and has a hard rind and an elastic texture with small, regular holes. It may be sold either *tenero* (fresh, mild), *mezzano* (medium-aged and more tasty), or *duro* (hard, to be used mainly for grating).

Bruz, brüs, or **brussu** (Piemonte) Ewe's milk cheese, packed in jars with *grappa,* sometimes with oil, vinegar, herbs, and seasonings, then left to re-ferment until super-strong; eaten spread on bread.

Caprino d'alpeggio (Liguria) Liguria's Valle Argentina is the source of tasty goat's milk cheeses aged in natural caves until hard and flavorful.

A selection of cheeses from Piemonte in the market in Alba

TRY TO SAMPLE

Bel Paese (Lombardia) This widely available and popular cheese is industrially produced from cow's milk and has a rich, creamy texture and a mild flavor. *Bel Paese* or "The Beautiful Country," the nickname for Italy, is derived from the best-seller by Antonio Stoppani whose portrait is used as a trade mark for the cheese.

Bra (Piemonte) One of the great cheeses of

Castelmagno, *one of the great cheeses of Piemonte*

Castelmagno (Piemonte) Cylindrical cow's milk cheese with a roughly textured rind that gets darker with age. The cheese, delicate and perfumed when young, gains in flavor and piquancy as it ages.

Fontina (Valle d'Aosta) Large, round, and extremely creamy cheese, made with full-fat cow's milk with the perfume and flavor of alpine meadows. *Fontina* is the classic cheese for melting, especially to make *fonduta.*

Gorgonzola (Lombardia) Italy's outstanding blue-veined cheese is a full-fat, whole-milk cheese made from creamy *stracchino* lightly layered to encourage the formation and growth of the tasty blue mold. *Gorgonzola* when young is defined as *dolce,* for it is indeed sweet, creamy, and mild; older cheese is deemed *piccante,* much fuller and sharper in flavor. *Gorgonzola* is a beautiful eating cheese, and is also widely used in the kitchen — delicious when made into a sauce for *gnocchi* or fresh *pasta.*

Grana padano (Lombardia) The only serious alternative to *parmigiano reggiano* comes from Lombardia (as well as parts of Veneto and Emilia-Romagna). *Grana padano,* like its great rival (see pp.144–145), is a semi-fat cooked cheese made from partially skimmed milk. It has a grainy texture that makes it both ideal for eating when young, and for grating when aged for a year or longer. Generally speaking, *grana padano* does not have the concentration or intensity of flavor of *parmigiano reggiano,* but it is still a very fine, high-quality cheese.

Magnuc or **mastusc** (Valtellina) Flavorful, softly textured cow's milk cheese from the province of Sondrio, widely used in cooking, especially to make *polenta taragna.*

Mascarpone (Lombardia) Incredibly rich, triple cream cheese with a texture like extremely heavy, almost whipped cream; widely used in making desserts, and delicious with a ripe, juicy pear.

Murazzano (Piemonte) Outstanding and flavorful sheep's milk cheese from the province of Cuneo.

Raschera (Piemonte) Sweet, mild, semi-fat, pressed cheese from cow's milk from the province of Cuneo. The best cheeses come from the higher sub-zone of Alpeggio and have a more intense flavor of the herbs and grasses of the high meadows.

Robiola di Rocca-verano (Piemonte) Small, cylindrical, fresh cheese, made from ewe's or goat's milk, with a soft texture and lightly acidic, full flavor; either eaten fresh or con-served in jars *sott'olio* (in olive oil).

Scimudin (Valtellina) Mountain cheese from the Alta Valtellina, made with partially skimmed cow's milk, sometimes with added goat's milk; used in cooking, and known locally as *casero.*

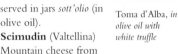

Toma d'Alba, *in olive oil with white truffle*

Stracchino Strictly speaking, *stracchino* indicates a family of slightly sharp cheeses made from two separate milkings. Tradi-tionally, the milk was from cows that had just returned at the end of summer from the high pastures to the valleys for winter. After the journey, their "tired" milk (*"stracco"* means "tired" in local dialect) was deemed to make particularly tasty cheeses, such as fresh *stracchino* itself, *gorgonzola,* and *taleggio. Stracchino* is the freshest version, extremely soft and runny, slightly sour yet beautifully creamy.

Taleggio Full-fat cow's milk cheese originally from Val Taleggio in Bergamo province but now produced throughout Lombardia. *Taleggio* has a soft, orange rind, and a creamy texture that gets more runny as it ripens. Assertive and full of flavor and aroma, this is one of the great cheeses of Lombardia.

Toma d'Alba (the Langhe) Small, fresh or aged round of sheep's milk cheese, often conserved in oil together with other flavorings, such as herbs, white truffles, black peppercorns, or *porcini* (cepe) mushrooms.

Grana padano, *a delicious cheese for both eating whole and grated*

I Dolci

CAKES, PASTRIES, AND DESSERTS

THE CONTRAST between the elegant chic of the great cities of the Northwest and the simpler, rustic traditions of the country is reflected in the range of sweets, pastries, and desserts of this vast region.

Amaretti di Saronno

TRY TO SAMPLE

Amaretti di Saronno (Lombardia) Well known, paper-wrapped almond macaroons. An almond flavored liqueur of the same name is also made.

Anello di Monaco (Mantova) Austrian-inspired, rich, ring-shaped yeast cake filled with a cream of toasted hazelnuts; generally made only in winter months.

Baci di dama (Piemonte) Two almond cookies joined together with apricot jam, and covered in chocolate.

Baxin (Liguria) Dense, fat cookies made with ground almonds and anise.

Bonet (Piemonte) The most frequently encountered dessert in Piemonte, a type of super-rich *crème caramel* made with coffee and Marsala.

Gianduiotti or **giandujotti** (Piemonte) Rich chocolates filled with *gianduia,* the hazelnut puree.

Marrons glacés (Piemonte and Lombardia) Chestnuts candied in sugar syrup.

Mataloc (Lake Como) Substantial, *brioche*-like cake filled with walnuts, hazelnuts, raisins, figs, and candied fruit.

Monte Bianco (Piemonte) Mound of sweetened chestnut puree covered with whipped cream "snow."

Pane di pescatore (Liguria) Rich, sweet bread studded with pieces of candied fruits and raisins.

Panettone (Milan and all Lombardia) Famous tall, feather-light cake filled with candied fruit; the traditional Christmas favorite throughout Italy.

Savoiardi (Piemonte) Light, sweet finger cookies; often used for making desserts (though our children love them as they are).

Torrone d'Alba (Alba and the Langhe) Nougat made from honey, toasted hazelnuts, and egg white, popularized by Giuseppe Sebaste earlier this century. Giuseppe's marketing coup was to sell *torrone* at local festivals from brightly colored horse drawn wagons: the modern motorized versions are still a familiar sight at local fairs in North Italy. Giuseppe's granddaughter and her husband continue to make traditional hand-made nougat at the Antica Torroneria Piemontese outside Gallo.

Torta elevezia (Mantova and all Lombardia) Layers of almond biscuits spread with *zabaione* and butter cream.

Torta alle nocciole (the Langhe and all Piemonte) Classic hazelnut cake, a delicious finish to meals in the Langhe wine country.

Torta sbrisolona (Mantova and all Lombardia) Very crumbly, rich, buttery almond cake.

Torta di tagliatelle (Mantova and all Lombardia) Shortcrust pastry filled with toasted almonds and butter, topped with very fine *tagliatelle* noodles, then doused with rum and icing sugar.

Zabaione or **zabaglione** (Piemonte) Favorite party piece of Italian restaurants: hot, foamy egg-yolk custard with sugar and Marsala wine (in the Langhe, Barolo is sometimes used).

An itinerant stand selling Sebaste torrone in Alba, a familiar sight at local fairs

Alba

PIEMONTE'S WINE AND TRUFFLE CAPITAL

ALBA IS TO THE LANGHE what St.-Emilion is to Bordeaux, Beaune is to Burgundy's Côte d'Or, and Haro is to Spain's Rioja: at once the central focus of a most prestigious wine zone, and a great and welcoming town for the visitor and wine lover. Rich in history, atmosphere, and warm *civiltà,* Alba is furthermore a gastronomic repository for the incredible wealth of fine things to eat as well as drink from the Langhe — truffles and truffle derivatives, *porcini* mushrooms, *salame* made with Barolo, *torrone d'Alba,* hand-pulled *grissini stirati a mano* still warm from the oven, local cheeses such as *bruz* and *toma d'Alba,* packed in jars, and, of course, wine.

The best time to come to Alba is during the fall, especially in October for the *Fiera del tartufo.* But Alba is worth visiting at any time of the year (an excellent market takes place on Saturdays). This former Roman town today is wholly medieval in feel, small, compact, consisting of two main avenues, the Viale Torino that leads from the fairground to the Piazza Risorgimento, and the main shopping street, the Via Vittorio Emanuele (known to locals as Via

Maestra) that leads from the Duomo to the Piazza Savona. In the truffle season, as you stroll down this pleasant, always crowded road, you can tell when you are near a shop selling that magical delicacy — several do — simply from the irresistible and overpowering aroma that emanates even through the walls and windows.

Alba street scene

Alba's Cattedrale di San Lorenzo is a rather austere building. It's worth popping inside all the same to view its frescoes from the 14th and 15th centuries. But Alba is not a city for art lovers or those who prefer to spend their time touring monuments. Its pleasures are wholly for the present moment. Enjoy, then, a house *aperitivo* or a goblet of wine sitting under the arches of the Caffè Calissano opposite the cathedral, before, literally, following your nose down the Via Maestra sniffing out a wealth of good things to eat and drink.

RECOMMENDED RESTAURANTS, BARS, AND FOOD SHOPS

Aldo Martino
Via V. Emanuele, 27
12051 Alba CN
tel: 0173/440614
Seasonal vegetables, white truffles, and out-standing cheeses.

Antico Caffè Calissano
Piazza Risorgimento, 3
12051 Alba CN
tel: 0173/442101
Good wines.

Bar Umberto
Piazza Savona, 4
12051 Alba CN
Local drinking hole for wine producers.

Cignetti
Via V. Emanuele, 3
12051 Alba CN
Hand-made regional sweets and pastries.

Osteria dell'Arco
Piazza Savona, 5
12051 Alba CN
tel: 0173/363974
Old favorite in new premises, with same genuine food.
$

Panetteria Tarable
Via V. Emanuele, 6
12051 Alba CN
Hand-made grissini.

Ristorante La Capannina
Strada Profonda, 21
12051 Alba CN
tel: 0173/442097
Located just outside Alba; outstanding regional foods and a warm welcome from Piergiorgio Gallina.
$$

Tartufi Morra
Piazza Pertinace, 3
12051 Alba CN
tel: 0173/290072
Fresh white truffles in season plus a range of good conserved truffle products.

I Vini
THE WINES OF NORTHWEST ITALY

Northwest Italy is an excellent part of the nation for wines: it can satisfy the discerning wine lover at every level with its wide range of styles and types of wines.

Piemonte and Valle d'Aosta

Arneis or **Roero Arneis DOC**
Excellent, perfumed, and sometimes rich and compact white wines of real class come from the Arneis grape grown in the Roero hills north of Alba.
Recommended producers: Ceretto, Deltetto.

Asti DOCG Popularly known as Asti Spumante, its pre-DOCG name, Asti is one of the world's favorite sparkling wines — light, usually fairly sweet, with the intense scent of the Moscato grape, and relatively low in alcohol. (See also Moscato d'Asti.)
Recommended producers: Martini, Fontana-fredda, Vignaioli di Santo Stefano.

Barbaresco DOCG One of Piemonte's (and Italy's) greatest red wines, from Nebbiolo grapes grown around Barbaresco. Complex, finely scented, and elegant, with body and tannin to age well.
Recommended producers: Gaja, Ceretto, Giacosa, Cigliuti, Castello di Neive, Marchesi di Gresy, Produttori del Barbaresco.

Barbera The great workhorse grape of Piemonte is capable of producing a range of different types and styles of wine, from fairly acid, slightly sparkling young wines that ably partner the rich foods (good examples come from Asti and Monferrato), to deep, serious, concentrated reds, as well as Barberas aged in new French *barriques*. Barbera is grown throughout the region and not all wines qualify for DOC status. The best DOC Barberas come from Asti, Alba, or Monferrato.
Recommended producers: Braida, Giacomo Conterno, Duca d'Asti, Guasti Clemente, Altare, Mascarello, Prunotto, Scarpa.

Barolo DOCG This legendary red wine, produced from Nebbiolo grapes grown in the Langhe can be immensely full bodied, even tough, tannic, and austere, though modern vinification and changing attitudes are resulting in lighter, more elegant wines with the fine, delicate perfume of the Nebbiolo. *Cru* wines from superior single vineyards can be outstanding.
Recommended producers: Ceretto, Altare, Giacomo Conterno, Aldo Conterno, Ratti, Cordero di Montezemolo, Giacosa, Voerzio, Gaja, Sandrone, Scavino, Prunotto, Mascarello, Cascina Fontana.

Castiglione Falletto

Brachetto d'Acqui DOC
Unusual, strawberry-scented, *frizzante* (slightly sparkling) or fully sparkling red wine from vineyards around the spa town of Acqui Terme.
Recommended producers: Braida, Correggia.

Carema DOC Northern Piemonte's best red wine, produced from Nebbiolo grapes: can be finely scented, elegant.

Roadside sign in a Barolo vineyard

Recommended producers: Ferrando, Cantina Sociale di Carema.

Cortese The workhorse white grape of Piemonte, producing pleasant, everyday white wines as well as exceptional white wines in the hills of Gavi (see below).

Dolcetto Another important and characteristic black grape of Piemonte, producing some outstanding red wines, especially in the wine hills of Alba (there are actually seven Dolcetto DOC zones). Wines produced from this ripe, juicy grape can range from the light, *frizzante*, soft and easy to drink to the deeply colored, intensely fruity wines of great, vivid concentration.
Recommended producers: Aldo Conterno, Fontanafredda, Moscarello, Cavallotto, Ratti, Vajra, Voerzio.

Donnaz Light, raspberry-scented red wine from Nebbiolo grapes grown in Alpine vineyards of Valle d'Aosta.

Erbaluce di Caluso DOC Dry white, sweet, and fortified wines are all made from the Erbaluce grapes grown on vineyards south of Ivrea. If you can find it, try Caluso *passito,* a delicious sweet wine made from semi-dried grapes.
Recommended producers: Ferrando, Boratto.

Favorita Light, fashionable white wine from vineyards of the Roero hills, north of Alba.

Freisa Light, usually *frizzante*, raspberry-scented red from the local Freisa grape. DOC in Asti and Chieri.

Gattinara DOCG
Characterful, sometimes elegant, red wines from Nebbiolo grapes grown in northern vineyards of Novara and Vercelli.
Recommended producers: Atoniolo, Travaglini.

Gavi DOC or **Cortese di Gavi DOC** At best, Gavi is probably Piemonte's finest white wine, for the rather mundane Cortese grape gains great character on the lime-rich foothills around Gavi and can result in modern, clean, bone-dry wines with structure, scent, and delicacy. Top wines from the classic heart of the zone may be labeled Gavi di Gavi. Many are overpriced.
Recommended producers: La Scolca, Bergaglio, San Pietro, La Chiara, La Giustiniana.

Grignolino One of my favorite red wines, rarely encountered outside the region, Grignolino should be sampled if you get a chance. Light in color, high in acidity, sometimes *frizzante*, it is excellent with rich local food. Best wines come from Vignale Monferrato and Asti.
Recommended producers: Cascina Alberta, Scarpa, Vietti, Il Mongetto.

Malvasia Interesting sweet, *frizzante* red wine from the Malvasia Nera grape which is good with local pastries and desserts. The best examples come from the DOC zones of Casorzo and Castelnuovo Don Bosco.

Moscato d'Asti DOCG Either *frizzante* or fully sparkling wines made from fragrant Moscato grapes. Light in alcohol, intensely grapy and sweet, and easy and pleasant to drink.
Recommended producers: Vignaioli di Santo Stefano, Ascheri, Fontanafredda, Arione, Braida, Vietti, La Spinetta-Rivetti.

Muscat *passito* di Chambave One of Valle d'Aosta's great wines, a dessert Muscat made from semi-dried grapes.
Recommended producer: E. Voyat.

Valle d'Aosta wine hamlet

Nebbiolo Good, everyday red table wines made from the Nebbiolo are produced and sold simply by the grape name (called Spanna in Northern Piemonte). Nebbiolo d'Alba DOC wines can be outstanding, something like lighter Barolo or Barbaresco, and also at a lighter price.

LOMBARDIA

Bonarda This unusual, juicy black grape thrives in the wine hills of the Oltrepò Pavese producing a rustic, country wine with a deep color and rasping finish.
Recommended producer: Castello di Luzzano.

Franciacorta DOC This small but important wine zone is located at the southern tip of Lake Iseo, west of Brescia, and is the source of both good white and prestigious sparkling wines from Pinot Bianco and Chardonnay, and outstanding full-flavored reds from an unusual mixture of Cabernet Franc, Merlot, and Barbera.
Recommended producers: Ca' del Bosco, Bellavista, Berlucchi.

Lambrusco Mantovano DOC Dry, foaming Lambrusco; goes well with the distinctive and delicious food of Mantova.

Lugana DOC Characterful, nutty white wines from Lake Garda vineyards; superb with fish.

Recommended producers: Ca' dei Frati, Zenato.

Oltrepò Pavese DOC This vast, still little-known wine zone south of Milan produces an astonishing range of wines — whites, sparkling, *rosato,* and reds — from a wide variety of grapes.

Basic Oltrepò red is made from a blend of grapes, but good varietals — almost always slightly *frizzante,* to drink while young and vivid — are made from Bonarda and Barbera. Buttafuoco is a deeply flavored, intense red wine. Sangue di Giuda is a *frizzante* red with a touch of residual sweetness. The fully sparkling wines of the Oltrepò Pavese are excellent and should be tried.
Recommended producers: Castello di Luzzano, L. Maga, Boatti, Valenti, Cantina Sociale di Santa Maria della Versa.

Valcalepio DOC Interesting and noteworthy red and white wines from hill vineyards west of Bergamo. Red Valcalepio is best, made from a classic Cabernet Franc-Merlot blend.
Recommended producer: Castello di Grumello.

Valtellina DOC Delicately perfumed, serious wines of character are produced from Nebbiolo grapes grown in the high alpine vineyards of the Valtellina just south of the Swiss border. Best wines come from four superior sub-zones: Grumello, Inferno, Sassella, and Valgella. Sfursat or Sforzato is made from semi-dried grapes, in character something like a local, rustic Amarone.
Recommended producers: Negri, Enologica Valtellinese.

LIGURIA

Cinqueterre DOC Light, dry white wine made from grapes grown on terraced vineyards of the southern Ligurian seaboard. Sciacchetrà is a rare *passito* version made from semi-dried grapes.
Recommended producers: Cantina Sociale di Riomaggiore, Cappellini.

Riviera Ligure di Ponente DOC
This *denominazione* covers vineyards running from west of Genoa to the French border. Try Pigato, a full, characterful white, Ormeasco, a fruity red, and Rossese, a perfumed, elegant red that has its own DOC around Dolceacqua.

PICK OF THE "SUPER" WINES
Chardonnay Gaja & Rey Angelo Gaja is a great winemaker and a great marketeer: all his wines, especially his single-vineyard *cru* Barbarescos, are in

The Castello di Luzzano, one of the most important estates in Oltrepò Pavese in Lombardia

great demand — and extremely expensive. Angelo's *barrique*-fermented Chardonnay is also an excellent example of his skills.
Bricco dell' Uccellone The late Giacomo Bologna demonstrated beyond doubt with this now-classic wine that Barbera when vinified properly and aged in French *barriques* is capable of greatness.

Cabernet Sauvignon La Bernardina
Bruno Ceretto demonstrates that anything the French (or Californians) can do, so can he. This wine is worth trying, though we personally prefer Bruno's elegant Barolos.
Maurizio Zanella Zanella's Ca' del Bosco sparkling wines are among Italy's finest. The red wine that bears the proprietor's name is produced from the classic blend of Bordeaux grapes; a well-structured wine of considerable class.

OTHER DRINKS
Amaro Though available nationwide, this bitter, almost black *digestivo,* flavored with herbs, spices, and peel is a favorite drink of the Northwest.
Barolo Chinato This is a fascinating drink, made from Barolo wine fortified with alcohol and flavored with herbs, spices, and sugar.
Grappa Some of the best *grappe* in Italy are distilled in Piemonte, in some cases using the wine-drenched *vinacce* (grape residue) from prestigious local wines such as Barolo, Barbaresco, Moscato, Arneis, or Gavi di Gavi.
Vermouth Though the vast quantities of aromatic herbs and spices needed can no longer be supplied locally, the best Italian Vermouths, both dry and sweet red versions, still come from Piemonte.

FOOD AND WINE COMBINATIONS
Affettati misti A platter of mixed sliced meats, including *salumi* from Lombardia and Piemonte, is best accompanied by a dry, young, slightly *frizzante* Barbera from Asti or Alba, or by a deeper, plummy Bonarda from the Oltrepò Pavese.
Grana padano A nugget makes a delicious finish to a meal. Try it with a glass of Erbaluce di Caluso *passito,* the dessert wine bringing out the sweet and nutty character of the cheese.

Pizzoccheri The classic buckwheat *pasta* from the Valtellina is a fine partner to the surprisingly deeply flavored local reds such as Grumello and Inferno.
Brasato al Barolo Braised in Barolo wine, this classic beef dish demands a mature Barolo from a top quality estate.
Tartufi bianchi The rather haunting, delicate after-flavor of white truffles can be brought out best by an equally delicate yet well-structured white such as Gavi di Gavi.

Castles, Vineyards, and Great Wines

THE WINE ROADS OF ALBA AND ASTI

As ITALY'S PREEMINENT wine region, Piemonte is well geared to welcoming visitors in search of wines and regional foods. *Strade dei vini* (wine roads) run throughout the region's extensive wine country. They are marked by signs illustrated with crenellations representing Piemonte's many castles, together with a bunch of grapes and a stylized winding road.

These wine roads, however, often overlap one another, and, in truth, they are not all that easy or necessary to follow in their entirety. A better bet is to concentrate on the region's principal wine zones and visit the outstanding *enoteche regionali,* official "wine libraries," often located in historic buildings, where wines can be tasted and bought, and which sometimes have good restaurants attached to them as well.

For touring the Langhe as well as the vineyards of Asti, either Alba or Asti make good bases.

Serralunga d'Alba

LA TERRA DI BAROLO

The Barolo wine zone, probably the most prestigious — and most beautiful — zone (see map) lies to the southwest of Alba, a relatively compact area extending across steep hills with hamlets ringed by concentric patterns of vines. This prestigious wine country can be toured most easily and enjoyably from Alba in a day (though wine lovers will wish to stay longer).

Leave Alba on the road to Gallo-Grinzane. Grinzane Cavour, located above Gallo, is the home of Piemonte's first *enoteca regionale,* and it is well worth visiting the castle for the wine and folk history displays and for its excellent restaurant. To continue the wine tour, return to Gallo, continue in the direction of Barolo and look for the turning to La Morra which leads immediately into the vine-covered hills. On the way, visit the wine museum and the modern *cantina,* Antiche Cantine dell' Abbazia dell'Annuziata, at L'Annunziata.

Dominating the town of Barolo, the 13th-century castle housing the enoteca regionale

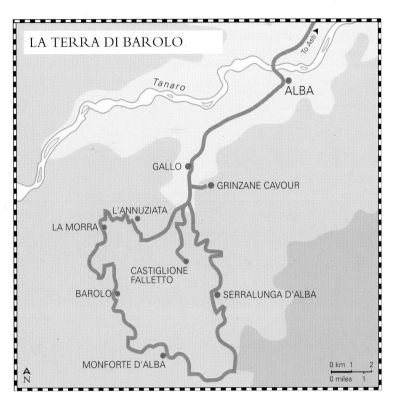

La Morra is the single most important wine commune in the Barolo zone. Enjoy spectacular views of the wine country, as well as regional foods and great wines at the Ristorante Belvedere before continuing on to Barolo itself, a modest and small wine hamlet with its own *enoteca regionale*.

From Barolo, find next Monforte d'Alba, another notable wine commune, whose wines are known above all for their great structure and body. No one makes more traditional, full bodied wines than Giovanni Conterno. Visit his *cantina* to taste and buy and, afterward, enjoy lunch or dinner at the Giardino da Felicin, one of the great restaurants of the Langhe.

Serralunga d'Alba is another particularly lovely wine hamlet to stroll around. From the top of the village, there are good views across to Castiglione Falletto, which should also be visited before returning to Alba.

Other wine tours from Alba strike into the Barbaresco wine hills to the northeast, and into the lesser-known wine country of the Roero to the north, source of both good, inexpensive red wines and the fashionable Arneis white.

ASTI AND THE MONFERRATO HILLS

If the vineyards of Alba's Langhe produce Italy's most prestigious wines, those of Asti and the Monferrato hills are an abundant source of pleasurable and easy-to-drink everyday wines, such as good Barbera and that ever popular vivacious sparkler, Asti Spumante. From Asti, itself a fine historic town, tour the wine hills south, by way of Costigliole d'Asti (home of an important *enoteca regionale*) through Nizza Monferrato, a quiet market town, and source of excellent Barbera wines, to Canelli. Canelli is the capital of Asti Spumante, its surrounding vineyards almost entirely given over to fragrant Moscato grapes. Though Asti may be scorned by would-be connoisseurs, this delightful sparkler is at its freshest and best when sampled on its home territory.

Another pleasant wine tour from Asti strikes north into the Monferrato hills. Find the main road to Casale Monferrato, then at Moncalvo, find the road to Grazzano Badoglio and Casorzo. Casorzo is the source of Malvasia di Casorzo, an unusual pale, lightly sweet, *frizzante* red wine.

Vignale Monferrato is the highlight of the tour — a stylish small wine town with an important *enoteca regionale* in the austere Palazzo Callori. Vignale is the center for Grignolino wine, one of our favorite Piemonte reds. Try it with local food in the farmhouse restaurant of Cascina Alberta.

ANDAR' PER LE VIGNE — INTO WINE COUNTRY

LA TERRA DEL BAROLO
Albergo Ristorante Italia
Piazza Cappellano, 3/A
12050 Serralunga d'Alba CN
tel: 0173/613124
Simple, inexpensive, authentic local foods.
$

Antiche Cantine dell'
Abbazia dell'Annunziata
Frazione Annunziata, 7
12064 La Morra CN
tel: 0173/50185
fax: 0173/509373
Wine museum and modern, stylish wines.

Bar La Terrazza
Via V. Emanuele, 6
12060 Castiglione Falletto CN
tel: 0173/62909
Enjoy simple home-cooked food on the terrace, with wines from this out-standing wine commune.
$

Cascina Fontana
Via Alfieri, 37
12060 Castiglione Falletto CN
tel: 0173/62963
Talented young winemaker Mario Fontana is a knowledgable and welcoming host.

Enoteca Regionale di
Barolo
Castello Comunale
Piazza Falletti
12060 Barolo CN
tel: 0173/56277
Barolo to taste and buy.

Enoteca Regionale
Piemontese Cavour
Castello di Grinzane
12060 Grinzane Cavour CN
tel: 0173/262159
Good display of wines, a museum, and restaurant.
$$

Giardino da Felicin
Via Vallada, 18
12065 Monforte d'Alba CN
tel/fax: 0173/78225
One of the finest country restaurants in the region.
$$–$$$

Giovanni Conterno
Località Ornati, 2
12064 Monforte d'Alba CN
tel: 0173/78221
Traditional Barolo of the highest quality.

Ristorante Belvedere
Piazza Castello, 5
12064 La Morra CN
tel/fax: 0173/50190
Classic foods as fine as the views of the wine country.
$$

ASTI AND THE
MONFERRATO HILLS
Antico Podere Conti della
Cremosina
Piazza Dante, 21
14049 Nizza Monferrato AT
tel: 0141/721273
fax: 0141/701706
Interesting wine museum.

Cascina Alberta
Ca' Prano, 14
15049 Vignale Monferrato AL
Farmhouse restaurant (evenings only, by reser-vation) serving good local foods and own wines.
$–$$

Enoteca Regionale del
Monferrato
Palazzo Callori
15049 Vignale Monferrato AL
tel: 0142/933243
Historic enoteca with restaurant.
$$

Enoteca Regionale di
Costigliole d'Asti
Castello di Costigliole
14055 Costigliole d'Asti AT
tel: 0141/966015
It's worth coming here not just to taste and buy wines but to eat at the restaurant in the historic castle.
$$

The Cinque Terre
VINEYARDS AND FISHING VILLAGES

FIVE TINY FISHING HAMLETS — Riomaggiore, Manarola, Corniglia, Vernazza, and Monterosso al Mare — make up the Cinque Terre, located on a stretch of rocky coastline in Liguria, between La Spezia and Levanto.

Their very inaccessibility and the fact that they cannot be further developed due to the harshness of the terrain means that the Cinque Terre have remained largely unspoiled, in spite of the hordes of tourists who make their way here during the summer season.

The tortuously steep terraced slopes that rise almost sheer from the water's edge are planted extensively with vines for the production of Cinqueterre DOC, a distinctive white wine that is consumed almost entirely in the popular bars and fish restaurants of this beautiful area. This is, without doubt, one of Italy's most beautiful and dramatic wine regions.

To reach the Cinque Terre, abandon your car and take the train from La Spezia or Levanto to any of the five fishing hamlets, then walk between them along the coastal footpath.

We suggest that you come first to Riomaggiore. Rising sharply from the waterfront, it looks both down to the sea as well as inland, with colorful houses climbing steeply toward the terraced vineyards above. The coastal footpath here, known as the *Via dell'Amore,* leads to Manarola, whose tiny harbor is so minuscule that the fishing boats have to be winched to shore each night.

Vernazza, one of the most beautiful of the Cinque Terre villages

To gain a perspective on the demands of viticulture on this harsh land, climb up from Manarola (follow signposted footpath No. 6) through the terraced vineyards to the wine cooperative at Groppo which has done much to preserve and modernize viticulture and winemaking. Reward yourself with a tasting (call first for an appointment), and perhaps a bottle of the rare Sciacchetrà dessert wine.

The coastal footpath continues through Corniglia and Vernazza to Monterosso al Mare, but you can catch the train in any of the villages whenever you wish.

RECOMMENDED WINE PRODUCER, ENOTECA, AND RESTAURANT

Cooperativa Agricoltura di Riomaggiore, Manarola, Corniglia, Vernazza e Monterosso Frazione Groppo 19010 Manarola SP tel: 0187/920435 fax: 0187/920076 *Try the superior cru wines of this modern cooperative.*	**Enoteca Internazionale** Via Roma, 62 19016 Monterosso al Mare SP tel: 0187/817278 *Cinqueterre and Sciacchetrà from small growers, plus good selection of wines from all over Italy.*	**Ristorante Aristide** Via Discovolo, 138 19010 Manarola SP tel: 0187/920000 *Restaurant located just a few steps from the harbor; try the outstanding* antipasti di mare *and local fish.* $

Indirizzi
USEFUL ADDRESSES

VALLE D'AOSTA
**Azienda Agrituristica
Lo Dzerby**
Frazione Machaby
11020 Arnad AO
tel: 0125/966067
*Farmhouse restaurant in
secluded mountain setting.*
$

**Azienda Vitivinicola Ezio
Voyat**
Via Arberaz, 31
11023 Chambave AO
tel: 0166/46139
*Valle d'Aosta's leading
private wine producer.*

Enoteca La Crotta
Via Circonvallazione, 102
11013 Courmayeur AO
tel: 0165/841735
*Source of hard-to-find
wines of Valle d'Aosta.*

Maison de Filippo
Località Entrèves
11013 Courmayeur AO
tel: 0165/869719
*Legendary restaurant; local
mountain foods.*
$$

*Trattoria Due Cavallini,
Mantova*

PIEMONTE
**Antica Torroneria
Piemontese**
Località Borgonuovo, 1
12050 Sinio CN
tel: 0173/263910
fax: 0173/263988
*Torrone d'Alba hand-made
on the premises.*

**Bar Pasticceria
Giordanino**
Corso Alfieri, 254
14100 Asti CN
tel: 0141/593802
*All the local sweet
specialties of Asti in this
town-center landmark.*

**Distilleria Santa Teresa
SRL dei Fratelli Marolo**
Case Sparse, 35
12067 Mussotto d'Alba CN
tel: 0173/33144
fax: 0173/361240
*Small artisan distillery,
producing some of Italy's
greatest single grape
variety grappe.*

Enoteca della Serra
Castello di Roppolo
13040 Roppolo VC
tel: 0161/98501
fax: 0161/987510
*Located above Lake
Viverone, this is the best
source of a range of wines
from northern Piemonte
vineyards. The castle
restaurant serves local food.*
$$

**Enoteca Regionale del
Barbaresco**
Via Torino 8/A
12050 Barbaresco CN
tel: 0173/635251
fax: 0173/635234
*Shrine for wine lovers in
deconsecrated San Donato
church.*

**Formaggi Giolito
Fiorenzo**
Via Umberto I, 138
12042 Bra CN
tel: 0172/412920
*Excellent farmhouse
cheeses from Cuneo.*

Gancia
Corso Libertà, 16
14053 Canelli AT
tel: 0141/8301
fax: 0141/835341
*Write in advance for an
appointment to visit this
famous sparkling-wine and
vermouth producer.*

**Giacoma Bologna
"Braida"**
Via Roma, 94
14030 Rocchetta Tanaro AT
tel: 0141/644113
fax: 0141/644584
*The finest Barbera wines
in Italy.*

La Contea
Piazza Cocito, 8
12057 Neive CN
tel: 0173/67126
fax: 0173/67367
*Stylish foods found in the
heart of the Barbaresco
vineyard.*
$$$

Osteria Boccondivino
Via Mendicità Istruita, 14
12042 Bra CN
tel: 0172/425674
*The Arcigola Slow Food
movement (see p. 9) was
born in this now-legendary
osteria.*
$–$$

Panetteria Fontana
Corso Langhe, 82
12051 Alba CN
tel: 0173/293256
*Great bread and grissini
stirati a mano.*

Pasticceria Bar Converso
Via V. Emanuele, 199
12042 Bra CN
tel: 0172/413626
*Outstanding local pasticceria
in a historic setting.*

Riseria Re Carlo
Via Molino, 1
13030 Albano Vercellese VC
tel: 0161/73124
*Highest quality artisan-
milled rice from paddies
north of Vercelli.*

**Ristorante Cantine del
Gavi**
Via Mameli, 67
15066 Gavi AL
tel: 0143/642458
*Elegant foods for
Piemonte's most elegant
white wine, Gavi di Gavi.*
$$–$$$

Torta sbrisolona, *a delicious crumbly cake*

Ristorante Da Giovanni
Via Fontana Riola, 3
10010 Quincinetto TO
tel: 0125/757927
fax: 0125/757447
Local trattoria in the wine village of Carema.
$$

Ristorante Pinocchio
Via Matteotti, 147
28021 Borgomanero NO
tel: 0322/82273
fax: 0322/835075
Elegant restaurant near Lake Maggiore serving regional and international foods.
$$$

Trattoria della Posta Da Camulin
Corso F.lli Negro, 3
12054 Cossano Belbo CN
tel: 0141/88126
fax: 0141/88559
Famous trattoria in heart of Moscato country, for classic foods of the Langhe.
$$–$$$

Trattoria I Bologna
Via Sardi, 4
14030 Rocchetta Tanaro AT
tel: 0141/644600
fax: 0141/644197
Family trattoria with wines of Bologna alongside excellent local food.
$$

LOMBARDIA
Albergo-Ristorante della Posta
Piazza Garibaldi, 19
23100 Sondrio SO
tel: 0342/510404
Oldest hotel-restaurant in

the Valtellina with outstanding restaurant, Da Sozzani, serving regional classics.
$$

Azienda Agraria M. e G. Fugazza
Castello di Luzzano
Località Luzzano
27040 Rovescala PV
tel: 0523/863277
fax: 0523/864786
The Oltrepò Pavese's leading wine producer.

Bistrot di Gualtiero Marchesi
Palazzo Rinascente
Duomo, 7th floor
Piazza Duomo
Milan MI
tel: 02/877120
fax: 02/877035
Super-star chef Gualtiero Marchesi's elegant "bistrot," with classic and imaginative foods plus views of the Duomo.
$$$

Ol Formager
Piazza Oberdan, 2
20124 Bergamo BG
tel: 035/239237
Great selection of cheeses from throughout Lombardia and North Italy.

Ristorante Vecchio Mulino
Via del Monumento, 5
27100 Certosa di Pavia PV
tel: 0382/925894
After visiting Pavia's certosa, one of Lombardia's great monuments, dine at this almost equally famous and elegant restaurant.
$$$

Trattoria Vecchia Lugana
Piazzale Vecchia Lugana, 1
25010 Sirmione BS
tel: 030/919012
fax: 030/9904045
This old, elegant favorite serves well-prepared lake fish, in fine weather in the garden over Lake Garda.
$$–$$$

LIGURIA
Antico Frantoio Sommariva
Via Mameli, 7
17031 Albenga SV
tel: 0182/559222
fax: 0182/541143
Outstanding Ligurian extra-virgin olive oil, plus a good range of other specialties, including fresh pesto.

Buco degli Artisti
Via Poggio, 6
Ligo
17038 Villanova d'Albenga SV
tel: 0182/580093
Quiet hideaway in the hills serving antipasti and grilled meats.
$–$$

BEST BUYS
• fresh and conserved white truffles and truffle derivatives (Alba)
• dried *funghi porcini* (Piemonte and Lombardia)
• Ligurian extra-virgin olive oil (Liguria)
• jars of *pesto* (Liguria)
• *torrone d'Alba* (Alba and the Langhe)
• *grappe*, especially single grape variety (Piemonte)
• bags of *riso canaroli* (Piemonte)
• *marrons glacés* (Piemonte and Lombardia)
• *amaretti di Saronno*
• *amaro*

Dried fungi porcini, *a great delicacy worth taking home*

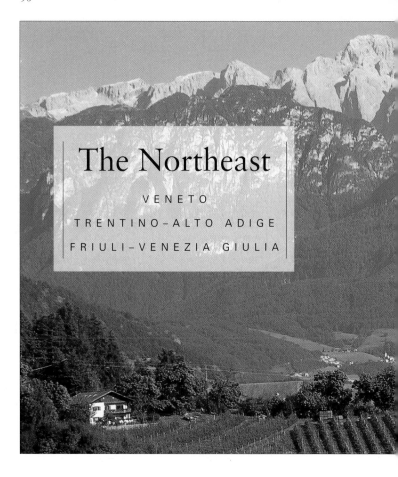

The Northeast

VENETO

TRENTINO–ALTO ADIGE

FRIULI–VENEZIA GIULIA

FROM THE FADED OLD-WORLD SPLENDOR of Trieste, across the alpine arc to the German-speaking Alto Adige, also known in German as the Südtirol, and from Venice along the wide Po Valley through cities, towns, and villages that retain the unmistakable stamp of the Lion of St. Mark, Northeast Italy is one of the most prosperous areas of the country. Once dominated by the powerful Venetian Republic and, later, the Austro-Hungarian Empire, influences from both of which remain throughout, Northeast Italy, in spite of its prosperity and industry, maintains its timeless beauty and serenity. This broad corner of the country is made up of three distinct regions known collectively as the Tre Venezie. They remain linked not only geographically but also historically and culturally: Veneto itself, together with the smaller autonomous regions of Trentino-Alto Adige and Friuli-Venezia Giulia.

VENETO — A BROAD, FERTILE HINTERLAND

The region of Veneto extends across the Po Valley from Lake Garda and Verona in the west, east through Vicenza and Padua to the Venetian Lagoon and the Adriatic Sea, as well as north from the flat, fertile plains of

Alpine landscape near Bolzano in Alto Adige

the Po River, up the Adige, Piave, and other valleys into the foothills and mountains of the Alps and the Dolomites.

If today's industrial prosperity centers on urban areas such as Verona, Vicenza, Padua, Treviso, and Mestre (Venice's *terra firma* counterpart), the surrounding countryside of Veneto is an unspoiled, quiet, and rural land, little visited by tourists. From Verona, strike off to the nearby but isolated, rugged, stone-terraced hills of Valpolicella (source not only of exceptional wine but also fine cherries and other fruits, as well as corn to be ground into *polenta* flour); or from Padua, head south to the volcanic ripple of hills known as the Colli Eugánei (where hot thermal springs are visited for therapeutic and recreational purposes), or north up the Brenta Valley to Bassano del Grappa, Asolo (the poet Robert Browning's favorite town), and Feltre; and from Treviso make for the wine hills of the Piave and the mountain resorts of Belluno and Cortina d'Ampezzo. From Venice itself, escape the tourists and explore the quieter, outer reaches of the Venetian Lagoon, beyond Murano and toy-like Burano, to the agricultural island of Sant'Erasmo, or across the lagoon to the fisherman's outpost of Chióggia, source of Adriatic fish and shellfish.

*Pretzels, the German
influence in Alto Adige*

TRENTINO-ALTO ADIGE — AUSTRIAN ITALY

After World War I and the defeat of the Axis powers, in return for supporting the Allies, Italy received, through the Treaty of Versailles of 1919, Trentino, South Tyrol, and the Brenner Pass, as well as Trieste and parts of Istria. The new and still fledgling nation was finally rid of the Austrian domination that had plagued it for over 200 years. Yet, if Italian speaking Trentino, the southern part of this now dual, autonomous region, on the whole welcomed the change, Alto Adige to the north clung tenaciously to its Tyrolean heritage. Today, Trentino-Alto Adige is one of the most fascinating of all Italy's regions to visit, not least because its bilingual cultural heritage remains so steadfastly intact.

Trentino, undoubtedly, is the more Italian of the two, though you might be forgiven for thinking otherwise if you come here up the western side of Lake Garda from Verona or the south. Indeed, the contrast with "Italian" Italy is immediate and evident in the Alpine scenery, styles of architecture, and Austrian-inspired cuisine. Further north, the contrast is even more striking, so much so that you may wonder if you are still in Italy: German is spoken everywhere, Italian only grudgingly acknowledged (unless they are trying to sell you something), men sport *lederhosen* and wool caps with feathers and the women wear pretty Austrian *dirndl* dresses and wool *loden* coats. The foods are wholly Germanic in style — smoked meats, *sauerkraut,* and dumplings — and the wines, unlike those of Trentino, are vinified in Germanic fashion to produce soft, easy-drinking wines that can be consumed in — well, Germanic quantities. No wonder the region is so popular with Austrians as well as Germans from nearby Munich who quickly pop over the Brenner Pass for their taste of Italy.

FRIULI-VENEZIA GIULIA

If Italy gained territory in the aftermath of World War I, she lost considerably at the end of the last war, when Tito moved his partisans to retake Istria and Fiume for Yugoslavia (though the Allies did stop him from seizing Trieste). Today, Friuli-Venezia Giulia, bordering both Austria and Slovenia, lies in the far northeastern corner of Italy, a historic and important region that is often overlooked by visitors. Trieste, located on its narrow spit of land just miles from the frontier, is today a beautiful, if out-on-a-limb, provincial outpost. No longer the strategic window on the Adriatic that it once was for the Habsburgs who made it a free port in 1715, it still remains wholly old world, even Central European, in feel. Trieste is well worth visiting not just from a historical perspective but because it is an old city in the process of regenerating itself, and there is a vibrant sense of young energy here that pulsates amid its monuments to the past. Wine lovers, of course, will wish to explore the wine hills of Friuli-Venezia Giulia, especially the Cóllio and Colli Orientali, source of some of the most exciting quality white wines in Italy today. Udine, the region's capital, suffered greatly in a devastating earthquake in 1976, though little evidence of that tragedy remains today. The mountains to the north of the capital provide a lovely backdrop, the source of one of Italy's greatest air-cured hams, *prosciutto di San Daniele,* and beyond, above Tolmezzo, lies the little-known and undervisited Carnia, home of an outstanding mountain *cucina.*

POLENTA — THE UNIFIER

As much as any cultural or historical factor, one gastronomic specialty undoubtedly unites the Tre Venezie. Whether enjoyed fresh from a copper cauldron as an accompaniment to a rich, meaty *gulasch* in a mountain refuge in Trentino or Alto Adige; sliced cold and grilled to accompany sardines in Chióggia, liver and onions in Venice, or grilled meats in farmhouse restaurants by Lake Garda: *polenta,* the staple cornmeal mush, is universally loved in all three regions.

Prodotti Regionali
REGIONAL PRODUCE

Northeast Italy rises from the flat, fertile plains of the Po Valley into the upper heights of some of Europe's most awe-inspiring mountain ranges. The plains are among the richest agricultural land in Italy, the source of *grano* (wheat), *granturco* (corn), *orzo* (barley), *fagioli* (beans), *riso* (rice), and *barbabiètole* (beets). From the rugged hills of Valpolicella to valleys that tumble down from the mountains, huge orchards provide superb *mele* (apples), *pere* (pears), *ciliegie* (cherries), *pesche* (peaches), and *susine* (plums) — fruits from northern climes that combine sweetness with crisp acidity.

Many towns and zones are famous for one or two particular local crops. The *radicchio di Treviso* (bitter, stalky, pale red lettuce), among the best known, is an outstanding salad vegetable available only

Radicchio di Treviso *(left) and* radicchio di Castelfranco Veneto

in winter, while the less distinctive round, red variety from Castelfranco Veneto or Chióggia can be found all year round. Bassano del Grappa is known not only for its fiery distillates but also for its exquisite *asparagi* (asparagus), and nearby Maróstica is equally renowned for its *ciliegie* (cherries). Friuli's Carnia is famous for its *fagioli* (beans), used in many soups, while the agricultural islands of the Venetian Lagoon yield *bisi* (baby peas), *carciofi violette* (tender baby artichokes), and *carote novelle* (new carrots).

Much of the higher ground in Friuli-Venezia Giulia and Trentino-Alto Adige is unsuitable for large-scale cultivation, but some vegetables grow in profusion, such as *cavolo* (cabbage), *patate* (potatoes), and *rape* (turnips), suitable partners for the heavy foods of these border regions.

APPLE TIME IN ALTO ADIGE

Almost as important as the grape harvest is the September harvest of apples that precedes it throughout the valleys of Trentino and Alto Adige. This is the most important region in Italy for apple production, and immense orchards line the valley floors as far as the eye can see.

Come here to purchase apples by the crate for a virtual pittance, enjoy them crisp off the trees, drink *apfelsaft* or *spremuta di mela* (freshly pressed apple juice), still cloudy and thick, a deliciously sweet and nourishing beverage.

Try to sample

Asparagi di Bassano Asparagus from Bassano del Grappa (May–Jun).

Bisi Venetian dialect for *piselli* — fresh peas (May–Jun).

Ciliegie Cherries; especially from Valpolicella, Maróstica, and Colli Eugánei (May–Jun).

Funghi di bosco (fall and winter) Wild mushrooms from the mountains, especially *porcini* (cepes) and *finferli* (chanterelles) from Trentino.

Radicchio di Treviso (winter) Bitter red lettuce from Treviso.

Al Mercato

MARKETS

Bringing produce into Venice

VENETO

Abano Terme	Wed
Asiago	Sat
Asolo	Sat
Bardolino	Thu
Bassano del Grappa	Thu
Belluno	Sat
Castelfranco Veneto	Tue, Fri
Chióggia	Thu
fish market	Tue–Sat
Conegliano	Fri
Cortina d'Ampezzo	Tue, Fri
Feltre	Tue, Fri
Garda	Fri
Isola della Scala	Fri
Montegrotto Terme	Thu
Negrar	Mon
Padua	Mon–Sat
San Pietro in Cariano	Fri
Soave	Tue
Treviso	Tue, Sat
Valéggio sul Mincio	Sat
Venice	Mon–Sat
Verona	Mon–Sat
Vicenza	Tue, Thu

TRENTINO-ALTO ADIGE

Bolzano (Bozen)	Mon–Sat
Bressanone (Brixen)	Mon
Caldaro (Kaltern)	Wed
Merano (Meran)	Fri
Rovereto	Tue
Riva del Garda	Wed
San Michele all'Adige	Tue
Trento	Thu

FRIULI-VENEZIA GIULIA

Cormons	Fri
Gorizia	Thu
Gradisca d'Isonzo	Tue, Sat
Grado	Sat (summer only)
Latisana	Wed
Palmanova	Mon
Pordenone	Wed, Sat
San Daniele del Friuli	Wed
Tarvisio	Mon–Sat
Tolmezzo	Mon
Trieste	Wed, Thu
Udine	Sat

POPULAR *FESTE*

VENETO

Bardolino *Festa dell'uva (wine)* end Sep

Negrar *Sagra del Recioto (wine)* Easter Mon

Padua *Sagra gastronomica (gastronomic)* early Dec

Chióggia *Sagra del Pesce (fish)* early Aug

Soave *Sagra dell'uva (wine)* end Sep

TRENTINO-ALTO ADIGE

Caldaro (Kaltern) *Settimana del Vino (wine week)* end Aug

FRIULI-VENEZIA GIULIA

San Daniele del Friuli *Sagra del prosciutto (ham)* end Aug

Below: Lazise, a lakeside port in Veneto

The Rialto Market in Venice

THE HUB OF DAILY LIFE

VENICE TODAY may appear to be a spectacle and a pastiche of its past, a city that seems unreal and dreamlike, but its principal market, the Rialto, is solidly down-to-earth, purveyor not of dreams but basic, everyday essentials. For us, it remains the greatest market in the world.

The Rialto has been at the heart of commerce and the daily life of Venice for centuries. Today, as you watch the heavy *mototopi* (work barges) being loaded and unloaded with crates of lettuce, cabbages, or vivid blood oranges, it is not at all difficult to half-close your eyes and imagine a similarly busy, sail-driven scene in one of Canaletto's paintings. We should remember that the prosperity of Venice was once based on trade monopolies in what were then rare and exotic foodstuffs, such as pepper and spices from the Orient, coffee, and sugar.

The Rialto is still an important market: a truly impressive emporium, the source, if no longer of the wonders of the Orient, then, certainly, of the best produce and products from throughout Italy. Yet a surprising amount of the produce on display is local: tender baby eggplants and new carrots from the island of Sant' Erasmo, round, red *radicchio,* and other vegetables from Chióggia, fresh tender peas for the Venetians' favorite *risi e bisi* (rice and peas), and, of course, all the fish and shellfish from the Venetian Lagoon, on display in the adjoining *mercato del pesce*.

A fruit stall in the Rialto market

In addition to its permanent and perambulatory stalls, the market winds through a maze of narrow, dark alleys lined with food stores of all types: *pastificii* selling homemade, fresh *paste;* bakeries offering bread, *biscotti,* and beautiful pastries still hot from the oven; butchers and fishmongers; general corner groceries; and little holes-in-the-wall.

The Rialto is where you really see and feel how the Venetians themselves live on a day-to-day basis. Come here early in the morning to soak in the scene, then afterward, wind your way to the Cantina Do Mori, our favorite Venetian drinking den. It will be packed with stall holders and market porters taking a mid-morning break after their early morning exertions, enjoying a tumbler of honest wine made from Raboso or Tocai grapes drawn direct from demijohns, together with simple but delicious snacks, such as *prosciutto* wrapped around bread sticks.

Cantina Do Mori
San Polo 429
tel: 041/5225401

Bread sticks wrapped in prosciutto, *a snack served with wine in bars around the market place*

Piatti Tipici

REGIONAL SPECIALTIES

THE COOKING of the Tre Venezie reflects the history of the region, its domination by, first, the Venetian Republic and, later, the Austro-Hungarians. As a result, it can range from the wholly Italian (as in tomato sauce and *pasta*) to foods that are Germanic and Middle European (steamed dumplings and *gulasch*, or apple strudel and other such pastries). Over all, the Venetian influence adds a touch of exotica and spice, while that of Austria provides a sober solidity to the diet of a northern people not overly given to Mediterranean excesses.

True local foods exist even in Venice, that most touristic of cities, though finding decent *fegato alla veneziana* or simply grilled sardines and *polenta* may take some tracking down. Elsewhere in Veneto, the simple, satisfying food of the country is most enjoyable — homemade *bigoli* (wholewheat pasta) and meats grilled over an open fire and served with fresh garden vegetables and grilled *polenta*, washed down with good jug wines.

The foods of Trentino-Alto Adige satisfy appetites made keen by walking in the Dolomites, or along *weinwanderweg* (signposted footpaths) that lead through the vineyards to welcoming guesthouses and farmhouses where foods, such as *speck* (smoked, air-cured ham), outstanding rye and other breads, or steaming platters of boiled meats and *sauerkraut* are served, accompanied by plentiful, easy-to-drink local wines.

Friuli-Venezia Giulia jealously guards and maintains its own local and regional food traditions, making no concessions to foreign tastes. Meals may start with sweet dumplings filled with cherries or plums and bathed in butter, or boiled *salame* sautéed in vinegar, followed by enormous servings of *stinco di vitello* (veal shank), or *gulasch*, both served up in generous Middle European helpings.

As for seafood, anywhere along the Adriatic seaboard, it is usually fresh, varied and outstanding.

ANTIPASTI

Affetatti misti   Mixed plate of local and regional *salumi*, including *prosciutto di San Daniele* (see p.109), *speck*, and *soppressa*, usually accompanied by vegetables conserved *sott'aceto* (in vinegar).

Antipasti di mare (Venice and the Adriatic Coast)   Selection of fresh fish and seafood appetizers.

Baccalà mantecato (Venice and all Veneto)   A classic preparation of air-dried stockfish (see p.24), soaked, then cooked to a creamy consistency with garlic, parsley, and olive oil.

Carne salà (Trentino)   Thinly sliced, brine-cured beef, dressed in olive oil and served with boiled beans.

Carpaccio (Venice and all Veneto) Famous dish, now served internationally, consisting of thinly sliced, raw tenderloin of beef, and dressed individually according to the establishment (often with lemon juice and olive oil), garnished with shavings of *parmigiano reggiano* or *grana* cheese, thinly sliced mushrooms, or even, in season, shavings of *tartufi bianchi* (white truffles).

Cevapcici (Friuli-Venezia Giulia) Small skewers of ground pork or veal, grilled, and served with chopped onions and chili sauce.

Fricò (Friuli-Venezia Giulia)   Fried cheese; eaten as an appetizer with wine.

Gefülltes Gemüse (Alto Adige) Stuffed, baked vegetables.

Granseola or **grancevola alla veneziana** (Venice and the Adriatic Coast)   Small, sweet spider crab, boiled and served cold, the flesh seasoned with garlic, olive oil, and chopped parsley.

Carpaccio, *at the Hotel Cipriani, Venice*

Boiled meats and sausages with crauti *and fresh horseradish at Buffet Da Pepi, Trieste*

Liptauer käse or **guarnito** (Alto Adige and Friuli-Venezia Giulia)   Cheese spread made with *ricotta* or *stracchino* mixed with chopped onions, cumin seeds, and plenty of paprika; to be spread on *pane di segale* (rye bread).

Moleche (Venice and the Adriatic Coast)   Tiny, soft-shell crabs, dipped in flour and egg, then fried in oil (available only seasonally when the crabs shed their shells — late spring and fall).

Prosciutto in crosta di pane (Friuli-Venezia Giulia)   Whole ham, baked covered in bread dough; usually served with grated horseradish.

Prosciutto di San Daniele (Friuli-Venezia Giulia)   Sweet air-cured mountain ham (see p.109).

Salame sott'aceto (Friuli-Venezia Giulia)   Hot, boiled *salame* cooked in vinegar with pickled onions.

Sfogie in saor (Veneto)   Baby sole coated with flour, fried, then marinated overnight in wine vinegar and spices.

Soppressa (Veneto)   Soft textured pork *salame*.

Speck (Trentino-Alto Adige)   Smoked air-cured ham (see p.108).

I PRIMI PIATTI

Bigoli (Veneto)   The most typical *pasta* of Veneto, a type of thick, wholewheat *spaghetti,* often served with a sauce of sardines or anchovies and breadcrumbs, or with *ragù* (meat sauce).

Brodetto (Trieste, Grado, Venice, and the Adriatic Coast)   Classic fish soup or stew, made with local fish, onions, garlic, and, optionally, tomatoes.

Canederli or **knödeln** (Trentino-Alto Adige) Large bread dumplings made with *speck,* poached, then gently fried in butter; eaten as a first course, or as an accompaniment to meats or stews.

Cjalzons (Friuli-Venezia Giulia) *Ravioli*-type *pasta* stuffed usually with mixtures of chopped vegetables, cheese, or, often, sweet ingredients, including chocolate, marmalade, and dried fruits.

Gnocchi di ciliegie or **di susine** (Friuli-Venezia Giulia)   Unusual sweet fruit dumplings filled with cherries or plums; to be eaten as a rich first course, smothered in melted butter.

Jota (Trieste)   Hugely substantial Central European-inspired *sauerkraut,* bean, and pork soup.

Pasta e fasoi (fagioli) (Veneto)   Dense soup made from *borlotti* beans and pork rind, with stubby *pasta* added at the end.

Polenta smalzada (Trentino)   *Polenta* made from a mixture of corn and buckwheat, mixed with butter, cheese, and anchovies, then baked in the oven.

Risi e bisi (Venice)   Famous but supremely simple Venetian specialty of rice cooked with fresh peas; the consistency of a *minestra,* i.e., quite soupy.

Risotti (Veneto)   *Risotti* are the favorite first courses in Veneto, even more so than *pasta asciutta.* The variations are endless, and include *risotto al mare* (with

Canederli *or bread dumplings with* gulasch

seafood and shellfish), *risotto al radicchio di Treviso*, *risotto ai funghi* (with fresh or dried *porcini* mushrooms), *risotto al amarone* (with Amarone wine), *risotto primavera* (with fresh spring vegetables), *risotto alla chioggiotta* (with fish from the Lagoon), *risotto all'isolana* (with chopped pork and veal seasoned with cinnamon), and *risotto nero* (with squid in its own ink).

Strangolapreti (Trentino)   "Priest stranglers" — *gnocchi* (small dumplings) made with bread, flour, and cooked vegetables, such as spinach or beet greens, served usually with butter and sage.

Tiroler speckknödelsuppe (Alto Adige)   Beef broth served with large bacon-and-bread dumpling.

Uardi e fasui (Friuli-Venezia Giulia)   Classic bean and barley soup.

Weinsuppe (Alto Adige)   Wine soup; usually made with white Alto Adige wine, broth, cream, and cinnamon.

I SECONDI PIATTI

Baccalà alla vicentina (Veneto)   Favorite preparation of air-dried stock-fish, simmered with onions, garlic, olive oil, and milk, then beaten to a smooth puree; often served as a main course with *polenta*.

Brasato all'amarone (Verona) Whole piece of beef, marinated in Amarone della Valpolicella and chopped vege-tables, cooked slowly, then sliced and served with a sauce of pureed vegetables.

Crauti con puntine di vitello e lucanica (Trentino)   *Sauerkraut* with cured belly of veal and boiling *salame*.

Fegato alla veneziana (Venice and all Veneto)   Thinly sliced calf's liver, cooked with plenty of sliced onions in butter and oil; this classic is usually served with grilled *polenta*.

Gulasch or **gulyas** (Friuli-Venezia Giulia and Trentino-Alto Adige)   Hungarian-inspired spicy beef paprika and potato stew.

Musetto con brovada (Friuli-Venezia Giulia)   Spicy boiled pork sausage;

usually served with sour, fermented turnips, a hearty winter warmer.

Seppia alla veneziana (Venice and all Veneto)   Cuttlefish stewed in its own ink, a grim-looking black dish that actually tastes much better than it looks.

Spezzatino di vitello (Veneto)   Stew of slowly cooked cubes of veal.

Fegato alla veneziana *with grilled* polenta

Stinco di vitello or **di maiale** (the Tre Venezie)   Shin of veal or pork, simmered in wine and seasonings; served whole — share one between two unless you are really ravenous.

Tafelspitz mit Kren (Alto Adige)   Boiled beef with grated horseradish.

Würstl con crauti (Alto Adige)   German-style sausage with *sauerkraut*.

Zwiebelrösbraten (Alto Adige)   Roast or braised beef with onions, served with gravy and dumplings.

I CONTORNI

Crauti (Friuli-Venezia Giulia and Trentino-Alto Adige) *Sauerkraut*.

Patate in tecia (Friuli-Venezia Giulia)   Boiled potatoes in their skins, sautéed in lard with onions.

Peperonata (Veneto)   Vegetable medley of stewed bell peppers, onion, eggplant, zucchini, and tomatoes.

Radicchio di Treviso (the Tre Venezie)   The famous red bitter lettuce is prepared in numerous ways, both raw and cooked. Delicious grilled over charcoal.

Topinambur (the Tre Venezie)   Jerusalem artichoke, a tasty tuber.

Verza (Veneto and Friuli-Venezia Giulia)   Savoy cabbage.

Riso Vialone Nano

THE ROLLS-ROYCE OF RICE

The short, fat grains of Vialone Nano rice

IN VENETO, a *risotto* is always *all'onda* ("wave-like") i.e., still fairly liquid, at times, even soupy, with a voluptuous, creamy texture, the fat, short grains of rice having absorbed more than double their volume of flavorful broth, yet still remaining wholly separate and *al dente*. For rice connoisseurs here and elsewhere, the finest rice for achieving such perfection is a rare and highly sought variety known as Vialone Nano, cultivated mainly in the lowlands below Verona around the small town of Isola della Scala.

In this small, prestigious rice zone, growers belonging to a select *consorzio* (a cooperative of growers and producers) cultivate their *risaie* (rice paddies) using no chemicals or pesticides. Carp are introduced into the canals and flooded paddies to eliminate unwanted insects and pests. By carefully regulating the flooding and draining of the fields, the rice growers ensure that a symbiotic equilibrium is established which allows this delicate and fickle rice variety to grow healthily. Once harvested in the fall, the first-choice rice is selected to be processed in a rice mill founded in 1650 and functioning since then. Today, it is run by Gabriele Ferron, one of Italy's acknowledged rice experts.

At the Ferron family's Antica Riseria, the selected Vialone Nano rice is worked very slowly and with great care, in some cases using the ancient, still water-driven machines that date from the foundation of the mill. Once the husk has been removed, the *pestelli* (pestles) move slowly up and down, gradually allowing the grains to polish themselves against each other while retaining as much as

possible of the rich starches and vitamins (industrial processes, though much faster, inevitably rob rice of much of its goodness, says Gabriele). Afterward, the final selection is made simply using *crivelli* (large, flat, hand sieves).

Vialone Nano is an exceptional rice with the capacity to absorb great quantities of cooking liquid. Its taste is exquisitely rich. Moreover, it cooks evenly throughout, maintaining its bite without even a hint of chalkiness, provided it is cooked properly.

The Antica Riseria has a rice restaurant where rice dishes such as the classic *risotto all'isolana* can be sampled. This rich and substantial dish made with pork and veal flavored with cinnamon (see p.105) is a staple of the people who work in the rice paddies. Gabriele Ferron also conducts rice cooking classes.

Antica Riseria Ferron
Via Saccovener, 6
37063 Isola della Scala VR
tel: 045/7301022

Using large sieves to make the final selection of Vialone Nano grains, at the Antica Riseria Ferron

Polenta

STAPLE OF THE TRE VENEZIE

Every diet — national, regional, or local — depends on a basic staple starch, whether bread, potatoes, rice, or *pasta* or other noodles. In the Tre Venezie, that staple is *polenta*, a nutritious mush made from coarsely ground white or yellow cornmeal.

As an agricultural crop, corn was introduced into Veneto in the 16th century by Conte Marc'Antonio Serègo on his estate in Valpolicella. The count may have been a visionary and a leader in agriculture, but it is doubtful whether even he could have foreseen how this originally North American crop would grow in popularity to become the staple food of Northeast Italy.

Polenta is the simplest of foods. Not long ago, it was prepared daily in many if not most homes throughout the Tre Venezie. And so it continues, though to a lesser extent today: the coarse yellow or white cornmeal is added to a large copper pan with the requisite amount of water and a dash of salt, then heated slowly, ever so slowly, and stirred all the while with a long wooden stick, *la mescola*.

As the cornmeal cooks, it thickens to the required consistency, and, at the same time, begins to spit as it simmers over the fire, sending hot bits of cornmeal onto the arms of the stirrer (this is why the wooden stick is very long). Once it begins to come off the sides of the pan, it is done (this can take 30–45 minutes), and the *polenta* is turned out onto a large wooden board.

At this point, the *polenta* may be served immediately by the spoonful. Alternatively, it is left to set, beaten with flat wooden paddles, then cut into slices with a piece of taut string and served with fish, meat, or just about anything else that is going that day.

Leftover *polenta* is delicious grilled over an open fire (something like an Italian "cornbread"). Or else, *polenta* cut into small rectangles is deep-fried into little *crostini* — crunchy morsels, topped

Cooking polenta *in a large cauldron outdoors, at a mountain refuge in Trentino*

sometimes with a *ragù* made from chicken livers — to enjoy as an appetizing snack with drinks.

Polenta is boiled, baked, or fried, eaten as a first course, a main course, even, sweetened, as a dessert. In whatever shape or form it is served, there is no getting away from *polenta* in the Tre Venezie: enjoy it in all its variety.

Visit *polenta* mills at:

Il Molino de March
Via Nongole
32024 Castion BL
Visit in the mornings to see the old mill working.

Il Mulino di Elio Urban
Loc. Piedim
Arta Terme UD
Their stone-ground *polenta* flour is highly regarded.

Mulin di Trus
Via Ruttars, 4
Loc. Trussio di Ruttars
34070 Dolegna del Còllio GO
tel: 0481/60546
Located just a few miles from the Slovenian frontier.

Salumi

CURED PORK PRODUCTS

Northeast Italy produces a wide variety of superb cured pork products: in the Italian tradition of *salami* and air-cured hams, in the Austro-Germanic manner of meats cured in *salamoia* (brine bath), and in the German style of sausages for eating boiled with *crauti (sauerkraut)* and potatoes.

Slices of soppressa *(left) and* coppa *(right)*

TRY TO SAMPLE

Coppa (the Tre Venezie)   Meaty, cured neck tenderloin.

Kaminwürzen (Alto Adige)   Small smoked sausage; often served with drinks.

Lingua (Friuli-Venezia Giulia and Trentino-Alto Adige)   Pig's or lamb's tongue, cured in brine.

Lucanica (Trentino-Alto Adige)   Boiling *salame,* sometimes smoked.

Mortandele (Trentino-Alto Adige)   Ground *salame* mixture, formed into large "meatballs" and smoked.

Ossocollo (Friuli-Venezia Giulia)   Similar to *coppa.*

Prosciutto del Veneto (Veneto)   A rather salty but tasty version of the air-cured classic.

Prosciutto di cinghiale (Friuli-Venezia Giulia and Trentino-Alto Adige)   Air-cured *prosciutto* made with the hind leg of wild boar.

Prosciutto di San Daniele   Veneto's prized ham (see opposite).

Prosciutto di Sáuris (Friuli-Venezia Giulia)   Highly prized smoked ham from the Carnia region.

Salame alla friulana   Boiling *salame,* usually served with vinegar and onions.

Soppressa (Veneto)   The most popular native *salame* of Veneto; large, rather fatty, and soft in texture.

SPECK TIROLESE

Speck is the great cured pork product of Northeast Italy's mountain regions. In the past, in every *maso* (upland farm), families would raise their own pig and slaughter it in winter, salt the hind legs, and hang them up to smoke in the farmhouse chimney. Today, superb *speck* is produced throughout Trentino-Alto Adige on both an artisan and semi-industrial scale.

The hind legs of select pigs are first cured for about three weeks in a mixture of dry salt, black pepper, crushed juniper berries, and bay leaves (the exact recipe varies considerably), then hung up to smoke over a smoldering fire of oak chips and juniper for three or four days. They are then left to age for a further

four or five months. The longer the *speck* is left to age, the better the taste.

A thick slice of chewy, wood-smoked *speck,* a piece of crunchy *schuttelbrot* (the traditional hard flat bread of Alto Adige), and a tumbler of fresh wine: this simple Tyrolean snack is hard to beat.

Prosciutto di San Daniele
THE SWEETEST OF HAMS

A SMALL RIPPLE of hills rises up gently from the Adriatic Sea toward the Alps that separate Friuli-Venezia Giulia from Austria. Here, in San Daniele del Friuli, are the ideal conditions for producing an exceptionally sweet, air-cured mountain ham that has few rivals in the world: *prosciutto di San Daniele,* which once graced the tables of the emperors and arch-dukes of Austro-Hungary.

The microclimate of this small community, where the humid air of the Adriatic mixes with the drier, lighter, and cooler air of the Alps, combined with centuries of expertise and skill, has resulted in the unique quality of the air-cured hams of San Daniele. Produced from the legs of fresh pork transformed with nothing else except pure sea salt and time, San Daniele ham is recognizable both by its characteristic pressed mandolin shape and the foot of the pig always left on.

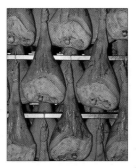

Prosciutto di San Daniele, *hung to age for at least one year*

Far less *prosciutto di San Daniele* than *prosciutto di Parma* (see p.141) is made. Here, it is still possible to find artisans working on a small scale. For ham lovers, therefore, it may be obligatory to come to San Daniele del Friuli to sample and buy this great ham.

The Castellani family are the smallest of the 25 producers of *prosciutto di San Daniele,* making only 2,500 hams a year. Unlike most producers, they still raise their own pigs and cure them by hand, using methods that have not changed for centuries. The fresh hams are dry-salted for only a brief period — perhaps just ten days — then carefully tended to make sure that the meat is properly cured: it is essential with such a brief salting period that the meat absorbs the salt completely; longer salting, on the other hand, results in hams that lose their sweetness.

Once salted, the hams are left to age in the attic above the shop, its tall windows opened and shut daily depending on the weather, humidity, and the direction of the wind.

Prosciutto di San Daniele must be aged for a minimum of 12 months, but according to Signora Caterina Castellani, who has been producing *prosciutto* for more than 40 years, it becomes really fine only after 16–18 months, during which time it loses almost completely any taste of salt and acquires instead its intense perfume, melting texture, and incomparable flavor.

The old historic town of San Daniele del Friuli is almost totally given over to its famous hams. Most of the large producers are located outside town and many are happy to sell direct to private customers. The Castellanis' *La Casa del Prosciutto* is the only *prosciuttificio* still located in the town center. In this shop-cum-bar, you can enjoy it by the plate, together with good, local Friuli wine, or buy a whole or half ham or vacuum packs of sliced ham to take away.

La Casa del Prosciutto
Via Teobaldo Ciconi, 32
33038 San Daniele del Friuli UD
tel: 0432/957422
fax: 0432/941412

Freshly sliced prosciutto di San Daniele *at La Casa del Prosciutto, San Daniele del Friuli*

Pesce e Frutti di Mare
FISH AND SHELLFISH

I N SPITE OF POLLUTION, the northern reaches of the Adriatic Sea and the Venetian Lagoon remain the source of a superlative, exceptionally varied, and often bewildering catch of fish and shellfish. Not only can the variety on offer be unfamiliar, matters are further complicated as, in markets and restaurants, fish and shellfish are often given their dialect names: names even vary between towns as near each other as Venice and Chióggia.

Visit Venice's Rialto fish market and also, if you have time, cross the lagoon to Chióggia, if only to look at the beautiful and varied catch on display and familiarize yourself with local species, or to buy some fish and shellfish if you have cooking facilities.

The following fish are often available at fish markets throughout Northeast Italy; we have given both Italian and local names that you may come across.

Triglie, *red mullet*

Marmora, *striped sea porgy or bream*

Scampi, *langoustines*

Baccalà   In Veneto, the term *baccalà* is used to indicate not dried salt cod but air-dried *stoccafisso* (stockfish; see p.24), the best of which is Norwegian *ragno*.

Bisato   Venetian name for *anguilla* (eel); the best come from the Venetian lagoon; sold live and still wriggling.

Bulli   Whelks.

Canestrelli   Tiny scallops from the lagoon (something like Bay scallops).

Canoce   Venetian for *cannocchie,* the delicious and prized mantis shrimp.

Caparozzoli   Venetian for *vongole* (clams); served over *spaghetti* or prepared *alla marinara* (steamed in wine).

Cape longhe   Venetian for *cannolicchi* (razor clams); long tube-like bivalves that are usually prepared *gratinati* (baked with breadcrumbs).

Capesante or **cappesante**   Scallops.

Cicala di mare   Flat lobster, small but highly prized shellfish, more expensive than *canoce.*

Coda di rospo   Tail of monkfish (angler-fish), a Venetian favorite.

Frittura   A mixed variety of small fish, dipped in flour, then deep fried.

Ghiozzo or **gô**   Goby, a spiny fish of the lagoon; usually fried or served *in saor* (fried then soused in vinegar).

Granseola or **grancevola**   Spider crab.

Granzoporo or **gransoporo** Venetian names for common edible crab.

Luserna   Tub robin or gurnard, a coarsely textured but tasty fish.

Marmora   Striped sea porgy or bream.

Moleche   Soft-shell crab.

Peoci   Venetian for *cozze* (mussels).

Sardelle   Sardines. The popular staple of fisherfolk, grilled over charcoal and eaten with *polenta.*

Scampi   Norway lobster or *langoustine.*

Seppie   Cuttlefish.

Seppioline   Baby cuttlefish. **Seppioline di burcelo**, tiny cuttlefish to fry, typical of Chióggia.

Sogliola   Dover sole. **Sogliola nostrale,** the local catch, tiny but very sweet.

Triglie   Red mullet.

Chióggia

A FISHING TOWN OF VENETO

CHIOGGIA, AN OLD VENETIAN outpost on the far fringe of the lagoon, is one of the most important and busiest fishing ports in the Adriatic. Connected to *terra firma* by a causeway, Chióggia looks inwards, across the lagoon to the mainland. The town is inhabited mainly by fisherfolk as well as by farmers, who work the surrounding rich, flooded alluvial plains.

Outside the high season, Chióggia is about as far from a tourist town as you can find in the lagoon. As you wander through its back alleys and along the side canals, it is easy to imagine that this is rather as Venice must have been before *La Serenissima* became a living museum.

It is not that easy to reach Chióggia. The trip from Venice is by bus and *vaporetto* (waterbus) from the Lido, and the journey takes about one and a half hours, but it's worth making your way here all the same to visit the remarkable fish market that takes place every day except Monday.

The traditional fishing boats of Chióggia, *bragossi chioggioti,* small and brightly painted, still land their catch directly at the market, on a side canal just behind it. Here, under the red canopies of the 50-odd permanent stone banks, you can see in all their glistening glory the fish and shellfish of the lagoon and surrounding waters.

Look out for Venetian specialties (see opposite), and especially the trays of tiny baby cuttlefish, stained black from their own ink; tanks of squirming eel, wet and glistening in the sunshine; the profusion of tiny sole, sea porgy, and mullet, so fresh they still wriggle. They are insistent, these fisherfolk of Chióggia and, as you pass by, they'll shout out, *"Canoce buone buone. Roba viva oggi!"* "Beautiful *canoce.* Caught live only today!"

When you have had your fill of the hectic scene, repair to a simple *trattoria* to enjoy a fresh seafood meal that is cheaper and better than most you would find in Venice. Or dine at the Ristorante El Gato, a stylish fish restaurant that is worth making the journey for in itself.

Ristorante El Gato
Campo Sant'Andrea, 653
30015 Chióggia VE
tel: 041/401806
fax: 041/405224
$$$

Traditional boats moored on a side canal near the market of Chióggia

Formaggi
CHEESES OF THE NORTHEAST

THE HERDS on the pastures and high Alpine meadows of the Tre Venezie yield plenty of milk, and good cheeses are made throughout the region. Alpine traditions persist in the small farm dairies on the lower slopes of the Alps and Dolomites, where shepherds and cowherds still take their animals to graze on lush mountain meadows in summer. And, down on the plains, cooperative dairies transform milk into cheese on a large scale.

Asiago mezzano, *a delicious and versatile cheese of Veneto and Trentino*

TRY TO SAMPLE

Asiago (Veneto and Trentino)   The great cheese of the Northeast, and a versatile one: a semi-fat, semi-cooked cheese made from cow's milk. When fresh and young, it is at its least interesting, rather rubbery and insipid in texture and flavor. **Asiago mezzano,** by contrast, is a medium-aged cheese (about six months) with a firm texture and deeper, fuller flavor. **Asiago stravecchio** is further aged for upward of 12 months, and is an outstanding, hard cheese, delicious for eating or grating.

Asin (Friuli-Venezia Giulia)   Fresh cow's milk cheese from the province of Udine.

Caciotta (Veneto)   Tasty, fresh cheese made from cow's, goat's, or ewe's milk in the commune of Sant'Ambrogio della Valpolicella. Good with Valpolicella wine.

Carnia (Friuli-Venezia Giulia)   Made from cow's milk, sometimes mixed with ewe's, this tasty cheese is good for eating as well as for grilling or frying to make *fricò,* as it does not melt too much.

Eisacktaler (Alto Adige)   Soft, fresh, or semi-aged cow's milk cheese with a light bloom of mold on the crust; from the Eisacktal Valley.

Grana trentina (Trentino)   Parmesan-type of cheese, hard and grainy; for eating or grating.

Montasio (Friuli-Venezia Giulia)   The great cheese of Friuli, a classic, hard-pressed cheese of great character, available either *fresco* (fresh, with a sweet taste of Alpine meadows) or *stagionata* (aged, with a full, *piccante* flavor and crumbly texture). Also known locally as *latteria.*

Piave (Veneto)   Semi-fat cooked cheese from the Piave Valley with a melting, sweet taste when fresh.

Ricotta affumicata (Friuli-Venezia Giulia, Veneto)   Smoked *ricotta* cheese, produced in the mountains, and aged; for eating and grating.

Vezzena (Trentino)   The greatest zone for the production of *asiago stravecchio* (see above). We consider *vezzena,* with its deep, rich, and complex flavor, one of the great cheeses of Italy.

FRICO

Wherever you visit in Friuli, you are apt to be offered *fricò,* which is no more than grated *montasio* or *carnia* cheese, fried gently in a *padella* (skillet), and served piping hot — *tenera* (soft) like an omelet, to be eaten as a meal with *polenta* (below), or *croccante* (crisp), to nibble as a tasty appetizer with a glass of chilled white wine.

Dolci

SWEETS AND PASTRIES

THE PEOPLE of Northeast Italy undoubtedly have a sweet tooth, for this area of the country probably provides a greater range of delicious pastries, cakes, and desserts than anywhere else (with the exception of Sicily). Austro-Hungarian influence certainly accounts for many of the delicacies, while the Venetians contribute their taste for highly spiced *dolci* flavored with nutmeg, cinnamon, cocoa, and candied fruits.

Krapfken, *fried pastries, typical of Alto Adige*

TRY TO SAMPLE

Ciosota (Chióggia) Delicious cake made with *radicchio di Chióggia;* in flavor and texture like a carrot cake.

Crostoli (the Tre Venezie) Fritters dusted with powdered sugar.

Gubana del Friuli (Friuli-Venezia Giulia) Sweet circular bread, filled with a mixture of dried and candied fruits, pine nuts, walnuts, and chocolate; typically enjoyed with a glass of *slivovitz* (plum brandy) for afternoon tea.

Kaiserschmarrn (Trentino-Alto Adige) Austrian-inspired sweet omelet spread with jam, fruit, and nuts, torn into pieces and rewarmed in a skillet before a dusting with powdered sugar.

Krapfken (Alto Adige) Jam-filled "sandwiches" of fried dough.

Kugelhupf (Trentino-Alto Adige and Friuli-Venezia Giulia) Light yeast cake with raisins and almonds, cooked in a traditional mold.

Lingua di suocera (Veneto) "Mother-in-law's tongue" chocolate biscuits.

Linzertorta (Friuli-Venezia Giulia) Raspberry jam pie covered with a lattice of pastry.

Ossi di morto (Veneto) "Bones of the dead" — little, irregular-shaped, anise-flavored cookies.

Pandoro (Verona and all Veneto) Verona's light yeast cake is a Christmas specialty; available nationally.

Pasta frolla (Verona and Lake Garda) Short-bread biscuit, delicious with a glass of Recioto della Valpolicella.

Polenta dolce di farina bianca (Friuli-Venezia Giulia) Sweet *polenta* made with white cornmeal, sugar, and milk.

Presnitz (Friuli-Venezia Giulia) Easter cake, originally from Castagnevizza (now in Slovenia); a spiral of flaky dough studded with walnuts, raisins, pine nuts, and spices. Popular in Trieste *caffès.*

Putizza (Friuli-Venezia Giulia) Similar to *gubana del Friuli.*

Sachertorte (Alto Adige) Super-rich Austrian chocolate cake.

Strucolo or **strudel** (Friuli-Venezia Giulia and Trentino-Alto Adige) Classic Austrian *strudel* pastry filled with a variety of ingredients; usually *apfel* or *mela* (apple), with grapes, pine nuts, and butter, as well as *ricotta,* nuts, and dried fruit.

Sugolo (the Tre Venezie) Fresh grape must cooked to a concentrate with flour and sugar; to be eaten as dessert.

Torta sabbiosa (Veneto) Plain, meltingly delicious cake made with flour, butter, and sugar; originally from Venice.

Gubana del Friuli, *made with nuts, dried and candied fruit, and chocolate*

Coffee Culture
GREAT COFFEE AND COFFEE HOUSES

WHEN THE VENETIANS began to import green coffee beans in the 17th century, coffee was a novel drink. It had been introduced by the Turks, who had discovered the process of roasting coffee beans in the 14th century. In Constantinople, they established *qahveh khaneh* — the world's first coffee houses. Such establishments were known as "schools of wisdom," because those who frequented them were scholars and poets, people who came as much to discuss important matters as to enjoy this stimulating beverage.

Europe's first great coffee houses were established in Vienna, after retreating Turks abandoned 500 sacks of coffee. The great European coffee houses that proliferated maintained the essential spirit of the coffee houses of Constantinople: they were not merely places of refreshment, but stylish, elegant salons, public drawing rooms where people gathered to to discuss art, literature, and politics. Venice's first great coffee house, Florian's, founded in 1720, still fulfills this role for locals and visitors alike.

Trieste, once Austria's principal port, is a city with a rich coffee culture. Today, some of Italy's leading coffee producers (such as Illycaffè) are located here, and the city still boasts some classic, old-world coffee houses that have remained unchanged for centuries. In Padua, the neo-classic Caffè Pedrocchi built in 1830 became one of the great, historic coffee houses of Europe, an important meeting place for the students, intellectuals, and politicians who aspired to a united Italy.

A table set outside Caffè Florian, Venice

TRIESTE COFFEE–SPEAK

Cappo A *cappuccino,* served in Trieste in a small, *demitasse* cup unless specified.

Cappo in bi *Cappuccino* served in a small glass not a cup.

Gocciato *Espresso* with just a drop or two of milk.

Macchiato *Espresso* "stained" with a little foamed milk, usually served in a large cup.

Nero *Espresso;* a concentrated mouthful of strong black coffee.

Viennese Weak *espresso* topped with whipped cream.

RECOMMENDED COFFEE HOUSES IN NORTHEAST ITALY

PADUA
Caffè Pedrocchi
Via 8 Febbraio, 15
tel/fax: 049/8762576
An institution; open until midnight.

TRIESTE
Caffè Pirona
Largo Barriera Vecchia, 12
tel/fax: 040/636046
Small caffè-pasticceria *frequented by James Joyce.*

Caffè San Marco
Via Battisti, 18
tel: 040/371373
Located behind the synagogue, this place has a pleasant old-world atmosphere.

Caffè Tommaseo
Rive Tre Novembre, 5
tel: 040/366765
On the seafront, a landmark of Trieste.

VENICE
Caffè Florian
Piazza San Marco, 57
tel: 041/5285338
Venice's first, and now famous, coffee house.

Caffè Quadri
Piazza San Marco, 121
tel: 041/5222105
Florian's great rival, on the opposite side of the square.

I Vini

THE WINES OF NORTHEAST ITALY

ONE THIRD of all Italian classified wines (DOC/DOCG) come from Veneto, Trentino-Alto Adige, and Friuli-Venezia Giulia.

The Tre Venezie is the source of vast quantities of sound, honest, "jug wines," sold by the demijohn direct from wine farms and cooperative wineries to bars, restaurants, and private customers. The fine wines that come from here include deeply flavored Valpolicella Classico and rich Amarone and Recioto from the vineyards of Verona; forceful, dry white wines and wood-aged reds from Friuli-Venezia Giulia; Cabernets from Veneto's Colli Eugánei and Treviso; aromatic white wines and soft reds from Trentino and Alto Adige; and vivacious, elegant sparklers such as Prosecco di Valdobbiádene, Cartizze, and elegant *spumante* from Trentino.

VENETO

Bardolino DOC   Light, fruity red and *chiaretto* (rosé) wines are produced from grapes grown on terraced vineyards above Lake Garda. Bardolino *novello* is Italy's answer to Beaujolais *nouveau*, to be drunk within weeks of the harvest.
Recommended producers: Guerrieri-Rizzardi, Masi, Colle dei Cipressi, Portalupi.

Bianco di Custoza DOC   This light dry white wine is most popular in bars and restaurants in Verona.
Recommended producers: Arvedi d'Emilei, Portalupi, Le Vigne di San Pietro, Zenato.

Breganze DOC   The Breganze DOC is less well known than the zone's leading producer, Fausto Maculan, who produces an outstanding range of white and red wines, including superb Cabernets. A rare *passito* wine, Torcolato, made

Vines on the Serègo Alighieri Estate trained as pergolas

from dried Vespaiolo grapes, is a world classic.
Recommended producer: Maculan.

Cabernet Franc   Though both Cabernet Sauvignon and Cabernet Franc are cultivated in Veneto, the latter is particularly well suited to Northeast Italy, producing red wines with a pungent, herbaceous character.

Clinton   This weird wine (known also as Fragola) made from American native grapes has acquired cult status, mainly because it is now illegal to sell it. Try it if you get a chance.

Colli Eugánei DOC   Come to the Colli Eugánei for its hot thermal springs and mud baths and while here, enjoy good zesty Serprina white, fragrant Moscato, and reds made from Raboso, Cabernet Franc, and Merlot.
Recommended producers: Villa dei Vescovi, Sceriman.

Lison-Pramaggiore DOC   This most easterly wine zone in Veneto extends to the border with Friuli. Worth sampling with Adriatic shellfish is the white Tocai di Lison, and with grilled meats, reds from Cabernet and Merlot.

Piave DOC   Piave is a vast wine zone centered on Treviso and extending along both sides of the Piave River valley, the source of much of the sound, everyday drinking wines of Veneto. Best whites are made from Pinot Bianco and Tocai, while the most distinctive red comes from the indigenous Raboso — rasping, vivid, and good with local food.
Recommended producer: Castello di Roncade.

Prosecco di Conegliano-Valdobbiádene DOC   Still, *frizzante* (lightly sparkling), and *spumante*

(fully sparkling) wines are produced from the characterful Prosecco grape on vineyards mainly between Conegliano and Valdobbiádene. The wine may be dry, medium dry, or quite sweet, and is probably Veneto's best and most popular sparkling wine. Select wines from the central classic zone may be labeled Cartizze.
Recommended producers: Case Bianche, Nino Franco, Canevel, Carpenè-Malvolti.
Soave DOC   The best wines come

from carefully tended hill vineyards in the *classico* zone around Soave itself, and have real character, depth of flavor, and a characteristic bitter finish.
Recioto di Soave DOC   Dessert wine made from *passito,* semi-dried grapes.

Grapes laid out to dry on straw-lined trays

Recommended producers: Pieropan, Anselmi, Masi, Tedeschi, Prà.
Valpolicella DOC   Both easy-to-drink as well as serious, well-structured red wines are produced from grapes grown on terraced hill vineyards north of Verona. *Classico* wines from top producers are a revelation of how good real Valpolicella can be: deep in color, intense fruity or floral aromas, with an aftertaste that is always a touch bitter.
Recioto della Valpolicella DOC and **Recioto della Valpolicella Amarone DOC** (the latter known more simply as Amarone) are unusual wines produced from grapes that have been left for months to dry on straw mats in well-ventilated lofts, thus concentrating flavor and intensity. The wines that result, Recioto, sweet; Amarone, completely dry; can be huge and complex with inimitable texture, weight, and bouquet.
Recommended producers: Masi, Quintarelli,

Serègo Alighieri, Allegrini, Tedeschi, Corte Aleardi, Boscaini, La Bionda, Brigaldara.

TRENTINO-ALTO ADIGE
Alto Adige (Südtiroler) DOC
Alto Adige produces a vast variety of red and white wines, from indigenous and international varieties grown at sub-alpine altitudes and vinified to suit local and Germanic tastes. The whites can be outstanding: enjoy those produced from Chardonnay, Riesling Renano (Rhein-riesling), Pinot Grigio (Rülander), Moscato Giallo (Goldenmuskateller), Traminer Aromatico (Gewürztraminer), Sylvaner, and Müller-Thurgau. The reds, from Lagrein, Schiava, and Cabernet, are usually soft, with little harsh tannin.
Recommended producers: Hofstätter, Grai, Haas, Tiefenbrunner, Lageder.
Colli di Bolzano (Bozner Leiten) DOC   Red Schiava wine from the hills around Bolzano.
Casteller DOC   This basic, everyday red wine of Trentino, made mainly from Schiava, is easy drinking and inexpensive.
Recommended producer: Cavit.
Lago di Caldaro (Kalterersee) DOC
Kalterersee is a typical Alto Adige red: soft and easy to drink. Wines from selected extra-ripe grapes may be labeled *Auslese* or *scelto.*
Recommended producers: Hofstätter, Lageder, Tiefenbrunner, Kettmeir, Prima & Nuova wine cooperative.

"ANDAR ALL'OMBRA"
The phrase *"andar all'ombra"* goes back to the time when wine, unloaded straight off boats docked by San Marco, Venice, would be sold from kiosks that moved around the square throughout the day, always staying in the shade — *all ombra* — to keep the wine cool. The term, which means "to go out for a quick one," is used throughout Veneto.

Meranese di Collina (Meraner Hügel) DOC   This light red Schiava wine comes from steep hill vineyards mainly to the north of Merano.

Santa Maddalena (St Magdalener) DOC   Ever since Mussolini praised this as one of Italy's top wines, it has been trying to live up to its reputation. In truth, it is little more than one of the best examples from Schiava grapes — light, soft, and easy to drink.

Sorni DOC   Obscure but interesting wines come from vineyards north of Trento. If you come across it, try the characterful white made from the local grape Nosiola.

Spumante   The Trentino vineyards have long specialized in the production of high quality and prestigious sparkling wines made by the classic method of secondary fermentation in the bottle (like Champagne), mainly from a blend of Pinot Nero, Chardonnay, and Pinot Bianco grapes.

Recommended producers: Ferrari, Equipe 5.

Teroldego Rotaliano DOC This powerful blockbuster is a rich, meaty red produced from Teroldego grapes grown on the Campo Rotaliano between San Michele all'Adige and Mezzolombardo.

Recommended producers: Dorigati, Cantina Sociale di Mezzolombardo, Foradori, Zeni.

Trentino DOC   This large regional *denominazione* covers most of the vineyards of Trentino, and applies to everything from fine premium varietals to inexpensive jug wines. Fine, strong, dry, aromatic white wines are made from Chardonnay, Pinot Bianco, Müller-Thurgau, and Riesling Renano. The most distinctive reds are Marzemino, packed with fresh, berryish fruit, and the sturdy, powerful Teroldego.

Recommended producers: Pojer e Sandri, Dorigati, Cantina Sociale di Mezzocorona, Cantina Sociale di Mezzolombardo, Bossi Fedrigotti, Cavit, Guerrieri Gonzaga, Foradori, Zeni.

Faedo, an important town in the Trentino DOC

Valle Isarco (Eisacktaler) DOC   The Isarco (Eisack) Valley that runs northeast of Bolzano to the Brenner Pass is the source of good white wines, especially Müller-Thurgau, Pinot Grigio (Rülander), and Traminer Aromatico (Gewürztraminer).

Recommended producer: Neustift (Abbazia di Novacella).

FRIULI-VENEZIA GIULIA

Cabernet   Both Cabernet Sauvignon and Cabernet Franc are grown throughout Friuli's vineyards. Elegant red wines, sometimes aged in *barrique* (new French oak) come from Cóllio and Isonzo.

Cóllio DOC   This relatively small wine zone, tucked against the national frontier with Slovenia, produces some of the finest and most exciting white wines in Italy, as well as, increasingly, fine red wines. Most wines come from named single-grape varieties, though some exciting and unusual blends are now emerging (such as Vintage Tunina; see p.119). Traditionalists prefer old varieties, such as the characterful Tocai and Ribolla Gialla. Good reds are made from Cabernet Franc, Merlot, and Pinot Nero.

Recommended producers: Russiz Superiore, Silvio Jermann, Schiopetto, Villa Russiz, Marco Felluga, Gravner, Princic, Gradnik, Puiatti, Conte Attems, Conti Formentini.

Colli Orientali del Friuli DOC
Together with Cóllio, Colli Orientali del Friuli is the most important Friuli wine zone in terms of quality. As in Cóllio, a large number of varietal wines are produced. We like the power and scent of white Pinot Grigio with full-flavored local foods, and juicy, ripe Merlot with meat. Picolit and Ramandolo (see below) are two rare dessert wines of the Colli Orientali worth sampling if you can track any down.
Recommended producers: Dorigo, Dri, L. Felluga, Abbazia di Rosazzo, Volpe Pasini.

Friuli Grave DOC Friuli's largest DOC wine zone extends over most of the southern half of the region, a vast source of sound and sometimes high quality red and white wines.
Recommended producers: Vescovo, Vigneti Le Monde, Plozner, Pighin, Ca' Bolani.

Isonzo DOC Try to sample deeply colored, berryish Isonzo Cabernets and dense, fruit-packed Merlots.
Recommended producers: Attems, Vescovo, Cantina Produttori di Cormons, Vie de Romans, Pecorari, Silvano Gallo.

Picolit Picolit is Friuli's rare and legendary dessert wine. A blight has almost destroyed the vine, and yields are sadly minuscule. The honeyed, floral wines are always expensive, but can be exquisite.
Recommended producer: Dorigo.

Ramandolo Another rare and unusual dessert wine, made from the Verduzzo grape in an amber, oxidized style.

Refosco Red wines made from this characterful local grape in Cóllio and Colli Orientali are deep in color with a rather pleasant, austere, bitter character.

Tocai friulano Much jug wine simply labeled Tocai is served throughout Friuli and Veneto, but this local grape can, at best, produce the finest white wine of the region, especially in the select vineyards of Cóllio and Colli Orientali: dry, full-bodied with a rich, creamy fruit, and a long finish.

I SUPER VINI DA TAVOLA — SUPER TABLE WINES
Foianeghe Rosso This long-established Cabernet/Merlot classic from

Vineyards around the beautiful Lago di Caldaro (Kalterersee), Alto Adige

Bossi Fedrigotti in Trentino is widely available and not expensive.

Pignolo di Dorigo   From the obscure, rare, indigenous Pignolo vine of Friuli, the Girolamo and rosetta Dorigo have created an astonishing, massive wine aged in French *barrique*.

Toar   Masi's sleek "super wine," produced from indigenous Veneto grapes vinified individually and aged in Slavonian and French oak, is a clean, intensely focused wine of great class.

Venegazzù Etichetta Nera   Conte Loredan Gasparini's long-established classic is produced from old vines yielding a mixture of Cabernet Sauvignon, Cabernet Franc, Malbec, and Merlot grapes grown in the wine hills of Treviso.

Vintage Tunina   Silvio Jermann is one of the most innovative winemakers in Friuli, and has demonstrated that great white wines can be created by blending unusual combinations of grapes. This compact, concentrated classic combines Sauvignon and Chardonnay with smaller amounts of Friuli varieties like Ribolla Gialla, Picolit, and Malvasia.

OTHER DRINKS

Amaro Praga   A distinctive, high quality herbal *digestivo* from Trieste.

Grappa   The alpine arc of the Tre Venezie is one of the traditional homes for this fiery distillate, produced from the *vinacce* or wine-drenched grape pomace left over after winemaking. Here, much *grappa* is distilled on a large, semi-industrial scale to satisfy the thirst of a mainly older generation who still find that a shot of the stuff is a daily requisite. However, fine, prestigious, artisan-produced *grappe* for connoisseurs are also distilled, notably in Friuli-Venezia Giulia, where the Nonino family, in particular, produce a highly regarded range of mono-varietal examples from the extensive range of grape varieties of the Friuli vineyards.

The overwhelming preference in the Northeast is for *grappa bianca,* or clear or unaged *grappa,* but wood-aged *riserve grappe* that take on an amber hue, and lose some of their raw, aggressive fire to gain a rich smoothness with time are definitely not to be sniffed at.

Recommended producers: Nardini, Nonino.

FOOD AND WINE COMBINATIONS

Affettati misti   A selection of *salame* from Veneto, including the always rather fatty *soppressa,* is neatly and most pleasantly complemented by a rasping, slightly *frizzante* Raboso del Veneto.

Antipasti di mare   Try a well-chilled Tocai from Friuli's Cóllio to accompany seafood appetizers.

Prosciutto di San Daniele   The exceptionally sweet taste of this great air-cured ham is exquisite when washed down with a creamy, soft Prosecco, especially from the *cru* Cartizze zone.

Brasato all'amarone   This beef-in-wine stew of Verona is best accompanied by — what else? — a fine Amarone della Valpolicella, of course.

Stinco di vitello   This big dish calls for a big wine: a wood-aged Cabernet from Veneto's Treviso or Friuli's Isonzo wine zones or Teroldego Rotaliano from Trentino.

Pasta frolla   This crumbly, not-too-sweet shortbread is the perfect partner for a rich Recioto della Valpolicella.

Gubana del Friuli   Partner this sweet, spiced bread not with wine but with a chilled glass of *slivovitz* (plum brandy).

Asiago stravecchio   We consider *asiago stravecchio,* especially that from the Vèzzena zone of Trentino, to be one of the great cheeses of the world — try it with a glass of an elegant but full wine such as Masi's Toar or Bossi Fedrigotti's Foianeghe Rosso.

Wine Roads of Verona
BARDOLINO, SOAVE, AND VALPOLICELLA

THE WINE COUNTRY outside Verona is some of the most charming and congenial in Italy. Those here for the summer opera season in the Roman arena, or for relaxing beside the shores of Lake Garda, should visit the vineyards. This is not, we stress, a wine tour only for the single-minded — the country is too pretty, too idyllic, too relaxing for that. Meander and explore at your own pace, covering as much as you care to.

WINES AND OLIVE OIL FROM THE SHORES OF LAKE GARDA

Bardolino is probably the most charming and easy Veronese wine zone to discover, its vineyards rising over gentle moraine slopes above Lake Garda. There is a signposted *strada del vino* (wine road), but it is not necessary to follow it. Come to Bardolino itself to visit wine cellars, explore the tiny, walled Venetian lakeside port of Lazise or the more cosmopolitan Garda, a popular tourist center, then, at any point, simply set off into the wine country, through Cisano to Calmasino, Cavaion Veronese, or Affi, all important wine growing centers.

These Lake Garda shores are also known as the Riviera degli Olivi, for they are noted not only for wine but also for fine, peppery, high quality olive oil produced from olives grown amid the vineyards. This *olio extra vergine d'oliva* from Garda is produced only in tiny quantities, but we rank it in the "premier division" of Italian oils. Visit the Museo dell'Olio in Cisano to see how it's made.

There are plenty of places at which to eat and drink in the lakeside towns, but instead try farmhouse restaurants in the wine country, where outstanding if simple local food is served in fine weather at outdoor tables set amid the vineyards.

VALPOLICELLA, A RUGGED LAND

Valpolicella, a wine zone to the east of Lake Garda, which produces the most serious wines (see map), is altogether

The lakeside town of Garda, Veneto

more hardy country, its classic heartland extending primarily over three north–south valleys, the Fumane, Marano, and Negrar. Though the cocktail of local grapes cultivated in Valpolicella is the same as that found in gentle Bardolino, the dry-stone terraced terrain and the higher altitude yield fruit that results in wines of considerable structure and elegance.

The inexpensive jug wines that made Valpolicella an international household name don't come from this classic heartland; rather, they are produced industrially in immense wineries from grapes grown prolifically on the fertile valley floor toward Verona. Low yields, of course, are one key to quality and, thus, the wines produced in the hills can be as serious and noteworthy as those from the plains are forgettable. This is why it is essential for the wine lover to come to the *classico* hill zone of Valpolicella.

From Verona, head northwest to the town of Sant'Ambrogio, and from there, climb to the little hill outpost of San Giorgio to visit its beautiful eighth-century church and to enjoy splendid views over all the Valpolicella vineyards. The Trattoria dalla Rosa Alda, which has a pleasant outdoor terrace, is the wine-growers' favorite and serves local foods and wines from all the best producers.

Go back down the hill and next find Gargagnago, home of the internationally known Masi winery as well as the Serègo Alighieri estate, founded in 1353 by the son of the poet Dante. Today, Count Pieralvise Serègo Alighieri produces fine traditional Valpolicella aged in cherry wood, as well as outstanding Recioto and Amarone, wines that benefit from Masi's technical supervision and marketing. You can buy or sample from the full range of wines on the estate and you can stay overnight in the beautifully restored farmhouse complex, La Foresteria.

From San Pietro in Cariano, make a loop into the high wine country by traveling first to Fumane, then cutting across to Marano, a drive that gives you a vivid demonstration of the classic and rugged Valpolicella terrain. Marano is a small, characteristic wine town and the home of some fine producers, including Boscaini, Valgatara, and Brigaldara. From Marano, continue down to San Floriano, whose simple but beautiful 12th-century church is worth visiting. Then continue through Pedemonte (the Tedeschi family is a notable producer here and can be visited for direct sales) and back up the

Negrar Valley to Negrar itself, where Giuseppe Quintarelli makes legendary wines almost entirely by hand, even down to hand-writing the labels. Guerrieri-Rizzardi is another good private wine estate in Negrar.

Finally, continue to the high, wine hamlet of Mazzano, then pick your way across to Torbe, at the top of the Negrar Valley. Grapes from both these small hamlets were deemed superior as far back as the 12th century when church documents specified them as tithes. Today, the top of this high valley is the source of some of the greatest Amarone and Recioto wines, produced from grapes dried in lofts and airy attics.

From Torbe return to Negrar, and from there back to Verona.

SOAVE, A FINE MEDIEVAL TOWN

Soave is one of the most charming, modest wine towns in Northeast Italy, still medieval in character, dominated by its Scaligero castle, and surrounded by its old town walls. Come here to visit the castle, sample wines, and have a simple snack in the *enoteca*.

Of course, Soave is so well known

VALPOLICELLA WINE COUNTRY

MAZZANO

MARANO   TORBE

FUMANE

SAN GIORGIO

Adige

NEGRAR

SANT'
AMBROGIO   GARGAGNAGO

SAN FLORIANO

To Verona   SAN PIETRO
IN CARIANO

A
N   PEDEMONTE

0 km 1   2
0 miles   1

Grape picking in the Valpolicella wine zone

today because of the immense quantities of wine that flooded international markets during an incredible boom in the 70s. Such wines, including those made by the giant firm Bolla, are generally well-made, clean, and inexpensive. But their shortcoming is that, at best, they are neutral, with little real character, because they are made from high-cropping grapes grown on the plains that fan down towards Verona. It is important, therefore, to come to Soave itself to discover the classic heartland where outstanding wines are produced in limited quantities.

Head southeast into the surrounding hills and make a circuit through the wine country to Monteforte d'Alpone, then north to Costalunga and Roncà and back to Soave via Castelcerino and Costeggiola. This beautiful country is the source of outstanding single vineyard *cru* wines, notably from Roberto Anselmi and Leonildo Pieropan. Recioto di Soave, a dessert wine made from semi-dried grapes, in some cases aged in *barrique,* is a great wine you should try while here.

ANDAR' PER LE VIGNE — INTO WINE COUNTRY

BARDOLINO
Azienda Agrituristica Camporengo
Loc. Camporengo
37010 Cavaion Veronese VR
tel: 045/6280673
Welcoming farmhouse trattoria in vineyards.

Conti Guerrieri-Rizzardi
Piazza Guerrieri
37011 Bardolino VR
tel: 045/7210028
fax: 045/7210704
Opportunities to taste as well as to buy wines.

Museo dell'Olio
Oleificio Cisano del Garda
Via Peschiera, 54
37010 Cisano di Bardolino VR
tel: 045/6229047
fax: 045/6229204
Museum of olive oil with working olive-oil mill; oils and wines for sale.

VALPOLICELLA
Fratelli Tedeschi
Via G. Verdi 4/A
37020 Pedemonte VR
tel: 045/7701487
fax: 045/7704239

A family concern producing world class wines.

La Foresteria di Serègo Alighieri
37020 Gargagnago di Valpolicella VR
tel: 045/7703622
fax:045/7703623
Direct sales of wines, farmhouse accommodation, wine-tastings, and cooking courses.

Masi Agricola S.p.A.
37020 Gargagnago di Valpolicella VR
tel: 045/6800588;598066
fax: 045/598066
Tradition and modern technology in brilliant harmony. Tutored wine-tastings for groups.

Ristorante Albergo dalla Rosa Alda
Strada Garibaldi, 4
Fraz. San Giorgio
Valpolicella
37020 Sant'Ambrogio Valpolicella
tel: 045/7701018
fax: 045/6800411
Local foods and great wine.

SOAVE
Azienda Agricola Anselmi
Via San Carlo, 46
37032 Monteforte d'Alpone VR
tel: 045/7611488
fax: 045/7611490
Taste cru Soaves and the exquisite and rare Recioto dei Capitelli, a dessert classic.

Azienda Agricola Pieropan
Via Camuzzoni, 3
37038 Soave VR
tel: 045/6190171
fax: 045/6190040
Exceptional Soaves, such as the single-vineyard cru Vigneto Calvarino.

Enoteca del Soave
Via Roma, 19
37038 Soave VR
tel/fax: 045/7681588
Good range of local Soaves to taste with simple snacks.

The Südtiroler Weinstrasse

WINE ROADS AND WINE GARDENS

IF YOU ARE in any doubt that Alto Adige is a tiny Austrian outpost in Italy, come to the region in spring, summer, and fall, when, literally, thousands of Austrians and Germans cross over the Brenner Pass and descend on this idyllic country to walk along beautiful Alpine and sub-Alpine footpaths, to eat well, and to quaff the plentiful, easy-drinking wines, all in a country where the first language spoken is German.

A short but lovely signposted wine road, the *Südtiroler Weinstrasse,* leads through some of the most beautiful wine country, through the hill villages along the Adige (Etsch) Valley below Bolzano (Bozen). It is the best wine road in Italy for beauty and enjoying wine in lovely, relaxed wine gardens.

If approaching from the south, leave the *autostrada* at Cortina all'Adige (Kurtinig) and there pick up the sign-posted wine road as it winds through Cortaccia (Kurtatsch), Termeno (Tramin, the original home of the Traminer grape), and Caldaro (Kaltern). Caldaro has become something of the unofficial tourist center due to its position above the deep, alpine lake known as the Lago di Caldaro (Kalterersee). From Caldaro, the route continues through the vine-yards of Appiano (Eppan), Girlan, and finally to Bolzano, atmospheric capital of

Footpath through the vineyards above Lago di Caldaro (Kalterersee), Alto Adige

the Alto Adige, and a fine, manageable city worth visiting.

TORGELLEN

From late October to December, visitors come to Alto Adige to walk in the wine country, and at guest houses and inns, to enjoy *törgellen,* a simple repast of *speck,* cheese, and roasted chestnuts accompanied by the new, still-fermenting wine.

You will come across *törgellen* along the *Südtiroler Weinstrasse* at establishments such as the Plattenhof in Sella, near Termeno; the Törglkeller in Caldaro; and the Wieser in Predonico, near Appiano; or at similar venues.

ANDAR' PER LE VIGNE — INTO WINE COUNTRY

Cantine J. Hofstätter
Rathausplatz, 5
39040 Tramin BZ
tel: 0471/860161
fax: 0471/860789
Obligatory for fans of the aromatic Gewürztraminer: stop here to sample Hofstätter's Kolbenhof cru.

Cantine Tiefenbrunner
Via Castello, 4
39040 Cortaccia BZ
tel/fax: 0471/880122

Try Tiefenbrunner's outstanding Müller-Thurgau and Traminer Aromatico.

Museo Enologico Südtirolese
Via dell'Oro, 1
39052 Caldaro BZ
tel: 0471/963168
fax: 0474/551764
An excellent wine museum, housed in a vaulted wine cellar.

Törglkeller
Bühel, 2
39052 Caldaro BZ
tel/fax: 0471/963421
Simple but tasty food to accompany a range of local wines in this welcoming wine garden.

Indirizzi

USEFUL ADDRESSES

VENETO

Al Granso Stanco
Lungomare Adriatico
30019 Sottomarina Lido VE
tel/fax: 041/491192
Near Chióggia, on the Adriatic lido, this is one of the best fish restaurants around. Bring your swim-suits for a dip afterward.
$$

Antica Locanda Mincio
Via Michelangelo, 12
Loc. Borghetto
37067 Valéggio sul Mincio VR
tel: 045/7950059
fax: 045/6370455
Traditional old favorite by the banks of the River Mincio; come here in fall for exquisite tortelli di zucca.
$$$

Bellinis at the Grand Canal Restaurant, Venice

Azienda Agrituristica Ca' Vignotto
Via Ca' Vignotto
Loc. Chiesa
30401 Sant'Erasmo VZ
tel: 041/5285329
Outstanding traditional farmhouse restaurant on Sant'Erasmo.
$

Caffè Gelateria Causin
Campo S. Margherita
30123 Venice
tel: 041/5236091
Sensational ice creams.

Cantinone Storico
San Vio, 660–661
30123 Dorsoduro VE
tel/fax: 041/5239577
Good Venetian home cooking in a quiet, peaceful neighborhood near the Guggenheim Collection.
$

Da Bruno
Calle Lunga San Bárnaba, 2754/A Dorsoduro
30123 Venice VE
tel: 041/5206978
This humble friggitoria *(fried fish house) is one of few still remaining serving good fried fish, polenta, and other local foods.*
$

Distilleria Nardini
Ponte Vecchio, 2
36061 Bassano del Grappa VI
tel: 0424/227741
fax: 0424/220477
One of Italy's oldest distilleries. A visit to the bar, located at one end of Palladio's famous bridge over the Brenta, to sample grappa *or the Nardinis' own bitter* aperitivo *is a must.*

Enoteca Da Severino
Via del Santo, 44
35100 Padua PD
tel: 049/650697
Atmospheric, classic wine bar and enoteca *serving a wide range of wines by the glass or bottle.*

Harry's Bar
Calle Vallaresso, 1323
San Marco
30124 Venice VE
tel: 041/5285777
fax: 041/5208822
This Venetian institution is worth visiting for the superbly prepared and presented food — mainly Venetian and regional specialties — and unique atmosphere.
$$$

Grand Canal Restaurant
Hotel Monaco e Grand Canal
Calle Vallaresso, 1325
Venice VE
tel: 041/5200211
fax: 041/5200501
Next door to Harry's Bar, the canalside tables are one of our favorite places in town. Come here to eat or simply to enjoy a Bellini while soaking in the sights.
$$$

Ristorante Albergo Posta Vecia
Via Strà, 142
37030 Colognola ai Colli VR
tel: 045/7650243;7650361
fax: 045/6150859
Historic coaching inn on the fringe of Soave vineyards; serves good local and national foods.
$$

Ristorante dell'Hotel Cipriani
Giudecca, 10
Venice VE
tel: 041/5207744
fax: 041/5203930
It is great fun to take the Cipriani private launch to the Giudecca. The elegant restaurant serves foods of the highest quality.
$$$$

Trattoria Buon Pesce
Stradale Ponte Caneva, 625
30015 Chióggia VE
tel: 041/400861
Another good fish restaurant in Chióggia.
$$

Trattoria Stella
Via Valpolicella, 42/A
37020 Arbizzano
Verona VR
tel: 045/7513144
Come here to enjoy true local foods — bigoli stracotto all'Amarone, polenta — in an authentic and welcoming trattoria.
$

Villa dei Vescovi
Via dei Vescovi, 33–39
35038 Livigliano di
Torreglia PD
tel/fax: 049/5211222
*In the wine hills of the Colli
Eugánei, this is a great
informal place to come to.
Sample the wines served
with simple snacks.*
$

TRENTINO–ALTO ADIGE
**Azienda Agrituristica
Maso Nello**
Via Pineta, 3
38010 Faedo TN
tel: 0461/650384
*Outstanding farmhouse
restaurant in the wine
country of Faedo.*
$

Bäckerei Franziskaner
Franziskanerstrasse, 3
39100 Bolzano BZ
tel: 0471/976443
*Alto Adige probably offers
the most varied range of
bread in Italy. Come here
to sample.*

Il Falchetto
Via Regole
Regole di Malosco
38010 Sarnónico TN
tel: 0463/870188
*Mountain refuge serving
exceptional polenta
accompanied by local
smoked meats.*
$

Locanda Port'Aquila
Largo Port'Aquila
38100 Trento TN
tel: 0461/982950
*Long-established source of
genuine foods of Trentino,
including canederli and
smoked meats served with
crauti and polenta.*
$$

FRIULI-VENEZIA GIULIA
Antica Trattoria Suban
Via Comici, 2/d
34100 Trieste TS
tel: 040/54368
fax: 040/579020

Hand-sliced prosciutto *at the
Hosterià Mulin Vecio*

*Historic Trieste institution
serving characteristic
Trieste and Middle
European specialties.*
$$$

**Azienda Agrituristica
Frasca al Cóllio**
Loc. Restocina, 12
34070 Dolegna del Cóllio
GO
tel/fax: 0481/639897
*Farmhouse restaurant
among the vineyards of
Cóllio, serving home-
cooked traditional foods.*
$

Buffet Da Pepi
Via Cassa di Risparmio, 3
34100 Trieste TS
tel: 040/366858
*Near the stock market, this
workers' buffet serves
typical boiled meats
straight from the caldaia
(boiling pot) with sauer-
kraut and horseradish,
washed down with local
Dreher beer.*
$

Hosterià Mulin Vecio
Via Gorizia, 2
34072 Gradisca d'Isonzo
GO
tel: 0481/99783
*This old water mill is a
popular and peaceful place
to visit to enjoy good
house wines, together*

*with superb prosciutto di
San Daniele and other
cured meats, cheese, and
simple snacks.*
$

La Subida
Loc. Monte, 22
34071 Cormons GO
tel/fax: 0481/60531
*Stylish and authentic local
and regional foods.*
$$$

Ristorante Al Bagatto
Via F. Venezian, 2
34100 Trieste TS
tel: 040/301771
*Excellent fish and shellfish
from the Adriatic.*
$$

BEST BUYS
• *grappe* (Veneto and
Friuli-Venezia Giulia)
• *riso Vialone Nano*
(Verona)
• *polenta* flour (the Tre
Venezie)
• *olio extra vergine d'oliva
di Lago di Garda* (Lake
Garda)
• *pandoro* (Verona, but
available everywhere)
• *amaro Praga* (Trieste)
• *speck* (Trentino-Alto
Adige)
• *wines* (Valpolicella, Friuli-
Venezia Giulia)
• *Asiago cheese* (Veneto)

*A canalside market stall in
Venice*

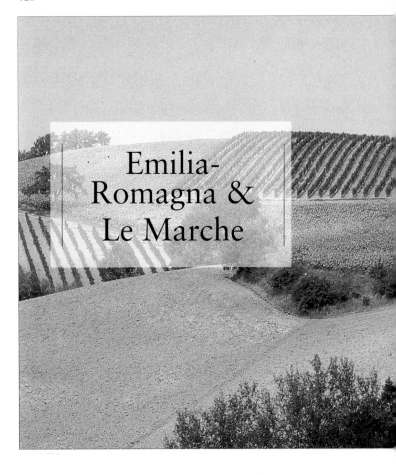

Emilia-Romagna & Le Marche

EMILIA-ROMAGNA AND LE MARCHE are two great gastronomic regions that stretch across almost the entire girth of Italy, from the northwest across to the northeastern seaboard of the Adriatic. In truth, the two regions are linked only geographically, and while the north of Le Marche may be an extension of Romagna's coast, sharing a similar dialect and even food, the rest of Le Marche has a character wholly its own.

Visitors come to both regions mainly in high summer, a time when coastal resorts such as Rimini, Riccione, and Cattólica should be avoided. But even during summer's busiest period, one needs to venture only a few miles inland to experience a quieter, rural world.

EMILIA-ROMAGNA — ABUNDANT AND GENEROUS

Emilia-Romagna is undoubtedly the belly of Italy, the source of so much of Italy's great gastronomic heritage. Many of the classic mainstays of Italian cuisine come from here, including *prosciutto di Parma* (Parma ham), *parmigiano reggiano* (parmesan cheese), homemade egg *pasta* served with *ragù* (meat sauce), *aceto balsamico tradizionale di Modena* (traditional balsamic vinegar), and *mortadella* (the original "baloney" from Bologna). The

Verdicchio vineyards in Le Marche

region was created during the unification of Italy when the hilly maritime province of Romagna was joined to the Emilian plain that extends along the flat Po Valley skirting the foothills of the Apennines. This is not, frankly, Italy's most appealing region to visit. It can be hellishly hot and humid in summer, damp and foggy in winter. Yet this broad, basically flat swath of land counts as one of Italy's most fertile, the source of grain for *pasta,* sugar beets, livestock for both fresh and cured meats, a profusion of good fruits and vegetables, and plentiful if not overly distinguished wines.

However, it is not simply the sheer abundance of fine foodstuffs and raw produce that makes Emilia-Romagna Italy's premier gastronomic region. More importantly, it is the ingenuity, the sheer imagination, the surprising gusto of its culinary heritage that is most remarkable, all the more so for the fact that the region is, on the whole, perhaps a little dull — prosperous, hardworking, yes, the solid backbone of the nation: but rarely a place visitors to Italy may feel compelled to visit.

What Emilia-Romagna lacks in physical beauty, though, she more than makes up for in gastronomic matters. Perhaps, in this industrious, workmanlike land of farmers, it was necessary to develop a diet at once filling and substantial (some might say a touch heavy) which was at the same time sophisticated, at times, almost frivolous. *Pasta,* for example, may be considered the national dish of Italy, but nowhere else in the nation are homemade egg noodles made with more care or in a greater variety of shapes. The undoubted favorite of them all is *tortellini,* a small, stuffed *pasta* said to have been modeled on the navel of the goddess Venus. We should remember, too, that this region is the birthplace of the composer Verdi as well as the most gifted operatic tenor of our era, Luciano Pavarotti, who comes from Modena — those same down-to-earth farmers, those lovers of belly-button *pasta,* are, apparently, among the most critical and hard-to-please of all opera lovers.

Punnets of freshly picked soft fruits from Emilia-Romagna

A great Roman road, the Via Emilia, extends as straight as an arrow across Emilia-Romagna, from Piacenza to Rimini on the Adriatic Coast. Most people today speed along the *autostrada* that parallels it with hardly a second glance. But lovers of Italian gastronomy should certainly pause for a while in towns along the way, such as Parma (famous for much more than merely ham), Reggio nell'Emilia, Modena, and Bologna. Indeed, this is a region that repays a little exploration, for in quiet towns, villages, and in the countryside itself, one finds a country at ease with itself, its natural rhythms a source of prosperity and seeming happiness.

LE MARCHE — A QUIET LAND WHERE THE LIVING IS EASY

Le Marche, so named because the Romans established marquisates in the border country of Ancona, Camerino, and Fano, remains something of a land apart. The mountains, as always, are the great divider, for the spiny range of the Apennines separates Le Marche from other central regions such as Tuscany and Umbria.

This is a region too, that, in its considerable length, bridges the divide between north and south. Certainly, if you arrive at Le Marche by way of either the Via Emilia through Emilia-Romagna to Pésaro or Urbino or by another great Roman road, the Via Flaminia that extends from Rome to the port of Fano (ancient Rome's Fanum Fortunae), the impression is that you are still in Northern Italy. Ancona to the south, with its gently beautiful Castelli di Jesi hinterland, is perhaps more like Central Italy. But by Macerata or Ascoli Piceno, bordering rugged Abruzzo, a subtle transition has undoubtedly taken us into Southern Italy.

The coastal resorts of Le Marche are where most people head to. Resorts stretching down the Adriatic, such as Fano, Senigallia, Portonovo, Grottammare, San Benedetto del Tronto, are all hugely popular (and overcrowded) in August. But even in the high season, life inland is

another world, rural Italy at its best, the rolling hills inevitably cultivated with both vines and olive trees, leading into high mountain passes and isolated, little-visited hill towns. So, even if you are staying on the coast, do try to head into the hills — you will not regret it.

The essential dual character of Le Marche, embracing both sea and land, is reflected in the foods of the region. Along the coast, there is a superlative catch of sweet fish and shellfish from the Adriatic. And, everywhere, this is put to use in the classic fish stew, *brodetto,* which varies considerably from town to town, household to household. Inland, however, the gastronomy of Le Marche is that which has long sustained people living on isolated upland farms — hearty, filling, mainly meat and *pasta* based. Wild foods, which include game such as *lepre* (hare), *coniglio selvatico* (wild rabbit), *cinghiale* (wild boar), as well as wild *funghi* (mushrooms), and black truffles, are everywhere enjoyed.

Fortunately, the wines of Le Marche prove equal partners to the task, the whites such as Verdicchio dei Castelli di Jesi, able to match to perfection the bounty from the sea, while robust reds, such as Rosso Cònero, match in stature and rustic power the full-flavored, hearty foods of the hinterland.

Reaping the harvest, medieval-style — detail from a church, Modena

Prodotti Regionali
REGIONAL PRODUCE

EMILIA-ROMAGNA'S broad, fertile, flat country is farmed intensively, and provides Italy with a large proportion of wheat (to be processed into dried *pasta* as well as fresh *pasta all'uovo*) and sugar beets, the latter processed industrially in immense sugar factories around Ravenna. Indeed, little seems to be done on a small scale, and the valley floor all along the Via Emilia is carpeted with densely cultivated fruit orchards, the source of excellent *pesche* (peaches), *susine* (plums), *albicocche* (apricots), *ciliegie* (cherries), *mele* (apples), *pere* (pears), and *uva* (grapes) both for eating and to be made into wine (most frequently on an industrial scale).

Sun-ripened peach

Le Marche, by contrast, is a region of individuals, not industrialists, of numerous smallholdings where a little bit of everything is cultivated. We have never eaten better fruit than the *pesche* of Le Marche, juicy, firm, exceptionally sweet, and still warm off the tree. And if Emilia-Romagna prefers to lace its cooking with butter or lard, Le Marche is olive country, its oils among the best (and most underrated) in the nation. *Olive ascolane* (enormous, fat olives) are also cured in brine, then stuffed, breaded, and deep-fried — delicious!

Here, wild mushrooms and truffles are gathered in season, but perhaps the most characteristic wild food of all is the *finocchio selvatico* (wild fennel) that grows freely just about everywhere. Its bulb is not eaten as a vegetable; rather, its stalk and seeds are used to flavor any number of foods, especially *porchetta* (roast suckling pig), one of the most characteristic foods.

Tastes here tend toward the strong and not particularly subtle. Wild greens, known simply as *erbe di campo,* and *spinaci* (spinach) are first boiled, then pressed hard, and sautéed *all'agro,* in olive oil with plenty of garlic.

TRUFFLES OF LE MARCHE

Le Marche is not the region most immediately associated with truffles of any sort, but even the Piemontese admit — albeit begrudgingly — that many of the white and black truffles on display at the *Mercato del tartufo* in Alba come from around Acqualagna, a small, unprepossessing town in the foothills of Le Marche's Apennines. Acqualagna is the source of the rarest and most prized of all, *Tuber magnatum pico* or white truffle (see p.72) as well as the *tartufo nero* (winter black truffle), and *bianchetto d'estivo* (summer truffle). These are available fresh as well as conserved in oil or truffle paste all year round. One reliable source is:

Marini Azzolini,
Viale Risorgimento, 26
Acqualagna PS
tel: 0721/798245

TRY TO SAMPLE

Asparagi di Altedo   Highly prized green Emilian asparagus (May–Jun).

Cavolfiore di Jesi   Cauliflower from Jesi (winter).

Ciliegie di Vignola   Cherries from Vignola, considered among the best in the nation (May–Jun).

Olive ascolane   Olives from Ascoli Piceno, best enjoyed in winter when freshly brine-cured. Older olives are stuffed, then deep fried.

Pesche   Peaches from Le Marche (Jun–Jul).

Susine   Plums from Le Marche and from Romagna (Jul–Aug).

Al Mercato
MARKETS

EMILIA-ROMAGNA

Bagno di Romagna	Fri
Bologna	Fri, Sat
Castell'Arquato	Mon
Castel San Giovanni	Sun
Cattólica	Sat
Cesenático	Fri
Comácchio	Wed
Dozza	Sat
Faenza	Tue, Thu, Sat
Ferrara	Mon, Fri
Forlì	Mon, Fri
Forlimpopoli	Sat
Imola	Mon, Thu
Langhirano	Mon
Modena	Mon
Parma	Wed, Sat
Piacenza	Wed, Sat
Ravenna	Sat
Riccione	Fri
Rimini	Wed, Sat
Savignano sul Rubicone	Tue
Ziano Piacentino	Sat

LE MARCHE

Acqualagna	Thu
Ancona	Tue, Fri
Ascoli Piceno	Wed, Sat
Civitanova Marche	Sat
Cupra Marittima	Sat
Cupramontana	Sat
Falconara Marittima	Mon
Fano	Mon, Sat
Grottammare	Thu
Jesi	Wed, Sat
Loreto	Fri
Macerata	Wed
Numana	Wed
Osimo	Thu
Pésaro	Tue
San Benedetto del Tronto	Tue–Fri
Senigallia	Thu
Sirolo	Fri
Stáffolo	Thu
Urbino	Sat

POPULAR *FESTE*
EMILIA-ROMAGNA

Bertinoro
Asta dei vini (wine) Sep
Cattólica
Sagra della rustida di pesce (fish roasting) Jun
Langhirano
Fiera del prosciutto (ham) end Jul
Pellegrino Parmense
Fiera del parmigiano (parmesan cheese) Jul
Vignale
Festa della porchetta (roast suckling pig) end Jul

LE MARCHE

Acqualagna
Mostra mercato del tartufo (truffles) 14–15 Aug and end Oct–beg Nov
Fano
Sagra delle sagre mid Aug
Numana
Sagra del pesce (fish) May
Senigallia
Sagra del pesce (fish) Jun
Stáffolo
Sagra del Verdicchio (Verdicchio wine) mid Jul

Below: Fano market

Piatti Tipici
REGIONAL SPECIALTIES

THE *CUCINA* OF Emilia-Romagna is the *bel canto* of the Italian gastronomic world. Rarely are foods presented unadorned, for this is not rustic country cooking: even seemingly simple, home-prepared foods belie a virtuosity in technique, a refinement in taste that is the hallmark of the region.

Much of what we consider fine Italian cooking comes from Emilia-Romagna, partly because, for a long time, the culture of Italian cooking was based on the precepts of cooks who worked in the courts of nobles and aristocrats in Ferrara, Parma, and Bologna.

Like its broad country, the cooking of Emilia-Romagna is both ample and expansive. Yet this is so vast a region in many ways, its foods so highly developed that one can speak equally not just of the foods of Emilia-Romagna but individually of the *cucine* of Parma, Piacenza, Modena, Reggio nell'Emilia, Bologna, Ferrara, or Ravenna (the provenance of *piatti tipici* is given below as specifically as possible, since some are rarely found outside their town or area of origin).

The *cucina* of Le Marche stands apart: it is the product of both land and sea, following the region's transition from north to south. The northern province of Pésaro comprises part of an area known as Montefeltro which includes not only

Romagna's Rimini but also the state of San Marino and parts of the Tuscan province of Arezzo. Naturally, its cooking reflects all these influences. To the south, by contrast, the foods of Macerata and Ascoli Piceno share traditions with neighboring Abruzzo, and inland areas, especially those connected by the Via Flaminia, share the influence of nearby Umbria.

As in Emilia-Romagna, food varies considerably from village to village. Nothing illustrates this more clearly than the great fish soup of the Adriatic, *brodetto*. Every village and town along the coast has its own way of preparing this magnificent celebration of the sea, each claiming its version as genuine.

ANTIPASTI

Affettati misti (Emilia-Romagna) So good and varied are the prepared, cured pork products of the region that, inevitably, a platter served at the start of a meal is a lavish and ample affair. Such a selection can include *mortadella, salame, coppa, prosciutto di Parma,* and much else (see p.140).

Antipasti di mare (Adriatic Coast) In Rimini, Riccione, Senigallia, Ancona, and all the resorts of the Adriatic Coast, good selections of mixed seafood and shellfish appetizers are offered. Ask to see what is available.

Batù d'oca (Romagna) Goose conserved in its own fat (something like an Italian equivalent of French *confit d'oie*).

Bocconcini alla modenese (Modena) Small "mouthfuls" of bread, layered with *prosciutto crudo, mortadella,* cheese, or truffles, dipped in egg and flour, then deep fried.

Bocconotti alla bolognese (Bologna) Little *vol-au-vents* filled with a rich mixture of chicken giblets or *ragù*.

Ciccioli (Emilia-Romagna) Morsels of pork or goose skin, first par-boiled, then deep fried until crispy, a typical nibble often served with drinks.

Women making stuffed pasta by hand, a labor-intensive task.

Mussels, for antipasti di mare

Crescente, crescentina, gnocco fritto
(Bologna and all Emilia-Romagna)
Yeast dough cut into squares and fried in
oil or lard, to accompany *affettati misti*.
The *gnocco fritto* is similar, studded with
ciccioli or nuggets of *prosciutto crudo* and
either fried or baked in a hot oven.
Crescione (Romagna)   Similar to
piadina (see p.136), this classic snack,
served with drinks, is a disk of
unleavened dough, first filled with any
number of ingredients (*prosciutto,
mozzarella, rucola, salame,* etc.), sealed
around the edges, then cooked on a
griddle so that the filling itself is heated
through.
Culatello di Zibello   This outstanding,
rare, cured pork product may be served
as a dish on its own (see p.142). Savor its
deep aroma and exceptional flavor.
Olive all'ascolana (Le Marche)   Fat,
large *olive ascolane* stuffed with *salame*,
grated cheese, and egg, then breaded and
deep fried.
Pane di Ferrara (Ferrara and all Emilia-
Romagna)   Not strictly an *antipasto*, but
mention should be given here to the
quite fantastically shaped breads of
Ferrara, such as *crocetta* (in the form of a
cross) and *ragnetto* (spider-shaped). The
white bread is always extremely soft and
light, in itself nothing we particularly
enjoy, but a necessary unfilling partner
to the always rich and heavy food of
Emilia-Romagna.
Prosciutto di Parma (Parma and all
Italy)   Though available world-wide,
this outstanding air-cured ham is always

deliciously sweet in its home region. A
plate of wafer-thin slices with bread and
wine is a meal in itself (p.141).

I PRIMI PIATTI
Anolini (Parma)   Parma's specialty is
ring-shaped *pasta* stuffed with a mixture
of ground beef, *parmigiano reggiano*
cheese, breadcrumbs, and seasoning;
usually served *in brodo* (see p.17).
Bomba di riso (Piacenza and Parma)
Mold of rice, filled with a rich mixture
of pigeon, eggs, mushrooms, and
sausage. Traditionally eaten on the *Festa
della Madonna*, August 15.
Cannelloni ripieni di tortellini
(Emilia-Romagna)   For real *pasta* lovers:

Crescione

fresh sheets of *pasta* filled and rolled with
a stuffing of *tortellini*, smothered in a
creamy cheese sauce, and baked.
Garganelli (Romagna)   Homemade
maccheroni, usually made *al pettine*, i.e., by
rolling over a special "comb."
Gramigna con la salsiccia (Modena)
Thick spirals of tube-shaped, *spaghetti*-
like *pasta;* usually served with a tomato
sugo (sauce) made with sausages.
Lasagne alla bolognese   This classic
dish has been "internationalized," but it
is no less delicious for that — sheets of
fresh *pasta sfoglia*, layered with *ragù* (meat
sauce) and a *besciamella* sauce, topped
with plenty of *parmigiano reggiano* cheese,
and baked.
Maltagliati e fagioli (Emilia-Romagna)
Irregular shapes of fresh *pasta* served in a
rich broth with *borlotti* beans.

Passatelli in bródo (Emilia-Romagna and Le Marche)   *Passatelli* are made from a soft paste of breadcrumbs, beaten egg, grated cheese, a little beef marrow, and nutmeg, forced through a sieve to make long *spaghetti*-like noodles. They are poached and served in a concentrated meat broth.

Pasticcio alla ferrarese (Ferrara) Another sumptuous, outrageously rich court dish consisting of a baked pastry case filled with *pasta* in a rich, truffled white sauce or meaty *ragù*.

Spaghetti con le moscioli (Ancona and the Riviera del Cònero)   Classic coastal *pasta* dish of *spaghetti* served in a tomato sauce with fresh mussels.

Strozzapreti (Romagna)   "Priest stranglers," made from a dough of flour, salt, and water, with no addition of egg,

Coniglio in porchetta

formed into long, squarish noodles, and served with a sauce of fresh vegetables or *ragù*. Rather heavy and hard to swallow, hence the name.

Tagliatelle asciutte con fagioli (Emilia-Romagna)   Very typical "poor people's" dish of fresh ribbon noodles served "dry" with boiled *borlotti* beans moistened with a little broth.

Vincisgrassi (Le Marche)   Classic and sumptuous baked *pasta* made with sheets of *lasagne* layered with a thick white sauce enriched with truffles and *prosciutto*.   The name comes from an Austrian general, Windisch-Graez, who served in the region during the Napoleonic Wars.

I SECONDI PIATTI

Agnello alla cacciatora (Montefeltro) A version of a national hunter's favorite: cubes of lamb stewed in olive oil or lard, white wine, and flavored with sage and wild fennel.

Agnello alla romagnola (Romagna) Cubes of lamb stewed in wine, with tomatoes, and, in season, fresh peas.

Bollito misto all'emiliana (Emilia-Romagna)   Many *pasta* dishes in the region are served with the rich cooking broth that results from *bollito misto;* here, an immense selection of boiled meats, including beef, pork, tongue, shin of veal, and boiling *salame* or *zampone*.

Coniglio all'aceto balsamico (Modena)   Wild rabbit stewed in wine, then finished with a spoonful or two of thick, flavorsome *aceto balsamico tradizionale di Modena* (see p.137).

Coniglio in porchetta (Le Marche) A great regional specialty — rabbit (boned or whole), stuffed with wild fennel, *pancetta* or lard, plenty of garlic and seasonings, then baked in a hot oven.

Frittata al balsamico (Modena)   One of the best vehicles for tasting real *aceto balsamico* — a simple *frittata* (omelet) over which a little *aceto balsamico* is dribbled.

Fritto misto all'emiliana (Emilia-Romagna)   Wide selection of foods, including chicken breast, sweetbreads, lamb chops, apple slices, and nuggets of cheese, coated in batter or egg and breadcrumbs, then deep fried.

Grigliata mista di carne (Emilia-Romagna and Le Marche)   This is meat-eating country, so great platters of grilled meats are often offered in restaurants — *castrato* (lamb or mutton chops), *costolette di vitello e maiale* (veal and pork cutlets), *salsiccie* (sausages) — usually served with hot *piadina* (see p.136). Dig in with your fingers.

Lattonzolo (Emilia-Romagna) Suckling pig, usually roasted.

Lumache in umido (Emilia-Romagna) Snails stewed in tomatoes and wine.

Spaccasassi *with fresh anchovies*

Oca in potacchio (Le Marche)
Another regional classic — pieces of
goose slowly stewed in wine, with garlic,
rosemary, and *peperoncini*. The same
method can also be used for *coniglio*
(rabbit) or *pollo* (chicken).

Porchetta alla marchigiana (Le
Marche)   *Porchetta* is popular
throughout Central Italy — a whole
suckling pig stuffed with wild fennel,
rosemary, garlic, and plenty of black
pepper, then roasted in a wood-fired
oven. Often available from street stalls.

Trippa alla parmigiana (Parma and all
Emilia)   Tripe that has first been boiled,
then slowly cooked in a casserole with a
sauce made from *prosciutto crudo*,
chopped vegetables, and tomatoes and
topped with grated *parmigiano reggiano*
and finished in the oven.

Zampone (Modena)   Modena's classic
boiling *salame*, a stuffed pig's trotter, is a
winter favorite throughout the region,
served most characteristically with lentils
and fruit mustard. It is almost obligatory
throughout the country to enjoy a slice
or two and a bowl of lentils during the
late night/early morning *Capo d'anno*
festivities, for it is said to be a harbinger
of good luck for the New Year.

I CONTORNI
Cardi alla parmigiana (Emilia-
Romagna)   Cardoons (delicious edible
thistles), boiled first, then baked either
with a topping of *ragù* or simply covered
with grated *parmigiano reggiano* cheese
and butter.

Erbe di campo (Le Marche)   Wild
edible greens, boiled, then squeezed out
and sautéed with olive oil and garlic.

Mischianza, misticanza (Emilia-
Romagna and Le Marche)   Salad made
from a variety of wild greens and herbs
(see Angelo's Herb Garden p.136).

Spaccasassi (Le Marche, especially
around Riviera del Cònero)   Type of
sea vegetable that clings to the rocks,
usually boiled then conserved in vinegar,
to accompany seafood *antipasti*.

I DOLCI
Bensone (Modena)   Sweet flat bread
studded with raisins and other dried fruits.
Delicious with a medium-dry Lambrusco.

Bonissima or **sarzenta** (Modena)
Shortbread pastry with nuts and honey
and covered in chocolate.

Castagnole (Emilia-Romagna)
Chestnut fritters.

Ciambella (Emilia-Romagna and Le
Marche)   Simple ring-shaped cake
made from flour, sugar, and eggs.

Piconi (Le Marche)   Shortcrust
"raviolo" filled with *ricotta* cheese, eggs,
sugar, nuts, chocolate, and rum.

Torta di ricotta (Emilia-Romagna)
Simple, delicious "cheesecake" made
with *ricotta* cheese and usually decorated
with fresh fruits.

Torta di tagliatelle (Emilia-Romagna)
Shortcrust pie base filled with a mixture
of dried fruits and nuts, then covered
with extremely fine *tagliatelle* noodles
and sugar and baked.

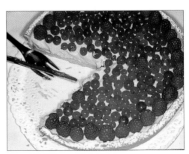

Torta di ricotta

La Piadina
LOCAL FAST FOOD

WHAT THE *PIZZA* is to other parts of Italy, the *piadina* is to Romagna and the north of Le Marche: not simply a fast food but a convivial, social one, eaten with the fingers, and accompanied with tumblers of fresh, local wines. Basically, it is no more than *pane schiacciato* or flat bread, patted out with the hands rather in the fashion of a Mexican cornmeal *tortilla,* then cooked briefly and quickly on a hot griddle. The Romagna version, made from no more than flour and water, is thickish and chewy, while that from Montefeltro and north of Le Marche, made with olive oil and lard, is both thinner and more flaky in texture.

Always cooked to order, the still piping-hot flat bread, scorched and all the more appetizing for the black, burned bits on the surface, is then simply layered with any number of toppings, including *prosciutto crudo, salame,* fresh salad vegetables such as *rucola* or *radicchio* dressed in olive oil, tomatoes and *mozzarella, squacquerone* (a bland, soft curd cheese), or *erbe di campo* (wild greens) stewed in garlic and olive oil. In short, *piadina* is a vehicle for whatever toppings and flavors you care to use. Most of all, it is a communal food that satisfies the appetite, promotes a healthy thirst for local wines, and contributes to a friendly and informal atmosphere.

Making piadina *at the Cá de Bé, Bertinoro, in the wine hills of Romagna*

ANGELO'S HERB GARDEN

Aromatic herbs are not usually associated with the cuisine of Emilia-Romagna. Yet, outside Modena, restaurateur Angelo Lancellotti has created an organic herb garden and *orto* (vegetable garden) around whose produce a particularly rich and imaginative *cucina* is based. Intensely perfumed herbs aromatize sides of *pancetta* (cured belly pork) and flavor wafer-thin slices of beef seasoned with the Lancellotti's own produced *aceto balsamico tradizionale di Modena.* Fine homemade *tagliolini* noodles are dressed with no more than an abundance of chopped herbs, together with a little butter and cheese. And, as a counterbalance to the otherwise heavy foods of Emilia-Romagna, Angelo has created a fresh, intensely flavored herb salad, *la mischianza,* consisting of a variety of fresh herbs and lettuce dressed simply in *aceto balsamico tradizionale di Modena* and extra-virgin olive oil.

Ristorante Lancellotti
Via Achille Grandi, 120
41019 Soliera MO
tel: 059/567406
fax: 059/565431
$$

Aceto Balsamico Tradizionale di Modena
TRADITIONAL BALSAMIC VINEGAR

The real thing

IN ANCIENT ATTICS in Modena that date from the Middle Ages, on noble estates and in farms throughout the outlying country, a secret treasure lies aging: *aceto balsamico tradizionale di Modena.* This is one of the greatest gastronomic specialties of Italy, and one of the most rare. Today, out of tradition and sheer passion, and certainly not for commercial reasons, *aceto balsamico tradizionale di Modena* continues to be produced by age-old methods in tiny quantities primarily for home use, as well as to be sold in limited amounts to the public — at great and seemingly exorbitant expense (a tiny flagon containing 100 ml. or 3¼ fl. oz. currently costs about 130,000 *lire*).

Real *aceto balsamico tradizionale di Modena* is a magnificent condiment that bears virtually no resemblance either to common vinegar or to the industrially produced fake. The genuine article is produced from the fresh juice of Trebbiano grapes, cooked in open copper cauldrons to reduce its volume by as much as two-thirds. This thick, concentrated grape must is then put into a series of wooden casks that vary progressively in size, all made of different woods (oak, chestnut, mulberry, cherry, juniper, and others). Over decades, the *aceto balsamico* passes through the battery of barrels, gently mellowing as it reduces, gaining in intensity of flavor and perfume. Only those vinegars that have aged sufficiently (for a minimum of 12 years but, in most cases, for far longer) and that pass a rigid tasting panel, organized by the *consorzio* that serves to protect it, are entitled to be sold as *aceto balsamico tradizionale di Modena.*

Concentrated and viscous, with a rare complexity of *agrodolce* (sweet and sour) and wood tones, this traditional product is unbelievably long and persistent in flavor. It is used in the smallest quantity only — a coffee spoonful is sufficient — over the simplest dishes, such as a vegetable *frittata,* boiled meats, a dish of *fior di latte* ice cream.

Sample the real thing when you are in the region, and visit a traditional *acetaia.* Remember, only *tradizionale* is sold in the special, uniform 100-ml. (3¼-fl. oz.) flagons, so beware of imitations.

However, producers of traditional *aceto balsamico* may part with younger samples (sometimes labeled *condimento balsamico*), that can demonstrate the character if not the concentration of the real thing, at affordable prices.

Conti Guidotti Bentivoglio
Corso Cavour, 60
41100 Modena MO
tel/fax: 059/234283

Italo Pedroni
Via Risaia, 2
41015 Rubbiara di Nonántola MO
tel: 059/549019
fax: 059/547514

Ermes Malpighi
Via A. Pica, 310
41100 Modena MO
tel: 059/280893
fax: 059/280361

The slow drip-drip as aceto balsamico tradizionale di Modena *makes its way through different barrels*

Pasta all'uovo

HAND-MADE EGG PASTA

EMILIA-ROMAGNA is Italy's foremost region for *pasta*. The immense and ingenious variety of *pasta* invented and regularly enjoyed here is unrivaled. Furthermore, Emilia-Romagna is the only region in Italy where such a vast assortment of *paste all'uovo* (egg *pasta*) is still produced fresh daily by hand, in simple and grand restaurants alike, as well as in many homes. Make no mistake: fresh *pasta* may be widely available nationally (indeed, internationally) but, good though it can be, it is not a patch on *pasta* hand-made from no more than flour and eggs (even water is shunned), using only a large wooden board, a long rolling pin, a knife, and perhaps some wooden instruments to help form special shapes.

Signora Ida Marverti Lancellotti, at the family *trattoria* in Soliera outside Modena (see p.136), makes *pasta sfoglia* (sheets of egg *pasta* dough) as often as three times a day. She demonstrated to us this deceptively simple art. "I calculate an egg per *etto* (100 g. or about ¼ lb.) of flour,"

she said as she proceeded to spoon out with her hand — with no recourse to even so much as a measuring cup — a pile of soft cake flour *(tipo 00)*. Into this, she made a well, broke in four eggs, then blended the mixture first with a fork then with her hands until it became a smooth, elastic, and extremely yellow dough. She worked this vigorously, turning and kneading and pressing and kneading. Then, only when she deemed it to be sufficiently smooth and elastic, did she begin to roll it out using a long wooden rolling pin: thinner and thinner, larger and larger, until the paper-thin sheet of dough virtually covered the large wooden board.

"Of course, in my day, if a young woman did not know how to make *pasta sfoglia* she had little chance of finding a husband. Here," she said, gripping us warmly, "feel my hands. Fortunately, I have always had warm hands. Much better for making *pasta*." Once the *pasta* had been rolled out, Signora Lancellotti proceeded to transform the sheet magically into scores of different forms and shapes: *maccheroni al pettine,* rolled around a little wooden dowel then over a ribbed wooden *pettine* (comb) to give it texture; *farfalle* (butterflies); and *cestini* (little baskets), "as they do in Bologna,"

Signora Ida Marverti Lancellotti demonstrating the fine art of making egg pasta: *(top left) eggs and flour, the sole ingredients; (bottom left) rolling out the dough on the table; (below) forming* maccheroni al pettine

she added. Once the sheet had dried out a bit more, she hand-cut *tagliatelle* and thinner, spaghetti-like *tagliolini,* and made the diamond-shaped *maltagliati* to serve with beans. She gathered up all the odd *pasta* scraps, then cut little *quadrucci* (squares) to add to soups. "Our generation never wastes anything. Not like young people today."

TRY TO SAMPLE

Capelli d'angelo   Fresh, extremely fine "angel's hair" *pasta,* usually served *in brodo.*

Cappellacci   Large, stuffed *pasta* (rather like *tortelli*) from Ferrara, usually filled with *zucca* (pumpkin) in season.

Cappelletti   This favorite *pasta* of Reggio nell'Emilia is similar to *tortellini,* filled with four types of meat, and served *in brodo.* Cappelletti are also popular in Northern Marche.

Maccheroni al pettine   This specialty of Modena (the same *pasta* in Bologna is called *garganelli*) is homemade *maccheroni* turned over a wooden "comb" to give it ribbing — usually served with *ragù.*

Tagliatelle   The simplest *pasta* of all — strips of noodles cut from the sheet of *pasta sfoglia.* When the dough is made with fresh spinach, it becomes *tagliatelle verdi. Tagliatelle* is usually served with *ragù* in winter, or with a sauce of fresh vegetables in summer.

Tortelli alla parmigiana   Another favorite of Parma, large stuffed squares of *pasta* filled with cooked mixed green vegetables, *ricotta* cheese, beaten eggs, and seasoning, served with melted butter and grated *parmigiano reggiano* cheese.

Tortellini   The famous "belly-button"-shaped *pasta* is best made fresh by hand and can have various stuffings. The usual mixture combines pork, *prosciutto crudo,* perhaps some *mortadella,* with eggs, *parmigiano reggiano* cheese, and nutmeg. *Tortellini* are most typically served *in brodo,* but can also be enjoyed *alla panna* (with cream) or *con ragù* (with meat sauce).

Ida Lancellotti proudly displaying the finished products: a variety of fresh egg pasta

Tortelloni   Large, fresh, stuffed *pasta,* often with *ricotta* cheese, spinach, and *parmigiano reggiano* cheese. Can be served *in brodo,* in a cream sauce or with butter, fresh sage, and grated cheese.

RAGU

The famous *ragù,* or meat sauce, of Emilia-Romagna is served all over Italy (and the world), but it is best in its homeland: a slowly simmered and richly concentrated mixture of hand-chopped meats (pork, beef, veal, *prosciutto crudo*) cooked with chopped onions, carrots, tomatoes, wine, seasoning, and broth. For *pasta* lovers, there is little that can beat hand-made egg noodles topped by homemade *ragù.*

Salumi
CURED PORK PRODUCTS

Emilia-Romagna is the kingdom of the pig. Most of the region's numerous cheese dairies maintain their own *porcile* (pig farm) just behind the cheese-making facilities, for the enormous quantity of whey that is a by-product of *parmigiano reggiano* cheese serves as an excellent, nutritious food for pigs. The pigs' meat subsquently makes the sweetest *prosciutto di Parma* and other cured pork products. Indeed, the range of such products in Emilia-Romagna, produced mainly on an industrial scale, is immense. Le Marche, on the other hand, makes smaller but no less delicious quantities of such cured meat products, more usually on an artisan scale.

Cubed mortadella *served with bread*

TRY TO SAMPLE

Cappello da prete (Modena) Unusually shaped boiling *salame* — tri-cornered like a "priest's hat," made with a mixture similar to that of *zampone* (see below).

Coppa (Emilia-Romagna) Cylindrical cured *salume* made with meat from the shoulder and head, seasoned with plenty of black pepper and spices, then aged for at least six months. The best comes from Piacenza.

Coppa marchigiana (Le Marche) Made from the pig's head, highly seasoned with peppers, nutmeg, and orange peel. Usually eaten warm.

Cotechino (Emilia-Romagna and Le Marche) Good boiling *salame* usually served with other boiled meats as part of *bollito misto* or with lentils and mashed potatoes.

Culatello di Zibello Rare, cured delicacy (see p.142).

Fiocchetto (Emilia-Romagna) Cut from the leg of pork similar to *culatello* (but inferior in quality), moderately salted, and aged for at least three months.

Lonza (Le Marche) Tenderloin of pork, cured in salt, black pepper, and garlic.

Mazzafegato (Le Marche) Ground pig's liver, lung, and other variety meats, highly seasoned and lightly smoked.

Mortadella (Bologna and all Emilia-Romagna) The best *mortadella* comes from Bologna and is made from a mixture of finely ground lean and fat pork in proportions of about 60 per cent lean to 40 per cent fat, studded with whole black peppercorns and (sometimes) pistachio nuts, and encased in a natural skin.

Prosciutto di Carpegna (Le Marche) Outstanding *prosciutto crudo* cured in salt, plenty of black pepper, vinegar, and sometimes juniper berries; usually, but not always, smoked.

Prosciutto di Montefeltro (Montefeltro) *Prosciutto crudo* cured in salt and pepper then covered in a paste of cooked grape must seasoned with garlic and rosemary. Aged for a minimum of 12 months.

Prosciutto di Parma Renowned air-dried ham (see opposite).

Salame marchigiana (Le Marche) Good, meaty *salame,* usually rather chewy and highly spiced.

Spalla cotta (Emilia-Romagna) Cooked shoulder of ham.

Zampone (Modena) Ground pork seasoned with salt, pepper, nutmeg, and saffron, stuffed into a pig's trotter; traditionally served boiled with lentils.

Prosciutto di Parma

THE MOST FAMOUS HAM IN THE WORLD

THE ROLLING HILLS that tumble down from the Apennines to the south of Parma between the valleys of the Enza and Stirone Rivers have been the source of cured hams since before the Roman era. The dry winds that arrive from the Tyrhennian Sea on the other side of the mountains, sweetened with the scents of olive groves and pine forests, provide the ideal climatic conditions for curing and aging of dried hams.

Today, in a small and strictly delimited area south of the Via Emilia and up to 900 m. (about 3,000 ft.) in altitude, around towns and villages, such as Langhirano, Traversétolo, and Lesignano de' Bagni, the aging lofts of specialist ham producers are easily identified by their tall, narrow windows that face the mountains, allowing the dry, scented air to pass through to air-cure the hams.

The process of curing Parma ham starts with fresh hams from selected pigs raised in a delimited area. The hams are dry-salted, with no other seasoning or preservative, then left to cure for a period of about three weeks. This phase, known as *la salagione,* is fundamental, for the salt is

slowly absorbed throughout the meat by a natural process of osmosis. By contrast with other air-dried hams, this salting is very light, which is why Parma ham remains incomparably sweet, the texture of the meat soft, not dried out and hard. Afterward, the excess surface salt is washed off and the hams are left in a cold, humid room for between two and three months, thus slowly allowing the salt fully to penetrate and cure the meat.

During the final phase, known as *la stagionatura,* the hams are hung up to cure in the airy ham lofts. Here, they ripen and mature, gaining in intensity and sweet-

ness of flavor for which Parma ham is renowned. The total period of aging for Parma ham is between ten and 12 months, depending on the size of the ham (an average *prosciutto di Parma* weighs 7 kg. or 15½ lbs. when finished). Only hams that have passed various con-

The ducal brand, a guarantee of quality

trols undertaken by the *consorzio* (the organization that oversees and ensures quality and promotion) are entitled to be branded with the ducal crown and to be sold as *prosciutto di Parma.*

Parma ham is undoubtedly one of the great gastronomic products of Italy. As it is widely available throughout the nation and, indeed, the world, it is not actually necessary to come to its zone of production to sample it. Ham connoisseurs, nonetheless, may wish to head into the hills south of Parma (especially around Langhirano) to track down this famous delicacy to its source. However, as most Parma ham producers operate on a fairly large scale (much larger, for example, than at San Daniele del Friuli, see p.109), opportunities for visiting ham lofts and purchasing direct are somewhat limited.

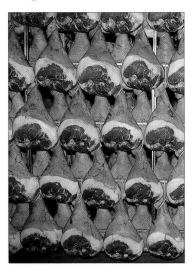

Prosciutti di Parma *aging in a ham loft in Langhirano*

Culatello di Zibello
A RARE PORK DELICACY

THE BASSA PARMENSE, to the north of Parma, lies in the basin of the great Po Valley, flat, interminably hot and humid in summer, and damp, cold, and foggy in winter. Verdi came from here, and scholars and musicians still descend on the tiny towns of Róncole Verdi and Busseto, where, respectively, the composer was born and later studied. Today, the Bassa is also known among *cognoscenti* as the source of Italy's rarest and perhaps greatest of all *salumi* products, *culatello di Zibello*. Indeed, so scarce, and so difficult to find, is genuine *culatello* that it is not going too far to say that a veritable cult has arisen around the production of this exalted pork product.

Cavaliere Colombo Ramelli inspects culatello *with the aid of a* tasto

"*Culo*" is a word not normally used in polite company, but it describes the cut of meat utilized to produce this most select product, which comes from the rump of a large, specially bred pig. As this nugget of pure meat is sliced out of the *prosciutto,* making it impossible to use the rest of the ham for that already highly valued product, one realizes why *culatello* is so rare and expensive. *Culatello,* moreover, cannot be made successfully on an industrial scale (commercial versions bear little resemblance to the original), so intuitive and delicate is its production and aging.

Whereas *prosciutto di Parma* traditionally gains its inimitable flavor and sweetness from curing in the dry, airy hills south of Parma, *culatello,* by contrast, must age slowly in the humid, foggy lowlands of the Bassa Parmense, in or around tiny towns such as Zibello, Polésine Parmense, and Roccabianca.

Only in this humid microclimate can the *culatello,* still warm from the freshly slaughtered pig, be successfully prepared: rubbed first in a secret *concia* (marinade) of salt, spices, and wine, then skillfully tied into a pear-shaped pig's bladder, and hung up to age slowly. In the process, a high proportion may spoil, but those that finally emerge successfully cured have acquired an intensity of flavor, a deep, pungent scent, and sheer sweetness that is unrivaled.

Cavaliere Colombo Ramelli, whose family has been making *culatello* for generations to serve at the Trattoria Colombo in Santa Franca, near Polésine Parmense, plunged a horsebone instrument, *il tasto,* into a mature *culatello* that had been aging for some 18 months, sniffed it critically, then laughed for sheer joy. The aroma was intense; the flavor, incredibly deep yet profoundly sweet; the texture firm but still soft, almost creamy. Come to the lowlands of the Bassa Parmense to sample this rare delicacy.

Trattoria Colombo
Via Mogadiscio, 119
Santa Franca
43010 Polésine Parmense PR
tel: 0524/98114
fax: 0524/98003
$$$

Trattoria La Buca
Via Ghizzi, 6
43010 Zibello PR
tel: 0524/99214
fax: 0524/99720
$$$

Sliced culatello, *deeper, more intense in flavor than* prosciutto di Parma

Pesce e Frutti di Mare

FISH AND SHELLFISH FROM THE ADRIATIC

THE ADRIATIC COAST south of the mouth of the Po River along Emilia-Romagna's seaboard and along that of Le Marche to its border with Abruzzo is the most important in Italy in terms of quantity of fish landed. Neither fish nor tourists seem to have been put off by the industrial pollution that mars these coastal waters, for the fish and shellfish from these waters are probably as sweet and tasty as those found anywhere in the Mediterranean.

Fritto misto di mare

Most towns along the coast have a daily fish market. Come to browse, and purchase if you have cooking facilities. Otherwise, sample some of the following in restaurants and *trattorie* on the coast.

TRY TO SAMPLE

Anguilla alla comacchiese (Romagna) Comácchio eels are reputed to be among the fattest and most tasty in Italy: this typical fisherman's stew combines them with a vinegar-laced tomato sauce.

Balleri (Ancona and the Riviera del Cònero)   Local name for *datteri di mare* (sea date), a rare bivalve that is delicious made into a rich seafood soup.

Brodetto (Adriatic Coast)   Classic fish stew of the Adriatic, with versions varying from town to town. Most famous is that of Ancona, made with no fewer than 13 different types of fish and shellfish. Usually the fish are tiny (no more than 6–7 cm. or about 3 in.), bought in mixed batches ready to cook. The concentrated broth, which may or may not include tomato and saffron, can be served with *pasta*.

Cannelli (Romagna)   Local term for *cannolicchi* (razor-shell clams), sometimes served *gratinata* (broiled with a topping of breadcrumbs), used to make a tasty soup, or served over hot *pasta*.

Fritto misto di mare (Adriatic Coast) A selection of small fish, floured, then deep fried.

Moscioli (Ancona)   Local name for *cozze* (mussels).

Poveracce, poverazze (Romagna) Local name for *vongole* (clams).

PESCE AZZURRO

The waters of the Adriatic are rich in *pesce azzurro* ("blue" fish) including the *acciuga* or *alice* (anchovy), *sardina* (sardine), *sgombro* (mackerel), and *suro* (horse mackerel). Such "blue" fish, rich in oil and highly nutritious, have traditionally been the staple of fishermen. One of the best places to enjoy such fresh fish is in Fano, a resort near Pésaro, where the Comarpesca fishing cooperative runs, in season, an excellent and inexpensive self-service restaurant.

Self-service Al Pesce Azzurro
Viale Adriatico, 48
61032 Fano PS
tel: 0721/803165
fax: 0721/805523
$

Parmigiano Reggiano
PARMESAN CHEESE

K NOWN THROUGHOUT the world simply as parmesan, *parmigiano reggiano* is one of the greatest and most distinctive of all of Italy's many gastronomic gifts to the world. *Parmigiano reggiano* is a wholly unique cheese, produced from unpasteurized cow's milk in strictly delimited zones (the provinces of Parma, Reggio-Emilia and Modena, as well as parts of the provinces of Mantova and Bologna), and is made almost entirely by hand.

The process begins early each morning, when the day's milk is brought to the *casello* (cheese dairy) to be

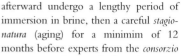

Parmigiano reggiano *cut in chunks for eating*

mixed with the partially skimmed milk from the previous evening. Some 1,100 liters (275 gallons) of milk are poured into each large copper-lined cauldron, whose inside is like the smooth, inverted interior of a bell. This huge quantity of liquid will, by the end of the morning, through the application of starter, rennet, heat, and much arduous manual labor, eventually yield two wheels of fresh cheese, each weighing about 36 kg. (80 lbs.). Such cheese may or may not become *parmigiano reggiano,* for it must

afterward undergo a lengthy period of immersion in brine, then a careful *stagionatura* (aging) for a minimim of 12 months before experts from the *consorzio* deem whether it merits their prestigious accolade.

Cheeses that do not make the grade have the rind defaced with Xs; such cheeses, however, are by no means inedible: they can be delicious, sold as *grana da pasto* to eat young, but are simply unsuitable for the lengthy aging necessary to become *parmigiano reggiano.* Especially good *parmigiano reggiano* cheeses are aged for up to three years and are designated *parmigiano reggiano stravecchio.*

There are some 600 *caselli* entitled to make *parmigiano reggiano,* ranging from small family enterprises turning out no more than one or two cheeses a day to cooperatives that may make as many as a dozen. It is worth venturing out into the country, on or off the Via Emilia, to visit a *casello* (preferably early in the morning) to witness the hand production of this great cheese, and to buy a large wedge.

We visited a cooperative dairy south of Modena where husband and wife

La spinatura: *Vitaliano Vignali cutting curds with* il spino

Maria and Vitaliano lifting the curds out of the whey in a cheesecloth

Vitaliano and Maria Vignali together with a few other helpers turn out between eight and 12 cheeses a day, every day of the year.

It was remarkable to witness the arduous process, as the milk was first heated, stirred, and curdled with rennet, separating into milk solids and whey. Vitaliano then rhythmically cut up the curds to the consistency of rice using a traditional, basket-like instrument known as *spino*. The curds were cooked again, the temperature allowed to rise to 55°C (131°F). When the curds had been cooked for long enough (Vitaliano constantly checked them by hand), the heat was turned off and the cooked curds eventually dropped to the bottom of the copper cauldron. After about half an hour, Maria and Vitaliano turned the curds with a wooden paddle and collected the heavy mass in a hemp cheesecloth, where it was left to further drain.

"*Ci vuole passione* — You need passion to be committed to this life," sighed Maria, as the morning drew toward its end (there was still *ricotta* to be made from the leftover whey). "It is very hard. It would perhaps not be so wearisome if we could lie in bed one Saturday, or perhaps occasionally have a Sunday free. Still, by the end of the year, when we count how many cheeses we have made, and when we see them lined up in the cheese store, yes, there is a sense of satisfaction."

So valuable is *parmigiano reggiano* considered that it is traditionally aged and stored in great cheese vaults owned by the region's banks.

OTHER CHEESES

Caciotta d'Urbino (Urbino and Pésaro)   One of the great cheeses of Le Marche, made from ewe's milk, to be eaten fresh.

Casècc (Le Marche)   Compact, aged cheese made from a mixture of cow's and ewe's milk, both for eating and grating, especially over *cappelletti*.

Castel San Pietro (Bologna)   A semi-fat fresh cheese made from partially skimmed milk.

Pecorino del Frignano (Modena)   Tasty ewe's milk cheese from flocks that graze in the Apennines above Modena.

Ricotta (Emilia-Romagna)   *Ricotta* is made throughout Italy, but that produced from leftover whey after the making of *parmigiano reggiano* has traditionally been used here in a variety of ways, especially to fill fresh *pasta* such as *tortelli*.

Slattato (Montefeltro)   Soft, creamy cheese to eat fresh; similar to *squacquerone*.

Squacquerone (Romagna)   Fresh, creamy, bland, curd cheese, often eaten spread on *piadina*.

Gathered curds hanging to drain over a vat of whey, each for a wheel of cheese

Wheels of parmigiano reggiano *left to age in a cheese vault*

The Via Emilia
A GREAT GASTRONOMIC ROMAN ROAD

LIKE ALL ROMAN ROADS, the Via Emilia, built in 187 B.C., runs straight and true. It crosses Emilia-Romagna diagonally, connecting its major cities and towns, from Piacenza in the northwest through Parma, Reggio nell'Emilia, Modena, Bologna, and Forlì, ending at Rimini on the Adriatic Coast. Most visitors today speed down the so-called *Autostrada del Sole* (A1) that parallels the old Roman road (N9) and leads to the popular resorts of the Adriatic. Gourmets and lovers of food and wine, on the other hand, should detour off the fast track from time to time to explore more closely this great gastronomic highway.

Piacenza, once a Roman fortified camp, is the northernmost town on the Via Emilia, and looks across the Po River to Lombardia. Though, today, it is an important industrial center, it retains its atmospheric *centro storico*. The Colli Piacentini wine hills to the south are not only the source of excellent and underrated wines but are also beautiful and idyllic wine country. Don't miss Castell'Arquato, one of Emilia-Romagna's loveliest medieval fortified towns. The wines of the area can be tasted and purchased at an *enoteca comunale* here.

Parma, of course, is best known for its superlative Parma ham and *parmigiano reggiano* cheese. In fact, this prosperous town retains the style and atmosphere of the former duchy that thrived in the 19th century under the patronage of the Empress Marie-Louise, and is still, today, a center of art and culture.

From Parma, excursions can be made to the Langhirano hills to the south, source of *prosciutto di Parma* (though visiting opportunities are limited) as well as to the Bassa Parmense, to Róncole Verdi, birthplace of the composer, and to Zibello and Polésine Parmense to seek out and sample *culatello di Zibello*. The N9 from Parma leads to Reggio nell'Emilia through country dotted with *caselli* (cheese dairies) that produce *parmigiano reggiano*.

Modena is a great gastronomic town, the source not only of *aceto balsamico tradizionale di Modena* but also fine *salumi, paste, parmigiano reggiano,* the best Lambrusco, and much else. Explore the old town, then strike off into the country to Nonántola, Soliera, and other small towns to taste genuine country foods.

Bologna, *"la Grassa"* ("the Fat"), Emilia-Romagna's administrative capital, is an important university town whose gastronomic traditions are legendary. It is almost impossible to eat badly in Bologna: once replenished, explore the historic center of the old town and search out some of its famous food stores.

The Via Emilia ends at Rimini, once a prosperous and important Roman port. Today, it is a popular holiday resort, unimaginably crowded in high season. Outside this period, though, Rimini is a fine, historic city with vestiges of both Roman and medieval eras.

In Modena, one of the great gastronomic towns of Italy, along the Via Emilia

I Vini

THE WINES OF EMILIA-ROMAGNA & LE MARCHE

THE AGONIZINGLY FLAT plain of Emilia-Romagna following the Po as it flows toward the Adriatic may be agriculturally rich, but flat terrain, on the whole, makes for flat and dull wines. Though an enormous amount of wine comes from the region, much is produced on an immense, industrial scale from the indigenous Lambrusco grape to satisfy a tremendous (and seemingly indiscriminate) international thirst. Yet, for even that most maligned of wines, the situation is somewhat different on home territory. Real Lambrusco — dry, vividly foaming, high in acid — is quite different from the soda-pop, screw-top bottled, exported versions.

Vineyards of Fattoria di Paradiso, Emilia-Romagna

Wherever the ground rises even slightly, better, more characterful wines are produced, such as those of the wine hills of the Colli Piacentini in the north of the region and the undulating hills of Romagna in the south.

Le Marche is one of the most underrated major wine regions in Italy, known internationally mainly for Verdicchio dei Castelli di Jesi, bottled in its "amphora" bottle. The Verdicchio, at best, is one of the most characterful of all Italy's indigenous white grapes. Superb, serious red wines are now being produced throughout the region too, including Rosso Cònero and Rosso Piceno, excellent partners to the robust, country foods of the region.

EMILIA-ROMAGNA

Albana di Romagna DOCG
Characterful quality white wine, produced in dry, *amabile* (medium sweet), and *dolce* versions. The latter, at best, is a light, beautifully perfumed, and delicately sweet marvel with an intense nutty aftertaste.
Recommended producers: Celli, Fattoria Paradiso, Ferrucci, Montericco, Nespoli, Zerbina.

Barbarossa VdT Made on one farm only, this is possibly Emilia-Romagna's greatest red wine, produced from a redis-covered indigenous grape; immensely dark, powerful, and very long-lived.
Recommended producer: Fattoria Paradiso.

Bianco di Scandiano DOC Fresh, light, zesty white produced mainly from the Sauvignon grape.
Recommended producer: Cantina Sociale di Scandiano.

Cagnina DOC Minor but pleasant, sweet, slightly *frizzante* red wine produced from the Terrano grape grown on the lower hills of Romagna — good with local *dolci* (sweets).

Colli Bolognesi DOC Good red and white wines from native and international grapes from wine hills to the south of Bologna: white Pignoletto, Pinot Bianco, and Sauvignon, and red Cabernet Sauvignon, Merlot, and Barbera.
Recommended producer: Terre Rosse.

Colli Piacentini DOC This large, important wine area is virtually contiguous with Lombardia's Oltrepò Pavese and produces a range of distinctive white and red wines from a variety of grapes, including Trebbianino di Val Trebbia, Monterosso Val d'Arda, and Val Nure (all three make zesty, light whites), Malvasia (good, refreshing *frizzante*), and Gutturnio, a characterful blend of Bonarda and Barbera, with light raspberry fruit and an appealing *frizzante* sparkle.
Recommended producers: Fugazza (Romito label), La Stoppa, Pusterla, Barattieri.

Lambrusco This is the most misunderstood wine in the world, scorned by connoisseurs. Suffice it to say that most of the millions of bottles of the sweet, fizzy red Lambrusco (as well as white, blush, even light or low alcohol versions) exported throughout the world is produced from Lambrusco grapes grown on high-yielding vines on the fertile, flat plains of Emilia-Romagna, with the addition of cheap grape musts from elsewhere. Such wines are little more than manufactured beverages, processed in immense cooperative wineries and private industrial firms, and often sold in screw-top bottles. This is not, we stress, the Lambrusco that is actually drunk in Emilia-Romagna.

Lambrusco di Sorbara DOC; Lambrusco Grasparossa di Castelvetro DOC; Lambrusco Salamino di Santa Croce DOC The top Lambrusco wines are made from the best three sub-varieties of this prolific grape, all grown in the province of Modena. Lambrusco di Sorbara comes

Vittorio Graziano in his Lambrusco vineyards above Castelvetro

from north of Modena and is the lightest in color, very acid, fresh, fruity, and fizzy. Lambrusco Grasparossa di Castelvetro, by contrast, comes from hill vineyards to the south; the wines produced are considerably deeper in color, lower in acid, highly scented, and with a light bite of tannin. Lambrusco Salamino di Santa Croce produces full, rather rich wines with a good dose of acidity which helps cut the fat of the local foods.

Recommended producers: Graziano, Bellei, Colombini, Cavicchioli, Cantina Sociale di Sorbara.

Lambrusco Reggiano DOC This is the largest delimited Lambrusco zone, extending over the province of Reggio-Emilia. The best wines, if not quite up to the character and quality of those above, can be good, pleasant (and, importantly, inexpensive) everyday partners to the rich foods of the region.

Recommended producer: Il Moro.

Pagadebit DOC The unusual name of this indigenous white grape, grown on the wine hills of Romagna, indicates

---

CA' DE BE' DRINKING HOUSES

The *Ca' de Be'* are informal wine taverns that provide locals and visitors alike with congenial places in which to enjoy a full range of Romagna wines, served with freshly cooked *piadina, crescione,* and other snacks. No visitor should miss them: even if you can't make it out to the wine country, visit the taverns in Rimini and Ravenna.

Ca' de Be'
Piazza della Libertà, 10
47032 Bertinoro FO
tel: 0543/445303

Ca' de Sanzves
Piazza Cavour, 18
47010 Predáppio Alta FO
tel: 0543/922410

Ca' de Vèn
Via Corrado Ricci, 24
48100 Ravenna RV
tel: 0544/30163

Chesa de Vein
Viale Dante, 18
47037 Rimini FO
tel: 0541/54180

Enoteca Regionale di Emilia-Romagna
Rocca Sforzesca
40050 Dozza BO
tel: 0542/678089
fax: 0542/678073

that its high yields in the past could be depended upon to help "pay the bills." Today, it produces nutty, characterful dry, *amabile,* and sweet wines.
Recommended producers: Celli, Fattoria Paradiso.

Sangiovese di Romagna DOC

Usually passed off as an inferior clone of the Sangiovese grape of Tuscany, Sangiovese, nonetheless, (when not over-cropped) can make meaty, deep red wines capable of aging. Otherwise, good, easy-to-drink, inexpensive, if fairly nondescript, younger versions are also widely produced.
Recommended producers: Fattoria Paradiso, Nespoli, Foschi, Spalletti, Mandorli.

Trebbiano di Romagna DOC

Never the most exciting of Italy's indigenous white grapes, Trebbiano di Romagna produces, at best, rather neutral, flat wines of little character.
Recommended producer: Fattoria Paradiso.

LE MARCHE

Bianchello del Metauro DOC
This light, sharp, lemony white, produced in the north of the region near Urbino, is refreshing and easy to drink, delicious with shellfish and seafood *antipasti.*
Recommended producers: Umani Ronchi, Giovanetti.

Rosso Cònero DOC
Outstanding, serious red wines are produced from Montepulciano grapes with the addition of up to 15 per cent Sangiovese grapes grown in the hills behind Ancona and on the Monte Cònero promontory. The best examples, aged in Slovenian or French oak, can rank among the top medium-priced red wines in the country.
Recommended producers: Moroder, Serenelli, Garofoli, Umani Ronchi.

Rosso Piceno DOC
Another characterful red from Le Marche, produced over a large area stretching from the lower slopes of the Apennines to the Adriatic, across the provinces of Ancona, Macerata, and Ascoli Piceno (the best zone). Produced from Sangiovese (mainly) and Montepulciano grapes, with the addition of some Trebbiano and Passerina, Rosso Piceno benefits from aging in wood.
Recommended producers: Villamagna, Cocci Grifoni.

Sangiovese dei Colli Pesaresi DOC
Undistinguished red wine produced in vineyards of Pésaro.

Verdicchio dei Castelli di Jesi DOC
In spite of its unserious, "sexy" bottle image, we consider Verdicchio dei Castelli di Jesi one of the great white

The vineyards of Castelli di Jesi

wines of Italy. The Verdicchio grape is capable of producing wines of real character, richly textured, with ripe — even overripe — fruit, and a clean, bitter aftertaste. Try the superior *cru* or single-vineyard wines from the *classico* zone. *Spumante* Verdicchio is also good.
Recommended producers: Umani Ronchi, Garofoli, Brunori, Bucci, Fazi-Battaglia, Monte Schiavo.

The cavernous cellar at Fattoria Paradiso storing thousands of bottles

Verdicchio di Matelica DOC
Verdicchio grapes grown in the much smaller delimited wine zone of Matelica produce high quality wines.
Recommended producers: La Monacesca, Benedetti, Mecvini di Enzo Mecella.

Vernaccia di Serrapetrona DOC
A traditional red sparkling wine, usually sweet; worth sampling if you can find it.

OTHER DRINKS
A huge range of homemade *liqueurs* and cordials is produced, often from local fruits, such as *ciliegie* (cherries), *more* (mulberries), *amarene* (bitter cherries), and *mirtilli* (bilberries); herbs, such as *lauro* (laurel); wild vegetables, such as *ortiche* (nettles); and *noci* (walnuts); all infused in alcohol with sugar and spices.
Nocino   The most popular of such household *liqueurs*, a traditional drink made by steeping immature green walnuts in alcohol with sugar and spices.
Sassolino   This anise-flavored liqueur from Sassuolo is a popular *digestivo*.
Vecchia Romagna   Italy's best brandy, smooth, well made, available nationally.

FOOD AND WINE COMBINATIONS

Affettati misti   The great variety of rich and sometimes fatty cured pork products of Emilia-Romagna is best accompanied by dry, high in acid Lambrusco di Sorbara.

Antipasti di mare   Splendid arrays of shellfish and fish appetizers all along the Adriatic Coast are ideally partnered by fresh, lemony Bianchello di Metauro, a light and refreshing summer white *par excellence*.

Coppa   The best *coppa* in Italy, say many, comes from Piacenza, where the locals enjoy it together with goblets of slightly *frizzante* Gutturnio red.

Coniglio in porchetta   Rabbit stuffed with wild fennel and garlic, then baked in a hot oven, is rustic fare

from Le Marche. Enjoy it with full-bodied Rosso Cònero or Rosso Piceno.

Fritto misto di mare   Sweet fish from the Adriatic, simply fried, goes well with a deeply flavored *cru* Verdicchio dei Castelli di Jesi.

Grigliata mista di carne   Char-grilled meats, eaten outdoors with the fingers, cry out for inexpensive, thirst quenching wines such as red Sangiovese di Romagna or a young Rosso Piceno.

Ciambella   This favorite ring-shaped cake is never overly sweet, so it makes a good accompaniment to sparkling Verdicchio or a lightly sweet and foaming Lambrusco.

Castelli di Jesi and Monte Cònero
THE WINE COUNTRY AROUND ANCONA

LE MARCHE IS ONE of Italy's most pleasant regions for visitors, primarily, we imagine, because so few come here. Its Adriatic Coast may be hugely popular in August (mainly with Italians and nowhere near as overcrowded as the beaches of Rimini, Riccione, and Cattólica to the north), but inland, as always, lies another, quieter world.

For Le Marche is really two separate regions, two separate personalities: the extrovert facing the sea, attracting tourists, the less attention-seeking looking inland toward the mountains. This essential dichotomy between sea and land is never far away in Le Marche.

Even its foods and wines reflect this, for, on the one hand, the wealth of Adriatic seafood is ably partnered by superb white wines, such as Verdicchio, while, on the other, robust wild foods and game are matched by gutsy, forthright reds.

Vines grow prolifically throughout the region, and its wine country is always congenial and pleasant to explore. However, the finest red and white wines come from Ancona's hinterland. The large protruding mountain that rises from Ancona's "elbow," known as Monte Cònero, is the source of the region's finest red wine, Rosso Cònero. A pleasant excursion into the wine country can be made from Ancona to Osimo, Castelfidardo, and Loreto, then around the mountain to the coastal resorts of Numana, Sirolo, and Portonovo (the latter has an exceptional fish restaurant, Ristorante Lelli, on the beach, see p.153).

Further inland, the classic area of the Castelli di Jesi, home of Verdicchio, is easily reached from Ancona by way of the *superstrada* that leads to Jesi, itself an impressive medieval town, still surrounded by its fortified walls, and the gateway to the wine country. In fact, the small towns that collectively comprise the *classico* zone, the select heart of the *denominazione,* are little visited and

The Verdicchio dei Castelli di Jesi country looking across to Montecarotto

unprepossessing, often located atop steep hills. This is wholly satisfying and enjoyable wine country to meander through, exploring from Jesi wine towns such as Stáffolo, Cupramontana, Monte Roberto, Castelbellino, Montecarotto, Monteschiavo, Móie, and Serra de' Conti.

INTO WINE COUNTRY

Casa Vinicola Garofoli
Via Arno, 9
60025 Loreto AN
tel: 071/7820163
fax: 071/7821437
Traditional quality wines, especially outstanding cru Verdicchio.

La Vite S.p.A.
Via Vivaio
Fra. Monteschiavo
60030 Maiolati Spontini AN
tel: 0731/700385
fax: 0731/703359
Highly regarded winery: formerly a cooperative.

Mario Brunori
Viale della Vittoria, 103
60035 Jesi AN
tel/fax: 0731/207213
Artisan-made wines.

Villa Bianchi Azienda Vinicola Umani Ronchi S.p.A.
Via Montecarottese
60030 Móie di Maiolati AN
tel: 0731/701674; 7108019
fax: 0731/7108859
Tasting room in the old family house.

Indirizzi

USEFUL ADDRESSES

Antica Salumeria di Giusti

EMILIA-ROMAGNA

Acetaia Ferdinando Cavalli
Via del Cristo, 6/AB
Loc. Fellegara
Scandiano RE
tel/fax: 0522/983430
Reggio nell'Emilia's balsamic vinegar may be less well known than Modena's, but it too is the real thing, produced by traditional artisan methods. Come here to discover and purchase it, as well as the younger, less expensive condimento balsamico.

Antica Salumeria di Giusti
Via Farini, 75
41100 Modena
tel/fax: 059/222533
An institution of Modena, for a range of good things to eat.

Cantine Cavicchioli
Piazza Gramsci, 9
41030 San Prospero sulla Sécchia Modena MO
tel: 059/90882
fax: 059/906163
Although this large family concern produces immense quantities of Lambrusco and other wines, its single-vineyard cru wines, made from 100 per cent Lambrusco di Sorbara, are serious and deserve to be tried.

Chicco d'Oro
Via F. Selmi, 27/A
41100 Modena
tel: 059/218216
Serves fresh pasta made daily on the premises.
$$

Coop. Casearia Nuova Martignana
Martignana, 281
Baggiovara MO
tel: 059/510217
Eight to 12 whole Parmigiano reggiano cheeses of great quality are made every day of the year in this cooperative cheese dairy just south of Modena.

Fattoria Paradiso
Via Palmeggiana, 285
47032 Bertinoro FO
tel: 0543/445044
fax: 0543/444224
Mario Pezzi is one of Emilia-Romagna's great winemakers. Come to the lovely and welcoming estate in the Romagna hills to taste wines or stay in farmhouse apartments.

Osteria di Rubbiara
Via Risaia, 2
Loc. Rubbiara
40105 Nonántola MO
tel: 059/549019
Italo Pedroni's country restaurant is informal and

Culatello, *a prized cured pork product from Emilia-Romagna*

serves home-cooked food, seasoned with Italo's own traditionally made balsamic vinegar.
$–$$

Ristorante Diana
Via Independenza, 24
40121 Bologna BO
tel: 051/231302
Famous Bolognese eating house serving the ample foods of Bologna — lasagne, tortellini di brodo, bollito misto.
$$

Ristorante Luis
Loc. Collinello, 541
47032 Bertinoro FO
tel: 0543/445120
In the wine hills of Romagna not far from Bertinoro, this simple but genuine trattoria serves home-cooked food, in summer, on the terrace.
$–$$

Salumeria Brandoli
Via Canalino, 11
41100 Modena MO
tel: 059/223127
The best place to stock up on goodies for a luxury picnic.

Specialità di Parma
Via Farini, 9C
43100 Parma PR
tel: 0521/233591
One of the oldest shops in Parma, selling all the gastronomic specialties of the town as well as home-cooked ones.

Tamburini Antica Salsamenteria Bolognese BO
Via Caprarie, 1
40100 Bologna
tel: 051/234726
fax: 051/232226
Outstanding old shop in Bologna, source of all the local specialties, including hand-made tortellini, mortadella, and prosciutto crudo.

Vecchio Molinetto
Viale Milazzo, 39
43100 Parma PR
tel: 0521/253941
A trattoria *serving traditional foods of Parma.*
$$

Vittorio Graziano
Via Ossi, 30
41014 Castelvetro MO
tel: 059/799162
Small, high-quality producer of genuine and characterful Lambrusco Grasparossa di Castelvetro.

LE MARCHE
Azienda Agrituristica La Quercia
Strada Falciraga, 55
61032 Fano PS
tel/fax: 0721/885646

This way for parmesan cheese

Outstanding farmhouse complex (swimming pool in summer) in the hills above Fano, with a great restaurant serving local foods, such as cappelletti *and* coniglio in porchetta.
$

Enoteca Vinovip
Viale Verdi, 78
61100 Pésaro PS
tel/fax: 0721/31011
Guido Praloran is an expert on the whole range of wines from Le Marche.

Grotta del Frate
Via Roma, 10
Stáffolo AN
tel: 0731/779260
On the wine itinerary of the Castelli di Jesi, a simple but authentic trattoria *in the grotto under the town walls.*
$

Ristorante Emilia
Via Portonovo
60020 Ancona AN
tel: 071/801109
Fisherman's restaurant on the beach of this popular spot on the Riviera del Conèro.
$–$$

Ristorante Lelli
Via Roma, 81
San Benedetto del Tronto
tel: 0735/587320
Old trattoria in the heart of this fishing town serving fish or shellfish, especially brodetto.
$–$$

Trattoria Anita
Via Fabio Filzi, 7
60034 Cupramontana AN
tel: 0731/780311
fax: 0731/789754
Enjoy local marchigiana *foods and wines in this characteristic Castelli di Jesi wine town.*
$

Trattoria La Quinta
Viale Adriatico
61032 Fano PS
You can still eat fresh fish and shellfish inexpensively at genuine trattorie *like this one near the fish market. Finish your meal with* murèta, *a spiked, spicy coffee drunk by Fanese fishermen.*
$

Villa Amalia
Via degli Spagnoli, 4
Falconara Marittima AN
tel: 071/9160550
fax: 071/912045

Signora Quinta of Trattoria La Quinta, Fano

Stylish and imaginative food in a popular resort north of Ancona.
$$$

BEST BUYS
• *aceto balsamico tradizionale di Modena*
• *parmigiano reggiano* (vacuum packed)
• real Lambrusco
• *zampone di Modena*
• Nocino, walnut liqueur
• *prosciutto di Parma* (vacuum-packed quarters)
• *culatello di Zibello* (whole pieces vacuum-packed)
• *Verdicchio and Rosso Cònero wines*
• extra-virgin olive oil

Pink marble lion at the entrance to Modena cathedral

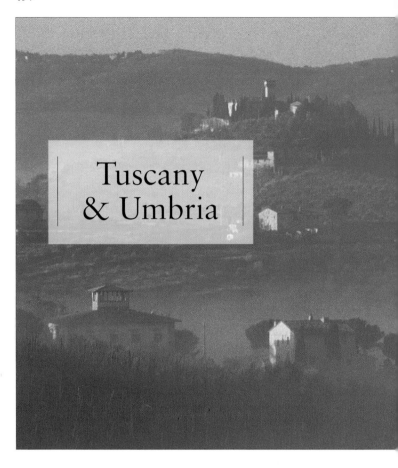

Tuscany & Umbria

THE LANDSCAPE OF Tuscany and Umbria embodies the classic Italian ideal. Seemingly unchanged for centuries, it recalls the backdrop of a Renaissance painting, with its steep, vine covered hills, interspersed with groves of olive trees and lines of tall cypresses. Old, isolated towns — sometimes little more than collections of stone houses, a fortified Romanesque church, and a town hall decorated with colorful plaques on its facade — dominate the hilltops, and Renaissance *palazzi* and *castelli* confront each other in splendid isolation from their lofty perches.

Here are the great cities of the Italian Renaissance, centers of art, architecture, culture, finance, and banking: Florence, birthplace of the Renaissance, Siena, Arezzo, Pienza, Montalcino, San Gimignano, and Pisa in Tuscany; Perugia, Orvieto, Assisi, Gubbio, and Spoleto in Umbria, to name just a few. However, in spite of a rich heritage that predates even the Romans, and the fact that in recent decades, as elsewhere in Italy, there has been an exodus from country to city, as young people have left the land in search of work in factories and new industries, both Tuscany and Umbria remain essentially rural in character, especially when it comes to matters gastronomic.

Castello Vicchiomaggio, a wine estate in Chianti Classico near Greve in Chianti

SIMPLE YET SOPHISTICATED

This section of the country, however, is neither rude nor rustic. In both regions, inhabitants display a quiet pride and satisfaction in the knowledge that the land yields more than its fair share of produce, to be transformed by them into products of world-class quality.

Italy's finest (and most expensive) extra-virgin olive oil comes from Tuscany, as does a profusion of superlative classic and new wave "designer" wines, the *super-toscani* (see p.177), and the native breed of Chianina cattle from the Val di Chiana, south of Arezzo, makes for exceptional beef. Luxury foods such as Umbria's black truffles contrast with simpler, everyday foods that are, nonetheless, of the highest quality — exceptional breads, a profusion of fresh, seasonal vegetables, an outstanding range of flavorsome, traditional cured meats and *salumi,* and probably the finest *pecorino* cheeses in the country.

From these essentials, a deceptively simple, Central Italian *cucina* has developed which manages to be at once rustic in character, yet classic, refined, sophisticated: simple appetizers of *crostini* (rounds of bread) spread with meat or vegetable paste; humble bean-and-bread soups seasoned

Basket of artichokes or carciofi

with precious olive oil, and meat cooked to perfection over a wood fire, the seared black stripes echoing the black and white marble bands of the Duomo of Siena. All these can be accompanied by simple wines served in unlabeled bottles or outrageously expensive *super-vini* with fancy — and fanciful — designer names and labels.

THE BEAUTY OF THE COUNTRYSIDE

Tuscany, of course, has been and remains one of the most popular of all Italian destinations. Certainly, Florence is a city that no visitor will want to miss, and Pisa and Siena are almost as popular. The chance to stay in rented villas or farmhouses, simply relaxing in the classic beauty and peace of the Tuscan countryside, can be equally rewarding: such opportunities allow you to experience life in Tuscany as the Tuscans do, shopping in local shops, eating local foods, trying out new wines, meeting the people. In addition to the classic Chianti country between Florence and Siena (so popular with British visitors that it has been dubbed "Chiantishire"), don't overlook less obvious areas such as southern Tuscany's wilder Maremma region in the province of Grosseto, the quiet country south of Siena towards the wine town of Montalcino, the Florentine hills to the west of the city in the wine zone of Carmignano, or to the north, the Rúfina's steep balcony of hills that leads up to the Apennines.

Terracotta orci *for the storage of olive oil*

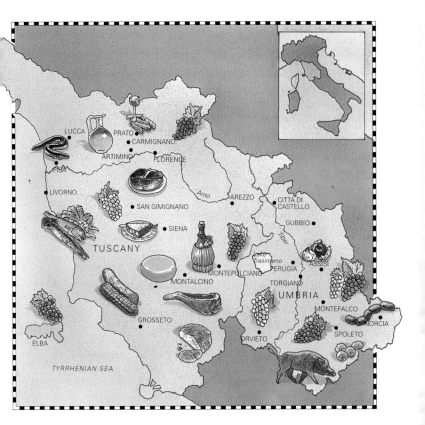

UNSPOILED AND SERENE

It is said that Umbria, popularly known as the "Green Heart" of Italy, is rather as Tuscany was some 30 years ago. Certainly, in contrast with parts of the latter, Umbria remains relatively untouched, a quieter, gentler variation of that same classic, Central Italian ideal. But make no mistake, Umbria has plenty to offer the visitor in its own right: cities and towns such as Perugia and Orvieto, with great art and culture; the pilgrimage town of Assisi; peaceful, unspoiled rural country; a superlative, essentially simple, country *cucina;* and outstanding wines from Torgiano, Montefalco, and Orvieto.

No matter where you go in Tuscany or Umbria, you are likely to eat well, amply, and at no great expense. Of course, there are temples of gastronomy here that rank among the finest in the nation — Umbria's Vissani, near Orvieto, one of the meccas for the so-called *cucina novella,* and the Enoteca Pinchiorri in Florence, quite simply one of the great classic restaurants of Italy — which charge prices to match. But to our way of thinking, the experiences that are most typical and unique to this lovely part of Central Italy are to be found in simpler *trattorie* and *osterie* in the cities and towns of both regions, as well as throughout the always beautiful and peaceful country.

Prodotti Regionali
REGIONAL PRODUCE

IF CENTRAL ITALY represents *la cucina italiana* at its purest and simplest, then it stands to reason that the primary ingredients of such a cuisine need to be of the highest quality — after all, it is far easier to mask second-rate produce in elaborate sauces and preparations. Tuscans lucky enough to live in the country or to have a garden often cultivate their own

Picking the cavolo nero *leaves off their stalks*

orto (kitchen garden) for their own supply of fresh vegetables, but even city dwellers make it a point to visit daily or weekly markets to purchase the best of seasonal produce. For a few weeks in April and May, you can find *baccelli* in the markets, young, tender fava beans to be eaten raw with fresh *pecorino* cheese. The season for *asparagi* (asparagus), a favorite in Florence, follows

in May and June. Fall is the time to enjoy *castagne* (chestnuts) and *funghi* (mushrooms) of all types, including *porcini* (*boletus edulis* or cepes) and the rare *tartufi neri* (black truffles) of Umbria. Winter, by contrast, brings that favorite Tuscan vegetable, the unique *cavolo nero*, flavorful dark green leaves of a yellow flowering plant, picked as needed.

No matter the time of year, there is always fresh produce to enjoy.

TRY TO SAMPLE
Asparagi (May–Jun)   Asparagus; **alla fiorentina** boiled, then served with melted butter, fried egg, and grated *grana* cheese.
Baccelli (Apr–May)   Baby fava beans.
Cardi (winter)   Cardoons.
Cavolo nero (winter)   Distinctive, strongly flavored, peppery, leaf vegetable.
Fagiolini di Sant'Anna (summer) Thin, tender, and extremely long green beans from Pescia.
Rape amare or **rapini** (winter)   Bitter turnip tops, usually added to soup or cooked with pasta.
Tartufi neri (Nov–Mar)   Black truffles.

THE BLACK TRUFFLES OF UMBRIA

Umbria is a great source of that most rare and prized fungus, the truffle. Though some white truffles are also unearthed, this is the foremost region for the *tartufo nero,* or black truffle.

Black truffles are pungent in flavor and aroma, with an intriguing, firm, *croccante* texture that is absolutely irresistible. The best come from Spoleto, Norcia, and the Val Nerina and, in season, are available fresh in markets and from specialist shops.

The finest black truffle, the *Tuber melanosporum,* is available only in winter (Nov–Mar), while the less distinctive *Tuber aestivum* is found in summer. Out of season, black truffles are conserved in brine (rarely worth buying), olive oil, or creamy pastes.

In season, black truffles are used with seeming abandon. Grated or coarsely chopped, they are sprinkled abundantly over homemade *umbricelli* noodles, eaten on *crostini,* and even wrapped in *pancetta* and roasted whole.

Al Mercato
MARKETS

TUSCANY

Arezzo	Sat
Carmignano	Tue
Chiusi	Tue
Cortona	Sat
Empoli	Thu
Fiesole	Sat
Florence	daily
Greve in Chianti	Sat
Grosseto	Thu
Impruneta	Sat
Lastra a Signa	Sat
Livórno	Mon–Sat
Lucca	Wed, Sat
Manciano	Sat
Marina di Pisa	Sun
Montalcino	Fri

Country fresh produce to tempt passsers-by at a street market in Cortona, Tuscany

The pick of eggplants

Montecatini Terme	Thu
Montepulciano	Thu
Orbetello	Sat
Pienza	Sat
Pisa	Wed, Sat
Pontassieve	Wed
Poggio a Caiano	Thu
Porto Azzurro	Sat
Prato	Mon
Radda in Chianti	last Mon of month
Rúfina	Sat
San Gimignano	Thu
Sansepolcro	Tue, Sat
Satúrnia	Sat
Scansano	Fri
Siena	Wed
Signa	Fri
Viareggio	Thu
Volterra	Sat

UMBRIA

Assisi	Sat
Bevagna	2 days in Aug, 1 day alternate months
Castiglione del Lago	Wed
Città di Castello	Thu, Sat
Gubbio	Tue
Montefalco	Mon
Norcia	Thu
Orvieto	Thu, Sat
Perugia	Tue, Thu, Sat
Spoleto	Fri
Terni	Wed, Sat
Todi	Sat
Torgiano	Wed (every fortnight)

POPULAR *FESTE*

TUSCANY

Carmignano: *Antica Fiera di Carmignano (folklore, wine)*   1st Tue Dec

Gaiole in Chianti: *Sagra dell'uva (wine)*   end Aug

Siena: *Mostra Mercato dei Vini (wine)*   early Jun

UMBRIA

Castellúccio: *Sagra delle lenticchie (lentils)*   Aug

Montefalco: *Settimana enologica (wine week)*   Easter

Norcia: *Sagra del tartufo (black truffles)*   Last week Feb

Succulent grapes, and peaches "fresh off the tree to your table"

Il Pane Toscano

TUSCAN BREAD

ONE OF the most distinctive features of the diet and cooking of Central Italy is the bread of this region. The large, dense, crusty loaves that are served at every meal are beautiful to look at — delicious, firmly textured, yet undoubtedly unusual in taste. This bread, you quickly realize, is unsalted, a singular omission that changes not just its taste but its entire character.

On first impression, this rather flavorless, even bland, bread may not be to your liking. But persevere, for *pane toscano* is a staple food, essential to the Tuscan diet, its neutral taste a necessary counterbalance to the highly salted and *saporito* (flavorful) foods of this region.

Pane toscano is a type of sourdough bread, made with a starter of dough left over from the previous day's baking. Free-form loaves weighing about 1 kg. (about 2¼ lbs.) emerge from the traditional, wood-fired baker's oven with a thick, hard crust, and a dense, yet chewy, interior.

This saltless, country bread is, of course, best fresh from the oven, but it can also last for upward of a week. Moreover, when slightly hard or even stale, Tuscan bread becomes the basis for a glorious range of foods, such as *crostini*, salads, and soups.

Umbria's bread, though not as well known as that of Tuscany, can also be outstanding. It too is usually unsalted.

Fettunta, *Tuscany's favorite garlic bread*

TRY TO SAMPLE

Crostini di fegatini   Small rounds of stale Tuscan bread, spread with a pungent paste made from chopped chicken livers, anchovies, and capers. Sometimes a bit of broth is dribbled over the bread (if it is really stale) or *crostini* can be baked in the oven and served hot.

Fettunta (known also as **bruschetta**) A slice of Tuscan bread toasted over a wood fire, rubbed with a cut clove of garlic, dribbled liberally with extra-virgin olive oil, and sprinkled with salt.

Pan col olio   No more than a large slab of Tuscan bread with a dribbling of extra-virgin olive oil and a sprinkling of salt: the classic after-school snack for children in Tuscany.

Panzanella   Stale Tuscan bread which is first soaked in cold water and vinegar, then mixed with chopped tomatoes, onions, basil and other herbs, and seasoned with extra-virgin olive oil. This unusual, cold first course is deliciously refreshing in summer.

Pappa al pomodoro   Bready mush made from stale bread cooked together with fresh tomatoes, a little onion, torn fresh basil leaves, and seasoned liberally with extra-virgin olive oil.

Ribollita   This classic vegetable soup, made with seasonal vegetables, white beans, and olive oil, and served layered with stale Tuscan bread, is actually tastier recooked the next day (hence the name).

Tuscan bread or pane toscano, *always unsalted and, thus, something of an acquired taste*

Olio Extra Vergine d'Oliva di Toscana
TUSCAN EXTRA-VIRGIN OLIVE OIL

THOUGH THE OLIVE TREE grows throughout the Italian Peninsula and olive oil is produced and consumed everywhere, it is widely acknowledged that Tuscany produces the country's finest: *olio extra vergine d'oliva di Toscana* (Tuscan extra-virgin olive oil).

Yet, as recently as 1985, a particularly severe cold snap virtually destroyed most of the olive groves of Tuscany, and, at the time, many wondered if they could ever recover. But the old plants eventually rejuvenated, and newly planted olive groves have since come into production.

Just as vines that produce the finest wines yield the smallest amount of grape, so too these olive trees yield minuscule amounts of fruit, especially when compared with the immense quantities harvested from the near oak-sized trees that bask in the sunny Mezzogiorno.

These smaller yields are harvested by hand (not collected from the ground) and the olives are then taken to the *frantoio* — the traditional olive oil mill. Here, the fruit is simply washed, then ground to a pulp by heavy, slow-revolving granite millstones. The olive paste is next layered between matting and cold-pressed only once to extract a mixture of oil and juice, which is subsequently separated into each component by decanting or in a centrifuge, resulting in pure, unfiltered olive oil that is traditionally stored in terracotta *orci* — large "Ali-Baba" style urns.

Estate-bottled extra virgin olive oils from Tuscany, some of the finest (and most expensive) in Italy

Tuscan *olio extra vergine d'oliva* has a fragrance and flavor — lean and elegant, peppery when new, and wholly ungreasy or fatty — that is, quite frankly, unrivaled by oils that we have tasted from anywhere else in Italy or, for that matter, the world. Often sold in designer bottles holding only ½ liter (1 pint), these aristocrats, especially from the select estates in Chianti Classico, Carmignano, and Lucca areas, or the wine country of Siena, are too good — and too expensive — to be used just for cooking. Rather, they are best employed to add a final magnificent flavoring to soups or grilled meats, or to form the simplest of dips — *pinzimonio* — to dunk raw vegetables in.

Olive trees in Tuscany

Every year, olive oil from *la nuova raccolta* (the new harvest) is as eagerly awaited as the year's new wine. It is best sampled simply dribbled generously onto a slice of Tuscan bread, rubbed in with the fingers, and sprinkled with salt. The hot piquancy that catches you at the back of the throat is the hallmark of fresh, extra-virgin olive oil straight from the *frantoio*. Even by spring, this will have diminished. For extra-virgin olive oil, unlike most wine, does not improve with age: it should always be consumed as young and as quickly as possible.

Recommended olive oil producers
Antinori, Selvapiana, Capezzana, Il Colle di Trequanda, Baccheretto, Capaccia, Uzzano, Volpaia, Badia a Coltibuono. The Laudemio trademark is used collectively by a handful of top estates and is reliable.

Salumi

CURED PORK AND OTHER MEAT PRODUCTS

CENTRAL ITALIAN expertise in the raising of pigs and the artisan-production of a varied and delicious range of cured pork products is widely acknowledged: indeed, the term utilized nationally for a pork butcher's shop that specializes in such products is *norcineria,* after the renowned pork butchers of Norcia, a town in Umbria noted for centuries for the excellence of its pork butchers and *salumi.*

Throughout Tuscany and Umbria, *norcinerie* proudly present an outstanding range of local and regional cured pork products. Such foods are delicious for a simple *merenda* (afternoon snack) or for picnics in the wine country. Indeed, there are few meals that can match paper-wrapped packets of *finocchiona* or *prosciutto toscano,* a dense loaf of unsalted *pane toscano,* and a bottle or two of Chianti Classico enjoyed in the open air.

TRY TO SAMPLE

Capocollo (Tuscany and Umbria) Outstanding regional *salame:* whole pieces of pork, usually from the upper shoulder and neck tenderloin, are seasoned with garlic, salt, and pepper, then tied in a *salame* shape and left to age for three months to a year.

Finocchiata (Montalcino and Siena) This exceptionally fine cured pork product is made from the same cut of

Wild boar sausages and other salumi *typical of Umbria*

meat as *capocollo,* i.e., the upper shoulder and neck tenderloin, though, in this case, it is salted and cured in a mixture of black pepper and wild fennel seeds, which impart a delicate anise flavor to the meat.

Finocchiona sbriciolona (Greve in Chianti and all Tuscany) Probably the most characteristic *salame* of Tuscany: soft textured, large, round *salame* made

Salame toscano, *in various sizes*

with fat and lean pork, flavored with wild fennel seeds. So soft is its texture that the meat usually crumbles apart as it is sliced, hence the name (from *sbriciolare,* "to crumble").

Guancia (Tuscany and Umbria) This fatty, inexpensive cut comes from the cheek of the pig. Salt-cured, it is used mainly for cooking.

Mazzafegati (Umbria) Unusual sweet sausage made with pork liver and flavored with pine nuts, orange peel, raisins, and sugar.

Prosciutto di cinghiale (Tuscany and Umbria) Salted, air-cured hind leg of wild boar.

Prosciutto di daino (Umbria) Salted and air-cured hind leg of fallow deer, a delicacy during the hunting season.

Rigatino (Florence and all Tuscany) The local name for *pancetta,* cured belly pork, usually covered in ground black pepper; to be used in cooking or eaten sliced, as a typical nibble with drinks.

Salame di cinghiale (Tuscany and Umbria) *Salame* made with finely ground lean and fat meat of wild boar.

Salame toscano (Tuscany)   This large typical *salame* is made from pure pork, and has large cubes of fat set in the ground lean meat; soft in texture, it is rather too rich for our taste, though it can be good with *pane toscano* and plenty of red wine.

Salsicce (Tuscany and Umbria)   Fresh sausages from Central Italy; can be outstanding. Meaty, and delicious grilled — specify *dolce* for mild taste or *piccante* for extra spicy and peppery.

Salsicce di cinghiale (Tuscany and Umbria)   Small wild boar sausages, cured for at least two weeks or longer so that they become dry and chewy; to be eaten uncooked.

Salsiccioli secchi   Small, soft textured sausages made from ground pork, salt, and pepper, cured for about two weeks, then eaten uncooked.

Rigatino, *cured belly pork, a favorite nibble to accompany drinks*

Soppressata (Tuscany and Umbria) Cured "head cheese," a pressed meat product utilizing meat from the pig's head and set in a gelatin.

Spalla (Tuscany and Umbria)   Salted shoulder of pork rubbed in black pepper and garlic — the same treatment as for *prosciutto,* but the meat is fattier and less refined in taste, so it also costs less.

PROSCIUTTO DI TOSCANA — TUSCAN HAM

There are two types of *prosciutto crudo* in Italy, *prosciutto dolce,* such as the sweet, air-cured hams of San Daniele and Parma (see pp.109 and 141), and *prosciutto salato.* Though the former is undoubtedly the finer of the two, as well as the more difficult to make, excellent, if saltier, hams are produced throughout the rest of Italy. Some of the best come from Tuscany.

At the *norcineria* at the Fattoria dei Barbi, for example, the hind legs of cereal-fed pigs raised on the estate are cured in a mixture of salt, garlic, and black pepper for upward of three weeks (as opposed to little more than a week for the curing of *prosciutto dolce* hams in Parma), then left to ripen further in a warm, humid room which

reproduces the conditions of the old farmhouse attic over the kitchen where such hams used to be stored. After a month there, the *prosciutti* are covered with ground black pepper and left to hang in a cool, airy loft for at least six months, and often longer.

Neither as delicate nor as sweet as *prosciutto di Parma* or *prosciutto di San Daniele,* this salty *prosciutto di Toscana* is nevertheless still very tasty, its robust flavor and chewy texture counterbalanced beautifully by unsalted Tuscan bread and ideally partnered with a lively, full red wine, such as the estate's own Brusco dei Barbi.

Fattoria dei Barbi
53024 Montalcino SI
tel: 0577/848277
fax: 0577/849356

Piatti Tipici
REGIONAL SPECIALTIES

THOUGH THE FLORENTINE Catherine de' Medici is credited with bringing culinary sophistication (and the fork) to France when she married Henry II, in truth, Tuscan cooking is essentially pure and simple. But Tuscans know more than most that such refined simplicity, the true hallmark of genius, is perhaps the hardest quality of all to achieve.

If purity and subtlety characterize Tuscany's country cooking, the foods of Umbria, though similar in essence, appeal to less delicate tastes. Here, there is a love of strong, robust flavors, of black truffles, chopped or grated, used generously, plenty of garlic and wild herbs, and the musty, deep flavors of the wild: mushrooms and game in season.

The preferred method of cooking in both regions remains grilling over an open fire. Thus, even in sophisticated and modern kitchens in city restaurants, as well as in rustic *trattorie,* great log fires blaze in summer as well as winter, and all manner of foods are cooked over them. Char-grilled meats, of course, are eaten in quantity, not just the *bistecca alla fiorentina* (see p.168), but also sausages, pork or veal chops, or ribs. Some places even boast a *girar-rosto,* a banked fire in front of which revolve mouth-watering rows of spits threaded with meats including chicken and guinea fowl or rolled loins of pork stuffed with fresh herbs and garlic.

Rustic-style kitchen of La Villa Miranda, Radda in Chianti

Kitchen of Vissani, near Orvieto, one of the most sophisticated restaurants in the country

ANTIPASTI

Antipasto alla toscana (Tuscany) Most typically consists of a plate of Tuscan cured meats, including *salame toscano, finocchiona,* and salty, local *prosciutto,* served with *crostini.*

Antipasto magro (Umbria) Cold salad of diced boiled potatoes, tuna, hardboiled eggs, capers, and olives, dressed with olive oil and vinegar.

Crostini al tartufo all'umbra (Umbria) Toasted rounds of stale bread spread with a paste made from chopped anchovies and black truffles, moistened with extra-virgin olive oil.

Crostini di fegatini Toasted rounds of bread with chicken liver spread (see p.160).

Crostini misti (Tuscany) Toasted rounds of bread with a selection of toppings, including chicken livers, finely chopped arugula mixed with olive oil, chopped tomatoes and basil, *radicchio di Treviso,* or a paste made from chopped olives and capers.

Fettunta or **bruschetta**   Toasted bread rubbed with garlic and soaked with olive oil (see p.160).

Pinzimonio (Florence and all Tuscany) A dip of no more than extra-virgin olive oil, salt, and pepper; to be dipped into with raw vegetables — fennel, celery, tomatoes, peppers, or carrots.

I PRIMI PIATTI

Acquacotta (Grosseto, Siena, and all Tuscany)   "Cooked water," a substantial soup made with any variety of vegetables, thickened with beaten egg, poured over slices of stale bread, and seasoned with olive oil. There are many variations.

Cuscusso alla livornese (Livórno) Of Arab derivation, made with steamed semolina and served with tomato sauce, vegetables, chickpeas, spices, and lamb; this can be eaten either as a first course, or as a substantial one-plate meal.

Frascarelli (Umbria)   Lightly textured *primo piatto* made from coarse grains of semolina formed into little bubbly dumpling shapes, boiled, and seasoned with olive oil, fresh tomatoes, and basil.

Pappa al pomodoro   Fresh tomatoes, stale bread, basil, and olive oil are combined in this classic mush (see p.160).

Pappardelle alla lepre (Tuscany and Umbria)   Homemade flat egg noodles seasoned with a hearty, strongly flavored sauce made from wild hare — a classic.

Pinci or **pici** (Montalcino, Montepulciano, and Siena) Sublimely simple homemade noodles made from hard durum wheat, water, and olive oil; in appearance rather like fat spaghetti. This traditionally poor people's dish should be served with a dressing of dry breadcrumbs, garlic, *peperoncini,* olive oil, and grated *pecorino* cheese. More often, it is served simply *al pomodoro* (with tomato sauce) or *al ragù* (with meat sauce).

Crostini misti *with assorted toppings*

THE *MANGIAFAGIOLI* OR BEANEATERS OF TUSCANY

It is perhaps not surprising that Italy, a country that lives by and for its stomach, should have any number of nicknames for people according to the foods that they eat. While those from the Mezzogiorno are known as *maccheroncini,* for their habitual consumption of huge quantities of dried pasta, usually flavored with tomato and garlic sauces, and those from Veneto are known as *polentoni,* after their favorite food, *polenta;* Tuscans, by contrast, are known to those from other parts of the country as *i mangiafagioli* — the

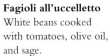

beaneaters. And, indeed, beans, usually small white cannellini, are used in any number of soups and *pasta* dishes, as well as stand alone as preparations in themselves. Two favorite Tuscan bean dishes are:

Fagioli al fiasco   White beans placed in a large, bulbous wine *fiasco* (flask), together with olive oil, garlic, sage, rosemary, pepper, and water, then left to slow-cook, preferably in a still-warm wood-fired oven.

Fagioli all'uccelletto White beans cooked with tomatoes, olive oil, and sage.

Ravioli *with arugula*

Ravioli (Tuscany and Umbria)   Fresh *pasta* parcels with *ricotta* and spinach, or other fresh seasonal vegetables, including arugula; often served simply *al burro e salvia* (with melted butter and fresh sage).

Ribollita   Thick, almost solid vegetable and bread soup (see p.160).

Spaghetti alla norcina (Umbria) *Spaghetti* served with a pungent sauce made from anchovies, capers, olive oil, and plenty of grated black truffles.

Spaghetti col rancetto (Spoleto) Umbrian equivalent of *bucatini all'amatriciana,* the pasta served with a sauce of tomato and *pancetta* or *guancia,* and a sprinkling of grated *pecorino* cheese.

Strozzapreti (Tuscany and Umbria) *Gnocchi* (dumplings) made with *ricotta* cheese and spinach or beet greens. The name means "priest stranglers," which, depending on your clerical standpoint, is because priests either choked on them through overindulgence — or fastidiousness, as the *gnocchi,* made without egg, would be too coarse for priestly palates.

Arista di maiale, *garnished with black truffles*

Tordelli (Tuscany)   Half-moon shaped hand-made *ravioli* stuffed with meat and *pecorino* cheese and served *al ragù.*

Umbricelli al tartufo di Norcia (Umbria)   Rustic, homemade *spaghetti* seasoned with a sauce made from olive oil, broth, and grated black truffles.

Zuppa alla frantoiana (Tuscany) Classic Tuscan bread soup made with *cavolo nero,* bread, and the new season extra-virgin olive oil.

Zuppa di fagioli (Montalcino and all Tuscany)   Simple but substantial bean soup made with dried cannellini beans, vegetables, stale bread, and olive oil.

Zuppa di funghi (Tuscany and Umbria) Mushroom soup — a real treat in fall, when wild mushrooms are available.

Umbricelli al tartufo di Norcia

I SECONDI PIATTI

Arista alla fiorentina (Florence and all Tuscany)   Loin of pork seasoned with wild fennel seeds, rosemary, and garlic, then roasted and served with potatoes and turnip tops or *cavolo nero.*

Arista di maiale (Tuscany and Umbria) Roast loin of pork; sometimes stuffed with herbs and garlic.

Bistecca alla fiorentina (Tuscany) The famous broiled Tuscan T-bone steak (see p.168).

Cacciucco (Livórno, Viareggio, and rest of the Tuscan seaboard)   Classic fish stew, with at least five types of fish, including red mullet and red gurnard, small Mediterranean fish such as *gallinelle* and *tracine,* and squid and octopus.

Cinghiale in umido (Umbria and Tuscany)   Fresh wild boar slow-cooked with sage, rosemary, *pancetta,* and wine.

Coniglio al vino bianco (Tuscany and Umbria)   Wild rabbit stuffed with rosemary, sage, and garlic, sautéed in olive oil, and braised in white wine.

Fritto misto alla toscana (Tuscany) One of the best and lightest "mixed frys" — small pieces of chicken, sweetbreads, artichokes, baby lamb chops, and zucchini, breaded, dipped in beaten egg, and fried in extra-virgin olive oil.

Palombacci (Umbria)   Small wild songbirds threaded onto spits and cooked over a wood fire; often served with *salsa ghiotta,* a characteristic sauce made with red wine, chopped herbs, garlic, and olives. A hunter's specialty, *palombacci* may not be available in restaurants due to conservation laws.

Pollo alla diavola (Tuscany)   "Devil's chicken" — a whole young chicken, butterflied, seasoned with olive oil, plenty of black pepper and *peperoncino,* then grilled over a hot wood fire.

Porchetta (Umbria)   Whole suckling pig stuffed with garlic, rosemary, wild fennel, salt, and pepper, then roasted in a wood-fired oven.

Rosticciana (Tuscany)   Pork ribs, an inexpensive but tasty favorite, when cooked over a wood fire.

Scottiglia (Montalcino, Arezzo, and Siena)   A mixture of meats, chicken, pork, rabbit, veal, or lamb, cooked in olive oil, with sage, rosemary, tomatoes, and *peperoncino.* Traditionally served to workers on a slice of bread.

Sfoglia di fegato grasso   Not, strictly speaking, a Central Italian dish; a refined, classic creation of duck liver in a *pasta* envelope, served with white truffle sauce.

Trippa alla fiorentina (Florence and Tuscany)   Cleaned and boiled tripe, cut into squares, cooked with vegetables, and finally topped with a tomato sauce and baked with *parmigiano reggiano.*

Coniglio al vino bianco, *rabbit in white wine*

I CONTORNI

Asparagi alla fiorentina (Tuscany) Boiled asparagus, topped with a fried egg, grated *parmigiano reggiano* (parmesan) cheese, and lashings of melted butter.

Cardi gobbi alla perugina (Perugia and all Umbria)   Cardoons, first boiled then dipped in flour, fried, and served with meat or tomato sauce.

Fagioli al fiasco, all'uccelletto (Tuscany)   Slow-cooked beans either cooked in a Chianti *fiasco* (flask), or simmered with tomato and sage.

Lenticchie di Castellúccio (Umbria) Italy's finest lentils are cultivated at Piano di Castelluccio, near Norcia: they are delicious served as a side dish with broiled meats.

Tartufi neri arrostiti (Umbria)   During the truffle gathering season in the Valle di Nera region, the best shaped specimens are covered in a slice of *pancetta* (bacon), wrapped in aluminum foil, and roasted slowly under the burning embers of a wood or coal fire.

Sfoglia di fegato grasso

La Bistecca alla Fiorentina

FLORENTINE T-BONE STEAK

UNLIKE MOST OTHER ITALIANS, who, on the whole, eat meat sparingly, Tuscans are unashamed, unreconstructed carnivores. They love nothing more than to enjoy, in quantity, both *affettati misti* — salty, cured pork *salumi* and *prosciutto* — and mouthwateringly char-broiled fresh beef, veal, pork, and sausages.

The biggest, literally, treat of all remains *la bistecca alla fiorentina*. Indeed, this massive T-bone is at once one of the most simple yet characteristic dishes of Tuscany. As with all simple food, however, the perfect *bistecca* may not be that easy to come across — and it is always an expensive treat, charged by the *etto* or *kilo*.

The perfect *bistecca alla fiorentina* is a T-bone cut from the triangular rack of

Bistecca alla fiorentina *cooking over wood embers*

the sirloin, and containing the nugget of tenderloin. The meat should come from the indigenous purebred Chianina, a powerful, muscular breed of beef cattle from the Val di Chiana near Arezzo, that is becoming increasingly rare. Moreover, it should be from an animal less than 18 months old whose meat is considered *vitellone,* more mature and flavorsome than veal, yet less red, and more tender than beef. And finally, this needs to be hung for at least three weeks to gain in flavor as well as tenderness.

Make no mistake: your average *bistecca alla fiorentina* is not for the fainthearted. It should be about *due* or *tre dita* (two or

three fingers) thick (ask for anything smaller, and you may well be scorned). It may weigh in at as much as 1–1¾ kg. (nearly 2¼–4 lbs.), though, admittedly, much of this is bone and fat. Although Tuscans with hearty appetites might easily manage this meat-feast on their own, don't be daunted by the size: it is quite in order to ask for a large steak to share between two or three people.

The art of cooking the *bistecca* is equally important. Red-hot embers are raked out from the fire, and a metal grill is laid over them. The unseasoned steak is placed on the grill for about five to seven minutes a side (depending on its thickness), and when it is deemed to be done (always *al sangue* — rare — unless you specify otherwise), it is laid on a platter, and seasoned with no more than salt, coarsely ground black pepper, and a generous sprinkling of extra-virgin olive oil. White Tuscan beans should always be ordered on the side as the classic accompaniment.

A *bistecca alla fiorentina,* when prepared and cooked perfectly, is the best steak in the world and demands to be accompanied by a top-class, Sangiovese-based super-Tuscan wine (see p.177).

For outstanding *bistecca:*

Antica Trattoria Sanesi
Via Arione, 33
50055 Lastra a Signa FI
tel: 055/8720234
Outside Florence, on the fringe of the Carmignano wine region.
$$

Cantinetta di Rignana
Via Rignana 13
Loc. Rignana
50022 Greve in Chianti FI
tel: 055/852601
This farmhouse restaurant is hard to find, but persevere, for young Massimo Abbarchini prepares authentic Tuscan foods, including *la bistecca,* with care and precision.
$$

Pecorino

EWE'S MILK CHEESE

CENTRAL ITALY IS noted for its superlative range of fresh and aged *pecorino,* cheeses made from pure ewe's milk, or from ewe's milk mixed in part with cow's.

In Etruscan times, ewe's milk cheeses were made from milk coagulated with wild artichoke flowers, a practice still carried out on a few farms in Chianti to produce outstanding *pecorino marzolino.*

More than likely, it was the *mezzadria* (see p.170) that led to the predominance of ewe's milk cheeses, for sheep rearing was more prevalent on smallholdings than cattle rearing.

Even today, the best *pecorino* cheeses are handmade along traditional lines. Small *caseifici* (cheese dairies), equipped with modern equipment to heat milk to the correct temperature (previously done, literally, by rule of thumb: by dipping in a finger), still use age-old methods of production. For example, some *pecorino* cheeses are rubbed with the dregs of olive oil to keep the crust from cracking, then wrapped in walnut leaves; some are smeared with tomato paste; and in Umbria, cheeses are aged in ash, a method that helped preserve cheese in the days before refrigeration.

If elsewhere in Italy, *pecorino* cheeses are often kept until very hard, to be used mainly as a sharp, flavorful cheese for grating, in Tuscany and Umbria, *pecorino* is a delicious cheese for eating. It is available either *tenero* or *dolce* — soft, sweet, young,

Pecorino *and* pecorino marzolino

with the flavor of herbs and grass from the meadows; or *semiduro* or *semi-secco,* i.e., not pressed but aged until it hardens and develops a dark brown crust, and more intense aromas and flavors.

TRY TO SAMPLE

Cacio, caciotto   Local name for *pecorino* cheese.

Marzolino (Chianti)   Oval-shaped *pecorino* cheese, traditionally made from pure ewe's milk coagulated with wild artichoke flowers, and in the spring time when the milk is at its most flavorful. *Marzolino* can be enjoyed *fresco* (fresh and young) or *stagionato* (aged).

Pecorino cenerino (Umbria) Traditionally made *pecorino* cheese aged in ash and wrapped in walnut leaves.

Pecorino delle crete senese (Siena and Montalcino)   Some of the finest *pecorino* cheeses come from the area known as *crete senese,* south of Siena toward Montalcino and across to Pienza.

Pecorino stagionato (Tuscany and Umbria)   *Pecorino* cheese aged for more than six months — the perfect partner for a glass of serious Tuscan red wine.

Pecorino tartufato (Umbria)   *Pecorino* cheese studded with black truffles.

Raviggiolo (Tuscany and Umbria) Extremely fresh, creamy curd cheese made from whole ewe's milk.

Ricotta (Tuscany and Umbria)   *Ricotta* cheese in this part of the country is invariably made with the rich whey of ewe's milk.

The crete senese *south of Siena, one of the finest areas for the production of* pecorino *cheeses*

Agriturismo
RURAL TOURISM

FOR CENTURIES, Central Italy had a system of sharecropping known as *mezzadria*. It was phased out only in the 1960s and 70s, which resulted in profound social and economic changes for both landowner and former tenant, but the evidence of the *mezzadria* is still there for all to see. Though much land has now been rationalized into specialized agriculture, you can still come across the old mixed system of so-called promiscuous culture, whereby a row of vines is trained up trees or other plants, interspersed with a few rows of grain, a vegetable garden, some olive trees, and so on. All of Tuscany and Umbria looked like this not that long ago, for the tenant farmers were not paid a wage and needed to be self-sufficient.

Barili, *the old measuring instruments of the mezzadria*

The old wooden measuring units of the *mezzadria,* now defunct, are still around, piled up haphazardly, gathering dust — the *barile* for wine, the *staia* for grain (one for the *padrone,* one for the *mezzadro,* each matched unit for unit as a means of measuring payment). And, of course, there still remain the simple, centuries-old *case coloniche* (tenant farmers' houses) where the *mezzadri* and their families lived and that are such a characteristic feature of the Central Italian rural landscape.

Today, these same houses, often located on lovely, sometimes internationally famous, wine estates, have been or are in the process of being restored and refurbished, to be rented out to Italians and foreign visitors who descend here each year in ever greater numbers. This is *agriturismo* (rural tourism) and, as such, it provides unrivaled opportunities to experience life in the Tuscan and Umbrian country.

Renting a farmhouse (for a long weekend, or for a week or longer) is a fine, relaxing way to get to know the region. In many instances, you can purchase local wine, olive oil, vegetables, cheese or meat from the farm you are staying on. You can also shop in local markets, and purchase local foods to cook yourself, preferably Tuscan-style, over an open fire. Indeed, we once spent a winter in just such an old farmhouse, enjoying nothing more most nights than warming ourselves in front of the fire while cooking meats, toasting Tuscan bread, then dribbling onto it the new year's oil from the farm — *our* oil, as we thought of it.

There are also further opportunities for enjoying life down on the farm in Tuscany and Umbria. Outstanding rural farmhouse restaurants serve local foods, utilizing produce from their own or neighboring farms, along with their own wines and olive oil. On some farms, you can also enjoy tutored wine tasting, and "hands on" cookery courses (see p.246).

Winemaker and food historian Giampaolo Pacini of the Podere Capaccia

Fattoria di Bacchereto, near Carmignano

AGRITURISMO — FAVORITE PLACES AND USEFUL ADDRESSES

TUSCANY
Associazione Agriturist Toscana
Piazza S. Firenze, 3
50122 Florence
tel: 055/287838

Castello Vicchiomaggio
Via Vicchiomaggio, 4
50022 Greve in Chianti FI
tel: 055/854079
fax: 055/853911
Weekend or weekly stays; Tuscan cooking courses; restaurant, by reservation.

Fattoria Castello di Volpaia
Loc. Volpaia
53017 Radda in Chianti SI
tel: 0577/738066
fax: 0577/738619
Hilltop estate: apartments, sensational wines and oil.

Fattoria dei Barbi
53024 Montalcino SI
tel: 0577/848277
fax: 0577/849356
Apartments; wines, meats, cheeses; trattoria, *La Taverna dei Barbi.*
$$

Fattoria di Bacchereto
Via Fontemorana, 179
Bacchereto
50040 Prato FI
tel/fax: 055/8717191
Accommodation; various courses; stylish rural restaurant, La Cantina di Toia.
$$

Fattoria Del Colle
53020 Trequanda SI
tel: 0577/662108
fax: 0577/849356
Apartments for weekend or weekly stays.

Podere Capaccia
Loc. Capaccia
53017 Radda in Chianti SI
tel: 0574/582426
fax: 0574/582428
Wine tasting; sampling of Tuscan dishes or historical Tuscan cuisine; courses; and at home with the Pacini family.

Podere Terreno
Via Terreno alla Via della Volpaia
53017 Radda in Chianti SI
tel/fax: 0577/738312

Farmhouse restaurant in the heart of wine country, serving excellent local foods; reservations only.
$$

UMBRIA
Agriturismo Poggio alle Vigne
Loc. Montespinello
06089 Torgiano PG
tel: 075/982944; 982129
fax: 075/9880294
Beautiful farmhouse apartments on the Lungarotti wine estate near Perugia.

Associazione Agriturist
Via Savonarola, 38
06121 Perugia
tel: 075/36665
fax: 075/32028

Azienda Agricola Belcapo
Loc. La Cacciata, 6
Fraz. Canale
05010 Orvieto TR
tel: 0763/92881
fax: 0763/41373
Rooms for short stays with the Belcapos; home-cooked meals on request.

I Dolci

SWEETS AND PASTRIES

L IKE VIRTUALLY EVERYTHING else in this sober and finely balanced region, the *dolci* of Tuscany and Umbria are not overblown, sickly sweet baroque creations, but, on the whole, simple, fruit-and-nut based cakes, *biscotti* and other cookies, and pastries to enjoy, rarely as desserts after meals, but for an afternoon *merenda* (tea), often accompanied with a glass of sweet Vin Santo.

Panforte di Siena

Umbria, with its monasteries, convents, and religious institutions, has a great range of individual *dolci,* produced, we imagine, by hardworking, sweet-loving monks and nuns. Perugia, its capital, is famous throughout the world for its chocolate *baci* (kisses).

TRY TO SAMPLE

Africani (Greve in Chianti)   Small, sweet cookies made from egg yolk, sugar, and butter, browned in the oven.
Baci di Assisi (Assisi)   Little, round meringue "kisses."
Brutti ma buoni (Tuscany and Umbria)   These irregular shaped, "ugly but nice" little cookies are usually made from sugar, egg white, and almonds.

Buccellato (Lucca)   Ring-shaped yeast cake with candied fruits and aniseed.
Cantuccini (Prato, Panzano, and all Tuscany)   The classic, hard, twice-cooked *biscotto* made with flour, egg, and almonds, to dunk in Vin Santo.
Pan coi santi (Siena)   Yeasty, sweet raisin-and-nut bread.
Pan nociato (Todi and Umbria)   Delicious and substantial bread made with walnuts, raisins, wine, and spices.
Ricciarelli (Tuscany and Umbria)   Soft, almond-and-honey cookies.
Schiacciata con uva (Panzano and all Tuscany)   Sweet, flat bread studded with fresh grapes in season or with raisins and nuts at other times.

SIENA'S SPICED CAKES

Pan pepato and *panforte* are two ancient Sienese specialties. *Pan pepato* dates from medieval times, when honey was used as a sweetener, and spices from the Orient were newly arrived flavorings. Medieval taste is evident, too, in the mixture of the sweet and spicy, for this flat, honey-sweetened cake is filled with an extravagant mixture of candied fruits and nuts, flavored with spices, and covered with a dusting of ground black pepper. The better-known *panforte di Siena* is a less peppery variation available in either black, cocoa- or white, sugar-dusted versions. The former is the older, while the more popular white version was created in the last century in honor of Queen Margherita.

Both *pan pepato* and *panforte* are characteristic tastes of Siena which you should not miss. And a possible added benefit: *"Pan pepato,"* a beautiful Sienese wine producer whispered to me *sotto voce,* "is the best aphrodisiac in

I Vini

THE WINES OF TUSCANY AND UMBRIA

Tuscany and Umbria are at once historic, noble, and traditional, as well as modern, international, and dynamic wine regions.

This essential paradox means that this is probably the most exciting part of Italy for both the casual wine drinker and the dedicated, intrepid oenophile. There is plenty of choice for sound, everyday, and medium-priced wines, such as Tuscany's Vernaccia di San Gimignano, Chianti, Barco Reale, Rosso di Montalcino, Morellino di Scansano, and Umbria's Orvieto, Rosso di Montefalco, and Torgiano. Outstanding DOCG reds include Brunello di Montalcino, Chianti Classico, Torgiano *riserva,* and Carmignano, while the so-called "super-Tuscans," produced outside the scope of DOC or DOCG, primarily from Cabernet Sauvignon or Sangiovese, continue to attract headlines and attention.

Harvesting Trebbiano grapes in the vineyards of Carmignano

TUSCANY

Bianco di Pitigliano DOC   If you are holidaying on the coast of Southern Tuscany's Maremma, this sound, if not overly exciting, local white wine produced from mainly Trebbiano Toscano is worth trying.
Recommended producer: Mantellassi.

Bolgheri DOC   Some say that this newly emerging wine zone on the Tuscan seaboard south of Livórno has the potential to become Tuscany's California; certainly, it has a prestigious pedigree, home of two of Tuscany's greatest super wines, Sassicaia, produced by Marchese Incisa della Rochetta, and Ornellaia, produced by Ludovico Antinori.

Brunello di Montalcino DOCG
One of Italy's greatest, most long-lived, and most expensive and prestigious red wines. It is produced from Sangiovese Grosso, grown in the commune of Montalcino, in the province of Siena where the grape is known as Brunello, and aged in large wooden casks for a minimum of four years.
Recommended producers: Barbi, Caparzo, Altesino, Col d'Orcia, Villa Banfi, Lisini, Biondi-Santi, Val di Suga.

Carmignano DOCG   This tiny wine zone west of Florence, extending into the Montalbano hills, produces outstanding wines. Red Carmignano, from Sangiovese and Canaiolo, with the addition of up to ten per cent Cabernet Sauvignon, is a silky, classic Tuscan red of great class. Rosato Carmignano (known also as Vin Ruspo) is a robust rosé made from the same grapes. Barco Reale is a young Carmignano red named after the Medici hunting preserve within which the Carmignano vineyard lies.
Recommended producers: Capezzana, Bacchereto, Calavria, Artimino, Ambra.

Radda in Chianti

Chianti DOCG Probably Italy's most famous red wine, produced widely throughout Tuscany, traditionally from Sangiovese (mainly), Canaiolo, and small amounts of white Trebbiano Toscano and Malvasia, but now, mainly without the white grapes. "Straight" Chianti is an uncomplicated red wine, best drunk young, and is produced through-out the provinces of Florence, Siena, Arezzo, Pisa, and Pistoia. There are also seven delimited subzones: Chianti Classico, the classic heartland, between Florence and Siena *(Antinori, Lamole di Lamole, Vicchiomaggio, Capaccia, Volpaia, Isole e Olena, Felsina Berardenga, Pagliarese, Castellina, Ama, Badia a Coltibuono, Cacchiano, Castello dei Rampola, Riecine, Castell'in Villa,*

Damigiane, *demi-johns*

Fontodi, Vignamaggio, Fonterutoli, Montsanto); Chianti Colli Aretini, east of Florence, along the Arno valley in the province of Arezzo; Chianti Colli Fiorentini, a zone that extends over hills mainly to the south and east of Florence between Val d'Arno and Val di Pesa; Chianti Colline Pisane, a zone southeast of Pisa, centered on Casciana Terme; Chianti Montalbano, a dramatic hill zone west of Florence *(Capezzana, Artimino);* Chianti Colli Senesi, a large zone that spreads over the wine hills of the province of Siena *(Avignonesi, Barbi, Poliziano, Cerro);* and Chianti Rúfina, a tiny, but prestigious wine zone east of Florence in the foothills of the Apennines above the Sieve valley *(Frescobaldi, Selvapiana).*

Elba DOC Tuscany's largest offshore island satisfies the thirst of locals and holidaymakers alike with Sangiovese based red and Trebbiano white.

Galestro This zesty, light, white wine has been created as a means of utilizing surplus white Trebbiano grapes. *Recommended producers: Antinori, Frescobaldi, Ruffino, Brolio.*

VIN SANTO

Vin Santo is one of Italy's oldest and most traditional wines. This unique sweet dessert wine is traditionally produced from grapes that have been laid out to dry on cane mats or hung by the bunch. Months later, the raisined grapes are pressed, and the sugar-rich grape must is trans-ferred to tiny *caratelli* (small barrels) that are sealed, then left to age in attics, suffering the cold of winter and the stuffy heat of summer. The wine that emerges from this brutal treatment as

much as three or four years later can be glorious: oxidized certainly, and varying in degrees of sweetness, yet with an underlying bitter aftertaste that keeps it from cloying, and a marvelous concentration of complex flavors of nuts, dried fruits, and caramel. Great Vin Santo is too good to dip *cantuccini* into, but we enjoy this Tuscan practice all the same.

Recommended producers

Avignonesi, Poliziano, Isole e Olena, Volpaia, Montagliari, Capezzana.

Montecarlo DOC   Undervalued white wine produced from Trebbiano (mainly), with the addition of Sémillon, Pinot Grigio, Pinot Bianco, Sauvignon, and Roussanne, from vineyards around Montecarlo, near Lucca, as well as lesser amounts of Sangiovese based red.
Recommended producers: Buonamico, Franceschini, Carmignani, Michi.

Morellino di Scansano DOC   This little-known wine zone south of Grosseto produces great, rustic but characterful and rich red wines entirely from the Morellino, a local name for Sangiovese.
Recommended producers: Mantellassi, Banti, Le Pupille.

Moscadello di Montalcino DOC
Sweet, grapy, sometimes *frizzante*, white wines are produced from Moscato Bianco grapes grown in the vineyards of Montalcino. A rare, concentrated *liquoroso* version, similar in weight to Sauternes, is also produced.
Recommended producer: Villa Banfi.

Parrina DOC   Southern Tuscany's select seaside community of Orbetello is the source of both Sangiovese based red, and Trebbiano based white.
Recommended producer: La Parrina.

Pomino DOC   This is a name that deserves to be better known: outstanding white and red wines are produced in this tiny but historic wine zone within the Chianti Rúfina area. Red Pomino is made from from Sangiovese and Canaiolo, with the addition of Cabernet and Merlot, while white Pomino comes from Chardonnay, Pinot Bianco, and Trebbiano. A good Vin Santo is also produced from semi-dried *passito* grapes left to wither on the vine.
Recommended producers: Frescobaldi, Petrognano.

Rosso di Montalcino DOC   Fine red wine produced from Brunello grapes with only one year's obligatory aging. However, serious, polished wines have emerged under this DOC that are by no means lightweight or second-string Brunello.

Lago di Corbara, near Orvieto

Recommended producers: Caparzo, Val di Suga, Altesino, Villa Banfi, Barbi, Costanti, Poggio Antico, Argiano, Talenti, Ciacci Piccolomini, Col d'Orcia.

Rosso di Montepulciano DOC
As in Montalcino, this relatively new DOC allows the producers of Vino Nobile di Montepulciano to produce younger, more supple styles of wine.
Recommended producers: Trerose, Avignonesi, Poliziano, Contucci.

Vernaccia di San Gimignano DOCG
Tuscany's most characterful white wine is made from indigenous Vernaccia grapes grown around San Gimignano.
Recommended producers: Terruzi & Puthod, San Quirico, Guicciardini-Strozzi, Monteniddi, Pietraserena.

Vino Nobile di Montepulciano DOCG   Distinguished red wine from vineyards entirely within the commune of Montepulciano, produced from Sangiovese (locally called Prugnolo), Canaiolo, and tiny amounts of Malvasia and Trebbiano Toscano.
Recommended producers: Trerose, Le Casalte, Avignonesi, Boscarelli, Contucci, Poliziano.

Umbria

Colli Altotiberini DOC Red, white, and rosé wines produced on slopes above the Upper Tiber Valley around Città di Castello.

Colli Perugini DOC Red, white, and rosé wines produced from vineyards along the Tiber Valley between Perugia and Todi.

Colli del Trasimeno DOC
Vast, sprawling vineyard extending over hills above the popular Lake Trasimeno and producing undistinguished red and white wines.

Montefalco DOC One of the great, though still little-known, wine zones of Umbria, source of an outstanding red wine (mainly Sangiovese). **Montefalco DOCG** The zone's greatest wine is a distinctive red *passito* made from semi-dried Sagrantino grapes; rich in the mouth and sometimes a touch sweet. It is an unusual and rare classic, also available in a dry version.

Recommended producers: Paolo Bea, Adanti, Caprai, Antonelli.

Orvieto DOC Famous and distinctive white wine from vineyards around Orvieto produced in both *secco* (dry) and *amabile* (medium-dry) versions. *Recommended producers: Barberani, Bigi (Vigneto Torricella), Castello della Sala, Decugnano dei Barbi, Palazzone.*

Torgiano DOC Umbria's greatest wines come from around the medieval town of Torgiano. A range of types and styles is produced, though the DOC applies only to some, including whites from Trebbiano, with a proportion of the distinctive Grechetto, and reds mainly from Sangiovese and Canaiolo.

Torgiano *riserva* DOCG We consider this Sangiovese based red one of Italy's greatest wines, richly textured, and with great aging potential. Production is almost entirely in the hands of the Lungarotti family.

Recommended producer: Lungarotti.

FOOD AND WINE COMBINATIONS

Affettati misti Salty Tuscan cured meats are best accompanied by a fresh, slightly acidic young Chianti.

Pappa al pomodoro
This bread-and-tomato mush may be favored by babies and the infirm, but we love it with a glass of cool Vernaccia di San Gimignano.

Ribollita The deep flavor of *cavolo nero* is best complemented by a deeply flavored Chianti Classico *riserva*.

Pappardelle alla lepre
Wide ribbon noodles with hare sauce cry out for a rustic but flavorful red, such as Morellino di Scansano or Umbria's Montefalco Rosso.

Vin Santo *with* cantuccini di Prato biscotti

Bistecca alla fiorentina Simple char-grilled meat, such as the *bistecca*, provides a perfect foil to a serious red wine: your choice should definitely be one of the super-Tuscans.

Cinghiale in umido
Rich, wild boar stew is another classic: try it with an old Brunello di Montalcino or, in Umbria, with Torgiano *riserva*.

Cantuccini di Prato
Don't miss the pleasure of munching on these crunchy almond *biscotti* while sipping a small glass of Vin Santo, the perfect finish to a meal in Tuscany.

I Super-Toscani
SUPER-TUSCAN DESIGNER WINES

THE SO-CALLED "super-Tuscans" are wines made outside the scope of either DOC or DOCG, and thus, to date, are entitled only to humble *vino da tavola* status.

Red super-Tuscans fall into two schools, those made from primarily the best clones of the indigenous Sangiovese grape (either 100 per cent or with the addition of other grapes), and those made primarily from the international superstar, Cabernet Sauvignon, as its principal component.

White super-Tuscans are made from Chardonnay and Sauvignon, sometimes used together with local grapes. Most super-Tuscans are aged (and sometimes fermented) in new French *barriques* — oak barrels containing 225 liters, or about 55 gallons, made with wood from the Tronçais, Allier, or Vosges forests of France. New French oak, when used judiciously, can add a voluptuous, silky character to such wines, smooth any rustic edges and give a glossy profile that is deemed more acceptable internationally. Presented with *nomi di fantasia* (imaginative names) on their beautiful, designer labels, and bottled in tall, heavy, "antique" bottles with deep punts in the bottom, the super-Tuscan *vini da tavola* are now an established part of the Tuscan (and Italian) wine scene, and many such wines rank among the greatest in the world. Here are some of our favorites.

SANGIOVESE BASED REDS
Camerlengo   Fattoria di Pagliarese
Cepparello   Isole e Olena
Coltassala   Castello di Volpaia
Flaccianello della Pieve   Fontodi
Pergole Torte   Monte Vertine
Querciagrande   Podere Capaccia
Ripa delle More   Castello Vicchiomaggio
Sangioveto di Coltibuono   Badia a Coltibuono
Sodi di San Niccolò   Castellare di Castellina
Tignanello   Antinori

Tignanello, *one of the first — and still one of the greatest — super-Tuscan wines*

CABERNET BASED REDS
Ghiaie della Furba   Tenuta di Capezzana
Mormoreto   Marchesi de' Frescobaldi
Ornellaia   Tenuta dell'Ornellaia
Sammarco   Castello dei Rampolla
Sassicaia DOC Tenuta San Guido
Solaia   Marchesi Antinori
Tavernelle   Villa Banfi

WHITE WINES
Chardonnay   Capezzana, Isole e Olena
Fontanelle   Villa Banfi
Il Marzocco   Avignonesi
Le Grance   Caparzo
Predicato del Selvante Castelgiocondo

Antinori cellars in the ninth-century Vallombrosan abbey at Badia a Passignano, Tuscany

In the Land of the Black Rooster

THE CHIANTI CLASSICO TRAIL

CHIANTI IS ONE OF ITALY'S single-most important wine regions, and one of its most welcoming. Between Florence and Siena, a sign-posted *strada del vino* (wine road) will take you through the heart of Chianti Classico country — the land of the black rooster, symbol of the Chianti Classico consortium.

To reach the wine country from Florence, exit the *auto-strada* at Firenze Certosa, then proceed through Impruneta to Strada in Chianti and the start of the wine road.

Greve in Chianti, a lively market town dominated by its irregularly shaped *piazza,* serves as the focus for the surrounding small communities and individual wine estates, many of which stand aloof on hilltops. One such is the Castello Vicchiomaggio, built in 957; today, it is owned by Englishman John Matta, and is one of the most welcoming estates to be found in this area.

From Greve, take the Via Chianti-giana, the old coach route linking Florence and Siena. Isolated wine estates lie off a complicated network of dirt tracks on either side of the route. To truly experience Chianti, it is essential to strike off now and then on these small roads.

Black rooster of Chianti

For example, find the track roughly between Panzano and Badia a Passignano to reach the Cantinetta di Rignana, an outstanding rural restaurant. Or make for Badia a Passignano and the Vallombrosan monastery. Its cellars (not open to the public) now house the most famous super-Tuscan wine of all, Antinori's Tignanello. Or, if you dare, outside Greve, find the back road that leads over the Monte dei Chianti to Radda, via Lámole.

From Greve, the next direct important wine community is Panzano. You can dine outside the town in Giovanni Capelli's farmhouse restaurant, Trattoria dei Montagliari.

Castellina in Chianti, further to the south, is still dominated by its medieval fortress. From Castellina, it is a short drive, through Fonterútoli, to Siena itself.

However, before you reach Castellina, look for the road on the left that leads to Radda in Chianti, a small but important wine town with plenty of character that lies surrounded by the zone's highest hills, now intensively cultivated with vines and the source of some of the greatest and most long-lived Chiantis. Incidentally, if you're feeling peckish,

---

ANDAR' PER LE VIGNE — INTO WINE COUNTRY

Azienda Agrituristica Pagliarese
Via Pagliarese, 4
53019 Castelnuovo
Berardenga SI
tel: 0577/359070
fax: 0577/359200
Warm fleshy wines and farmhouse accommodation.

Badia a Coltibuono
Loc. Badia a Coltibuono
53013 Gaiole in Chianti SI
tel: 0577/749498

fax: 0577/749235
12th-century stone complex and great wines.

Castello Vicchiomaggio
(address, p.171)
English owned; fine Chianti Classico and super-Tuscan Ripa delle More.

Enoteca del Gallo Nero
Piazzetta S. Croce, 8
50022 Greve in Chianti FI
tel: 055/853297
Best wine shop in Chianti.

Fattoria Castello di Volpaia
(address, p.171)
The vendita diretta *is "always open"; there is also a bar selling drinks and simple snacks.*
$

La Cantinetta di Rignana
(address, p.168)
Authentic Tuscan food, especially bistecca alla fiorentina.
$$

before reaching Radda, the Ristoro a Lucarelli is an excellent bar-cum-shop. There are also many atmospheric and authentic restaurants around Radda.

Between Radda and Gaiole, there are several historic monuments and castles, an indication of this area's importance and prosperity over the centuries. The 12th-century Badia a Colti-buono is one such, today, a famous wine estate owned and run by the Stucchi-Prinetti family (direct sales, *trattoria,* and cooking classes by Lorenza de' Medici).

South of Gaiole, the Castello di Brolio has been home to the Ricasoli family since the 11th century and the Casa Vinicola Barone Ricasoli. Barone Bettino Ricasoli, Prime Minister after Cavour, formulated the original "recipe" of grapes and production methods for Chianti.

While the countryside between Radda and Gaiole is rugged in the extreme, with some of the highest

vineyards in Chianti, the wine country to the southeast, around Castelnuovo Berardenga, is an immediate contrast — lower, softer, and more fertile. Its wines are similarly warm and full-bodied. From Castelnuovo Berardenga, you can reach Siena by the N73.

THE CHIANTI CLASSICO TRAIL

To Florence

IMPRUNETA

STRADA IN CHIANTI

Arno

CASTELLO VICCHIOMAGGIO

BADIA A PASSIGNANO

GREVE IN CHIANTI

PANZANO

LAMOLE

BADIA A COLTIBUONO

RADDA IN CHIANTI

CASTELLINA IN CHIANTI

GAIOLE IN CHIANTI

To Castelnuovo Berardenga

N

FONTERUTOLI

0 km 2 4
0 miles 2

INTO WINE COUNTRY (CONTD)

La Villa Miranda
53017 Radda in Chianti
tel: 0577/738021
fax: 0577/738668
Popular inn with accommo-dation, shop, and trattoria.
$–$$

Podere Capaccia
(address, p.171)
Weekends for direct sales; tastings and courses by arrangement. The Pacini family are usually "at home".

Ristoro a Lucarelli
Loc. Lucarelli
53017 Radda in Chianti SI
tel: 0577/ 733538
To stock up for a picnic .

Ristorante Le Vigne
Podere Le Vigne
53017 Radda in Chianti SI
tel/fax: 0577/738640
Charming friendly restaurant in old house among vineyards.
$

Taverna del Guerrino
Castello di Montefioralle
50022 Greve in Chianti FI
tel: 055/853106
Simple food; great views.
$

Trattoria dei Montagliari
Strada del Vino
50020 Panzano FI
tel: 055/852014
fax: 055/852804
Stylish, popular farmhouse restaurant.
$$–$$$

The Rest of the Best
OTHER TUSCAN WINE TRIPS

THE VINE GROWS prolifically throughout virtually all of Tuscany, so the whole region is, in effect, wine country. However, these suggested destinations are so congenial that they are well worth hunting out even if wine is not your principal interest.

CARMIGNANO
The Carmignano wine country lies just to the west of Florence, on a steep, limestone balcony of hills. This was once the playground of the Medici, who constructed villas at Poggio a Caiano, Artimino, Capezzana, and Bacchereto.

It is worth coming here not only to discover Carmignano's fine red wines (which have recently been elevated to select DOCG status), but also to explore this still unspoiled wine country. From Poggio a Caiano, visit the Medici villa at Artimino, a tiny but lovely walled town, and dine at the outstanding and stylish Ristorante Da Delfina. Or else, head for Carmignano (stopping to view Pontormo's "Visitation" in the church of San Michele). Then climb into the hills to Tenuta di Capezzana, the finest wine estate in the zone, and to the isolated hamlet of Bacchereto. Here, La Cantina di Toia, a fine restaurant, was once the home of Leonardo da Vinci's grandmother.

Carmignano vineyards

SAN GIMIGNANO
It is worth coming to San Gimignano just to approach the remarkable medieval skyline of steep towers rising above the classic Tuscan landscape. San Gimignano's wines have always benefited from its unique "high profile." In truth, they deserve to, for while most whites produced from indigenous Tuscan grapes are insipid at best, Vernaccia di San Gimignano is full-flavored and characterful.

SIENA
Located in the historic Medici fortress, Siena's Enoteca Italica Permanente provides the Italian wine lover with the unique opportunity to tour all of Italy in a glass. The *enoteca* is an official, perma-

---

ANDAR' PER LE VIGNE — INTO WINE COUNTRY

CARMIGNANO
La Cantina di Toia
Via Toia, 12
50040 Bacchereto FI
tel/fax: 055/8717135
Stylish regional foods.
$$$

Ristorante Da Delfina
Via della Chiesa, 1
50042 Artimino FI
tel: 055/8718074
fax: 055/8718175
Famous trattoria *over-looking wine hills.*
$$$

Tenuta di Capezzana
Via Capezzana, 100
50040 Seano FI
tel: 055/8706005
fax: 055/8706673
Carmignano's finest wines and olive oils.

SIENA
Enoteca Italica Permanente
Fortezza Medicea
53100 Siena SI
tel: 0577/288497
fax: 0577/42627
Wines from all over Italy.

SAN GIMIGNANO
Enoteca Il Castello
Palazzo Gonfiantini
Via del Castello, 20
53037 San Gimignano SI
tel: 0577/940878
The best place in town to sample wines accompanied by simple nibbles and local foods.
$–$$

nent exhibition of wines from every corner of Italy, all clearly displayed and available for tasting at the adjoining bar (open afternoons and evenings only).

MONTALCINO AND MONTEPULCIANO

Montalcino and Montepulciano may be often linked together as fine, classic wine towns, but they are worlds apart.

Montalcino, with its grand *fortezza* (the Enotecca La Fortezza is located within its walls) is essentially a medieval country town. Though its Brunello wines rank among the most famous and expensive in Italy, the wine country is quite unspoiled.

Don't miss visiting the Fattoria dei Barbi not only to sample wines, but also to purchase outstanding homecured *salumi* and hand-made *pecorino* cheeses. There is also a good restaurant on the farm. Afterward, continue to Sant' Antimo, one of the most beautiful Romanesque chapels in Central Italy.

In contrast, Montepulciano is a fine Renaissance hill town, its central avenue lined with grand palaces. Below ground is an extensive network of cellars that has traditionally served as a store for its noble wines. Visit the Azienda Agricola Contucci cellars below the Palazzo Contucci if you are feeling thirsty.

MAREMMA

Tuscany's deep south, the Maremma, is a relatively little visited area (with the exception of coastal areas in the summer season of July and August). Come here to find the hot springs of Saturnia, which emerge from the bowels of the earth at some 38°C (100°F) and are located in the middle of a field.

After luxuriating in the hot water and mud, make your way (smelling strongly of sulphur) to the Enoteca Bacco e Cerere for warming goblets of Morellino di Scansano, one of the great undervalued wines of Tuscany. Or else, repair to Montemerano to enjoy simple, authentically prepared foods at the Antico Frantoio, the restaurant of wine producer and local character Erik Banti.

La Fortezza, *Montalcino's fortified castle*

INTO WINE COUNTRY (CONTD)

MONTALCINO AND MONTEPULCIANO

Azienda Agricola Contucci
Palazzo Contucci
Via del Teatro, 1
53045 Montepulciano SI
tel/fax: 0578/757006
Cellars under palazzo.

Castello di Banfi
Villa Banfi
53020 Sant'Angelo Scalo SI
tel: 0577/840111
American owned, one of the most modern wineries in Italy.

Fattoria dei Barbi
53024 Montalcino SI
tel: 0577/848277
fax: 0577/849356
Brunello, salumi, cheeses, and a good restaurant.
$$

Enoteca La Fortezza
Piazzale Fortezza
53024 Montalcino SI
tel/fax: 0577/849211
Located in the 13th-century fortress, serving wines and snacks.
$

MAREMMA

Antico Frantoio
Piazza Solferino, 7
58050 Montemerano GR
tel: 0564/602615
Local foods and a good selection of wines.
$$

Enoteca Bacco e Cerere
Via Mazzini, 4
58050 Saturnia GR
tel/fax: 0564/601235
Good selection of wines. Restaurant serves local food.
$–$$

The Wines and Wine Roads of Umbria
ORVIETO, MONTEFALCO, AND TORGIANO

UMBRIA IS NOT for the single-minded wine tourist: the country is far too easy, too pretty, too relaxing to make hard work of. But visitors staying in Italy's "Green Heart" may certainly wish to make excursions into the wine country, both to stock up for their own needs and to visit three outstanding and atmospheric wine towns.

Orvieto's splendid Duomo *dominating the skyline*

ORVIETO

Orvieto is a hugely atmospheric town that is well worth visiting, not just for the delightful wines that are produced here. It is strategically sited on a tufa mesa that rises dramatically from the valley floor, and its magnificent *Duomo,* visible for miles from the surrounding country, is one of the most beautiful in Italy, most notable for its magnificent facade with bas-relief sculpture and striking mosaics depicting scenes from the Old and New Testaments. The tufa bedrock on which Orvieto has been built has, over the centuries, been carved into a maze of caves interconnected with tunnels, a process that began in Etruscan times and continued through the Roman and medieval eras. The cool caves of Orvieto were perfect for the storage of wine, one factor, certainly, that contributed to the fame and prosperity of the town. For, if the natural, cool ambience of the caves kept the wine well, it futhermore had the effect often of stopping fermentation, and, thus, the wines of Orvieto have

always retained a slight residual sweetness that makes them particularly delightful to drink as an *aperitivo*. Try them for yourself at the Cantina Foresi, a small bar on the corner of the Piazza del Duomo, and ask to see the hand-carved cellars where the wines are stored.

Outside Orvieto, tour the wine country, especially around the lovely Lake Corbara. The Barberani winery can be visited, while Vissani, located on the shores of the lake, is one of the most famous restaurants in Italy, a mecca for lovers of fine, creative cuisine.

MONTEFALCO

Montefalco, located some 12 km. (7½ miles) south of Foligno, is, as yet, a little-known wine town that deserves to be visited. The small town itself is known as the *"Ringhiera dell'Umbrie"* — Umbria's balcony — because of its commanding, strategic position looking down on the old Roman Via Flaminia. Climb up to

---

MUSEO DEL VINO

Torgiano's *Museo del Vino,* the most important wine museum in Italy, has 20 rooms of well-presented archeological, historical, ethnographic, artistic, technical, and ceramic displays relating to wine and viticulture not just in Umbria but throughout Italy and the Mediterranean. As such, it successfully serves to place the subject of wine within the broad historical and cultural context of the Western world. After visiting the museum, the full range of Lungarotti wines can be tasted and purchased in the adjoining *Osteria del Museo.*

Museo del Vino
Palazzo Baglioni
Corso Vittorio Emanuele, 11
06089 Torgiano PG
tel: 075/9880200
fax: 075/9880294

the belltower of the Palazzo Comunale to enjoy astonishing views of the surrounding country.

Montefalco is the source of outstanding red wines, as well as of a rare *passito* red wine made from dried grapes, Sagrantino di Montefalco. It is one of the greatest, if most unusual, wines of this type. Sample it in the Ristorante Coccorone, or visit the Antica Azienda Paolo Bea, one of the leading traditional producers in this area.

Over the rooftops of Montefalco

TORGIANO

Torgiano, another small medieval town just 10 km. (6 miles) south of Perugia, has come to be recognized as one of the great wine areas of Italy, the source of an immense and very high quality range of white, red, and sparkling wines.

This has been achieved entirely through the efforts of the Lungarotti family, who transformed the zone after World War II. Torgiano itself is certainly worth coming to to visit the Cantine Lungarotti and the *Museo del Vino* (see opposite), as well as to sample wines and regional foods in the luxury of the restaurant of the Lungarotti's Tre Vaselle hotel. It makes a most pleasant base for touring Umbria and visiting nearby towns such as Perugia, Assisi, and Gubbio, as well as Lake Trasimeno.

ANDAR' PER LE VIGNE — INTO WINE COUNTRY

ORVIETO

Barberani
Az. Ag. Vallesanta
Loc. Cerreto
Baschi
05023 Orvieto TR
tel: 0744/950113
fax: 0763/40773
Ultra-modern new premises above Lake Corbara.

Cantina Foresi
Piazza del Duomo, 2
05018 Orvieto TR
tel: 0763/41611
An obligatory stop for a glass of the family's own Orvieto enjoyed within the shadow of the Duomo.

Vissani
(address, p.185)
Super-chef Gianfranco Vissani's famous restaurant.
$$$$

MONTEFALCO

Antica Azienda Paolo Bea
Via Cerrete, 8
06036 Montefalco PG
tel/fax: 0742/378128
Outstanding wines made by the Bea family.

Ristorante Coccorone
Largo Tempestivi
06036 Montefalco PG
tel/fax: 0742/379535
Good local foods and wines.
$$

TORGIANO

Cantine Giorgio Lungarotti
Via Mario Angeloni, 16
06089 Torgiano PG
tel: 075/9880348
fax: 075/9880294
One of Italy's leading family wine estates. The special cru wines are not easily available elsewhere.

Le Tre Vaselle
Via Giuseppe Garibaldi, 48
06089 Torgiano PG
tel: 075/9880447
fax: 075/9880214
Elegant restaurant serving traditional and regional food.
$$$$

Chef Roberto Vitali of Le Tre Vaselle, Torgiano

Indirizzi
USEFUL ADDRESSES

TUSCANY
Antica Macelleria Falorni
Piazza Matteotti, 69–71
50022 Greve in Chianti FI
tel: 055/853029
fax: 055/8544521
*Long-established
butcher's, with an
extensive range of both
fresh meat and out-
standing Tuscan salumi.*

**Caffè Fiaschetteria
Italiana**
Piazza del Popolo, 6
53024 Montalcino SI
tel: 0577/849043
*This popular central bar
serves an excellent range
of Rosso and Brunello di
Montalcino by the glass or
bottle.*
$

Cantinetta Antinori
Palazzo Antinori
Piazza degli Antinori, 3
50123 Florence
tel: 055/292234
fax: 055/2359877
*This stylish wine bar, a
popular hangout for
Florence's beau monde, is
worth visiting to sample
the full range of Antinori
wines by the glass or
bottle, along with snacks
or light meals.*
$$–$$$

*Panificio Flli. Cennini,
Panzano in Chianti*

**Enoteca del Chianti
Classico**
Via G. Verrazzano, 8–10
50020 Panzano in Chianti FI
tel: 055/852003
fax: 055/852128
*The best wines not only
from Chianti Classico but
all Tuscany.*

Enoteca Pinchiorri
Via Ghibellina, 87
58100 Florence
tel: 055/242777
fax: 055/244983
*One of the great restaurants
of Italy, serving refined
cuisine of the highest
order, accompanied by an
outstanding and extensive
list of Tuscan, Italian, and
French wines.*
$$$$

Fattoria Buca Nuova
Strada per Pienza, 34
53045 Montepulciano SI
tel/fax: 0578/758338
*Excellent marzolino, cacio,
and fresh pecorino
sott'olio cheeses.*

Gastronomia Porciatti
Piazza IV Novembre, 1
53017 Radda in Chianti SI
tel: 0577/738055
fax: 0577/738234
*Excellent homecured
salumi and cheeses and
good ready-to-eat food.*

Hosteria Il Carroccio
Via Casato di Sotto, 32
53100 Siena
tel: 0577/41165
*In the shadow of Siena's
belltower, this trattoria
serves good local foods.*
$

**Hotel La Cisterna –
Ristorante Le Terrazze**
Piazza della Cisterna, 24
53037 San Gimignano SI
tel: 0577/940328
fax: 0577/942080
*Beautiful views from the
dining room of this
perennial favorite.*
$$–$$$

**Hotel Paggeria Medicea –
Ristorante Biagio
Pignatta**
Viale Papa Giovanni XXIII
50040 Artimino FI
tel: 055/8718081;8718086
fax: 055/8718080
*Famous Medici villa with
hotel and restaurant.*
$$–$$$

**Il Cantinone del Gallo
Nero**
Via S. Spirito, 6R
50125 Florence
tel: 055/218898
fax: 055/7322793
Authentic Tuscan foods.
$

*View of Artimino from its
Medici Villa*

La Taverna dei Barbi
Fattoria dei Barbi
53024 Montalcino SI
tel: 0577/849357
fax: 0577/848356
*Stylish restaurant using
own farm products and
the great Barbi wines.*
$$–$$$

Panificio Flli. Cennini
Via XX Luglio, 60
50020 Panzano in Chianti FI
tel: 055/852223
fax: 055/852730
*Source of not only
outstanding pane toscano,
but also schiacciata con
uva and good homemade
biscotti.*

Sagrantino *grapes laid out to dry for the rare passito wine*

Pasticceria Nannini
Via F. Tozzi, 2
53100 Siena
tel: 0577/41301
For the best panforte *in town, as well as other Sienese dolci, such as* ricciarelli, colomba, fave di morte, *etc.*

Ristorante-Albergo Giovanni da Verrazzano
Piazza Matteotti, 28
50022 Greve in Chianti FI
tel: 055/853189
fax: 055/853648
Popular hotel-restaurant in Greve's market square.
$$

Caffè *Fiaschetteria Italiana, Montalcino*

Ristorante La Mangiatoia
Via Mainardi, 5
53037 San Gimignano SI
tel/fax: 0577/941528
Good local foods, including homemade pasta, *and game in season.*
$$

UMBRIA
Bottega di Pasticcerie
Via Portica, 9
06081 Assisi PG
tel: 075/812392
Wonderful selection of typical dolci.

Dai Fratelli
Via Duomo, 11
05018 Orvieto TR
tel: 0763/43965
Full range of Umbrian specialties, including fresh truffles in season. Stop here to make up a special picnic or to buy goodies to take back home.

Enoteca La Loggia
Via Loggia dei Mercanti, 6
05018 Orvieto TR
tel/fax: 0763/44371
Laura Punzi makes outstanding fruit preserves, as well as vegetables conserved sott'olio.

Enoteca Provinciale
Via Ulisse Rocchi, 18
06100 Perugia
tel: 075/5724824
Behind the cathedral in the historic heart of Perugia, this is a good source for the wines of Umbria.

Ristorante Umbra
Vicolo degli Archi, 6
06081 Assisi PG
tel: 075/812240
fax: 075/813653
This restaurant, in the hotel of the same name, is probably the best in this always busy pilgrim town.
$$$

Vissani
SS 448
Baschi
05020 Todi TR
tel/fax: 0744/950396
Though Vissani's is located in the middle of nowhere, knowledgeable diners flock here to one of Italy's greatest and most famous temples of creative gastronomy. Gianfranco's cuisine is imaginative, deftly prepared, sometimes astonishing.
$$$$+

Salume *produced by the* norcineria *at Fattoria dei Barbi*

BEST BUYS
- extra-virgin olive oil
- *cantuccini* and Vin Santo
- super-Tuscan wines
- local wines from wherever you are staying, such as Vernaccia di San Gimignano, Chianti, Brunello di Montalcino, and Orvieto
- fresh black truffles in season
- *panforte, pan pepato,* and other typical Sienese dolci, such as *ricciarelli*
- *pecorino* cheese (vacuum-wrapped for traveling long distance)
- chocolates from Perugia

The South

LAZIO, CAMPANIA,
CALABRIA, BASILICATA,
ABRUZZO & MOLISE,
PUGLIA

S OUTHERN ITALY, also known as the *Mezzogiorno* or land of the midday sun, is more a concept than a region, an amorphous entity whose boundaries vary considerably, depending on your point of view.

To listen to many Northerners, the *Mezzogiorno* (and with it, to their way of thinking, all the ills that plague modern Italy) may well begin somewhere not too far south of Milan. To Romans, who still believe proudly that their Eternal City is the center of Italy, it probably begins somewhere closer to Naples. Neapolitans, however, have no problems with this matter: their great, noisy, chaotic city is undoubtedly the capital of *Italia Meridionale* — Southern Italy — and they are proud of it.

What is indisputable is that, as you travel down the narrow, spiny Italian Peninsula, you inevitably reach a point when you know that you have arrived in the South. For us, that point probably occurs somewhere within the region of Lazio. For while Lazio's northern provinces undoubtedly have much in common with Central Umbria and Tuscany, somewhere along the way, as you approach Rome, and certainly to the south of the capital, you know that you are in the *Mezzogiorno*. It is not just a question of climate and geography (important though these two elements are); it is also the noise, the vivacity, the smells (good and bad), a vague but exciting thrill that here life is lived on the edge.

Inland Calabria, surprisingly lush and beautiful

DOLCE FAR NIENTE

In the South, it is far too hot — too hot and too poor — for its inhabitants to take life overly seriously. Thus, the fine art of *"dolce far niente"* has developed: not merely the art of "doing sweet nothing" but, rather, of appreciating the moment, the pleasure of being alive, of feeling the sun on your back. But make no mistake: the people of the South, contrary to what most Northerners would have us believe, are by no means averse to hard work. They do work hard, must work hard, simply to survive, for urban and rural poverty still exists on a large scale. But the difference between North and South, we imagine, is more a state of mind, an attitude toward work and life: for if Northern Italians seem to live to make money, Southerners, on the other hand, make money in order to enjoy living — and to enjoy it, under that glorious Mediterranean sun.

LAZIO — ALL ROADS DON'T LEAD TO ROME

The region that encompasses Rome and its environs, Lazio, extends from the coast north and south of the capital and inland to the Apennines. It retains the elements and atmosphere of its rich and historic past, from Etruscan towns such as Viterbo, to the Roman ruins of Ostia Antica and Tivoli. To the south of the Eternal City, on the ancient Via Appia, lie the

Colli Albani (Alban Hills), a particularly congenial wine zone, to which Romans have been escaping for centuries. Further south are the fertile plains of the old Roman *campagna felix,* the former breadbasket and vineyard of the empire.

CAMPANIA — A HOT LAND UNDER THE VOLCANO

To the south of Lazio, Campania doesn't just smoke, it sizzles with unrestrained vivacity, noise, and energy. A sense of danger — real or imagined — is never far away. The ruins of Pompeii and Herculaneum are vivid reminders of the volcanic eruptions of Vesuvio (less evident, but even sadder are the still-ruined towns in the Avellino hills, victims of the earthquake of 1980). Naples, old, crumbling, and former capital of the Bourbons, is so noisy a city that it may be difficult to keep your wits about you, let alone handbags or cameras, though this unsavory aspect has apparently improved in recent years. On the other hand, the fabled Amalfi Coast, with its steep and picturesque towns, such as Positano, Ravello, and Amalfi, continues to exert its timeless charm, making this one of the most popular and visited parts of Italy. The isle of Capri is one of the most perfect and beautiful in the Mediterranean.

CALABRIA — THE FORGOTTEN TOE OF ITALY

With its unspoiled stretches of Ionian beaches along Italy's instep, in addition to its lengthy Tyrrhenian coastline, Calabria should be a region ideal for vacationers. Unfortunately, its hastily built, often half-finished seaside towns sprawl one into another, and its coastal development leaves much to be desired. More interesting by far and well worth coming to explore are the isolated and ancient hilltop villages of this rugged and beautiful land, villages that cling tenaciously to their rocky outcrops, inward-looking, suspicious, unpenetrated. From the forested Sila to the inhospitable Aspromonte Mountains, few such untouched corners remain in Western Europe. Reggio Calabria, the region's earthquake-ravaged capital, is worth visiting for its splendid and important collection of Greek artifacts.

BASILICATA — A RUGGED, MOUNTAIN LAND

That Southern Italy is an area of contrasts is attested to by Basilicata. The popular image of endless southern sun, for example, is given the lie by this mountainous region, whose inhospitable winters are as long and fierce as in Alto Adige. Time seems to have all but stood still in this poor land once known as Lucania, where, in the inland villages, women in black still prod donkeys. Basilicata is hardly on-the-beaten-track Italy, but for the true traveler, it is a region that rewards a visit. Maratea, on the Tyrrhenian coast, is a dramatically sited hill town.

Local produce for sale on the Amalfi Coast

ABRUZZO & MOLISE —
SECLUDED FORESTS AND CROWDED BEACHES

Two regions linked administratively and historically, Abruzzo and Molise, lie along the Adriatic Coast between Le Marche and Puglia. As elsewhere, while beachside resorts are popular to the point of being overrun in summer, inland lies another world. In particular, Abruzzo's Gran Sasso National Park is a vast and wild area of great natural beauty. There is plenty of good walking here, especially along old pastoral tracks that once served for the annual transhumance of millions of sheep.

PUGLIA — THE DEEP, DEEP SOUTH

In many ways, Puglia stands apart from the rest of the South. For a start, it is one of the few regions in Italy not dominated by the Apennines. The land, as a result, is softer and abundantly fertile. Far away and remote though Puglia seems, this is a well-trodden land, for since Roman times, ports such as Bari and Brindisi have served as gateways to the Eastern Mediterranean. The stamp of foreign influence — Byzantine, Spanish, and Norman — is evident in architecture and even food, a reminder of Puglia's rich past. With its outstanding, still unspoiled coastline, its warm, friendly people, and its wealth of fine foods and generous wines, Puglia is among the most appealing of southern destinations.

Prodotti Regionali
REGIONAL PRODUCE

THE AGRICULTURAL SOUTH may be poor compared to the industrial North, but it is immeasurably wealthier when it comes to an abundance of fine, sun-ripened produce.

All those vegetables and fruits associated with the Mediterranean are found in Southern Italy, and the searing heat combined with rich volcanic soil give an unrivaled intensity of flavor to *pomodori* (tomatoes); a wealth of different types of *melanzane* (eggplant) — from bulging, pregnant, and purple to albino white; zucchini; *peperoni* (green and red bell peppers); *cipolle* (onions); and *peperoncini* (chili peppers). Fruits include enormous *cocomeri* (watermelons), *susine* (plums), *pesche* (peaches), *pere* (pears), *uva* (grapes), *fichi* (fresh figs), and that most characteristic fruit of hot countries, the *fichi d'India* (prickly pear).

It is almost impossible to imagine Italian cooking, especially Southern Italian cooking, without the *"pomo d'oro"* — the golden apple, as the tomato was called when it was first introduced to Italy in the 16th century on its arrival from the New World. Indeed, fresh tomatoes, barely cooked in olive oil with a touch of garlic, served over steaming hot *spaghetti* that is *al dente* — firm to the bite, is at once the most characteristic as well as the most delicious of all southern foods.

Whether grown intensively in fields and acres for the canning industry, or on a

Peperoncini, *fiery chili peppers, an exciting feature of Southern Italian cooking*

domestic scale, with just a few rows of plants in every home garden, a pot or two on every sunny balcony, tomatoes color the foods of the South.

In fact, until you come to Southern Italy, you may not have realized or remembered what a real tomato actually tastes like. Enjoy, then, a vine-ripened tomato, still warm from the sun, simply sliced and interleaved with hours-old *mozzarella di bufala* cheese topped with some pungent hand-torn basil leaves, and dribbled with green extra-virgin olive oil: this simple *antipasto* is known as *caprese* and, at best, is one of the most exquisite salads in the world.

The sheer riot of colors, scents, and flavors which permeates the outdoor markets of the South in spring, summer, and fall has to be seen to be believed. And, of course, the glut of super-fresh, seasonal produce ensures that prices remain low to the point of giveaway. Indeed, many Italians purchase fruits and vegetables not by the kilo but by the tray or sack, then take such produce home to conserve it, either by traditional means or in the freezer.

The profusion and abundance of fresh produce, moreover, means that an exceptional vegetarian cuisine has developed throughout the South, unself-consciously. Indeed, *pasta* topped with mixtures of fresh vegetables, vegetables stuffed or layered in sauce and cheese then baked in the oven, or fresh, uncooked vegetable *antipasti* are so tasty

Crates of ripe plum tomatoes in the Martina Franca market, Puglia

and full of flavor that we defy the most ardent carnivore not to enjoy them!

TRY TO SAMPLE

Carciofini   Baby artichokes (especially *mammole* or *cimaroli* varieties), so tender and free of spines that they can be boiled or fried and eaten whole (spring and early summer).

Cipolle di Tropea   Sweet red onion from Calabria (winter and spring).

Lampascioni or **lampasciuoli**   Small variety of wild onion highly prized throughout the South, usually boiled then marinated in olive oil, to eat as an *antipasto* nibble.

Limone   Thick-skinned, fresh, unwaxed lemons from the Amalfi Coast and throughout Campania and Calabria are available in summer months; utilized to make tart *granita* ices, refreshing *spremuta* (freshly squeezed) drinks, or infused in alcohol to make the popular aromatic liqueur, *limoncello*.

Melanzane   Eggplant, after the tomato, the most characteristic vegetable of the South (summer).

Peperoncini   Different types of hot chilies appear in profusion in markets during the summer and fall months, and are strung up to dry for use throughout the year.

Pomodori   Tomatoes. Some of the best for sauces are reputed to come from San Marzano, and, for salads, those from Torre del Greco are highly valued. In the fall, strings of *pomodori col pizzo* (tough-skinned round tomatoes with a pointed nipple at one end) are hung outdoor, and remain fresh and delicious even through the winter (summer months for best fresh tomatoes).

Fragrant lemons from the Amalfi Coast, used to refresh in a variety of ways

---

VEGETABLES PRESERVED *"SOTT'OLIO"*

Summer in the South brings all at once a glut of the most flavorsome vegetables in the world — tomatoes, of course, red and yellow bell peppers, zucchini, eggplant, among others. Traditional methods of preserving such an abundance of produce naturally developed in the era before refrigerators and freezers became commonplace.

Drying vegetables in the sun, then preserving them *sott'olio* — bottled in olive oil — was one of the most effective methods, and remains so even today. Thick-skinned plum tomatoes are split, salted, laid out to dry in the sun for upward of ten days, then preserved in jars of olive oil. Strips of eggplant, sun-dried zucchini, roasted red bell peppers, artichoke hearts, tender fava beans, cauliflower, or prized wild foods such as *porcini* mushrooms or the rare *lampascioni* are similarly preserved. Jars of vegetables *sott'olio* are one of the best food gifts to take home as a reminder, in the depths of winter, of the summer sun of Southern Italy.

Al Mercato
MARKETS

LAZIO

Albano	Thu
Civitavecchia	Wed
Frascati	Wed
Genzano	Tue
Marino	Wed
Ostia	Mon–Sat
Terracina	Thu
Tivoli	Wed
Velletri	Thu
Viterbo	Sat

CAMPANIA

Amalfi	Wed
Avellino	Sat
Battipaglia	Thu
Caserta	Wed, Sat
Ischia	Mon–Sat
Naples	daily
Paestum	Thu
Ravello	Tue
Salerno	Mon–Sat
Sorrento	Tue

CALABRIA

Catanzaro	Sat
Cirò	2nd Fri of month
Cosenza	Mon–Sat
Diamante	Sat
Reggio Calabria	Mon–Sat
Scalea	Mon

BASILICATA

Maratea	Sat
Matera	Sat
Melfi	Mon–Sat
Metaponto	1st Sun of month
Potenza	Mon–Sat

ABRUZZO & MOLISE

Chieti	Tue, Wed
L'Aquila	Mon–Sat
Pescara	Mon
Teramo	Sat

PUGLIA

Alberobello	Thu
Bari	Mon–Thu
Bríndisi	Thu
Foggia	Fri
Gallipoli	Wed
Lecce	Mon, Fri
Locorotondo	Fri
Manduria	Tue
Martina Franca	Wed
Ostuni	Sat
Otranto	Wed
Táranto	Wed–Fri

POPULAR *FESTE*

LAZIO

Marino
Festa dell'uva (grapes) 1st Sun of Oct
Montefiascone
Sagra del vino (wine) end July–beg Aug
Nemi
Sagra della fragola (strawberries) Jun

CALABRIA

Diamante
Peperoncino festival (chili pepper) 1st week Sep

PUGLIA

Bari
Fiera del Levante (wines and other regional products) Sep
Locorotondo
Sagra del vino novello (new wine) Nov

Below: Watermelons at the Martina Franca market, Puglia

Il Peperoncino
CHILI PEPPERS OF THE SOUTH

ONE OF THE MOST colorful sights encountered throughout the *Mezzogiorno* is that of strings of red chili peppers hanging out to dry in summer, from windows and balconies, on washing lines, spread out on the hoods of cars, nailed to trees in the country. In markets, old women in black sit beside their piles of produce, patiently sewing up strings of chilies with a needle and thread.

The *peperoncino* adds spice and flavor to the essentially simple foods of the South, and it is encountered in virtually everything: added to *pasta* sauces, ground and used in *salumi,* preserved in oil or vinegar to eat just so, or dried for a year or more then fried in hot oil until crunchy. Of course, the smaller the pepper, the hotter it is. Peppers as large as 10 cm. (4 in.) are usually quite sweet and not at all hot. Small, pointed chilies and round cherry chilies, on the other hand, can be devastatingly scorching. But the hottest of all are the tiniest examples, no more than 2 cm. (less than 1 in.) long, called *diavoletti,* which are indeed "little devils," to be eaten at your peril.

Though the *peperoncino* is widely consumed throughout Southern Italy (traditionally, hot countries have developed hot cuisines as a means of cooling down the body naturally through perspiration), the region most associated with this fiery foodstuff is Calabria, traditionally one of the poorest of all the regions. Calabrians learned to utilize the *peperoncino* extensively in their cuisine in times when there was little else to add flavor to foods. Poverty and unemployment, furthermore, led to a high degree of emigration from Calabria to other parts of Italy, as well as abroad, especially to the United States and South America. And, of course, the Calabrians took their

Peperoncini *for sale at a roadside stand on the Amalfi coast*

favorite food with them. Thus, today, the *peperoncino* has become something of an emotive symbol for Calabrians throughout the world, inextricably linked not only to its cuisine but to the very soul of the people.

The *Accademia del peperoncino,* for example, is an organization with local chapters around the world which serve primarily as a focus for Calabrian communities far from home, using the humble but fiery *peperoncino* as its rallying

Strings of peperoncini *drying in the sun*

standard. In Diamante, a seaside town on Calabria's Riviera del Cedro (named for the *cedro* or citron fruit that grows in profusion here), there is an annual *peperoncino* festival (first week of September). This serves not only as an excuse to celebrate the spicy, outrageous power of the chili in all its myriad manifestations (a different "hot" menu is served each night to the public) but also as a festival for "hot" or erotic art and satire in whatever manifestation. And, believe me, much of what is on show is *molto piccante* (very spicy) indeed.

Enzo Monaco, the organizer of Diamante's "hot" festival, has a shop selling an extensive range of *peperoncino* products, and can supply further information about both the festival and the *Accademia del peperoncino.*

Centro Gastronomico Sapore Calabria
Via Amendola, 3
87023 Diamante CS
tel: 0985/81130
fax: 0985/87168

Piatti Tipici
REGIONAL SPECIALTIES

We state categorically and unhesitatingly: you can eat better in Southern Italy than you can almost anywhere else in Europe. The food is fresh, genuine, and bursting with flavor. And like most of the great poor or peasant cuisines of the world, the home cooking of Southern Italy is intricate and elaborate, a labor-intensive *cucina* that relies on manual ingenuity and time-consuming skills to transform readily available, locally produced — and thus inexpensive — ingredients into real everyday feasts. Few here eat badly. No wonder the so-called Mediterranean diet, the envy of the Western world, is modeled almost entirely on the diet of the people of Southern Italy.

Puglia's deliciously fresh vegetarian cuisine

Of course, emigrants have taken the delights of the Southern Italian diet to people throughout the world, so much so, that what are considered essentially local foods, especially tomato-based *pasta,* not to mention *pizza,* the original fast food of Naples, have become internationalized. But foods transplanted from their native soil quickly lose their true essence, acquiring in their place a fusion of influences that may be interesting in its own right but by definition is no longer wholly authentic.

A visit to Southern Italy, therefore, provides an opportunity to dissect — quite effortlessly and enjoyably — the delicious and healthy elements of the Mediterranean diet at source. Moreover, the dishes of the South demonstrate clearly that "Southern Italian cooking" is actually a misnomer, for regional and local styles vary so considerably across this vast section of the country, that there is not a single but rather myriad cuisines for

us to discover and enjoy. Indeed, as elsewhere throughout Italy, local food traditions are clung to tenaciously, a means of maintaining contact with one's roots in this era of extreme social mobility when families have had to emigrate to search for work.

Though there is great variety throughout Southern Italy, wherever you are, the food, we guarantee, will satisfy. Enjoy the great abundance of superlative fresh fruits and vegetables whenever you can — you may never have them so good again. Feast on an ingenious and always delicious array of magnificent *pasta* dishes, but remember to leave room for the always substantial main courses, consisting of either fish and shellfish from Tyrrhenian, Adriatic, or Ionian waters (*pesce spada,* swordfish, is the prize specialty here) or meat, including lamb and kid, and an array of stews and casseroles made from inexpensive but flavorful cuts. The food of the South is not fussy, finicky, or for the lily-livered: it is genuine, hearty, and filling, for appetites made keen by hard work or hard play in the sun.

Antipasti

Antipasti pugliese (Puglia)   No region in Italy, except perhaps Piemonte, offers a more outstanding and varied selection of appetizers than Puglia. Even simple *trattorie* can offer a selection of 30 or more *assaggi* — little bite-sized tastes — of mainly vegetable creations, some of which are listed below. If you see a good array displayed in a restaurant, make a meal of it.

Bruschetta (Lazio)   Slice of country bread, toasted over a wood fire, rubbed with a cut clove of garlic, and soaked in extra-virgin olive oil.

Caprese (Campania and all the South) Salad of freshly sliced tomatoes interleaved with slices of *mozzarella* (preferably *di bufala*), torn basil leaves, and dressed in extra-virgin olive oil.

Friselle or **frise** (Campania and all the South)   Hard, twice-cooked bread roll (often, like a split doughnut), first soaked in water then dressed with tomatoes, oregano, and extra-virgin olive oil — a delicious snack with a glass of wine.

Insalata all'abruzzese (Abruzzo) Mixed salad of raw and cooked vegetables with tuna or anchovies, dressed with olive oil and vinegar — a type of rustic *salade niçoise*.

Melanzane (all the South)   Eggplant is one of the favorite and characteristic foods of Southern Italy, eaten regularly and in enormous quantity, as *antipasti* (marinated, fried, or baked), on *pasta,* and as a main course.

Mozzarella in carrozza (Campania) A slice of fresh *mozzarella* sandwiched between slices of bread, dipped in egg, then deep fried.

Novellame or **rosamarina** or **mùstica** (Calabria)   Known also as *"il caviale del Sud"* — the caviar of the South — this distinctive and pungent specialty consists of the small fry of anchovy salted and conserved in a fiery *peperoncino* sauce, to be spread on bread to eat as *antipasto.*

Panzerotti (Puglia, Campania, and Calabria)   Little semi-circles of deep-fried dough filled with a variety of mixtures, including meat, cheese and tomato, anchovies, and parsley.

Pomodori secchi sott'olio   Sun-dried tomatoes in olive oil, a favorite *antipasto* throughout the South.

Purea di fave con cicoria or **n'capriata** (Puglia)   Puree made from

Char-grilled eggplant and tomatoes tossed in extra-virgin olive oil in Puglia

Mozzarella *and fresh tomatoes*

boiled fava beans, dressed with plenty of extra-virgin olive oil and served with raw wild chicory.

Zucchine a scapece (Campania) Fried zucchini strips marinated in vinegar, garlic, oregano, and fresh mint.

I PRIMI PIATTI

Bucatini all'amatriciana (Rome and Lazio)   Long, thick *spaghetti*-like *pasta* with a bore, served with a robust tomato and *guanciale* (cured pork cheek) sauce, topped with *pecorino romano* cheese.

Cavatelli or **cavatieddi** or **cecatelli** (Puglia, Abruzzo, Molise, and Basilicata) Sort of rustic *pasta* made only from durum wheat and water, best served in summer with a sauce of fresh, uncooked tomatoes, arugula, basil, and olive oil.

Lagane e ceci (Calabria)   Hand-cut, rather wide, ribbon noodles served with chickpeas cooked in broth.

Maccheroni (all the South) Confusingly, this word in Southern Italy may be used to signify any number of different types of *paste,* including *spaghetti, fusilli, bucatini,* and others, not just the stubby, tube-like *pasta* we know by that name.

Maccheroni alla chitarra (Abruzzo) This specialty of Abruzzo is everywhere else known as *spaghetti alla chitarra,* a sort of squarish homemade egg noodle made by rolling a sheet of dough across a steel-wire-strung instrument to cut it, hence the name. Typically, it should be served with a *ragù* made from *castrato* (mutton), tomato, and *peperoncino.*

Orecchiette con le cime di rapa
(Puglia) "Ears" of hand-made *pasta*
served with boiled turnip greens stewed
in olive oil and *peperoncino* — a classic.
Spaghetti aglio, olio or **ajo e ojo**
(all the South)   Simplest of *pasta* dishes
— *spaghetti* dressed with sizzling olive oil
and plenty of chopped garlic and chilis.
Spaghetti alle vongole (all the South)
Spaghetti served with clams on the shell
sautéed in olive oil with garlic, with
wine added. The best and tastiest clams
are designated *vongole veraci*.
Spaghettini alla puttanesca (Ischia and
all Campania)   *Spaghetti* served with a
sauce of tomatoes, garlic, anchovies,
capers, and olives. No one seems to know
why "the women of the night" have
been credited with this delicious dish.

Zucchini flowers

Hand-made orecchiette *with a simple, fresh
tomato and basil sauce*

I SECONDI PIATTI

Agnello al forno (all the South)
Lamb, or more usually, mutton, baked
with wine and herbs.
Abbacchio (Lazio)   Milk-fed baby lamb.
Brasciole alla barese (Puglia)   Thin
slices of veal rolled around *prosciutto,*
breadcrumbs, *pecorino* cheese, and parsley,
and simmered in a tomato sauce.
Brodetto pescarese (Abruzzo)
Outstanding fish soup, made with a variety of fish, depending on what is available, cooked with onion, peppers, and
wine, but no tomatoes.
Capretto alla silana (Calabria)   Hearty
stew made from cubes of kid, cooked
slowly with onions, pototoes, tomatoes,
and wine.

Coniglio alla cacciatora (Campania)
Wild rabbit stewed with tomatoes,
olives, garlic, and herbs.
Costata or **bistecca alla pizzaiola**
(Campania)   Thin slice of beef cooked
with a tomato, garlic, and oregano sauce.
Costolette d'agnello alla calabrese
(Calabria)   Fried lamb or mutton chops
simmered in a tomato sauce flavored
with onions, peppers, and olives.
Luganega (Basilicata)   Meaty pork
sausage, usually flavored with *peperoncino*
and grilled.
Parmigiana di melanzane (Campania
and all the South)   Slices of eggplant
first fried, then layered with tomato
sauce, hardboiled eggs, slices of
mozzarella, and topped with grated parmesan cheese, then baked in the oven.
Pesce spada alla griglia (Calabria and
Campania)   Thick swordfish steak
grilled over charcoal and seasoned with
olive oil and garlic.
Scamorza alla griglia (Basilicata,
Puglia, and Calabria)   Thickly sliced
scamorza cheese grilled briefly and served
as an alternative to meat.

I CONTORNI

Ciambotta or **cianfotta**   Typical
southern vegetable stew combining
eggplant, zucchini, tomatoes, bell peppers,
onions, celery, potatoes, olives, and
garlic, simmered in olive oil.
Cicoria   Wild chicory, a characteristic,
bitter salad vegetable.
Fiori di zucchine   Zucchini flowers
usually dipped in batter and fried.

Pasta, Bella Pasta

PASTA MADE WITH DURUM WHEAT AND WATER

THE IMPOVERISHED South has traditionally subsisted on a staple diet of dried *pasta* flavored with sauces based on the ever-present tomato. At its simplest and best, this may be just a bowl of *spaghetti* served with no more than sieved fresh tomatoes simmered in a bit of olive oil and garlic. In hard times, dried *pasta* might be seasoned only with crumbled breadcrumbs, olive oil, and copious amounts of fiery *peperoncino* to give some flavor. In summer, meanwhile, a virtual symphony of sauces based on fresh vegetables in all their glorious abundance — eggplant, zucchini, bell peppers, not to mention tomato — is served over huge bowls of steaming-hot dried *pasta*.

Making fusilli calabresi *by hand*

Vast quantities of dried *pasta* are made industrially in factories around Naples and Salerno, and in Puglia, Abruzzo, and Molise, all sources of a rich harvest of high quality durum wheat. Thus, dried *pasta* in any number of shapes, forms, and sizes is readily and cheaply available throughout the country.

Even so, homemade *pasta* southern-style is still prepared regularly in many homes and restaurants in the South. Here, in contrast to the fresh *pasta* of Emilia-Romagna (see pp.138–139), the dough is made with only hard durum wheat flour and water. Nothing even so luxurious as a single egg is used. Yet, from this basic dough, a remarkable range of beautiful and delicious *pasta* shapes are made, using traditional instruments, such as the *chitarra* in Abruzzo to cut *maccheroni alla chitarra,* the *ferro* in Calabria to make *fusilli calabresi* (a sort of homemade *bucatini* made by rolling noodles around a piece of wire), or simply the fingers in Puglia to make *orecchiette* (ear-shaped); *cavatelucci* (hand-made small shell type); *cavatelli* (large flat shells); and *frciid* (hand-formed *fusilli* twists).

Even when fresh, such homemade *paste* take longer to cook than their egg-based equivalents from the North. Artisan-made versions left to dry in the sun then packaged for sale may take 15–20 minutes to cook.

Two of our favorite artisan *pastifici* whose products are available throughout Italy are:

Pastificio La Golosa
Via Don Minzoni, 12
87029 Scalea CS
tel/fax: 0985/90030
Outstanding artisan *paste,* especially *fusilli calabresi* as well as fiery versions spiked with *peperoncino.*

Pastificio dei Trulli
Viale Apulia, 18
70011 Corréggia Alberobello BA
tel/fax: 080/9324888
Artisan-produced *orecchiette, cavatelli, cavatellucci,* and *frciid.*

Selection of artisan-made Apulian paste: frciid, orecchiette integrale, cavatelli, *and* cavatellucci

Pane e Pizze
BREADS AND *PIZZE*

THROUGHOUT SOUTHERN Italy, bread is, on the whole, far better than the often mushy, airy loaves and rolls of the North. In Puglia, enormous loaves made entirely from *semolino di grano duro* (semolina flour milled entirely from the heart of the amber-colored durum wheat grain) emerge from the *forno a legna* (wood-fired oven) with thick, crunchy crusts and a dense interior as yellow as egg yolk. We have enjoyed a wonderful array of *panini* (bread rolls) in Calabria hot out of the oven, and in Campania virtually any bakery worth its salt offers *pizze* alongside the daily loaves.

Remains of a bakery in Pompeii

Throughout the South, there is one specialty that is unique, *friselle* or *frisellini* — hard rolls in various forms (doughnut or slipper shapes are most common), split, then baked again, until hard as rock. These breads seem to last forever, an important consideration in a hot climate, where soft, fresh bread would go stale in hours. *Friselle* are reconstituted with a sprinkling of water; then, once soft, but still slightly crunchy, the bread is piled with chopped tomatoes and dressed with plenty of olive oil and a dusting of *origano*.

A selection of pane pugliese, *breads from Puglia, in front of a* trullo

Pizza, known and loved internationally, had its origins in the back streets of Naples, though flattened bread made tasty with the addition of flavorings had probably been enjoyed elsewhere in Italy, in Puglia, Abruzzo, and Sicily, long before the Neapolitans came to claim it as their own. Yet, few deny that the best *pizzaiuoli* (*pizza* chefs) come from Naples, nor that throughout Campania *pizza* is at its purest and most delicious.

The essential *pizza* is very simple. For true lovers of *pizza,* only two varieties exist: *pizza alla marinara* and *pizza margherita*. The former — so-called, not because it is made with seafood, but because it the sailor's favorite — is no more than bread dough flattened out by hand into a circular disk, topped with tomato sauce, sprinkled with a little raw, chopped garlic, doused with a sprinkling of olive oil, then baked in a wood-fired oven for no more than two minutes. *Pizza margherita* seems positively baroque in comparison, made with tomato sauce, *mozzarella* cheese, and torn fresh basil leaves. Created in homage to Queen Margherita, consort of Vittorio Emanuele II, the red, white, and green symbolize the colors of the Italian flag.

Though most *pizzerie* in Campania produce outstanding *pizze,* our Neapolitan friends particularly recommend:

Brandi
Salita Sant'Anna di Palazzo, 1/2
80100 Naples
tel: 081/416928
The most historic *pizzeria* in Naples, and the source of the original *pizza margherita*.

Antica Pizzeria da Michele
Via Cesare Sersale, 1/3
80100 Naples
tel: 081/5539204
Genuine backstreet *pizzeria,* serving only the classic *marinara* and *margherita*.

Rome

A GASTRONOMIC CAPITAL

Rome is nothing if not direct, robust, yet vigorously exciting, a marvelous cosmopolitan capital that is super-charged with vitality and energy and an over-layering of two millennia of history, making it one of the most enjoyable and stimulating cities to visit in Italy.

Millions flock here throughout the year, to pay a pilgrimage at the Vatican, to wonder at the remains of ancient Rome, to enjoy the Renaissance, baroque, and neoclassical monuments, squares, palaces, and mansions, and to wander and shop along the Via Veneto. Yet, though undoubtedly cosmopolitan, Rome, charmingly and in spite of the hordes of visitors, manages to retain something of the feel of a provincial town, a character that is — well, wholly Roman.

Though Rome has more than its share of highly reputed international res-

Bucatini al pomodoro

taurants, as well as scores serving food from every Italian region, a true, authentic, and unselfconscious *cucina romana* remains that is delicious and unique, consisting of foods not found even in towns just outside the capital. The true taste of Rome is assertive, virile, and strongly flavored, and the best areas to find authentic Roman cooking are neighborhoods such as Trastevere and Testaccio (the butchers' quarter), where it is possible to eat not only well but also cheaply at simple *osterie* and *trattorie*.

I PRIMI PIATTI

Bucatini all'amatriciana   *Bucatini* are thick *spaghetti*-like noodles with a bore, typically served in a pungent sauce made from tomatoes, *guanciale* (cured pork cheek), plenty of black pepper, and topped with grated *pecorino romano* cheese.

Fave con pecorino   Springtime favorite of tender fava beans eaten with fresh *pecorino* cheese.

Fettuccine alla romana   Thin, freshly made ribbon noodles, generally served with a meat sauce.

Gnocchi alla romana   Unlike potato *gnocchi*, these are made from semolina; boiled, then cut into disks, they are baked with butter and cheese.

Pasta alla carbonara   Though *carbonara* has become internationalized, the real dish is worth sampling in Rome. Any type of *pasta* may be used, including *rigatoni* (ribbed macaroni), *bucatini,* or *spaghetti*. The sauce is made from beaten eggs, fried *guanciale* or *pancetta,* garlic, grated *pecorino romano* and *parmigiano reggiano* cheeses, and plenty of black pepper. The hot *pasta* is tossed in this sauce, which lightly cooks the egg.

Cooling off on a hot day in the fountains of Piazza Navona, Rome

Penne all'arrabbiata Quill-shaped *maccheroni,* served in a fiery tomato sauce made with garlic, *pancetta* or *guanciale,* and plenty of *peperoncino. Penne infuocate* is similar but even hotter!

Rigatoni con la pajata *Pajata* or *pagliata* is a wholly Roman specialty consisting of a section of intestine from a milk-fed calf, stewed gently, and served over *rigatoni.*

Spaghetti a cacio e pepe *Spaghetti* topped with grated *pecorino romano* and plenty of freshly ground black pepper.

Stracciatella alla romana Boiling meat broth to which is added beaten egg mixed with grated parmesan cheese and semolina.

Supplì al telefono Little balls made from left-over *risotto,* filled with a nugget of *mozzarella,* then deep-fried. So called, because, when the balls are split apart,

Rigatoni alla carbonara *as served at Perilli al Testaccio*

"telephone wires" of melted cheese stretch out.

I SECONDI PIATTI

Abbacchio Milk-fed baby lamb. Tiny lamb chops may be broiled, or leg meat cubed and stewed in olive oil, rosemary, and wine vinegar.

Baccalà Strips of salt cod, most typically enjoyed deep-fried in batter.

Coda alla vaccinara Oxtail stew, with garlic, wine, tomato, and celery.

Coratella Romans love variety meats, such as, in this case, lamb's or kid's

intestines, heart, lungs, and liver threaded onto a skewer and grilled over a direct fire.

Saltimbocca alla romana Delicious Roman dish of thin slices of veal layered with *prosciutto crudo* and a sage leaf, then quickly fried in olive oil, which just "jump into the mouth."

Vitello arrosto *as served at the Trattoria Lilli*

Scottadito Baby lamb chops, grilled or fried quickly, to be picked up and eaten with the fingers.

I CONTORNI

Carciofi alla giudìa Tender, tiny artichokes, flattened and fried in olive oil, a traditional favorite from the Jewish ghetto.

Fagioli con le cotiche Slow-cooked beans with flavorful pieces of pork skin.

Fave al guanciale Older fava beans stewed slowly with cured pork cheek.

I DOLCI

Bignè Choux pastry filled with custard or *zabaione.*

Tartufo Famous super-rich chocolate ice cream with a cherry in the middle. Best is served in Piazza Navona.

THE BEST OF ROME'S DAILY STREET MARKETS

Campo dei Fiori
Mercato Andrea Doria
Mercato di Testaccio
Mercato del Trionfale
Mercato di Piazza Vittorio Emanuele
Piazza delle Coppolle (near the Pantheon)
Piazza San Cosimato, Trastevere
Via della Pace (near Piazza Navonna)

Indirizzi

USEFUL ADDRESSES IN ROME

Typical Roman restaurant

Checco er Carrettiere
Via Benedetta, 10
tel: 06/5800985
This loud, large, always crowded, and atmospheric eating house in Trastevere serves genuine Roman foods — antipasti di mare, bucatini all'amatriciana, coda alla vaccinara — stylishly and well prepared, accompanied by a superior wine list of the best of Italy.
$$$

Enoteca Trimani
Via Goito, 20
tel: 06/497971
fax: 06/4468351
Rome has no shortage of local wine shops anywhere in the city, but Mario Trimani's is singled out, for it is one of the most important private enoteche in the country, source of an outstanding range of not only local wines, but the best from throughout Italy.

Tartufo and coffee in the Piazza Navona

E. Volpetti
Via Marmorata, 47
tel: 06/5746986
fax: 06/5747629
Located in the atmospheric Testaccio butcher's quarter: excellent cheeses, meats, and prepared dishes. Good panini made to order.

Filetti di Baccalà
Largo de' Librari
Simple hole-in-the-wall near Campo dei Fiori, selling strips of deep-fried salt cod to eat with the fingers and washed down with gutsy house white wine: something of an institution of Old Rome.
$

Forno Campo dei Fiori
Campo dei Fiori, 22
tel: 06/68806662

Campo dei Fiori market

Peek inside this traditional bakery near the market and enjoy the busy scene, as long pizze, loaves of bread, and panini enter and come out of the huge ovens — strangely reminiscent of imagined scenes in the ruined bakeries of Pompeii. Try the delicious biscotti.

Ristorante Perilli al Testaccio
Via Marmorata, 39
tel: 06/5742415

Old, traditional eating house in the Testaccio butcher's quarter serving the classic meat specialties of Rome, including coda alla vaccinara and coratella.
$$

Sant'Andrea della Valle

Tre Scalini
Piazza Navona, 30–35
tel: 06/6879148
fax: 06/6861234
It is probably obligatory, when in Rome, to sit outside in Piazza Navona, admiring Bernini's amazing statue to the four rivers, while enjoying a tartufo gelato. This hand-made chocolate ice cream, incredibly rich and scandalously expensive, was invented here more than 50 years ago. The restaurant itself at Tre Scalini's is adequate.
$$

Trattoria Lilli
Via Tor di Nona, 26
tel: 06/6861916
This simple, centrally located trattoria near the Tiber is one of our favorites, serving simple but authentic Roman foods: rigatoni con la pajata, bucatini all'amatriciana, and saltimbocca alla romana.
$

Salumi

PORK AND OTHER CURED PRODUCTS

THE HOTTER and more humid the climate, the more difficult it is to preserve meats by salting. Yet Southern Italy defies logic, for throughout the region, there is a great tradition of cured pork products almost as rich and varied as from anywhere else in the country. Naturally, the climatic conditions have meant that such products are traditionally strongly flavored with plenty of salt, garlic, *peperoncino,* black pepper, or wild fennel, flavorings so assertive, that in the past they masked successfully the taste of meats gone off in the heat. Today, of course, such products are made under hygienic and temperature-controlled conditions and the robust and assertive flavorings are used out of choice not necessity. The finest range of *peperoncino-*spiked *salumi* comes from Calabria.

TRY TO SAMPLE

Capelomme (Abruzzo)   Artisan-cured pork tenderloin, traditionally home-smoked in the chimney, then left to age in a humid place.

Capocollo or **capicollo** (Calabria, Basilicata, and Puglia) Made with the pork neck tenderloin or part of the upper shoulder, kept in a whole piece, and cured with salt, garlic, black pepper, and, in Calabria, *peperoncino*. It is aged from three months to a year, and is usually chewy to the point of toughness, but very tasty.

Capocollo, *a tasty, chewy salame.*

Guanciale (Lazio)   Pork cheek or jowl, cured with salt and plenty of black pepper — essential for Roman *pasta* dishes such as *all'amatriciana.*

Lucanica or **luganega** (Basilicata and all the South)   Coarsely textured, spicy pork sausage for broiling.

Mulette (Molise) Molise's version of *capocollo,* cured with *peperoncino:*

'Nduja or **'ndugghia** (Calabria) Mushy Calabrian sausage, made with finely ground meat, fat, liver, and lungs, highly seasoned with *peperoncino.*

Salame napoletana   Like *milanese* and *genovese, salame napoletana* is widely made throughout Italy. To be authentic, it should contain ground pork meat and fat

Calabrian *salumi, including* capocollo, soppressata dolce, salsiccia piccante, *and* soppressata piccante

with the addition of some beef, flavored with pepper and garlic.

Salsicce leccese (Lecce and all Puglia) Veal-and-pork sausages delicately perfumed with lemon rind and cinnamon.

Salsiccia or **sazizza** (Calabria)   Spicy, dried sausage made with pork — lean and fat — cured with salt, black pepper, fennel seeds, and *peperoncino.*

Scammarita (Lazio)   Pork neck tenderloin, cured in salt, pepper, and wild fennel. *Dolce* versions are milder than *piccante.*

Soppressata calabrese (Calabria) This rustic Calabrian *salame* is made from pork meats traditionally coarsely cut by hand with a knife, seasoned with red wine, salt, pepper, and (of course) lots of *peperoncino,* then pressed under a weight.

Tarantello (Táranto and all the South) Curious cured product made from seasoned belly of tuna.

Ventricina (Abruzzo)   This local *salame* is typical of Chieti, made with lean and fat pork cured with salt, *peperoncino,* wild fennel seeds, and, unusually, orange peel.

A Tale of Three Seas
FISH AND SHELLFISH

THE SOUTH IS LAPPED on all sides by the sea: the Adriatic to the east, the Tyrrhenian to the west, and the Ionian to the south. Every region has a stretch of coast, and fish and shellfish are widely and regularly consumed, at least in coastal towns. The climate has meant that fresh fish are rarely transported too far inland, but as most visitors to the South stay near or by the sea, there is ample opportunity to visit fish markets as well as to enjoy fish and shellfish in seaside restaurants.

The great tradition of *brodetto,* that most classic and variable of all Adriatic fish soups, continues along the coast of Abruzzo and Molise. Puglia has the longest coastline of any region in Italy, and a fine catch of fish and shellfish is landed not only along the Adriatic but also in the Ionian Gulf of Táranto. Calabria is famous, above all, for its enormous *pesce spada,* and indeed a thick, red swordfish steak, laced with garlic, seasoned with olive oil, and cooked over an open fire, is one of its typical dishes. Campania, meanwhile, delights in a profusion of excellent, fishy *pasta* dishes, and in Lazio, the most characteristic fish is still *baccalà*.

TRY TO SAMPLE

Alici   Fresh anchovies; much loved throughout the South.

Alici a scapece   Fresh anchovies, boned, dipped in flour, and fried, then marinated in a mixture of vinegar, herbs, and spices.

Baccalà in guazzetto (Lazio) Fried strips of salt cod, simmered in a tomato sauce flavored with anchovies, pine nuts, and raisins.

Brodetto abruzzese (Abruzzo)   Both "white" and "red" (with tomatoes) versions of the classic seafood soup are enjoyed, usually made with fish such as whiting, sole, ray, and squid, and shellfish such as mussels and clams.

Cozze   Mussels. **Cozze alla leccese** are steamed in oil and lemon juice.

Orata alla pugliese (Puglia)   Porgy or sea bream baked with potatoes, garlic, and olive oil.

Ostriche alla tarantina (Puglia) Good oysters are raised in the shallow lagoon by Táranto. They are enjoyed locally, covered with bread crumbs and parsley, then baked briefly in the oven.

Pesce alla marinara (Campania) General fisherman's method of stewing any inexpensive variety of fish with garlic, olive oil, tomatoes, and oregano.

Pesce spada (Calabria and all the South)   Swordfish, usually grilled in thick steaks. **Pesce spada alla bagna-rese** gently steamed with olive oil, lemon juice, capers, and oregano.

Polpo   Octopus is much loved, especially stewed in wine and herbs, and the sight of fishermen beating this cephalopod on the ground to tenderize it is a common one around the fishing ports of Southern Italy. **Polipi sott'aceto**   boiled octopus cut into pieces and marinated in vinegar and garlic: a popular *antipasto* nibble.

Spaghetti alle vongole   *Spaghetti* with clams.

Sauté di vongole (Campania)   The usual term here for *vongole alla marinara,* i.e., clams steamed in olive oil and wine, with garlic and freshly chopped parsley.

Fishermen repairing their nets in old Gallipoli on Puglia's Salentine Peninsula

Mozzarella di Bufala
THE FRESHEST CHEESE IN THE WORLD

Made from the rich milk of water buffalo that graze on the plains of Campania, *mozzarella di bufala* is, at its best, the simplest, freshest, and most fragrant cheese in the world. It is also one of the most delicate and perishable. For, whereas elsewhere, making cheese is essentially a way of preserving milk, which is quickly prone to spoilage in a hot climate, the hand-made production of *mozzarella di bufala* results in a sublimely delicious cheese that is possibly even more delicate than the very milk from which it has been made.

Weaving "una treccia," a braid, of mozzarella di bufala

Today, though *mozzarella di bufala*, vacuum-packed in brine, may sometimes be found outside the region and even outside Italy, inevitably, after no more than 48 hours, such cheeses begin to lose the inexpressible fragrance and light texture that are the hallmarks of real *mozzarella di bufala*.

The water buffalo was probably introduced into Italy from India, possibly as long ago as the early Christian era. Though it adapted well to its Southern Italian habitat, this formidable looking beast is more difficult to keep than the cow, and its females yield far less milk. Today, therefore, much more *mozzarella* is produced from cow's milk or from cow's milk mixed with water buffalo's than from pure water buffalo's milk. However, pure water buffalo's milk is extremely rich and flavorful, containing up to three times the fat content of cow's milk, and it, undoubtedly, makes the finest *mozzarella*, with a distinctive, yet delicate, taste and a light, not rubbery, texture which is exquisite. The main centers for the production of *mozzarella di bufala* are in the province of Caserta, north of Naples, and around Battipáglia, near Salerno.

To make *mozzarella di bufala*, the curds of fresh unpasteurized buffalo's milk, once coagualated with rennet and after reaching the requisite degree of acidity, are crumbled and torn apart by hand, then cooked in small wooden vats in boiling water. This is a remarkable process to watch: the dense, glistening, elastic mass of yellow-white cheese is turned and swirled skillfully by hand with a wooden stick and bowl, the excess whey and water drained off through a small sieve.

Once the desired consistency and texture are reached, balls of *mozzarella* are then formed by hand, as the cheesemakers, working in pairs, tear off the cheeses with their fingers, forming the burning hot, elastic mass into individual forms, and dropping them into trays of brine. It is always possible to tell a hand-made *mozzarella* from an

Herd of water buffalo on the Campania plains near Céllole

Stirring and turning mozzarella *in boiling water*

Hand-made (right) and machine-made (left)
mozzarella di bufala

industrial one by the torn lines left by the cheesemakers' fingers on the cheeses.

At the Caseificio Pietro La Torre near Céllole in the province of Caserta, Pietro and his three sons, Antonio, Umberto, and Michele, daily transform the milk from their herd of 50 water buffalo, about 1,000 liters (250 gallons), into some 200 kg. (440 lbs.) of fresh *mozzarella di bufala*. Various forms and sizes of the cheese are made, including *bocconcini* (little balls weighing no more than 40–50 g. or 1½–1¾ oz.), to *mozzarelle,* weighing anything from 100 g. (about ¼ lb., the ideal portion for one person) up to 700–800 g. (1½–1¾ lbs.). *Mozzarella* is also braided into *trecce. Mozzarella* made from cow's milk is known as *fior di latte. Fior di latte* is usually the type widely used for cooking, both as a topping for *pizze* and in baked *pasta* and vegetable dishes, as it is delicate in flavor as well as less expensive than *mozzarella di bufala.*

Wherever you are in Campania, sample fresh, hand-made *mozzarella di bufala,* for we doubt that you will ever find anything elsewhere that can compare in freshness and fragrance with the real thing.

Caseificio Pietro La Torre
Via Casammare
81030 Campo Felice di Céllole CE
tel: 0823/706220

OTHER SOUTHERN CHEESES

Southern Italy has a great and varied tradition of cheesemaking, for in this poor part of the country the hand-production of cheese from the milk of cows, buffaloes, sheep, or goats has always been a traditional means of preserving milk and an essential source of protein in the daily diet.

The most important class of cheeses in the South is the so-called *pasta filata* (strung or stretched out), made (as with *mozzarella*) by cooking the curds in boiling water until elastic, then cutting or tearing them into strips, and forming them into cheeses. *Caciocavallo, scamorza, provola,* and *provolone* are all such cheeses.

While much cheese is made to be consumed when it is extremely fresh (at most, within hours or days), cheeses are also dried in the sun until hard, to be used for grating *(ricotta salata* and *cacioricotta),* and also smoked, a process that not only adds distinctive flavor but which also

Caseificio Pietro La Torre

preserves the cheese for longer. *Pecorino romano,* made in this manner, is one of the great ewe's milk cheeses of Italy.

TRY TO SAMPLE

Bocconcini (all the South)   Tiny balls, or "mouthfuls," of *mozzarella.*

Burrata (Puglia) One of the freshest and most delicate of all cheeses, made from *mozzarella* curds, stuffed with a mixture of chopped *mozzarella* mixed with heavy cream and salt.

Caciocavallo (Campania, Basilicata, Puglia, and Calabria)   Large, pear-shaped cheese tied together in pairs and slung over a piece of wood known as the "*cavallo*" or horse. Like *scamorza* and

Burrata, *a fresh* mozzarella-*type cheese mixed with rich cream, served here with fresh tomatoes*

provolone, *caciocavallo* is sometimes smoked. In Puglia and Basilicata, this compact, firm cheese is often grilled over charcoal and eaten as a main course.

Cacioricotta di capra (Puglia)   Small disks of goat's milk *ricotta,* left to age in the sun; used for grating over *pasta.*

Casiello (Basilicata) Small, fresh, goat's cheese.

Fior di latte (all the South)   *Mozzarella* made from cow's milk.

Pecorino romano (Lazio)   This outstanding cheese is made entirely from ewe's milk, traditionally curdled with lamb's rennet, and aged for upward of a year. This hard, *piccante* cheese is delicious for eating and for grating over *pasta* and is used widely in Rome and throughout Lazio.

Pecorino di Potenza (Basilicata)   Good ewe's milk cheeses — hard, for both eating and grating — come from the province of Potenza.

Provola (Campania)   Similar to *provolone,* but always made from buffalo's milk.

Provolone (all the South)   Perhaps the most characteristic cheese of the South;

made in a process similar to *scamorza,* but formed into any number of different shapes, including long, fat sausages, little pigs, melons, and pears. *Provolone dolce,* the mildest version, is aged for no more than two or three months; *provolone piccante,* much sharper in flavor and harder in texture, is aged for up to a year; *provolone affumicato* is lightly smoked for about a week, then aged for a further three months.

Ricotta (all the South)   This fresh, mild soft cheese is made from the leftover whey from the milk of cows, sheep, goats, and buffaloes; generally eaten with sugar or salt, and used widely in cooking.

Ricotta forte (Puglia)   Strong, fermented *ricotta,* sometimes mixed with herbs; to be eaten as a spread on bread.

Ricotta salata (Campania, Calabria, and

Unsmoked provola *and smoked* caciocavallo, *two typical cheeses of Southern Italy*

Basilicata)   *Ricotta* cheese, usually made from ewe's milk, conserved in salt, then left to age until hard. Pleasantly salty yet creamy in flavor. A favorite for grating over *pasta.*

Scamorza (all the South)   Important regional *pasta filata* cheese. It is made by first slicing curds made from cow's milk into strips with a *mezzaluna* (two-handled crescent-shaped knife), leaving them to ferment and develop flavor for at least a few days, then cooking the curds in boiling water, forming them into large balls that are tied up at one end (or placed in nets), then soaked in brine. *Scamorza* is sometimes smoked.

Trecce (throughout the South) Braided strings of *mozzarella* or *scamorza* cheese weighing up to a kilo or more.

I Dolci

SWEETS AND PASTRIES

Pine nuts, walnuts, almonds, candied citrus fruits, and honey: these ingredients, all plentiful in Southern Italy, are used to produce an astounding and imaginative range of *biscotti,* cakes, pastries, and other *dolci.*

A popular means of escape from the intense summer heat is a visit to the *gelateria* (ice cream parlor). The South offers a wide range of homemade ice creams and *granite* (flavored ices). But an even simpler way of cooling down is *grata-grata,* a cupful of ice shaved off a large frozen block with a two-handled razor knife, to which is added a generous splash of mandarin or orange syrup.

TRY TO SAMPLE

Bignè (Rome and Lazio)   Choux pastries filled with *zabaione* (egg yolks, sugar, and Marsala wine) or custard cream; a sort of Roman *profiterole.*

Biscotti di mandorle (Campania and Calabria)   Hard, twice-cooked biscuits made with almonds (similar to Tuscan *cantuccini*).

Cannariculi (Calabria)   Fried sticks of dough immersed in either concentrated grape must and/or honey.

Carteddate or **cartellate** (Puglia) Light pastry formed with the fingers into various shapes, deep fried, then either soaked in honey or dusted with confectioner's sugar.

Cumpittu (Calabria)   Soft nougat made with honey, almonds, and sesame seeds.

Fichi ripieni alla sibarita

Fichi ripieni alla sibarita (Calabria) Dried figs stuffed with almonds or walnuts, covered in concentrated grape must, and cooked in the oven. Very sticky and delicious — wooden boxes of this treat make a good gift to take home.

Panzerotti alla marmellata (Puglia) Small pastry turnovers the size of a *raviolo,* filled with fruit conserves and baked in the oven.

Pastiera napoletana (Naples and all Campania)   Naples's famous Easter cake, a large pastry filled with *ricotta* cheese, rice, corn, or barley cooked in milk, candied fruits, sugar, orange-blossom water, and spices.

Pizza dolce (Campania)   A flat, sweet tart, usually topped with *ricotta* cheese, sugar, and almonds.

Sproccolati (Amalfi Coast)   Dried figs, sometimes soaked in honey, stuffed with fennel seeds, and threaded on wooden skewers.

Strangolapreti lucani (Basilicata) Dough mixed with egg and lemon rind, rolled into strips, and deep fried, a favorite accompaniment to sweet wines.

Struffoli (Campania)   This Neapolitan favorite (probably of Greek origin) consists of deep-fried pastry balls mixed with honey, candied peel, and chocolate, formed into a ring-shaped cake.

Zuppa inglese (Campania and Puglia) Italy's version of English trifle: layers of sponge cake soaked in orange or coffee liqueur spread with *crema pasticciera,* a rich, sweet, creamy custard.

Cooling off with a large bowl of gelati misti, *enough for two*

I Vini
THE WINES OF SOUTHERN ITALY

For LONG, the wines of Southern Italy were scorned by wine connoisseurs, dismissed as coarse and high in alcohol, sunbaked and suitable only for blending.

But a quiet revolution has occurred, as both private and cooperative wineries have invested in new technology, replanted vineyards, and set out to harvest early. The result? Today, Southern Italy is the source of modern, well-made, clean white wines as well as fine red wines that combine power and finesse.

What is more, such wines are available at a fraction of the price of similar but more prestigious wines of the North. Now Southern Italy has some affordable surprises for lovers of Italian wines.

That said, we feel compelled to issue a warning: in simple inns and *trattorie* throughout the South, we have been served more undrinkable homemade wines — brown, oxidized whites, crude, overly alcoholic, headbanging reds — than anywhere else. The situation is often made even more embarrassing, because, as you taste the wine, the innkeeper, standing beside you and beaming proudly, declares, *"L'ho fatt'io — I made it myself."* What can you say?

Harvesting grapes in the vineyards of Falerno, Campania

LAZIO

Castelli Romani The ridge of wine hills south of Rome, known as the Castelli Romani, encompasses such famous names as Frascati and Marino, but vast quantities of unclassified wine are produced here too, rarely bottled but served in carafes.

Colli Lanuvini DOC This small wine zone centered on Lanuvio and Genzano is the source of some characterful and undervalued white wines.

Est! Est!! Est!!! di Montefiascone DOC The story of the greedy German prelate who drank so much of Montefiascone's local wine that he passed away (he is actually buried in the town churchyard) is well remembered, though sadly today's wine is mainly forgettable: clean, neutral, made from Trebbiano and Malvasia grapes, but generally lacking in much real character.
Recommended producer: Cantina Sociale di Montefiascone, Falesco.

Frascati DOC One of the best-known Italian white wines in the world, produced from Trebbiano and Malvasia grapes. While most export bottlings from the large companies, though clean and well made, are often neutral at best, Frascati when drunk on home territory is altogether different: a gutsy, full-flavored wine with an intriguing nutty character. Frascati *cannellino* is the traditional sweet version.
Recommended producers: Colli di Catone, Villa Simone, Pallavicini.

Marino DOC Marino is a neighbor to Frascati, and its vineyards produce similar white wines from Trebbiano and Malvasia grapes. Some good, individual, *vino da tavola* reds are also produced.
Recommended producer: Di Mauro.

Torre Ercolana Made on one estate only at Anagni, north of Frosinone, Torre Ercolana is often cited as Lazio's finest red wine: dense, concentrated, sometimes austere, from local Cesanese grapes with some Cabernet and Merlot.
Recommended producer: Colacicchi.

Velletri DOC Velletri, a large wine zone in the Castelli Romani, produces plenty of sound white and red wines that are usually less expensive (but rarely more exciting) than better-known names.

CAMPANIA

Falerno DOC The ancient Falanghina grape, researchers have proved, was the source of the Romans' favorite Falernum wine. Today, the

DOC applies to both white from the Falanghina and red from Aglianico. White Falerno is clean, fresh, and sometimes richly flavored. The red is a deep, rich, velvety wine of great character and class.
Recommended producer: Villa Matilde.

Fiano di Avellino DOC   One of the rarest but finest white wines of Italy, an intensely concentrated, rich, and elegant wine produced in minuscule quantity from the ancient Fiano grape.
Recommended producers: Mastroberardino, Vadiaperti.

Greco di Tufo DOC   Another rare but distinguished white wine, made from Greco grapes grown in the earthquake-ravaged Avellino hills; full-bodied, with an opulent, creamy fruit, and a compact, nutty richness.
Recommended producers: Mastroberardino, Di Marzo.

Taurasi DOCG   This distinguished red wine is produced from Aglianico grapes grown in the Avellino hills. Though hailed as one of the great red wines of Italy, it can be notoriously slow to develop, so ensure that you try a bottle with plenty of age (at least a decade, if possible).
Recommended producer: Mastroberardino.

CALABRIA

Cirò DOC   The vineyards of Calabria's best and best-known wine were in ancient times known as Krimisa, a wine much loved by the ancient Greeks. Today, white Cirò is Calabria's best, and only reliable, white wine, made from the characterful Greco grape. It is fresh, zesty, with a nice bitter orange finish: but drink it young, for, like all southern whites, it has the tendency to oxidize quickly. Red Cirò is made from the beefy Gaglioppo grape, a weighty, concentrated wine that is good with stews and roast meats.
Recommended producers: Ippolito, San Francesco, Librandi.

Greco di Bianco DOC   This unusual, rare, and hard-to-find dessert wine is a classic. Made from Greco grapes laid out in the sun to dry, it is at once powerful yet delicately sweet.
Recommended producer: Ceratti.

BASILICATA

Aglianico del Vulture DOC   One of the great, but still little-known, red wines of Italy, produced entirely from the characterful Aglianico grape grown at altitude on the eastern flanks of Monte Vulture, near Potenza. Best wines have color, concentrated bouquet (licorice, herbs, tar), and intensity of flavor allied with power and elegance.
Recommended producers: D'Angelo, Paternoster.

ABRUZZO AND MOLISE

Biferno DOC   Molise's best-known wines are Trebbiano-based whites and Montepulciano-based reds.
Recommended producer: Di Majo Norante.

Montepulciano d'Abruzzo DOC Punchy, dense, fruit-packed red wines from the characterful Montepulciano. Cerasuolo is the *rosato* (rosé) version.
Recommended producers: Valentini, Nicodemi, Illuminati, Emidio Pepe, Cornacchia.

Trebbiano d'Abruzzo DOC Abruzzo's white wines are generally less

The wine country of the Colli Lanuvini, south of Rome

distinguished than its reds, but sound if
rather neutral wines.
*Recommended producers: Valentini,
Illuminati, Emidio Pepe.*

PUGLIA

Bríndisi DOC   Distinguished red
wines produced chiefly from the
characterful Negroamaro grape. Best
wines are Il Patriglione (Taurino) and
Vallone's La Graticciaia, a sort of Puglian
Amarone, made from semi-dried grapes.
Recommended producers: Taurino, Vallone.

Castel del Monte DOC   Named for
the octagonal stone castle built in the
13th century by Emperor Frederick II,
this DOC applies to a fine, smooth, full-
bodied red wine as well as to good
rosato. Il Falcone is the best name.
Recommended producer: Rivera.

Copertino DOC   Copertino is the
source of good, still inexpensive, richly
flavored red wines mainly from the
Negroamaro grape.
*Recommended producer: Cantina Sociale di
Copertino.*

Five Roses   Named by an American
general during World War II, this full-
flavored, wood-aged *rosato* is a classic.
Recommended producer: de Castris.

Locorotondo DOC   One of the
cleanest and most reliable white wines of
the South. Drink as
young as possible.
*Recommended producer:
Cantina Sociale di Loco-
rotondo.*

**Primitivo di
Manduria DOC**
This near legendary
DOC applies to
walloping, hugely
alcoholic wines from
the local Primitivo
grape, which is one and
the same as California's
Zinfandel.

Rosa del Golfo   One
of Italy's finest *rosato*

Vineyards of Puglia, near Locorotondo

wines; compact, full-bodied, fruity.
Recommended producer: Rosa del Golfo.

Salice Salentino DOC   One of the
great red wines of the South, a rich,
powerful wine with a concentration of
complex flavors. Ages well.
*Recommended producers: Taurino, Candido,
Vallone, de Castris.*

OTHER DRINKS

Cedro (Calabria)   A large, knobbly,
and aromatic citrus fruit, *cedro* (citron) is
used to make Calabria's great regional
liquore.

Limoncello (Amalfi Coast)   Fresh
lemons from the Amalfi Coast, infused
with sugar and alcohol, result in this
pretty and delicately perfumed *liquore*.

*Limoncello, an
aperitivo of the
Amalfi Coast*

FOOD AND WINE COMBINATIONS

Antipasti pugliese   Puglia's magnificent array of mainly vegetable-
based appetizers is ably partnered by
a full-bodied *rosato*, such as Rosa del
Golfo or the wood-aged Five Roses.

Pesce spada   Calabria's char-grilled
swordfish is best with a white Cirò
(if you can get a young bottle). Alternatively, enjoy its rich flavor and
meaty texture with an aged red Cirò.

Porchetta   This garlicky fast food
cries out for a gutsy white from Colli
Albani or Castelli Romani.

Colli Albani
ROME'S ALBAN HILLS

THE COLLI ALBANI, a series of volcanic ridges that lies approximately 20 km. (13 miles) to the southeast of Rome, have for 2,000 years served as a favorite retreat for the citizens of the capital. Visitors to Rome who are weary of the city, or in search of peace, relaxation, and good, genuine local foods and wines, should do as the Romans do. But be warned: avoid weekends and Italian holidays when, it seems, virtually everybody in the capital has the same idea.

To reach the Colli Albani, leave the city on the ancient Via Tuscolana (N215) to arrive eventually at Frascati, Rome's most famous wine town, and since ancient times a popular and fashionable resort. The nearby ruin of ancient Tusculum was the birthplace of Cato, while Cicero, Pompey, and Tiberius all had

Wild strawberries from Nemi

houses here. In later times, wealthy patricians built splendid villas in Frascati, such as the Villa Aldobrandini. Yet, Frascati is still mainly medieval in feel: explore its small streets and alleys, and hunt down *cantine* — underground drinking dens, where you can enjoy simple foods and gutsy, golden wine by the carafe.

In truth, the Colli Albani is not a wine zone for serious wine touring and few opportunities exist for cellar visits. After all, you don't come here to study wine or to pontificate about it. You come here simply to drink the wine and take in the atmosphere, to enjoy touring towns such as Grottaferrata (visit the fortified Byzantine abbey, with views from its terrace), and Marino, the best-known wine town after Frascati. Here, during the wine festival in early October, the town fountain flows with free wine.

Nearby, Castel Gandolfo is where the Pope has his summer residence, so, not surprisingly, its streets are packed at weekends. Arricia is more pleasant: while there, don't miss sampling *porchetta*, reputed to be the best in the area. Genzano is famous above all for its splendid festival held after Easter, when the main avenue is carpeted with flowers arranged in beautiful patterns. Little medieval Nemi is another favorite, located above Lake Nemi and famous for its delicious wild strawberries.

ANDAR' PER LE VIGNE — INTO WINE COUNTRY

Azienda Agricola Tre Palme
Strada Muti, 73
Loc. I Muti
00045 Genzano RM
tel/fax: 06/9370286
Farmhouse accommodation and meals, and Colli Lanuvini wines.
$

Enoteca Frascati
Via Armando Diaz, 42
00044 Frascati RM
tel/fax: 06/9417449

Rustic enoteca, open evenings only — good selection of local wines, simple snacks, and good local foods.
$

Paolo Di Mauro
Via Colle Picchioni, 46
00040 Frattócchie di Marino RM
tel: 06/3360217
Artisan winery producing highly regarded white Marino and red Colle Picchioni wines.

Trattoria dei Cacciatori
Via del Municipio, 13
00040 Nemi RM
tel: 06/9368096
Simple hunter's trattoria.
$

Villa Simone
Via Frascati-Colonna, 29
00040 Monte Porzio Catone RM
tel: 06/9449717
Outstanding traditional Frascati, especially the rare cannellino version.

Wines in Antiquity
THE PAST ALL AROUND US

VIRGIL, HORACE, and Ovid all wrote about their favorite wines, and Pliny and Cato both composed analytic and precise treatises on vine growing and winemaking.

Amphorae have been recovered from the sea bed from laden Roman galleys that sank in storms. And in Pompeii, that evocative and most direct link with the ancient world, the remains of wine-growing estates that have been excavated have allowed archeologists to discover how Roman *cantine* were organized.

It is no surprise that the Romans had their own highly rigid hierarchy of local wines, the *grands crus,* as it were, of the ancient world. Praise was heaped in verse and prose on wines such as Falernum (considered the foremost), Caucinium, Alba (from the Colli Albani of Rome), Rhaetic (from Verona,

Roman amphorae found at Pompeii

a probable precursor of Recioto), and scores of others.

The Roman wines of old probably bear little if any resemblance to their counterparts of today (the Roman taste was for very old, concentrated, and bitter wines, often flavored with spices, aromatic herbs, honey, and diluted with water). Nonetheless, vineyards and grape varieties that were highly valued by the Romans in many cases today are capable of producing wines of world class.

Antonio Mastroberardino, one of Italy's most famous winemakers, has built an international reputation on a trio of wines all produced from indigenous grapes whose roots go back, literally, thousands of years. The great red wine Taurasi, vinified from Aglianico, and the

white Greco di Tufo, are both produced from grapes grown on the hills of Avellino and whose names indicate their Greek origins. Fiano, a grape Pliny favored (he called it Appianum because its high sugar content attracted *api* — bees), meanwhile, produces one of the rarest and most individual white wines of Italy.

Dr. Francesco Avallone, a classical scholar and lawyer in Naples, continually came upon references to Falernum wine in his readings. His passion both for the classics and for wine led him to purchase Villa Matilde, an old wine estate in the heart of the ancient Falernum wine zone, on the Roman Via Domiziana near Mondragone.

There, he propagated the nearly extinct Falanghina grape variety from which the name Falernum derives, and, today, the family estate produces fine white wines with the character, scent, and body of the Falanghina, as well as good, sturdy red Falerno from the Aglianico grape.

In a wine world increasingly made uniform through the creeping dominance of "international" grapes such as Cabernet Sauvignon and Chardonnay, such efforts and wines are to be applauded. Enjoy these wines whenever you get the chance; they rank among the finest in Southern Italy

Azienda Vinicola Mastroberardino
Via Manfredi, 75–81
83042 Atripalda AV
tel: 0825/626123
fax: 0825/624151
Antonio Mastroberardino's wines are available internationally; wander into and discover the rugged, earthquake-ravaged country where they come from.

Fattoria Villa Matilde
SS Domitiana, 18
81030 Cellole CE
tel: 0823/932088
fax: 0823/932134
Direct sales plus farmhouse accommodation and children's summer camp.

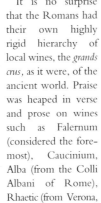

The Wine Roads of Puglia
INTO THE LAND OF THE TRULLI

Puglia is the great, undiscovered surprise of the South. A rich agricultural land at ease with itself, it presents a striking contrast to other, more rugged, and impoverished regions of Southern Italy. Its beaches, extending along the Adriatic Coast as well as the Ionian Gulf of Táranto, remain, on the whole, unspoiled and unpolluted. The region can boast one of the most varied and original of all southern cuisines, based primarily on its array of superlative vegetables. And it is the source of a good range of still inexpensive but always satisfying wines. No wonder this is a region that is increasingly becoming popular with both Italians and foreigners.

Visitors to the beaches of Puglia may well wish to make a brief excursion inland into the wine country of the Murge, between Bari and Bríndisi. Alberobello is the most striking town to head for, an unusual, really bizarre place, consisting almost entirely of conical *trulli*, white-washed dry-stone dwellings made from soft tufa blocks, blindingly white in the midday sun (see p.215).

Nearby, Locorotondo is the center of an important vine-growing zone, its wine cooperative something of a model for others throughout the South, for it has demonstrated that, by using modern technology and harvesting grapes early, clean, sound, and inexpensive white

Locorotondo

wines can be produced here that appeal not only locally but internationally. Locorotondo itself is an atmospheric maze of tiny alleys, and tall, whitewashed houses.

Just south of Locorotondo the 18th-century baroque town of Martina Franca also deserves to be visited, not least for its remarkable outdoor market that takes place on Wednesdays. In the past, most local wines were sent north to be made into Vermouth. Though this industry has declined, Martina Franca's most distinctive wine is still the old-style fortified *bianco di Martina*: ask for it in any of the local bars.

From Martina Franca, return to the coast at Ostuni, another startling white town that is almost African in feel. Then finish the tour at Bríndisi, today, a busy, workmanlike port, and still the gateway to the Eastern Mediterranean. Bríndisi's surrounding vineyards are the source of some exceptionally fine red wines. Purchase a bottle or two and you will be able to *"fare un bríndisi,"* "make a toast."

ANDAR' PER LE VIGNE — INTO WINE COUNTRY

Cantina Borgo Canale
Viale Canale di Pirro, 23
72015 Fasano BR
tel: 080/9331351
fax: 080/9331505
Clean white wines.

Cantina Sociale di Locorotondo
Via Madonna della Catena, 99
70010 Locorotondo BA
tel: 080/9311644

fax: 080/9311213
Well-made white Locorotondo from this model cooperative.

Enoteca Internazionale
Via C. Battisti, 23
73100 Lecce
tel: 0832/22832
One of the best wine stores in Puglia; in the center of the beautiful, baroque city of Lecce.

Enoteca Puglia
Largo Martellotta, 84
70011 Alberobello BA
tel: 080/9325558
Local wines and olive oil.

Trattoria Centro Storico
Via Eroi di Dogali, 6
70010 Locorotondo BA
tel: 080/9315473
Authentic local foods and wines.
$

Indirizzi

USEFUL ADDRESSES

Greek temple at Metaponto, Basilicata

CAMPANIA

Azienda Agricola Di Marzo
Via G. Di Marzo, 17
83010 Tufo AV
tel: 0825/998022
fax: 0825/998383
Earthquake-ravaged Tufo is still the source of some good, traditionally made wines. Come here to taste and buy them at source.

Bar-Pasticceria La Zagara
Via dei Mulini, 10
84017 Positano SA
tel: 089/875964
Delicious lemon granita plus a range of pasticceria and cakes.
$

Ristorante La Cambusa
Piazza A. Vespucci, 4
84017 Positano SA
tel: 089/875432
Probably the best restaurant in town. Overlooks the sea and serves excellent fish and shellfish.
$$$

Ristorante Malaga
Via Francesco Tedesco, 347
83100 Avellino
tel: 0825/626045
fax: 0825/626045
Serving a menu based entirely on fish, accompanied by local wines like Greco and Fiano.
$$

I Sapori di Positano
Via dei Mulini, 6
84017 Positano SA
tel: 089/811116
Sandra Russo makes the best limoncello *on the Amalfi Coast, hand-made in small batches from fresh lemons from her own gardens. "The secret," she says, "is to drink* limoncello *when it is very fresh, so that it maintains its beautiful color and the perfume of our fresh lemons of Positano."*

Villa Maria
Via Santa Chiara, 2
84010 Ravello SA
tel: 089/857255
fax: 089/857071
A lovely base for visiting the Amalfi Coast, with a highly regarded restaurant.
$$$

Peaches from the South

CALABRIA

Centro Gastronomico Sapore Calabria
Diamante CS
(see p.193)

Fattoria San Francesco
Casale San Francesco
88071 Cirò Marina CZ
tel: 0962/32228
fax: 0962/32987
Fine Cirò wines aged in barrique, *olive oil, and* pecorino *cheese.*

Hotel-Ristorante Il Gabbiano
Punta Alice
88072 Cirò Marina CZ

tel: 0962/31338
fax: 0962/31339
Friendly family beach hotel with a good restaurant serving seafood pasta, *fresh fish, and shellfish.*
$$

Il Mulino
Contrada Maucera
87020 Buonvicino CS
tel: 0985/85188
Farmhouse restaurant in the hills, straddling the mill stream; genuine, well-prepared country foods.
$

Pastificio La Golosa
Scalea CS
(see p.197)

Rifugio Piano di Lanzo
Piazza Mercato
87010 San Donato di Ninea CS
tel: 0981/63369
fax: 0981/952033
Mountain refuge with guided walks, mountain foods, and simple rustic accommodation.
$

BASILICATA

Casa Vinicola d'Angelo
Via Provinciale, 8
85028 Rionero in Vúlture PZ
tel: 0972/721517
fax: 0972/723495
Donato d'Angelo is one of Southern Italy's great winemakers. Discover here Aglianico del Vulture and the silky Canneto (Aglianico aged in barrique).

Hotel-Ristorante La Pergola
Via Lavista, 27/31
85028 Rionero in Vúlture PZ
tel: 0972/721179;720391
fax: 0972/721819
Best base for seeking out Aglianico del Vulture; restaurant serves good, spicy local foods.
$

Taverna Rovita
Via Rovita, 13
85046 Maratea PZ
tel: 0973/876588
Maratea is one of poor Basilicata's few beauty spots. Come up here to the old town and reward yourself with the very best of local foods from both land and sea.
$$

ABRUZZO & MOLISE

Albergo-Ristorante Villa Donna Lisa
Via Senatore De Castris
73015 Salice Salentino LE
tel: 0832/732222
fax: 0832/732224
The Leone de Castris family, one of the most important wine producers in Puglia, run this modern, friendly hotel-restaurant in this one-street wine town. Regional and international foods accompanied by the de Castris wines: try the famous "Five Roses" (rosé), and ask to tour the impressive and extensive wine cellars.
$$$

Cantina di Majo-Norante
Contrada Ramitelli, 4
86042 Campomarino CB
tel: 0875/57208
fax: 0875/57379
The best wines of Molise plus good home-conserved jams and vegetables sott'olio.

Cooperativa Agricola Cerere
Via Trichiano, 11
03040 Alvito FR
tel/fax: 0776/509110
Located in the Parco Nazionale d'Abruzzo (though officially in Lazio), this cooperative sells prodotti tipici *and also serves good home-cooked foods including* maccheroni alla chittara *and broiled lamb and kid.*
$

Alberobello in Puglia, home to hundreds of trulli *dwellings*

Ristorante Leon d'Or
Via A. Moro, 55/57
64014 Martinsicuro TE
tel: 0861/797070
fax: 0861/797695
This is one of the greatest fish restaurants in Italy.
$$

Ristorante Ribo
Calle da Malecoste, 7
86034 Guglionesi CB
tel/fax: 0875/680655
In deepest Molise, this stylish restaurant on the road from Térmoli serves genuine local foods.
$$

PUGLIA

Antico Frantoio Oleario
Via Monte Sabotino, 6
70011 Alberobello BA
tel: 080/721538
Puglian extra-virgin olive oil is green, richly flavored, and inexpensive compared to designer oils from Tuscany and elsewhere.

Forno dei Fratelli di Gesù
Via E. Pimentel, 15
70022 Altamura BA
tel: 080/842737
Altamura is famous for its breads, and the town boasts many traditional bakeries like this one, still using a wood-fired forno a legna.

La Masseria
Loc. Torre Sabea
73014 Gallipoli LE
tel: 0833/202295
Good traditional wines at Carlo Coppola's agriturismo complex. Apartments, camping, and beach.
$

Latticini Fragnelli
Via E. Toti, 5
74015 Martina Franca TA
tel: 080/8807241
The full range of pasta filata cheeses made fresh daily on the premises.

Ristorante Trullo d'Oro
Via Felice Cavallotti, 27
70011 Alberobello BA
tel/fax: 080/721820
Imaginative vegetarian antipasti in a trullo.
$$

BEST BUYS
• *friselle* (Puglia, Calabria, and Campania)
• *limoncello* (Amalfi Coast)
• strings of *peperoncini* (Calabria, Basilicata, and Campania)
• dried *paste* and *paste* made with *peperoncini* (Puglia and Calabria)
• extra-virgin olive oil (Puglia and Calabria)
• dried tomatoes (Puglia, Campania, and Calabria)
• *cedro* liqueur (Calabria)

Menu at Ristorante Trullo d'Oro, Alberobello, Puglia

Sicily

SEPARATED FROM THE MAINLAND by the narrow Straits of Messina, Sicily is a world apart from the rest of Italy. Over the centuries, a torrent of armies and influences — Phoenician, Greek, Roman, Arab, Norman, Angevin, Spanish Bourbon — has invaded, conquered, ruled, left, or been kicked out: yet, an essential Sicilian character remains. The largest island in the Mediterranean, Sicily has an insular mentality — at once suspicious, at once proud and self-satisfied. Though poverty and an iniquitous feudal system based on absentee landowners led to mass emigration, few Sicilians, we imagine, would not want to come back home given the chance. For Sicily, in spite of its problems, is a place that gets under your skin, a hot, volatile land, exciting, often troubling, but one of the most hospitable places in all Italy.

TAORMINA AND THE EAST COAST

Most visitors to Sicily make for the East Coast, and Taormina is undoubtedly the jewel in Sicily's touristic crown. This charming medieval hill town overlooking the sea across to mainland Calabria, dominated inland by the always brooding, often smoking presence of Mount Etna, has been important since at least Greek times, as the magnificent ruins of

Mount Etna, in background, viewed from Taormina on the East Coast of Sicily

the third-century B.C. amphitheater testify. Today, its narrow alleys, packed in high season, spill onto scores of hotels and good *trattorie* and restaurants.

No visit to Taormina would be complete without an excursion to the summit of Mount Etna, at 3,340 m. (nearly 11,000 ft.) Europe's highest active volcano. Earthquake-ravaged Messina and sprawling Catania lie on either side of Taormina, interconnected by lush agricultural land that thrives on the mineral-rich soil that spreads down from the broad flanks of the smoldering volcano. Syracuse, an ancient Greek city that rivaled even Athens, deserves to be visited for its classic ruins and its medieval port, a maze of dark, winding alleys on the Ortigia Peninsula. The baroque town of Noto is also worth visiting, and the Greek ruins of Agrigento are some of the finest outside Greece.

PALERMO AND WESTERN SICILY

The chaotic, baroque capital of the island, Palermo was once home to Norman kings and Spanish viceroys. Today, it is an intriguing, exciting, sometimes dangerous city. Visitors here will certainly wish to see monuments such as the Palazzo dei Normanni and the cathedral, but don't miss the Vucceria market, a sheer riot of color and smells, and crazy

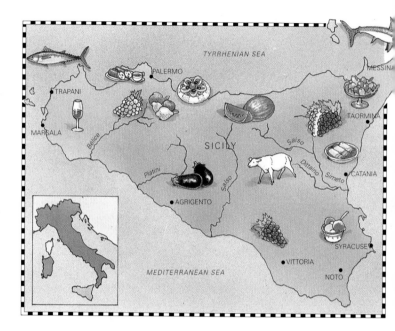

activity as can only be found in Sicily. From Palermo, head out to quieter Monreale, or to the West Coast, to Trapani, Erice (a former Greek and Phoenician colony), and Marsala, one of the historic wine towns of Italy. From Trapani, there are ferries to Pantelleria, an island off the north coast of Africa most famous for its fragrant and powerful Moscato dessert wines, as well as to Sardinia. Palermo also has regular ferry services to Naples, Genova, Sardinia, Livorno, and the Aeolian Islands.

A RICH MIX OF ARISTOCRATIC AND PEASANT FOODS

The curious mix of cultures and influences has, naturally, left its imprint on Sicilian cuisine. The Arabs planted extensive and lush citrus groves and

left a taste for sophisticated and intricate pastries and desserts. The Norman and Spanish aristocracy left a heritage of elaborate, ornate foods that contrast with the simpler *cucina povera* of the working classes. On the one hand, extravagant dishes were created to titillate the palates of the jaded (usually foreign) aristocracy; on the other, delicious and imaginative foods appeared almost magically out of basic and meager provisions to satisfy the appetites of peasant, fishermen, and working people. Today, both traditions provide a fascinating contrast in a diet that is never less than exciting and delicious.

Detail from the typically ornate baroque architecture of Noto

Prodotti Regionali
REGIONAL PRODUCE

THE ARABS introduced intricate systems of irrigation to this hot, volcanic island, and even today, there is extreme contrast between areas where there is water and the mainly arid interior.

Where there is water, there is an abundance of luxuriant vegetation — flowers, fruits, and vegetables — and there is prosperity. Where there is none or only little, the landscape is bare, and rural people are con-

Cocomeri, *watermelons*

demned to poverty, in some cases, living barely above subsistence level.

Sicily's southerly position means a climate that is able to provide not only Sicily but also the rest of Italy and Northern Europe with the season's first, early harvested fruits and vegetables. Indeed, the *tarocco* "blood" oranges that arrive in Northern Italy by Christmas — vivid in color, full of flavor, and sweet, red juice and pulp — bring in the depths of winter a sense of warmth and the southern sun. Grapes are cultivated almost throughout the year (in winter, under plastic covering), and the *uva regina*

is one of Italy's best.

Because of its harsh terrain, Sicily has never been an island for the widescale raising of livestock, so its cuisine has remained based very much on vegetables supplemented only occasionally with meat and fish. The range of fruits, vegetables, and nuts is impressive: citrus fruit, tomatoes, eggplant, olives, zucchini, capers (grown widely on the Aeolian Islands), bell peppers, almonds, figs, pistachios, melons, and watermelons.

TRY TO SAMPLE

Capperi Capers (fresh in summer; preserved, all year). Sample also *i cucunsi* (flowers from the caper plant), preserved *sott'aceto* (in vinegar).

Citrus fruits (all year round) Fresh, off-the-tree oranges, lemons, and citron.

Cocomero or **anguria** (summer) You'll never taste better watermelon. Don't miss *granita di cocomero*, a delicious, slushy watermelon ice.

Melanzane (summer and fall) Eggplant, the most characteristic vegetable.

SICILY'S CITRUS GROVES

The Conca d'Oro, the dense, fertile plain that surrounds Palermo, planted almost exclusively with orange and lemon groves, is a splendid sight, especially looking down from the hill town of Monreale. Citrus groves abound throughout Sicily, and not just *arance* (oranges) and *limoni* (lemons) are cultivated, but also *mandarini* (mandarin

oranges), *cedro* (citron, an important fruit that is candied and used in confectionary and cakes), and *pompelmo* (grapefruit).

Spremuta di arancia — freshly pressed orange juice — is delicious, but *spremuta di limone* is even more refreshing in summer, the juice of one or two lemons topped up with seltzer and a dash of salt.

The Kingdom by the Sea
SICILY'S FISHING TRADITION

IN SICILY, fishing traditions have long been an important way of life for those living by the coast. Great shoals of tuna (today, no longer so prevalent) used to be caught in bloody expeditions known as the *tonnare* off the shores of the western part of the island from the ports of Trapani and Mazzara del Vallo.

Fishermen would lay their nets to channel the fish into a central death chamber where they would be speared with harpoons, a brutal and bloody spectacle. So many fish were caught that the sea would turn red from the blood.

In the east of the island, by the narrow Straits of Messina, the traditional hunt, again using harpoons and nets, was and continues to be for *pesce spada* (swordfish) and *ricciola* (amberjack).

All along the coast in Sicily, you will come across good fish and seafood dishes as well as a fine selection on view and for sale in local markets.

The harbor at Lipari, a popular destination on the Aeolian Islands

TRY TO SAMPLE

Acciughe Fresh anchovies.

Alalunga or **alalonga** Albacore or longfin tuna, considered the finest.

Bottarga Salted and wind-dried tuna roe.

Capone Gurnard.

Cicina Mixture of tiny fish; to fry or use in soups.

Pesce spada Swordfish.

Ricciola Amberjack.

Tonnetto Little tunny; a mackerel-sized tuna, a favorite on the island.

Totano Flying squid, a large reddish-yellow species.

Vongole veraci Carpetshell clams; the finest and most expensive.

AL MERCATO — MARKETS

Arcireale	Sat	Marsala	Mon, Fri
Agrigento	Tue, Fri	Messina	Mon–Sat
Caltagirone	Sat	Milazzo	Fish market
Caltanissetta	Sat		daily
Cefalu	Sat	Modica	Thu
Enna	Tue	Monreale	Thu
Erice	Mon	Noto	Mon
		Palermo	Mon–Sat
		Pantelleria	Tue, Fri
		Piazza	
		Armerina	Wed
		Ragusa	Wed
		Segesta	Fri
		Syracuse	daily
		Taormina	Wed
		Trapani	Thu
		Vittoria	Sat

POPULAR *FESTE*

Lipari: *Sagra del dolci eoliani (traditional Aeolian sweets)* Oct

Noto: *Infiorata (flowers)* 3rd Sun May

Chiaromonte: *Sagra della salsiccia (sausages)* Feb

Piatti Tipici
REGIONAL SPECIALTIES

THE *CUCINA* OF SICILY, like the island itself, stands alone from the rest of Italy, a unique development from its history and geography.

The Arabs introduced citrus fruit, ice cream, desserts and sweets based on nuts and dried fruits, as well as African foods such as *cuscusu*. The Normans brought a love of *baccalà* (dried cod) to an island whose waters are the abundant source of fresh fish. The Spaniards introduced an intricate baroque style not only to architecture but to elaborate, colorful, sometimes whimsical foods. The French Angevins reinforced a native love of garlic and introduced sophisticated techniques for pastry-making. All these influences have left their mark and shaped the foods of Sicily. The unique genius of the Sicilians melded these diverse influences to result in cuisine that is at once colorful, sometimes exotic and sophisticated, but never less than appetizing and appealing.

Antipasti siciliani

An array of Sicilian *antipasti* ranks among the finest in the country, fresh fish is excellent, and the desserts and pastries are irresistible.

ANTIPASTI

Antipasti siciliani　A good array of Sicilian *antipasti* may consist of a variety of vegetable dishes, such as roasted, grilled, and stuffed zucchini, red onions, bell peppers, and tomatoes; a *giardiniera* salad of raw chopped vegetables dressed *sott'aceto* (in vinegar); *caponata* (see below); and *melanzane* (eggplant) prepared in several ways — grilled slices dressed with garlic and oil; deep-fried cubes; baked, then shredded and dressed in olive oil; or *alla parmigiana*: layered with *mozzarella* and parmesan cheeses,

then baked. Fish *antipasti* often include marinated anchovies; mussels on the half-shell covered with breadcrumbs and baked; and strips of raw *pesce spada* (swordfish) "cooked" with lemon juice and *peperoncini*.

Arancini or **arancini di riso**　Little balls of rice stuffed with meat, peas, and cheese, then coated in breadcrumbs and deep fried.

Bottarga　Salted, dried, and pressed roe of tuna or gray mullet, cut into thin slices, then dressed with olive oil and plenty of lemon juice.

Caponata　Island specialty of eggplant, onion, tomatoes, bell peppers, cauliflower, celery, capers, pine nuts, raisins, and almonds dressed in an *agrodolce* (sweet-and-sour sauce) of vinegar, sugar, and orange juice.

Insalata di mare　Seafood salad of shrimp, boiled squid, pieces of octopus, and chopped vegetables, dressed in olive oil and vinegar or lemon juice.

Musseddu　Air- and sun-dried fillet of tuna (dolphin was once preferred), cut into thin strips or slices.

Schiacciate　Flat breads layered or filled with a variety of ingredients, including anchovies or tuna, stewed and dressed vegetables, or cheese.

I PRIMI PIATTI

Cannelloni alla siciliana　Dried or fresh *cannelloni* (large tubes of *pasta*) filled with a *ragù* (meat sauce), covered with tomato sauce and cheese, and baked.

Cozze alla marinara　Mussels steamed in wine with garlic and parsley.

Cuscusu　Sicilian *couscous* made from coarse semolina first steamed, then moistened with fish stock, and served usually with a spicy fish stew on top.

Maccaruni di casa
Sicilian term for homemade *pasta* — usually a long, flattish noodle made only from hard durum wheat and water.

Maccu   Thick, soupy puree of dried beans, soaked then boiled, and seasoned with extra-virgin olive oil and wild fennel.

Cozze alla marinara

Pasta al forno   A Sicilian specialty: any type of *pasta* and sauce (tomato, meat *ragù,* or vegetables) mixed together, usually layered with cheese, then baked.

Pasta alla Norma
Pasta (either homemade *maccaruni* or dried *spaghetti* or *penne)* served with a tomato sauce made with basil and strips of fried eggplant, and topped always with *ricotta salata* cheese. This specialty comes from Catania, where Bellini, composer of the opera *Norma,* was born, hence the name.

Pasta alla Norma

Pasta con le sarde
Classic, simple dish of *pasta* served in a tomato sauce made with sardines and flavored with capers, raisins, pine nuts, and vinegar.

Spaghetti all'isolana
Spaghetti with tomatoes, capers, and olives.

Spaghetti alle cozze
Spaghetti with mussels.

Spaghetti alla siracusana   *Spaghetti* with a sauce with slices of dried *bottarga* (salted tuna or mullet roe).

Spaghetti alle vongole veraci
Spaghetti with clams (of many varieties, *vongole veraci* are considered the finest), steamed in wine, with garlic, olive oil, and parsley.

Zuppa di cozze   Mussel soup.

I SECONDI PIATTI

Coniglio alla stimpirata   Rabbit stewed with olive oil, garlic, celery, bell peppers, carrots, and olives.

Costoletta alla siciliana   Thin slice of beef or veal covered with grated parmesan cheese and chopped garlic, then dipped in breadcrumbs and fried.

HONEY

Zafferana Etnea is a small town on the volcanic slopes of Mount Etna. Many of its inhabitants keep bees either as a livelihood or as a hobby.

We met Signor Caruso nearly at the summit of Etna, where he takes his van to sell his honeys and honey products. He explained how he transports his hives to different parts of the island for the bees to gather nectar from different plants, as each results in a unique

honey. *Miele di arancia* (orange-blossom honey) is marvelously fragrant, *miele di timo* (thyme) has an intriguing herbal tang, whereas *miele di eucalipto* (eucalyptus) is particularly full flavored.

At Apicultura Caruso-Barbagallo, Signor Caruso also offers *pappa reale* (royal jelly), and his own specialties, such as *frutta secca mista al miele d'arancia* — almonds, pistachios, and pine nuts mixed with orange-blossom honey (address p.227).

Farsumagru or **falsomagro**   Sicily's best-known meat dish — the name means "false lean," for this is a rich and substantial dish made from a large slice of beef or veal rolled around boiled eggs, sausage, grated cheese, *prosciutto*, pine nuts, and raisins, which is tied securely with string, then stewed slowly in a tomato sauce. It is then thinly sliced and served with the sauce on top.

Ghiotta di pescestocco   Dried salt cod, soaked, then cooked with tomatoes, capers, pine nuts, olives, celery, and raisins.

Pepata di cozze   Mussels cooked in a sauce made with fresh tomatoes.

Pesce alla griglia   Freshly caught fish of the day, char-grilled to order.

Pesce spada   Swordfish; often center-cut into thick steaks, then grilled over charcoal. **Pesce spada alla ghiotta** is cooked with tomato, capers, onion, celery, and potatoes.

Involtini di pesce spada are little fried rolls of swordfish stuffed with pine nuts, breadcrumbs, and anchovies.

Char-grilled ricciola

Ricciola Amberjack, one of the great fishes of Sicily; usually cut into steaks and char-grilled.

Sarde a beccafico Boned sardines, stuffed with raisins, pine nuts, breadcrumbs, anchovies, and cinnamon, and baked with lemon or orange juice.

Tonnetto   Mackerel-sized silvery fish of the tuna family; in appearance and taste like a very small tuna.

Tonno fresco   Tuna, either prepared **in umido** (stewed in wine with garlic) or **alla brace** (char-grilled).

Spaghetti alle vongole veraci

I CONTORNI

Caponata   Medley of vegetables in a sweet-and-sour sauce.

Fritella or **fritedda** Fried mixture of artichokes, peas, shallots, and fava beans in a sweet-and-sour sauce.

SICILIAN CHEESES

Sicily has a tradition of cheesemaking that goes back to when the island was part of ancient Greece. Ewe's milk cheeses are Sicily's most important, and a wide selection of them is made. Especially noteworthy are those from the province of Ragusa. A full range of typical southern cheeses — *mozzarella, caciocavallo, provola* — is also made (see pp.204–206).

Pecorino canestrato Ewe's milk cheese made

from curds drained in wicker baskets or molds and usually aged until hard, with a yellow to dark orange rind.

Pecorino pepato *Canestrato* cheese with whole black peppercorns.

Ricotta fresca di pecora Ewe's milk *ricotta;* eaten fresh and used widely in sweets and pastries as well as savory dishes.

Ricotta salata   Aged *ricotta* (sometimes dried in the sun), generally used for grating over *pasta* dishes.

I Dolci Siciliani

THE SWEETEST OF THE SWEET

AN ESSENTIAL PART of visiting Sicily is the chance to sample its range of wonderful *dolci* — pastries, sweets, and desserts.

Sicily also makes some of the finest ice creams you will taste anywhere. *Cassata* is, of course, the most famous, but best of all are *granite* — slushy ices made with purees of fresh fruit pulp, such as *limone* (lemon), *pesca* (peach), *anguria* (watermelon), *fragola* (strawberry), or from *espresso* (coffee) — usually served in glasses and eaten with a *brioche,* the yeasty bun, dipped into the ice.

Cassata alla siciliana

TRY TO SAMPLE

Biscotti A vast assortment of twice-cooked biscuits and cookies is available, usually made with honey, almonds, hazelnuts, and figs.

Bucce d'arancia and **bucce di limone** Fresh orange and lemon peel cut into thin strips and candied in sugar syrup — a delicious, fragrant nibble. Sometimes the candied peel is covered in chocolate.

Cannolo The classic pastry of Sicily; a crunchy tube of pastry filled with *ricotta* cheese studded with candied fruits, pistachio nuts, and bits of chocolate.

Cassata alla siciliana This famous cake, not to be confused with *cassata al gelato,* is a layered sponge cake moistened with orange liqueur or Marsala, and filled with *ricotta* cheese, pieces of candied fruits, chunks of chocolate, covered with icing, and, often, decorated with marzipan or marzipan fruit shapes.

Cassata al gelato Elaborate frozen dessert made with pistachios and hazelnuts, candied fruits, and bits of chocolate in a vanilla-flavored frozen custard.

Torrone A nougat made with honey, egg white, and sugar, and usually studded with pistachio nuts or candied orange and lemon peel.

A cannolo and caffè at the Pasticceria Chemi Antonino, Taormina

---

PASTA REALE

The art of making both fantastic and realistic shapes from *pasta reale,* the name given to marzipan made from a  paste of ground almonds, sugar, and egg whites, was probably introduced to Sicily by the Arabs. Today, producers vie with one another to make the most beautiful and true likenesses of fruits, such as prickly pears, figs, pomegranates, blood oranges, or peaches. Shaped by hand, then decorated painstakingly with food colorings, they are so realistic that you want to reach out and touch them.

Pasta reale is an expensive treat; once, it was made only on special saints' days, but, today, it is one of the best edible souvenirs of Sicily you can take back home.

I Vini

THE WINES OF SICILY

Beware of lava-encrusted wine bottles in Taormina

A s with so many other things, Sicily is a paradox when it comes to wine. It boasts the largest area in Italy under vines and sometimes produces the most wine of any Italian region, yet little of this ever reaches the bottle. The local taste is for huge, powerful, highly alcoholic wines made from overripe grapes from this sunbaked land, but the wines that have gained most attention are light, clean, and modern to the point of neutrality.

Many DOC wines are so rare that they are virtually unobtainable. Safer and better wines come from recognizable brands that are widely available not just throughout the island but even internationally.

Try to sample

Alcamo DOC   One of Sicily's best DOC wines, a dry white of some character made from the Catarratto grape. When young, it has a fresh, lemony character, but like many Sicilian whites it does have a tendency to oxidize quickly, so always drink the youngest wines available. *Recommended producer: Rapitalà.*

Cerasuolo di Vittoria DOC   Deeply colored and flavored red wine from the southeast of the island. *Recommended producers: COS, Coria.*

Corvo   Good, well-made, and consistent red and white wines made by the Duca di Salaparuta winery from grapes grown throughout the island.

Donnafugata   Another good, private, and reliable brand for both fresh white wine and full-bodied red from grapes grown in the center of the island at Contessa Entellina.

Duca di Salaparuta   Sicily's largest and most important winery, and the source of not just reliable Corvo but of superior bottlings such as the fresh, aromatic white Colomba Platino and the classy Duca Enrico, a super *vino da tavola* aged in new *barriques*.

Etna DOC   Ignore the lava-encrusted bottles — both good white and red

Mount Etna vinescape

wines are produced on the volcano's mineral-rich flanks. *Recommended producer: Barone di Villagrande.*

Malvasia delle Lipari DOC   A unique island wine produced from Malvasia grapes grown on the Aeolian Islands; a rich, sunbaked dessert wine with an amber color and intriguing flavors of dried fruits. *Recommended producer: Hauner.*

Marsala   Sicily's best-known wine (see p.226).

Moscato di Pantelleria DOC; Passito di Pantelleria   We consider this to be one of the great but undervalued dessert wines of the world, produced from Zibibbo grapes (a variety of Moscato) on the island of Pantelleria, just a stone's throw from the coast of North Africa. For the *passito* version, the already sunbaked grapes are further laid out to dry in the wind and sun, concentrating sugar, flavor, and aroma to result in sweet, concentrated yet intriguingly delicate wine with an almost floral, orange-blossom character.

Recommended producers: Cantina Sociale di Pantelleria (Tanit), De Bartoli (Bukkuram).

The vineyards of Alcamo

Rapitalà Fine, well-made Alcamo white and spicy, rich red made by Frenchman Comte Hugues de la Gatinais.

Regaleali The Tasca d'Almerita family produces fine wines under the Regaleali label. Straight wines are good and reliable, while superior bottlings — fresh, zesty white Nozze d'Oro and ripe, fleshy red Rosso del Conte — rank with the best from Sicily.

Settesoli This large cooperative winery produces and markets a range of sound inexpensive white, red, and rosé wines that demonstrate the great, still unfulfilled potential of the island. Most wines from this cooperative are reliable, but, as always in Sicily, check vintage dates and drink the youngest.

Terre di Ginestra Modern, high-quality wines: white, mainly from local Catarratto, and rich, spicy red from Nero d'Avola.

Vecchio Samperi Marco De Bartoli makes Marsala as it used to be — unfortified and aged by the traditional *solera* system of dynamic aging through fractional blending (as opposed to aging single vintage years). The results are some of the finest wines of this type. Try the Vecchio Samperi and the exquisite, dry Josephine Doré.

MARSALA

Like Portuguese Madeira and Spanish Malaga, Marsala is a wine from another age, created in the 18th century not for local consumption but mainly for export to London and the British Empire. Fortified with grape brandy to make it more robust and able to withstand the voyage, and sweetened with *sifone* (grape must and brandy) or thick *cotto* (cooked grape must), it became hugely popular in the 19th century, especially after Nelson had it supplied to his fleet

instead of rum.

Marsala is still produced in the town from where Garibaldi began the struggle that led to the unification of Italy and where, today, whitewashed warehouses hold thousands of barrels.

Marsala is available in many styles and types. Try outstanding and individual dry *vergine* or *solera* or richly sweet, smooth, old *superiore riserva*.

Recommended producers: Florio, Pellegrino, Rallo, Vecchio Samperi.

Indirizzi
ADDRESSES

Antica Pasticceria Siciliana
Via Maestranza, 39
Syracuse SR
tel: 0931/67303
The oldest pasticceria in the city, famous for its intricate sugar work and also typical specialties such as cassata alla siciliana.

Apicultura Caruso-Barbagallo
Via IV Novembre
95019 Zafferana Etnea CT
tel: 095/7081947
Outstanding honey and honey products direct from the producer.

Azienda Agricola Carlo Hauner
Via Umberto I
98050 Lingua di Salina ME
tel/fax: 090/9843141
Outstanding wines from the tiny island of Salina.

Azienda Agricola COS
Piazza del Popolo, 34
97019 Vittoria RG
tel: 0932/864042
fax: 0932/869700
Some of the best wines of Southeast Sicily.

Barone di Villagrande
Via del Bosco, 25
95010 Milo CT
tel: 095/7082175
fax: 095/7894339
The most important private winery in the zone, with excellent red and white wines.

Caffè Sicilia
Corso V. Emanuele, 125
96017 Noto SR
tel: 0931/835013
fax: 0931/839781
Historic bar/caffè in this remarkable baroque town.

Cantine Florio
Via Vincenzo Florio, 1
91025 Marsala TP
tel: 0923/781111
fax: 0923/982380

It's worth making an appointment to visit this great, historic winery.

Da Nello Il Greco
Via Roma, 105
90010 Porticello PA

Ceramic mask

tel: 091/957868
fax: 091/958062
One of the great restaurants of Sicily; Porticello is located 18 km. (about 11 miles) east of Palermo.
$$$$

Fattoria delle Torri
Via Nativo, 30/32
97015 Módica RG
tel: 0932/751286
fax: 0932/751086
Outstanding Sicilian foods carefully researched and prepared by Beppe Barone and family.
$

Pasticceria Chemi Antonino
Corso Umberto, 102
98039 Taormina ME
tel/fax: 0942/24260
For the obligatory cannolo and cappuccino, also other dolci and pasta reale.

Ristorante Filippino
Piazza Mazzini
98055 Lipari ME
tel: 090/9811002
fax: 090/09812878
Best restaurant on island for Aeolian specialties.
$$$

Ristorante Giova Rosy Senior
Corso Umberto, 38
98039 Taormina ME
tel/fax: 0942/24411
Good local foods and a sunny outdoor terrace.
$

Ristorante Il Delfino
Loc. Mazzarrò
Via Nazionale
98039 Taormina ME
tel: 0942/23004
The best seafood in town.
$$

Ristorante Zio Ciccio
Lungomare Mediterraneo, 211
91025 Marsala TP
tel: 0923/981962
On the seafront, serving fresh fish and cuscusu.
$$

Taverna Aretusa
Via Santa Teresa, 32
96100 Siracusa SR
tel: 0931/68720
Atmospheric trattoria serving good, authentic local foods.
$

Trattoria Caprice
Via Panoramica dei Templi, 51
92100 Agrigento AG
tel/fax: 0922/26469
Outstanding antipasti.
$$

Trattoria d'Oro
Via Umberto I°, 28–32
98055 Lipari ME
tel/fax: 090/9811304
Good seafood pasta and grilled fish.
$

BEST BUYS
• salted capers and Malvasia wine from the Aeolian Islands
• *pasta reale* marzipan
• bottles of fruit syrups
• almond pastries and *biscotti*
• candied citrus peel

Sardinia

STILL LARGELY UNSPOILED AND UNDISCOVERED, Sardinia, the second largest island in the Mediterranean (after Sicily), supports only a million-and-a-half inhabitants (plus more than twice that number of sheep). But both exclusive and mass tourism have come — and are coming quickly — to the island: the Costa Smeralda, a stunningly beautiful stretch of rocky coastline in the northeast, is one of the most expensive, exclusive, and chic international resorts in Europe. Elsewhere along the coast, at Alghero and Cagliari, in particular, hotels and holiday complexes proliferate. But the great body of the island, mountainous in the extreme, covered with the characteristic *macchia mediterranea* — maquis, the primarily evergreen Mediterranean scrub bush — remains as it has for centuries, isolated, remote, starkly beautiful, a land mainly of *pastori* (shepherds), who still drive their flocks into the high slopes in summer to find cooler, fresher grazing, as they have done for centuries.

As in Sicily, the influences of invaders who have come to Sardinia over the millennia have undoubtedly shaped its character. No one knows for sure who or where the original Sards came from, though the 4,000-year-old *nuraghi* — circular stone buildings that are both dwellings and fortresses — are striking evidence of the aboriginal peoples who settled

The rugged mountains of the Sopramonte in Central Sardinia

here. Later, the island's strategic Mediterranean location meant that, in ancient times, the Phoenicians traded here, and Carthaginians and Romans also settled in Sardinia. The Romans made the island a province, but its inhospitable interior was never conquered, and it was to here, mainly in the center of the island, that the Sards retreated. This land is still known as La Barbágia, or land of the barbarians (to the Romans, any who resisted Roman conquest and rule were considered barbarians).

In the Middle Ages, Muslims from North Africa continually raided the shores of Sardinia, further causing its people to turn inland, away from the sea that always brought danger. Pisans and Genoans later settled here, and, in the 15th century, the island became a colony of Spain. The Spaniards remained for 250 years, and the evidence of their presence is still strong: in Alghero, for example, locals still speak Catalan. Later, Sardinia played its role in the foundation of the modern, unified Italian state, for that great liberator of the South, Giuseppe Garibaldi, came from the small Sardinian island of Caprera, and embarked on his ultimately successful expeditions from there.

Yet, through the centuries of invasion and conquest, and in spite of the new wave of "invaders" who are investing in the development of luxury,

international tourist resorts, Sardinia manages to retain a character that is as unchangeable as the stone *nuraghi* themselves, testimonials to a proud people who have always refused to capitulate to foreigners or invaders. It is this strong sense of separateness that is most striking for the visitor. For, although part of Italy, Sardinia remains somehow a world or more apart from the mainland, a rugged, genuine, unsentimental land that displays the far-reaching influences of a checkered multi-faceted past.

Undoubtedly, as a vacation destination, Sardinia has a great deal going for it: fine, sandy beaches, clean sea, and a beautiful rocky coastline. Most tourists come to the island in search of sun and sea and little else. Alghero and Cagliari are well developed for this type of tourism, while the Costa Smeralda jealously guards its exclusivity (its establishments achieve this, quite practically, by charging extortionate prices). But other attractions extend well beyond the beaches: trekking in the mountains of the Gennargentu, archeological excursions, camping and farmhouse holidays, and simply exploring the interior of the island where tourism has yet to come and where life has changed very little over the centuries. Here, the foods and wines, like almost everything else, compromise little to foreign or international tastes. Names of Sardinian foods can be baffling even for Italians for they are usually written in Sardinian, and the preference remains above all for the types of basic foods that have satisfied the appetites of herdsmen and shepherds for centuries if not millennia. It is inland, too, where you will taste the real Sardinia, where outstanding and unique flat breads are still cooked in wood-fired ovens in homes and bakeries, and where the diet is based on homemade *paste,* meats grilled on spits over an open fire, and *pecorino* and other fine, hand-made cheeses.

Sardinia has four international airports and frequent ferry connections with mainland Italy and with Sicily. Main roads are good, so touring by car is easy and it is feasible to drive around the whole island in no more than a week.

Prodotti Regionali
REGIONAL PRODUCE

S ARDINIA'S LANDSCAPE is as varied as the historical influences that have shaped the island's character. From the high and dramatic limestone mountains of the interior to the sandy beaches lapped by an aquamarine-colored sea; from tortured basaltic rock formations that are evidence of the volcanic origins of the island to verdant valleys and high, hidden plains where goats and sheep nibble the grass and provide a gentle but ever-present symphony of music from the jangle of their bells; and from lush, almost tropical gardens to the arid *macchia:* Sardinia is a land of extreme contrast.

Much of the island is simply too harsh, and the climate too hot and dry, to support the large-scale cultivation of agricultural crops. But, as throughout the Mediterranean, the olive and the vine grow where little else will, and provide the basis of the island's diet. Sardinian olive oil, particularly from central areas such as Dorgali and Oliena, is quite underrated and of a high and individual quality. The profusion of wild plants and herbs, gathered in the scrub bush, have often formed an important element of the diet, as well as served as the source of

Sardinian olive groves near Dorgali, Central Sardinia

herbal remedies for any variety of ailments. *Finocchio selvatico* (wild fennel) grows everywhere, literally, all along the roadside, and adds its characteristic flavor to stuffed *pasta,* stews, and roast meats.

IN SEASON
Favette   Tender fava beans, stewed in olive oil *con la menta* (with wild mint) (Apr–May).

Olio d'oliva extra vergine   The new olive oil, straight from the *frantoio* (oil press), is a treat not to be missed (Nov–Feb), dribbled on *pane carasau* (see p.232) with a little salt.

Spinosi   Small, spiny but tender baby artichokes (May–Jun).

SARDINIAN *PASTE*

Sardinians enjoy a range of outstanding homemade *paste*. As in Southern Italy, such *paste* developed out of necessity as the staple food of the poor, and they are made from the simplest dough of hard durum wheat, water, and salt. *Gnocchetti* are made everywhere, though the precise form and size vary — shaped into shells with thumbs or given texture by pressing against a sieve or rolling the dough against a straw basket. *Maccarrones de*

busa are a type of homemade *bucatini* made by rolling the dough around a piece of wire. *Filindeu* is like a fine lacework of noodles. Also, an immense variety of stuffed *ravioli*-like *paste* are found, filled with mixtures of *pecorino* and vegetables, or, in the case of *culingiones,* stuffed with potato and wild mint. Favorite sauces include *sugo di cinghiale* (a *ragù* of wild boar) as well as *pomodoro* (tomato) and *ragù* (meat sauce).

Pane Carasau
SARDINIA'S "MUSIC PAPER" BREAD

THE NATIONAL BREAD of Sardinia is its famous *pane carasau,* known also as *carta da musica* ("music paper"), an apt description, for the large, round disks of bread are as thin and yet as durable as composer's vellum. This tough, flat, crunchy bread can be kept for, literally, months, provided it is stored in a dry place, and it has always served as the bread of the *pastori* (shepherds) who take it with them into the high slopes where they travel for months at a time for the annual transhumance of sheep.

Puffed pane carasau *emerging from the oven, ready to be slit into two sheets*

Pane carasau is served throughout the island, but the finest is still prepared almost entirely by hand, baked not on commercial premises but in wood-fired ovens, often at home. It is remarkable to witness the process, for *pane carasau* is at once one of the simplest, most primitive, yet sophisticated of all breads. We spent a morning in Oliena with Annamaria and Graziana Bette, who bake *pane carasau* three or four times a week to supply a few private customers. They begin at 2 a.m., making the dough from durum wheat, yeast, water, and salt. The dough must be worked until it is extremely elastic and smooth, then, once it has risen and rested, it is rolled into large, thin disks. These are then taken upstairs to the traditional *forno a legna* (wood-fired oven) where the women, seated on the floor or on crude, low stools, working in pairs or with one or more assistants, bake the bread. The disks

Pressing down pane carasau *to flatten it, before it is baked again*

of uncooked bread are slid into the super-hot oven for no more than 20–30 seconds, during which time they first bubble, then blow up into airy, pillow-like balls. When these are taken out, the steam immediately escapes, so deflating the bread. Using kitchen knives, the women then slit each oven-hot bread into two separate sheets which are layered in piles and pressed under a cork weight to keep them flat. At this point, the bread is fully cooked but still soft and pliable. After the first baking has been completed (on a full day, Annamaria and Graziana might make about 650 *sfoglie* or sheets of bread from 70 kg. or 155 lbs. of flour), the wood fire is reduced, and each separated sheet is *"biscottato"* — baked a second time — to make it hard, crunchy, and durable.

Pane carasau is eaten in many ways. The simplest breakfast is *pane carasau* dunked in hot milk or *caffelatte.* Outdoors, it serves as a "plate" for shepherds and picnickers alike, topped with *ricotta* cheese and honey, or grilled meats and salads. Dribbled with olive oil and salt, then popped into a hot oven for only a minute, it becomes *pane guciau,* delicious with drinks. If the bread becomes too dry and hard, it is softened by soaking in water or milk; indeed, one of the most tasty first courses is *pane frattau,* the bread soaked in boiling water, then topped with *ragù* (meat sauce), *pecorino* cheese, and, if you are really hungry, a poached egg.

Food for the Gods

SARDINIAN HONEY

SARDINIA'S RUGGED TERRAIN is something of a paradise for wild flowers, herbs, and aromatic shrubs. Many such plants are visited by the island's bees in search of pollen, so the quality and individuality of Sardinian honey is very high indeed.

The slopes of Monte Arci, near Oristano, a designated national park, are a particularly propitious source of pollen. Luigi Manias, one of the great honey experts of Sardinia, transports his hives here to gather a mixed cocktail of honeys for his fine *millefiori del Monte Arci* ("thousand" flowers of Monte Arci), as well as for distinguished *monoflora* (single-variety) honeys from *erica* (heather), *lavanda* (lavender), *eucalipto* (eucalyptus), and the rare and prized *corbezzolo* (arbutus), which yields a most distinctive bitter honey — *miele amaro* — which is exquisite, with a fine, almost lemony aftertaste.

A favorite Sardinian snack is honey dribbled over ewe's milk *ricotta* cheese piled on a slice of crunchy *pane carasau*. Or else, try honey spooned onto lettuce leaves, a traditional finish to meals in Central Sardinia.

Luigi Manias
Via Amisicora, 27
09091 Ales OR
tel: 0783/91477

Honey with fresh ricotta *on* pane carasau — *a simple snack in Sardinia*

AL MERCATO — MARKETS

		Dolianova	Thu
		Dorgali	Mon, Thu
		Gavoi	Wed
		Macomér	Tue, Fri
		Nuoro	Thu
		Olbia	Mon, Sat
		Oliena	Sat
		Orgosolo	Thu
		Oristano	Tue, Fri
		Orosei	Tue, Fri
		Palau	Fri
		Porto Rotondo	Tue, Sat
Aglientu	Tue	San Antioco	Tue
Alghero	Wed	Santa Teresa Gallura	Thu
Arzachena	Wed	Sássari	Mon–Sat
Baia Sardinia	Wed		
Bosa	Tue		
Cagliari	Mon–Sat		
Calasetta	Wed		
Carloforte	Wed		
Castelsardo	Fri		
Cúglieri	Sat		

POPULAR *FESTE*

Calasetta *Sagra del pesce* (fish)   Jul–Aug

Désulo *La Montagna Produce (mountain cuisine)*   31 Oct–5 Nov

Meana Sardo *Sagra del formaggio (cheese)*   25 Jun

Orgosolo *Sagra del miele (honey)*   3 Sep

Santa Teresa Gallura *Sagra del pesce (fish)*   early Aug

Piatti Tipici
REGIONAL SPECIALTIES

IN SPITE OF THE FACT that Sardinia is an island, the outlook here is definitely rooted toward land not sea. The Sards, after all, have long lived by the maxim *"furat chi de su mare venit"* — "those who come from the sea come to rob us." Thus, they have traditionally been shepherds, not fishermen.

True, if you are staying anywhere near the coast, you can eat good, fresh fish and shellfish, especially *aragosta* (spiny lobster), one of the great luxury foods of Sardinia. But the real taste of the island revolves around meats cooked *allo spiedo,* basted with flaming lard and spit-roasted over or in front of a wood fire. This simple cooking method finds its greatest expression in *porceddu,* roast suckling pig, truly the national dish of Sardinia.

Cooking porceddu *over an open fire in the dining room of Hotel-Ristorante Su Gologone*

ANTIPASTI

Antipasti alla sarda   Usually a mix-ture of local *prosciutto, salame,* and *coppe* served with olives, vegetables preserved *sott'olio* (in olive oil), and *fritelle* or fritters (see below).

Bottarga or **buttàriga**   Salted, pressed, and aged roe of *muggine* (gray mullet) or *tonno* (tuna). This popular appetizer is usually thinly sliced, seasoned with oil and lemon, and added to salad or served as *spaghetti alla buttariga,* the salted roe grated over hot pasta.

Burrida   Ligurian-inspired cold fish preparation usually made with *pesce palombo* (a type of shark), first fried, then served cold in a tomato sauce with pickled vegetables and olives.

Fritelle   Fritters; made with vegetables such as *carciofi* (artichokes) or *funghi* (mushrooms) or with shellfish such as *cappesante* (scallops) or *gamberetti* (shrimp).

Impanadas or **panadas**   Spanish-inspired baked savory turnovers filled usually either with meat or mixtures of vegetables and cheese. **Impanada di agnello e maiale** is filled with ground lamb and pork. **Impanada di anguillas** is eel pie.

Insalata di mare   Seafood salad, usually containing a mixture of boiled shrimp, cuttlefish, mussels, and octopus, mixed with chopped vegetables and seasoned with oil and vinegar.

Pane carasau or **carta da musica**   Wafer-thin, crunchy bread (see p.232).

Pane frattau   *Pane carasau* bread, first soaked in boiling water, topped with tomato or meat sauce, then with grated *pecorino* cheese and a poached egg. To eat, you mash the egg, and roll the whole thing up.

Pesce scabecciau   Small fish, first fried in oil, then marinated in oil, vinegar, garlic, parsley, and tomato; eaten cold.

Polipi in insalata con gamberi e calamari   Cold seafood salad of boiled pieces of octopus with shrimp and squid.

Prosciutto di cinghiale   Air-cured hind leg of wild boar, eaten raw in thin slices, like Parma ham.

I PRIMI PIATTI

Angiulottus or **anzolottos**   The island's *ravioli*-type *pasta,* at best, freshly hand-made with a variety of fillings, including fresh *pecorino,* cooked vegetables, *ricotta,* potatoes, and sometimes (though rarely) meat. Usually served with simple *sugo di pomodoro* (tomato sauce) and grated *pecorino* cheese.

Cascà   Island version of Arab *couscous,* made with steamed semolina topped with a spicy mixture of lamb or kid and stewed vegetables.

Culingiones or **cullurzones**
Sardinian *ravioli*-type *pasta;* usually made in fat half-moon shapes with a filling of cheese, potato, and wild mint.

Farru or **farro**   Barley soup made with rich meat stock thickened with barley flour and seasoned with wild mint.

Filindeu   Very fine, hand-made *pasta* noodles; usually served in a rich lamb broth with *pecorino* cheese.

Gnocchetti alla sarda   Probably the most popular and ubiquitous of all the island's various first courses: small dumplings made from semolina, water, and a little salt, formed by hand into shell shapes, and served either *alla barbaricina* (with a sausage *ragù*), *al sugo di cinghiale* (with wild boar sauce), or *al punios* (with *pecorino* cheese).

Maccarrones de busa or **maccarrones a ferritus**   Characteristic fresh, home-made *pasta* rather like thick *spaghetti,* hand-formed around a wire to give the noodle a bore through the middle. Usually served with *ragù* (meat sauce) topped with *pecorino* cheese.

Malloreddus   Variation of *gnocchetti:* little shell-shaped dumplings made from semolina, water, salt, and saffron; traditionally served with a lamb or pork *ragù* topped with grated *pecorino* cheese.

Ravioli   Whether known as *angiulottus* or *culingiones* or simply *ravioli,* fresh, usually hand-made, stuffed *pasta* is enjoyed throughout Sardinia, usually filled with mixtures of cheese and cooked vegetables.

Risotto al pescatore   Fisherman's *risotto;* usually made with the catch of the day in a rich fish broth. More extravagant versions may include shellfish.

Spaghetti alla buttariga   Hot spaghetti seasoned with grated *bottarga* (see p.234).

Zuppa di mare or **zuppa di pesce**   This usually substantial fish soup can be eaten as either a *primo* or a substantial one-plate main course.

Pane frattau, *eaten rolled up, the egg mashed*

THE LOBSTER COAST

The northwestern coast of Sardinia is known as the Costa dell'Aragosta, or lobster coast, but you don't have to come to Alghero to sample this great delicacy. All around its rocky shores, *aragosta* (spiny lobster), as well as *astice* (lobster), and *cicala* (flat lobster) are caught and enjoyed.

Spiny lobster does not have claws (unlike *astice,* which is similar to Maine lobster and does), but *aragosta* is considered one of the most finely flavored of all Mediterranean crustaceans, its densely textured but tender meat from the tail exceptionally sweet.

In Alghero, *aragosta* may be served in the Catalan style — stewed with

olive oil, white wine, tomatoes, and peppers. A simpler but no less delicious version (below) simply takes the boiled spiny lobster, still tepid from the cooking pot, and serves it with a sauce made from the pounded coral, olive oil, vinegar, and chopped parsley.

Grigliata mista di pesce, *mixed grill of fish*

I SECONDI PIATTI

Agnello or **angioni**   Lamb, preferably new season (Dec–late May), traditionally cooked like *porceddu,* whole, on spits in front of a blazing wood fire.

Angioni cun finugheddu   Cubes of lamb stewed with wine and wild fennel.

Anguilla   Saltwater eel; served *arrosto* (roasted) or *in umido* (stewed with wine and tomatoes).

Aragosta   Spiny lobster (see p.235).

Capretto al finocchietto in umido Kid stewed in wine with wild fennel; the flavor of the young goat, which grazes on a diet of grass and herbs, is beautifully accentuated by the intense anise flavor of the fennel.

Cinghiale   Wild boar.

Cinghiale in agro   Wild boar stewed in wine and vinegar.

Grigliata mista di pesce   All along the coast, a variety of fresh fish is simply served char-grilled.

Cordula   Lamb's or kid's intestines roasted on a spit in front of a wood fire.

Cunillu   Rabbit; usually stewed in wine, garlic, and olive oil.

Favata   Substantial winter stew of pork or wild boar slowly cooked with beans.

Lepre   Hare; stewed in wine, garlic, and olive oil.

Porceddu or **porcetto**   Whole suckling pig, roasted on a metal spit over or in front of a wood fire (traditionally, juniper should be used for its aroma), and continually basted with flaming lard.

Salsiccia arrosta   Large, coarsely ground, meaty Sardinian sausage,

seasoned with plenty of salt and garlic, cooked before an open wood fire.

Tonno alla carlofortina   Fresh tuna cooked in an earthenware casserole with tomatoes, wine, vinegar, and bay.

Trota   Trout; most typically cooked in Vernaccia wine.

I CONTORNI

Carciofi con patate or **cauiofa cun patatas**   Artichokes stewed in wine with potatoes.

Favette con la menta   Fava beans stewed with wild mint.

Lattuga al miele   A leaf of stiff, fresh lettuce dribbled with honey; an unusual finish to rustic meals.

Verdure alla griglia   Mixed vegetables, including eggplant, zucchini, and bell peppers, grilled over a wood fire.

I DOLCI

Dolci sardi   An enormous range of sweets and pastries is produced, primarily using almonds, honey, pine nuts, and sometimes *pecorino* cheese. Commonly encountered are *caschettas* (thin "tubes" of meringue filled with honey and almond paste), *gattò e mendula* (diamond-shaped pieces of almond tart), *coricheddos* (heart-shaped almond cookies), *casadinas* (little tartlets filled with *pecorino* cheese), and *aranzada* (candied orange peel).

Sebada or **seada** or **sevada al miele di corbezzolo**   Large *ravioli*-like pastry filled with *pecorino* cheese, fried in hot oil, and served covered with honey.

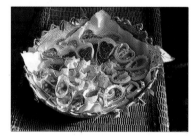

Sardinian sweets. Top: coricheddos*; left:* gattò e mendula*; right:* caschettas*; center:* casadinas

Pecorino Sardo

EWE'S MILK AND OTHER SARDINIAN CHEESES

S ARDINIA'S MOST DISTINCTIVE cheeses are made from the milk of sheep that graze on the scrubby bush and limestone plateaus of the island, as well, to a lesser extent, from the milk of *capre* (goats).

Pecorino sardo, *one of the great ewe's milk cheeses of Italy*

TRY TO SAMPLE

Bonassài   Large, square ewe's milk cheese; rather soft, delicate, and slightly acidic, to be eaten very young.
Caciottina di latte di capra   Small, cylindrical goat's cheese, to be eaten while young and mild.
Dolce sardo   Pale, soft, cylindrical cheese most usually made from ewe's milk, with a sweet, perfumed flavor of wild herbs and grasses. Enjoy within at most a month of production.
Pecorino pepato   *Pecorino* cheese made with whole peppercorns inside.
Pecorino romano   Rome's great, hard, aged *pecorino* is also allowed to be made in Sardinia; must be aged for at least nine months.
Pecorino sardo   The traditional Sardinian *pecorino* cheese is a cylindrical, semi-

cooked cheese with a compact interior with small holes. *Dolce* (sweet), aged up to three months, is delicately perfumed. *Semi-dolce* or *media stagionata* cheeses, up to nine months old, gain a piquant flavor but are never overly strong. *Stagionata* (well-aged) cheeses, a year old or more, are hard and more pungent.
Ricotta   Usually made from ewe's milk; light, with a distinctive flavor.
Spalmabile   Smooth, fresh cream cheeses made from ewe's and goat's milk, sometimes spiked with *peperoncini* (chilies) or mixed with herbs.

LUNCH WITH A SHEPHERD

In parts of Central Sardinia, tourists can join organized excursions into the high mountains, either on foot or in four-wheel-drive vehicles, to visit prehistoric sites and appreciate the beauty of the country, followed by lunch cooked outdoors by a shepherd with the help of the guides.

We joined a group of Italians from the mainland, toured parts of the Sopramonte mountain range both in Land Rover and on foot, and so worked up an immense appetite. Afterward, we retired to a cool, shady glade in the secluded Lanaitta Valley, where shepherd Nicolà had a wood fire blazing with spits laden with meats. We enjoyed this simple repast eating the good, homemade sausage

and chunks of veal with our fingers off sheets of *pane carasau* in lieu of plates, washed down with gutsy Cannonau wine, and followed by slabs of *pecorino* cheese made by Nicolà himself.

Mountain excursions with meals can be arranged through the Hotel Su Gologone, Oliena (address, p.239).

I Vini

THE WINES OF SARDINIA

A RANGE OF BOTH TRADITIONAL and modern, light, "new-wave" wines are produced in Sardinia. Both indigenous and Spanish grapes predominate. The most widely available (and reliable) wines come from the private winery of Sella & Mosca, while the island's co-operative wineries are today turning out sound wines.

Cannonau vineyards in the Lanaitto Valley near Dorgali

TRY TO SAMPLE

Anghelu Ruju   One of Sardinia's finest dessert wines, made by Sella & Mosca, from semi-dried Cannonau grapes: hefty in alcohol, lusciously sweet, with a nutty finish.

Cannonau di Sardegna DOC
Cannonau, introduced by the Spanish (it is the same as Garnacha, an important grape in Northern Spain, including Rioja), is widely grown throughout the island and makes warm, fleshy red wines.
Recommended producers: Cantina Sociale di Dolianova, Cantina Sociale di Oliena.

Malvasia di Bosa DOC   Rich and distinguished dessert wine with an intriguing aftertaste of apricots and nuts.
Recommended producer: Cantina Sociale della Planargia.

Monica di Sardegna DOC   Juicy, fruity red wine to be drunk while young.
Recommended producer: Cantina Sociale di Dolianova.

Moscato di Sardegna DOC   Try this distinctive, fragrant, and grapy dessert wine with a nugget of aged *pecorino*.
Recommended producers: Cantina Sociale di Dolianova, Meloni Vini.

Tanca Farrà Vdt   Probably the island's finest red wine, made from a blend of Cannonau and Cabernet Sauvignon grapes and aged for at least three years in oak casks: a powerful, velvety, rich wine.
Recommended producer: Sella & Mosca.

Torbato di Alghero Vdt   Torbato, another grape of Spanish origin, makes pale, fresh, clean, white wines. Terre Bianche, a selected *cru* wine that is richer, with more scent and depth of flavor, is one of Sardinia's finest white table wines.
Recommended producer: Sella & Mosca.

Vermentino di Gallura DOC
Mainly light, fresh, modern white wines, produced from Vermentino grapes in the north of the island. Dry *frizzante* versions are refreshing.
Recommended producers: Cantina Sociale di Gallura, Cantina Sociale di Vermentino.

Vernaccia di Oristano DOC
Famous, traditional wine of Sardinia, perhaps the island's most characteristic, aged in wood for upward of a decade or longer, with a character something like a rich, nutty amontillado sherry.
Recommended producer: Attilio Contini.

OTHER DRINKS

Filu e ferru   The island's finest *grappe*, it is said, used to be distilled illegally, the contraband liquor buried in the ground and marked with a metal wire, *un filo di ferro*, or *filu e ferru* in the Sard dialect. This after-dinner firewater, therefore, celebrates the island's renowned anti-authoritarian character, but be warned: some home-made examples can be horrible.

Mirto   Characteristic *digestivo* of the island; comes in two versions: one clear, made from the leaves of the myrtle shrub, the other dense, almost black, made from the berries, with a distinctive bitter herbal scent and flavor.

Indirizzi

USEFUL ADDRESSES

Al Tonno di Corsa
Via Marconi, 47
09014 Carloforte CA
Isola di San Pietro
tel: 0781/855106
*The islands of San Pietro
and Sant'Antioco, to the
southwest of Sardinia, are
home to fisherfolk who
originally settled here
from Liguria. The narrow
straits between the
islands provide a bloody
spectacle each May when
tuna is caught in the
thousands. Come here to
enjoy the catch in*
spaghetti alla buttariga
(with tuna roe) and tonno
alla griglia *or* alla
carlofortina.
$$

**Cooperativa Olivicoltori
del Parteolla**
Via Emilio Lussu, 43
09041 Dolianova CA
tel/fax: 070/741329
*High-quality extra-virgin
olive oil.*

**Hotel-Ristorante Su
Gologone**
Loc. Su Gologone
08025 Oliena NU
tel: 0784/287512
fax: 0784/287668
*Possibly the finest hotel-
restaurant in all Sardinia for
regional foods, serving
outstanding homemade*
gnocchetti *and other*
paste, *meats roasted over
a spit in the dining room,
and* dolci sardi. *In the
center of the island, so,
ideal as a base for moun-
tain trekking (see p. 237).*
$$$$

La Lepanto
Via Carlo Alberto, 135
07041 Alghero SS
tel: 079/981570
*The place to come to
sample* aragosta *prepared
in a variety of ways. Also
good seafood* antipasti *and*
paste *dishes.*
$$$$

*Entrance to the Hotel Su
Gologone, Oliena*

Prodotti Alimentari Sardi
Via Einstein, 9
08022 Dorgali NU
tel: 0784/96307
*This small, friendly shop on
the outskirts of Dorgali
sells wines, cheese, and
olive oil from Dorgali's
cooperatives at keen
prices, plus good cured*
salumi *and* pane carasau. *If
you are in this area, it's
worth coming here both to
get the essentials for
picnics in the mountains
and to stock up on good
things to take home.*

Ristorante Il Pescatore
Via Acquadolce, 7
08022 Cala Gonone NU
tel: 0784/93174
*This seafront restaurant is
run by a family of fisher-
folk, so the fish and
shellfish on offer are
always impeccably fresh.
Come here to enjoy
seafood* antipasti, risotto
alla pescatora, *and
excellent* aragosta *(when
available). Afterward take a
boat ride to the Cala Luna
beach, one of the most
beautiful on this stretch
of the coast.*
$–$$

Salumificio Puddu
Via Chironi, 24
08025 Oliena NU
tel: 0784/288457
fax: 0784/287057

*Outstanding source of
hand-cured traditional
Sardinian meats —*
prosciutto crudo, pancetta,
coppa, *and* salsiccia
stagionata.

**Soc. Coop. Dorgali
Pastori**
Regione Golloi
08022 Dorgali NU
tel: 0784/96517
fax: 0784/94260
The full range of Sardinian
pecorino *cheeses are
made and sold at this
cooperative dairy, and
vacuum-packed cheeses
are on sale.*

Tenute Sella & Mosca
Loc. I Piani
07041 Alghero SS
tel: 079/997700
fax: 079/951279
*The wines of Sardinia's
leading producer are
widely sold throughout
the island, but visitors in
Alghero may wish to make
an appointment to visit
the winery itself.*

Trattoria CK
Corso Martin Luther
King, 2/4
08025 Oliena NU
tel: 0784/288024
*Serves good, traditional
foods of Sardinia plus
excellent* pizze *in the
evenings.*
$

BEST BUYS
• dolci sardi (traditional
  sweets from throughout
  the island)
• pecorino sardo (vacuum-
  wrapped whole cheeses)
• pane carasau
• dried malloreddus pasta
• olio d'oliva extra vergine
• miele (honey), especially
  the rare and distinctive
  miele amaro di
  corbezzolo.

Basic English-Italian Food Glossary

ITALIAN PRONUNCIATION
When speaking Italian, a good guide is to pronounce every letter. The Italians are generous by nature and will try to understand even the worst attempts at their language. Remember, too, that there are "soft" and "hard" consonants: **c** and **g**, before i or e, sound like **ch** or **j** respectively, as in church or jelly. Before a, o, or u, they become **k** or **g**, as in sky or goal.

Almond Mandorla.

Anchovies Acciughe/alici.

Apple Mela.

Apricot Albicocca.

Artichoke Carciofio.

Arugula Rucola.

Asparagus Asparagi.

Banana Banana.

Basil Basilico.

Beef Manzo.

Beer Birra.

Bell pepper Peperone.

Bread Pane; **bread roll** panino.

Butter Burro.

Cabbage Cavolo.

Cake Torta.

Can Latta; **canned** in scatola.

Capers Capperi.

Carrot Carota.

Cauliflower Cavolfiore.

Celery Sedano.

Cheese Formaggio.

Cherries Ciliegie.

Chestnuts Castagne.

Chicken Pollo; **chicken breast** petto di pollo.

Chickpeas Ceci.

Chocolate Cioccolata.

Cinnamon Cannella.

Coffee Caffè; **coffee beans** caffè in grano; **ground coffee** caffè maccinato.

Cold cuts Affettati misti.

Cookies or **sweet, hard biscuits** Biscotti.

Crab Granchio.

Cream Panna.

Cucumber Cetriolo.

Dates Datteri.

Dessert Dolce.

Duck Anitra.

Egg Uova.

Eggplant Melanzana.

Fennel Finocchio.

Fig Fico.

Fish Pesce.

Flour Farina.

Fruits Frutta.

Game Selvaggina.

Garlic Aglio.

Grapefruit Pompelmo.

Grapes Uva.

Green beans Fagiolini.

Ham Prosciutto.

Honey Miele.

Ice cream Gelato.

Lamb Agnello.

Leek Porro.

Lemon Limone.

Lemonade Limonata.

Lentils Lenticchie.

Lettuce Lattuga.

Liver Fegato.

Mayonnaise Maionese.

Meat Carne.

Melon Melone.

Milk Latte.

Mushrooms Funghi.

Mussels Cozze/vongole.

Mustard Senape.

Nectarine Pescanoce.

Nutmeg Noce moscato.

Oil Olio.

Onion Cipolla.

Orange Arancia.

Oyster Ostrica.

Parsley Prezzemolo.

Pasta Pasta.

Peach Pesca.

Pear Pera.

Peas Piselli.

Pepper Pepe.

Pineapple Ananas.

Plum Susina.

Pomegranate Melagrana.

Pork Maiale.

Potato Patata.

Radish Ravanello.

Raspberries Lamponi.

Rice Riso.

Rosemary Rosmarino.

Salad Insalata.

Salmon Salmone.

Salt Sale.

Sausage Salsiccia.

Shellfish Frutti di mare.

Shrimp Gambero.

Spinach Spinaci.

Squid Calamari.

Steak Bistecca.

Strawberries Fragole.

Sugar Zucchero.

Tea Tè.

Tomato Pomodoro; **tomato paste** conserva di pomodoro.

Truffle Tartufo.

Tuna Tonno.

Turkey Tacchino/dindo.

Veal Vitello.

Vegetables Ortaggi/legumi.

Vinegar Aceto.

Walnut Noce.

Water Acqua.

Watermelon Cocomero.

Wild boar Cinghiale.

Wine Vino.

Italian-English Food Glossary

Acciughe Anchovies.
Aceto Vinegar.
Affumicato Smoked.
Aglio Garlic.
Agnello Lamb.
Agrodolce Sweet and sour.
Albicocche Apricots.
Alici Anchovies.
Ananas Pineapple.
Anguilla Eel.
Anitra Duck; **anitra selvatica** wild duck.
Antipasto Appetizer or first course.
Arancia Orange.
Arrosto Roast.
Asparagi Asparagus.
Banana Banana.
Barbabietola Beet.
Basilico Basil.
Biscotti Sweet, hard biscuits or cookies.
Bistecca Steak.
Bollito Boiled.
Brace, alla Char-grilled.
Braciola Thin slice of beef, pork, or veal.
Branzino Sea bass.
Brasato Braised.
Brodo Clear broth or bouillon, often chicken; **pasta in brodo** small *pasta* shapes in broth.
Budino Pudding.
Burro Butter.
Cacciatora, alla Hunter's style; usually in tomato sauce with wine and mushrooms.
Caffè Coffee.
Calamari Squid.
Caldo Hot.
Capperi Capers.
Cappesante Scallops.
Cappone Capon.
Capretto Kid.
Carciofo Artichoke.
Cardo Cardoon.

Carne Meat.
Carota Carrot.
Carrello, al Served from the trolley.
Cartoccio, in Baked in parchment paper or foil.
Casalinga Homemade.
Castagne Chestnuts.
Castrato Mutton (from a castrated sheep).
Caviale Caviar.
Cavolfiore Cauliflower.
Cavolo Cabbage; **cavolo nero** dark, leafy winter vegetable, used freshly picked.
Ceci Chickpeas.
Cedro Citron.
Cena Evening meal.
Cervelle Brains.
Cervo Venison.
Cetriolo Cucumber.
Ciabatta Slipper bread, a flat loaf.
Cicoria Wild chicory.
Ciliegie Cherries.
Cinghiale Wild boar.
Cipolla Onion.
Cocomero Watermelon.
Coniglio Rabbit; **coniglio selvatico** wild rabbit.
Consommé Consommé or bouillon.
Contorno Side dish or vegetable dish.
Costoletta/costata Rib or chop.
Cotto Cooked.
Cozze Mussels.
Crauti *Sauerkraut*.
Crema Creamed soup; **crema di asparagi** cream of asparagus.
Crema caramella Crème caramel.
Crocchette Croquettes.
Crudo Raw.
Dattero Date.

Dattero di mare Sea date.
Dindo Turkey.
Dolci Desserts/sweets.
Erbe Herbs.
Fagiano Pheasant.
Fagioli Beans.
Fagiolini String beans.
Faraona Guinea hen.
Farfalle *Pasta* butterflies.
Fegato Liver.
Ferri, ai/alla griglia Cooked on a ribbed, iron griddle.
Fettuccine Thin ribbon noodles.
Fichi Figs (usually fresh).
Filetto di manzo Tenderloin of beef.
Finocchio Fennel.
Focaccia Flat, *pizza*-like bread, usually dimpled.
Formaggio Cheese.
Forno, al Baked.
Fragole Strawberries.
Fragoline Small wild strawberries.
Freddo Cold.
Frittata Italian "omelet," usually quite thick, made with vegetables or *pasta*.
Frittelle Fritters.
Fritto Fried.
Frutta Fruits.
Frutti di mare Shellfish.
Funghi Mushrooms.
Gambero Shrimp.
Gelato Ice cream.
Ghiacciato Iced.
Ghiaccio Ice.
Gnocchi Dumplings made from potatoes and flour, or from semolina.
Granchio Crab.
Granita Slushy fruit ice.
Granseola Spider crab.
Gratinato Baked with a breadcrumb topping.
Grissini Breadsticks.

Insalata Salad; **insalata di mare** mixed seafood salad.

Lamponi Raspberries.

Lasagne Sheets of egg dough, layered, and baked. Can also be used as a general term for *pasta* in the South.

Lattonzolo Suckling pig; usually roasted.

Lattuga Lettuce.

Lenticchie Lentils.

Lepre Hare.

Limone Lemon.

Lingua Tongue.

Liquore, al With liqueur.

Lumache Snails.

Maccheroni Stubby macaroni *pasta;* term is also used to indicate any long *pasta* shape in the South.

Macedonia di frutta Fresh fruit salad.

Magro, di Usually indicates made without meat.

Maiale Pork.

Maionese Mayonnaise.

Mandarino Tangerine.

Manzo Beef.

Marinara, alla Fisherman's style.

Marinata Marinated.

Mascarpone Rich cream cheese.

Melagrana Pomegranate.

Melanzane Eggplant; **melanzane alla parmigiana** baked eggplant layered with *mozzarella* cheese and tomato sauce.

Mela Apple.

Melone Melon; **melone con prosciutto** melon with slices of *prosciutto crudo.*

Miele Honey.

Minestra Soup.

Minestrone Thick vegetable soup.

Misto Mixed.

More Blackberries or mulberries.

Mostarda or **senape** Mustard.

Mozzarella Very fresh cheese, made from cow's or buffalo's milk.

Mugnaia, alla Miller's style; dredged in flour, then pan fried.

Muscoli Mussels.

Noce Walnut.

Noce di cocco Coconut.

Nocciole Hazelnuts.

Nostrale/nostrano Local, home-grown.

Oca Goose.

Occhio di bue Fried egg.

Olio Oil; **olio d'oliva** olive oil; **sott'olio** preserved in oil.

Olive Olives.

Origano Oregano.

Ossobuco Pieces of shin or shank of veal.

Osteria Simple inn.

Ostrica Oyster.

Paglia e fieno "Straw and hay" — green and white ribbon noodles.

Pancetta Cured belly pork.

Pane Bread; **panino** bread roll; roll filled with meat or cheese.

Panna cotta Rich cream custard.

Panna, con With whipped cream.

Pappardelle Thick ribbon noodles.

Parmigiano reggiano Parmesan cheese.

Passato Puree.

Pasta *Pasta* or pastry; **pasta frolla** shortbread.

Pasticciata Baked *pasta.*

Patata Potato.

Pepe Pepper.

Peperoncini Small chili peppers.

Peperone Bell pepper.

Pera Pear.

Pesca Peach.

Pescanoce Nectarine.

Pesce Fish.

Pesto Fresh basil sauce with garlic, pine nuts, and olive oil.

Piacere, a To be prepared as you like it.

Piatto Dish/plate; **piatto del giorno** daily special.

Piccione Pigeon.

Pinolo Pine nut.

Piselli Peas.

Pizzaiola, alla Usually served in a tomato sauce with oregano and garlic.

Polenta Cornmeal mush.

Pollo Chicken; **petto di pollo** chicken breast.

Polpetta Meatball.

Polpo/polipo Octopus.

Pomodoro Tomato; **pomodori secchi** sun-dried tomatoes.

Pompelmo Grapefruit.

Porchetta Roast suckling pig.

Porcino *Boletus edulis* or cepe mushroom.

Porzione Portion or serving.

Pranzo Midday meal; **sala di pranzo** dining room.

Prezzemolo Parsley.

Prima colazione Breakfast.

Profiteroles Choux pastries, filled with cream

and covered in hot chocolate sauce.

Prosciutto Ham; **prosciutto crudo** raw, Parma-style ham; **prosciutto di cinghiale** wild boar ham.

Quaglia Quail.

Rabarbaro Rhubarb.

Radicchio Red lettuce.

Ragù Classic meat sauce, served over *pasta*.

Rane Frogs or frog's legs.

Ravioli Stuffed *pasta*.

Ribes nero Blackcurrants; **ribes rosso** redcurrants.

Ricciola Amberjack.

Ricotta Fresh curd cheese.

Ripieno Stuffed or filled.

Riso Rice.

Risotto Italian rice cooked with broth and various ingredients.

Ristorante Restaurant.

Rognone Kidney.

Rosbif Roast beef.

Rosmarino Rosemary.

Salame Ground and cured meat sausage.

Sale Salt.

Salmone Salmon; **salmone affumicato** smoked salmon.

Salsa Sauce.

Salsiccia Sausage; **salsicce** sausages.

Salumi General term for cured meats.

Salvia Sage.

Sardine Sardines.

Scaloppa/scaloppine Escalope/s.

Scampi Dublin Bay prawn or Norway lobster.

Sedano Celery.

Seppia Small cuttlefish.

Sgombro Mackerel.

Sogliola Sole or flounder.

Soppressa Soft-textured pork *salame*.

Sorbetto Sorbet or sherbet ice.

Speck Smoked, air-cured ham.

Spezzatino Stew made from cubes of meat.

Spiedo, allo Spit-roasted.

Spinaci Spinach.

Spremuta Freshly squeezed fruit juice.

Stagione, di Seasonal.

Stoccafisso Stockfish or air-dried cod.

Stracotto Slow-cooked stew.

Susine Plums.

Tacchino Turkey.

Tagliatelle Flat, egg noodles.

Tagliolini Very fine, hand-cut noodles.

Tarocco "Blood" orange.

Tartufo Truffle; **tartufo bianco** white truffle; **tartufo nero** black truffle; **tartufo gelato** chocolate ice cream in the shape of a truffle.

Tavola calda Self-service restaurant; usually offering pre-cooked foods.

Tiramisù "Pick me up" dessert of sponge cake soaked in liqueur, layered with *mascarpone* cheese, and dusted with cocoa.

Tonno Tuna.

Torrone Honey, egg white, and nut nougat.

Torta Cake or tart; **torta della casa** home-made cake.

Tortellini Small, meat-stuffed *pasta*, usually served *in brodo*.

Tramezzini Crustless sandwiches, usually with mayonnaise-based fillings.

Trancia Slice.

Trattoria Family-style restaurant, often serving set meals.

Triglia Red mullet.

Trippa Tripe.

Trota Trout; **trota affumicata** smoked trout.

Umido, in Stewed in wine, with vegetables and herbs.

Uova Egg; **uova al piatto** eggs fried in butter; **uova in camicia** poached eggs; **uova in padella** pan-fried eggs; **uova mollette** soft-boiled eggs; **uova soda** hard-boiled eggs.

Uva grapes; **uva passita** raisins.

Vitello Veal; **vitello all'uccelletto** slices of veal fried with garlic and fresh sage; **vitello ton-nato** boiled veal, thinly sliced, then covered with a rich tuna and mayon-naise sauce.

Vitellone Meat from animal too old to be veal but not yet beef.

Vongole Clams.

Zabaione/zabaglione Dessert made with egg yolks, sugar, and Marsala.

Zampone Ground pork stuffed in a pig's trotter.

Zucca Pumpkin.

Zucchine Zucchini.

Zuppa Soup.

Zuppa inglese Italy's version of English trifle: sponge cake soaked in Marsala and layered with cream, custard, candied fruit, and nuts.

Italian–English Drinks Glossary

Abboccato Medium dry to slightly sweet wine.

Acido Acid.

Acqua minerale Mineral water; **acqua minerale gassata/non gassata** carbonated/still mineral water.

Amabile Lightly sweet wine.

Amaretto Sweet, almond flavored liqueur.

Amaro Bitter. Also a bitter, herbal *digestivo*.

Analcolica/o Non-alcoholic.

Annata Year of vintage.

Aperitivo A drink to enjoy before a meal; **aperitivo della casa** house aperitif; **aperitivo analcolico della casa** non-alcoholic alternative.

Aranciata Orange soda.

Asciutto Dry wine.

Azienda agricola Private wine estate.

Barrique New oak barrel for wine (generally made from French oak) containing 225 liters (55 gallons).

Bellini Cocktail of fresh white peach juice and sparkling Prosecco wine.

Birra Beer; **birra alla spina** draft beer.

Caffè *Espresso* coffee; **caffè corretto** *espresso* "corrected" with *grappa* or other strong liquor; **caffelatte** *espresso* topped up with large amount of scalded milk; **caffè lungo** slightly weaker *espresso* coffee; **caffè macchiato** *espresso* "stained" with just a dapple of milk; **caffè**

decaffeinato decaffeinated coffee.

Caldo Wine that is high in alcohol.

Campari Classic Italian bitter *aperitivo*.

Cantina sociale, cantina cooperativa Cooperative winery.

Cappuccino *Espresso* coffee topped up with steamed, frothy milk, often dusted with cocoa powder.

Cascina Farm or wine estate in Piemonte.

Classico Wines from the historic heartland of the DOC zone.

Corposo Full-bodied wine.

Dolce Sweet.

Duro Hard, high in tannin wine.

Enoteca Wine shop or official wine "library" promoting wines of a region or area.

Fermentazione naturale Natural fermentation.

Fondo Wine dregs.

Fresco Fresh wine, with refreshing acidity.

Frizzante Slightly fizzy wine; usually from a natural secondary fermentation in the bottle.

Gradevole Pleasant wine.

Grappa Liquor made by distilling the grape pomace (residue of skins, pulp, etc., left over after the winemaking process); **grappa di monovitigno** *grappa* made from single grape variety (usually aromatic).

Imbottigliato all' origine Estate-bottled wine (bottled by the producer at the source).

Imbottigliato nella zona di produzione Wine bottled in the region or zone, but not estate-bottled.

Invecchiamento Aging wine.

Latte Milk.

Leggero Light, but pleasing wine.

Limonata Lemon soda.

Limoncello Fresh lemons infused in alcohol.

Liquoroso Dessert wine, usually fortified.

Maturo Mature, bottle aged wine.

Metodo classico Classic method of making sparkling wine by secondary fermentation in the bottle.

Muffa Mold; **muffa nobile** noble rot, a beneficial fungus that contributes to the making of sweet, dessert wines.

Nervoso "Highly strung," wine that is rich in acidity.

Nocino Homemade walnut liqueur.

Ossidato Oxidized wine.

Passito Wine made with semi-dried grapes.

Profumo Bouquet that comes from fermentation and aging of wine.

Ricco Rich wine, with plenty of body, color, and flavor.

Riserva Reserve wine; **riserva speciale** special reserve wine.

Sambuca Anise-flavored liqueur.
Sapore Flavor, taste.
Secco Dry wine.
Spremuta Freshly squeezed fruit juice; **spremuta di arancia** freshly squeezed orange juice; **spremuta di limone** freshly squeezed lemon juice, to be topped up with water or seltzer, and sweetened to taste.
Spumante Fully sparkling wine.
Stravecchio Very old wine.
Succo di frutta Thick, bottled fruit juice.
Superiore Wine with a higher specified degree of alcohol than minimum.
Super vino "Super" wine made outside the bounds of DOC or DOCG.
Tannico Tannic; wine rich in tannin.
Tappo Cork; **tappato** corked wine.
Uva Grape.
Vasche Wine tanks; fermentation vats.
Vecchio Old wine.
Vellutato Velvety wine.
Vendemmia Harvest; indicates year of harvest or vintage.
Vermouth Classic, fortified herbal *aperitivo*.
Vignaiolo Vine grower.
Vinacce Dregs of pressed grapes; used to make *grappa*.
Vinificazione Vinification.
Vino Wine; **vino bianco** white wine; **vino da tavola** basic table wine; **vino passito** dessert wine made from semi-dried grapes; **vino rosso** red wine; **vino sfuso** wine sold on tap unbottled.
Violaceo Purple color of some young red wines.
Vite Vines.
Viticoltura Vine cultivation.

VINTAGE YEARS FOR WINES

This chart indicates the best years for wines that age well. In years not included, the wines were not very good or are now too old to drink.

PIEMONTE	94	93	92	91	90	89	88	87	86	85	82	79	78
Barolo, Barbaresco, Gattinara	7❱	6❱	5❱	6❱	10❱	9❱	8●	6★	7★	9●	10●	7★	9★
Barbera	6❱	6❱	7❱	6●	10●	9●	8★	6★	6★	9★	9★		

VENETO	94	93	92	91	90	89	88	87	86	85	83	81	
Amarone, Recioto, Ripasso	7❱	8❱	5❱	5❱	10❱	6●	9●	4★	8●	9●	8★	9★	

TUSCANY	94	93	92	91	90	89	88	87	86	85	83	82	
Chianti (Classico, Rufino) Riserva, Carmignano	9❱	7❱	6❱	7❱	10❱	6★	9●	6★	8★	10★	8★	8★	
Vino Nobile di Montepulciano	9❱	7❱	6❱	8❱	10❱	6●	9❱	7●	8●	10●	8★	8★	
Brunello di Montepulciano	9❱	8❱	6❱	8❱	10❱	8●	9❱	7●	8●	9●	8★	9●	

KEY TO NUMBERS
0 = worst   10 = best
These numerals represent an overall rating for each year, based on a score out of ten.

KEY TO SYMBOLS

❱ = Needs more time
● = Ready but will improve
★ = At its peak

Useful Addresses

ITALIAN GOVERNMENT TOURIST OFFICES (ENIT)
Head Office
Via Marghera, 2
00185 Rome
tel: 06/49711
fax: 06/4463379

In United States
Suite 1565
630 5th Ave
New York
NY 10111
tel: (212) 245 4822
fax: (212) 586 9249

Suite 550
12400 Wilshire Blvd
Los Angeles
CA 90025
tel: (310) 820 0098
fax: (310) 820 6357

In Canada
Suite 19141
Place Ville Marie
Montréal
Québec H3B 2C3
tel: (514) 866 7667
fax: (514) 392 1429

In United Kingdom
1 Princes Street
London W1R 8AY
tel: (0171) 408 1254
fax: (0171) 493 6695

COOKING SCHOOLS
Castello Vicchiomaggio
Via Vicchiomaggio
50022 Greve in Chianti FI
tel: 055/854079
fax: 055/853911
Residential courses on a historic wine estate in Chianti Classico

Giulano Bugialli's Cooking in Florence
P. O. Box 1650
Canal Street Station
New York
NY 10013-1650
tel: (212) 966 5325
fax: (212) 226 0601
Classic Tuscan cuisine from a renowned master and great food writer.

Hazan Classics
P.O. Box 285
Circleville
NY 10919
tel: (914) 692 7104
fax: (914) 692 2659
The Hazans' popular cooking and wine courses

Hotel Cipriani
Giudecca, 10
30133 Venezia
tel: 041/5207744
fax: 041/5203930

Cooking courses with master chefs in this world-class hotel-restaurant.

La Cucina Italiana, Inc.
Maria Battaglia
P.O. Box 6528
Evanston
Ill 60204
tel: (708) 328 1144
fax: (708) 328 1787
Wine and food courses based in the Valpolicella wine hills.

Le Tre Vaselle
Via Giuseppe Garibaldi, 48
06089 Torgiano PG
tel: 075/9880447
fax: 075/9880214
Cooking classes are held at the Lungarotti's hotel complemented by wine-tasting courses based on the great wines of Torgiano.

Podere Capaccia
Loc. Capaccia
53017 Radda in Chianti SI
tel: 0574/582426
fax: 0574/582428
Historical Tuscan cooking and tutored wine tasting with winemaker and food historian Giampaolo Pacini (see p.171).

NATIONAL HOLIDAYS AND SOME FEAST DAYS

Most shops are closed on national holidays and many may close on certain feast days. Check with your hotel or the local tourist office.
National holidays: 1 and 6 January; Easter Sunday and Monday; 25 April (Liberation Day); 1 May; 15 August *(Ferragosto);* 1 November; 8 December; 25 and 26 December (Christmas).

Feast days in main cities:
Bologna: 4 October (St. Petronio); Florence: 24 June (St. John); Genoa: 24 June (St. John); Milan: 7 December (St. Ambrose); Naples: 19 September (St. Gennaro); Palermo: 11 July (St. Rosalia); Rome: 29 June (St. Peter); Turin: 24 June (St. John); Venice: 25 April (St. Mark).

Recommended Reading

Anderson, Burton, *Vino* (New York: Little, Brown, 1980, 1987);
> *The Wine Atlas of Italy* (New York: Simon & Schuster, 1990);
> *Treasures of the Italian Table* (New York: William Morrow and Co. Inc, 1994)

Ashley, Maureen, *Italian Wines* (London: Websters International Publishers, 1990)

Boni, Ada, *Cuciana Regionale Italiana* (Milan; Arnoldo Mondadori Editori, 1975)

Bugialli, Giuliano, *Foods of Italy* (New York: Stewart, Tabori & Chang, 1984)

Bugialli, Giuliano, *The Fine Art of Italian Cooking* (New York: Times Books, 1979)

Chianti Locations Culture Itineraries Wines (Milan: Edizioni Tecniche Moderne)

David, Elizabeth, *Italian Food* (New York: Penguin, 1985)

Davidson, Alan, *Mediterranean Seafood* (London: Penguin Books, 1981);
> *North Atlantic Seafood* (London: Penguin Books, 1979)

Del Conte, Anna, *Gastronomy of Italy* (New York: Prentice Hall Press, 1988)

Eyewitness Travel Guide Rome (New York: D.K. Inc., 1993)

Freson, Robert, *Savoring Italy* (New York: Callaway Editions Inc., 1992)

Guida all'Italia gastronomica (Milan: Touring Club Italiano, 1984)

Guida dell'Ospitalità Rurale (Rome: Agriturist, annual)

Harris, Valentina, *Traveler's Guide to the Food of Italy* (New York: Henry Holt and Co., 1988)

Hazan, Marcella, *The Classic Italian Cookbook* (New York: Alfred A. Knopf, Inc.,1976)

I Formaggi di Fattoria in Italia (Rome: Atlante, 1993)

Il Buon Paese (Bra: Slow Food Editore, 1994)

Il Ponente Ligure (Bra: Slow Food Editore, 1993)

La Costiera Amalfitana (Bra: Slow Food Editore, 1994)

Le Cose Buone di Veronelli (Milan: Georgio Mondadori & Associati, 1989)

Le Strade del Barolo (Bra: Slow Food Editore, 1993)

Lintner, Valerio, *A Traveler's History of Italy* (New York: Interlink Publishing Group, 1995)

Michelin: Italy (Clermont-Ferrand: Michelin et Cie., annual)

Millon, Marc & Kim, *The Wine Roads of Italy* (New York: HarperCollins, 1991)

Mistretta, Giorgio, *The Italian Gourmet* (Des Moines: Sedgewood Press, 1992)

Montefeltro e Valmarecchia (Bra: Slow Food Editore, 1993)

Nel Cuore delle Marche (Bra: Slow Food Editore, 1993)

Osterie d'Italia (Bra: Slow Food Editore, annual)

Piccinardi, Antonio, *Dizionario di Gastronomia* (Milan: Biblioteca Universale Rizzoli, 1993)

Ricette delle Osterie di Langa (Bra: Slow Food Editore, 1992)

Ricette di Sua Maestà Il Raviolo (Bra: Slow Food Editore, 1993)

Ristoranti d'Italia (Rome: Gambero Rosso Editore, annual)

Ristoranti di Veronelli (Bergamo: Veronelli Editore, annual)

Root, Waverly, *The Cooking of Italy* (Virginia: Time-Life Books Inc, 1977)

Sartoni, Monica Cesari, *Dizionario del Ghiottone Viaggiatore Italia* (Bologna: Fuori Thema/Tempi Streti, 1994)

Slow Food Guide to the Wines of the World (Bra: Slow Food Editore, 1993)

Treviso e i Colli Asolani (Bra: Slow Food Editore, 1993)

Valtellina e Valchiavenna (Bra: Slow Food Editore, 1993)

Vini d'Italia (Rome: Gambero Rosso Editore, annual)

Index

ACKNOWLEDGMENTS

Author's acknowledgments:
It would not have been possible to put together this book without the considerable assistance of many people. In Italy, we owe an enormous debt to all who welcomed us into their lives, taught, and showed us so much, and were so generous with sharing foods, wines, and good times. Extra special thanks are due to Sandro Boscaini, Count Pieralvise Sèrego Alighieri, Donatella Cinelli Colombini, the Lungarotti family, Michele Bernetti, Carmen Wallace, Silvio Barbero, Giampaolo Pacini, John Matta, Riccardo Illy, the Lancellotti family, Mario Pezzi, Stefano Martinelli and family. Friends in Italy who have shared countless meals and wines with us over the years include Giulano and Agnese Corti, Elda and Elia Rossetti, Alder Zonari, Ralph and Danila Church, Mario Fontana.

In England, our good friend Nello Ghezzo, a great regional Italian chef, advised and assisted us by preparing foods in his restaurant, as well as in lengthy discussions while cycling through the Devon countryside. John Bradbury kept our office ticking over while we were on the road, and assisted us in practical tasks too numerous to recount here.

Putting this volume together has been an immense practical task, and I would particularly like to acknowledge our editor Shirin Patel who has been so efficient, thorough, and sensitive; and our book designer Joanna Pocock, who has done such a magnificent job in making the book look so good. I would also like to thank our agents, Rivers Scott and Gloria Ferris, for their considerable support.

Finally, we would like to thank Pauline Redford, who accompanied us during our lengthy research travels in Italy, helped us to look after our young children Guy and Bella, and became such a part of our family.

Publisher's acknowledgments:
Websters International Publishers would like to thank the following for their assistance: Arcigola Slow Food Editore S.r.l., Bra, Italy; Keith Banbury; Lorna Bateson; Carluccio's, Specialists in Italian Food, 28A Neal Street, London W.C.2; Andrew Carton-Kelly; Jonathan Harley; Tim Lewis; David Lucas; Kim Parsons; Anna Pauletti; Daphne Trotter; Phillip Williamson; Martha Worthington.